Narrative Interventions in Post-modern Guidance and Career Counseling

AF793851

Annamaria Di Fabio · Jean-Luc Bernaud
Editors

Narrative Interventions in Post-modern Guidance and Career Counseling

A Review of Case Studies and Innovative Qualitative Approaches

Springer

Editors
Annamaria Di Fabio
Department of Education and Psychology
University of Florence
Florence, Italy

Jean-Luc Bernaud
Inetop
Conservatoire National
des Arts et Métiers
Paris, France

ISBN 978-3-030-07480-7 ISBN 978-3-319-98300-4 (eBook)
https://doi.org/10.1007/978-3-319-98300-4

© Springer Nature Switzerland AG 2018
Softcover re-print of the Hardcover 1st edition 2018
This work is subject to copyright. All rights are reserved by the Publisher, whether the whole or part of the material is concerned, specifically the rights of translation, reprinting, reuse of illustrations, recitation, broadcasting, reproduction on microfilms or in any other physical way, and transmission or information storage and retrieval, electronic adaptation, computer software, or by similar or dissimilar methodology now known or hereafter developed.
The use of general descriptive names, registered names, trademarks, service marks, etc. in this publication does not imply, even in the absence of a specific statement, that such names are exempt from the relevant protective laws and regulations and therefore free for general use.
The publisher, the authors and the editors are safe to assume that the advice and information in this book are believed to be true and accurate at the date of publication. Neither the publisher nor the authors or the editors give a warranty, express or implied, with respect to the material contained herein or for any errors or omissions that may have been made. The publisher remains neutral with regard to jurisdictional claims in published maps and institutional affiliations.

This Springer imprint is published by the registered company Springer Nature Switzerland AG
The registered company address is: Gewerbestrasse 11, 6330 Cham, Switzerland

To Jean Guichard, Magister and extraordinary colleague as a concrete example of reflexivity, courage and integrity

Foreword

I am honored to be asked to write a Foreword for this important new book edited by Professors Annamaria Di Fabio and Jean-Luc Bernaud on accountability in career development interventions. The unique contribution of this outstanding volume is its focus on narrative interventions, which are becoming more and more common and important in this era of great complexity and challenge in the world of work. Indeed, this book provides a perfect blend of new ideas, practices, and methods for narrative approaches in career counseling and education. Interestingly, this book comes at a time when the demands for accountability are increasing due to financial constraints in providing resources for needed services for clients facing career and work-based problems. Moreover, our field (and many related disciplines in the social and behavioral sciences) is in the midst of a strong push by quantitative methodologies, which are often viewed as more rigorous or precise than qualitative and narrative tools.

Into this complex landscape, Professors Di Fabio and Bernaud and their talented chapter authors have bravely contributed their time and effort to not just affirming the importance of qualitative and narrative tools as viable means of ensuring accountability, but also of elevating the discourse in these approaches. The interesting dialectic that is taking place in our field is the growing popularity of qualitative and narrative approaches to counseling and career education at the same that funders and administrators are expecting quantitative evaluation methods. As noted throughout this book, the need for qualitative counseling approaches is particularly relevant during an era of such massive transformations in the world of work. For many clients, narrative tools provide the sort of relativistic solutions that are optimally relevant for this period of such uncertainty in the world of work. The chapters of this book provide wonderful counterpoints to the growing hegemony of quantitative evaluation tools and also link the evaluation efforts seamlessly to the interventions that have been so creatively described in this book.

I also would like to use the space provided for me in this Foreword to make a plea to scholars in our field to be respectful of both qualitative and quantitative approaches to both counseling and evaluation. I have observed a growing rancor in our discourse from advocates from both sides of the qualitative–quantitative continuum, which has troubled me. In many ways, I find this debate to be irrelevant at best and harmful at worst. The challenges that beset working people currently and in the coming years are serious and are having a profoundly negative impact on individuals and communities. The underlying frameworks of our theories, research, and practices have multiple intellectual and methodological influences, which are appropriate given the complexity of the issues that we are studying. To create battles over the ostensible superiority of one set of methods over another is an unnecessary distraction. We need to focus on resolving the problems that exist for people and nations as they grapple with a working context that is increasingly unpredictable. At times, quantitative methods are appropriately called for, and at other times, qualitative methods are optimal.

This excellent book will soon emerge as a classic resource for counselors, educators, practitioners, and policy analysts who will be relying upon the very creative and thoughtful strategies and perspectives that have been shared by these leading scholars. I congratulate the entire team of contributors of this book, who have given us a great gift that will resonate in our field for many years to come.

Lexington, MA, USA David L. Blustein
December 2017

Preface

This book presents *A Review of Case Studies and Innovative Qualitative Approaches* with the aim of enhancing accountability in post-modern guidance and career counseling narrative interventions under the UNESCO UNITWIN Network Life Designing Interventions (counseling, guidance, education) for decent work and sustainable development. The book has two parts. The first part includes theoretical perspectives and new interventions in different contexts. The second part is focused on accountability and shows new qualitative tools for evaluating the effectiveness of post-modern guidance and career counseling interventions in the twenty-first century. This volume responds to the call, made some years ago (Blustein, Kenna, Murphy, DeVoy & DeWine, 2005), for new qualitative tools to detect change in clients' narratives and to evaluate the effectiveness of narrative career counseling interventions. Yet, years after the rise of narrative career counseling for the twenty-first century, there have been a few responses to the call for methods of evaluation. Rehfuss' (2009) *Future Career Autobiography: A narrative measure of career intervention effectiveness* is a notable exception.

The book begins with the chapter by Annamaria Di Fabio and Jean-Luc Bernaud. This first chapter introduces the principles of accountability and the issue of evaluating the effectiveness of post-modern guidance and career counseling narrative interventions for the twenty-first century. The chapter is focused on the necessity to create specific tools to fully capture the depth and nuance of changes brought about by narrative interventions. Furthermore, the guidelines for accountability are presented as a positive preventive perspective.

The second chapter by Kobus Maree is articulated in two parts. The first part of the chapter introduces the construct of career indecision and provides a brief overview of the research into this construct. Maree examines key aspects of career construction that enable career counselors to help clients manage and resolve their career indecision. The second part of the chapter presents a case study that demonstrates the value of career construction counseling for a postgraduate student in psychology who is facing career indecision, and highlights how career construction counseling can be used to deal with similar challenges.

The third chapter by Jean-Luc Bernaud and Dominique Guédon describes a new approach to individualized counseling for job decency analysis and career development through a case study of a manager working in an establishment for the elderly. The case study shows in particular the use of a quali + quanti approach to the assessment of psychosocial risks and proposes a counseling method to assess work-related resources and dangers. The chapter underlines the importance of not only doing the diagnostic work relating to risk, but also doing the work of individualizing resources. Identifying resources provides companies opportunities for exploration, allows employees to put their situations into perspective, and redefines their relationships to their jobs.

The fourth chapter by Lin Lhotellier, Caroline Arnoux-Nicolas, and Laurent Sovet reveals an innovative framework for career intervention that is focused on meaning. The chapter presents a case study with a special focus on analyzing the interactions between the counselor and the client, and the qualitative effectiveness of the career intervention. The contribution discusses the importance of exploring both qualitative and quantitative effects of a meaning-centered career intervention and highlights the challenges of career counseling within a post-modern context.

The fifth chapter by Peter McIlveen and Allison Creed introduces an approach to case formulation and metaphor. It is through case conceptualization that the counselor reveals (consciously or unconsciously) the rhetoric used to objectify the life of another. The focus is on the professional practice of case formulation as a highly specialized aesthetic of counseling practice.

The contribution by Afonso Ribeiro, Guilherme de Oliveira Silva Fonçatti, and Maria da Conceição Coropos Uvaldo concludes the first part of the volume. Their chapter describes a case study about the impact of a group-based career counseling model for unskilled adults in crisis in the Brazilian context. The effectiveness of the intervention was qualitatively evaluated by a non-structured method based on the participants' life and working narratives, and changes to those narratives throughout the group process. The results indicated an increased reflexivity and a clear process of narrative change during the counseling.

The second part of the present book widens horizons through the lens of accountability that is focused on new qualitative tools for evaluating the effectiveness of post-modern guidance and career interventions in the twenty-first century. This second part of the book presents some case studies from the *International Research and Intervention Laboratory of Psychology for Vocational Guidance, Career Counseling and Talents* (*LabOProCCareer&T*), within the Department of Education and Psychology, Section of Psychology, at the University of Florence. These case studies involve collaborative work with international colleagues. The focus is on different narrative career interventions for the twenty-first century and new qualitative tools to evaluate the effectiveness of such interventions.

The seventh contribution by Maureen E. Kenny and Annamaria Di Fabio introduces the second part of the book. Taking into account the characteristics of work in the twenty-first century (e.g., globalization, rapid spread of technology, instability), the chapter firstly introduces the relevance of adaptability, purposeful identitarian awareness, grounded reflexivity, fluidity management, and then the shift from career development to career management through self and relational management. This chapter also describes some post-modern guidance and career counseling interventions and innovative tools that qualitatively detect a change (or lack of change) in narratives produced by clients before and after their interventions.

The eighth chapter by Ornella Bucci, Allison Creed, and Annamaria Di Fabio presents a case study of an Italian Ph.D. student. The case study involves the Career Interest Profile (CIP), as a life design counseling intervention, and the Future Career Autobiography (FCA). In addition, the Life Adaptability Qualitative Assessment (LAQuA) is described as an innovative narrative tool. The results of the study revealed the more specific life and occupational goals after the intervention as well as narrative changes in the adaptability dimensions. The life design counseling intervention using the CIP helped the participant to increase self-awareness to develop future career and life paths.

The ninth chapter by Letizia Palazzeschi, Allison Creed, Alessio Gori, and Annamaria Di Fabio presents two case studies. The first is a case study of a young male physiotherapist who graduated in France and then decided to move to Italy some months after graduation to find a job in his field of specialization. The client participated in a life design counseling intervention. The effectiveness of the intervention was qualitatively evaluated through the Life Adaptability Qualitative Assessment (LAQuA). The second is a case study of a personnel director of a big company in the center of Italy who participated in a narrative career counseling intervention. The client completed two new qualitative tools before and after the intervention: the Life Adaptability Qualitative Assessment (LAQuA) and the Career Counseling Innovative Outcomes (CCIO). The results showed the importance of using a life design counseling intervention in helping people to understand themselves more deeply, to identify their actual objectives, and to take the necessary steps toward their future.

The tenth chapter by Annamaria Di Fabio and Maureen E. Kenny presents the case study of an operator of an employment office in Tuscany who participated in a life meaning intervention. The client completed two qualitative instruments before and after the intervention: the Life Adaptability Qualitative Assessment (LAQuA) and the Career Counseling Innovative Outcomes (CCIO). The results of the study underscored the effectiveness of the life meaning intervention in helping the client to increase self-awareness, life meaningfulness, and deep values.

The eleventh contribution by Peter McIlveen and Annamaria Di Fabio describes a case study that addresses the effectiveness of Intrapreneurial Self-Capital Training for a final-year female biology student. The case study involves a qualitative instrument, the Life Adaptability Qualitative Assessment (LAQuA). The results of the analysis using the LAQuA coding system describe improvements in the participant's awareness about her personal intrapreneurial resources.

The twelfth chapter by Violetta Drabik-Podgórna, Marek Podgórny, and Annamaria Di Fabio presents a case study of an Italian worker. This case study addresses the effectiveness of a new life construction dialogue intervention, "Constructing My Future Purposeful Life," using three different qualitative evaluation tools: the Future Career Autobiography, FCA; the Life Adaptability Qualitative Assessment, LAQuA; and the Career Counseling Innovative Outcomes, CCIO. The results of the case study underscore the effectiveness of the Constructing My Future Purposeful Life intervention and highlight the value of enhancing new dialogue interventions to strengthen the client's reflexivity and increase purposeful identitarian awareness.

The last chapter by Annamaria Di Fabio and Peter McIlveen introduces a new qualitative tool, the Qualitative SIFS Evaluation For Future (QSEF), for evaluating the effectiveness of dialogue interventions. The chapter describes a case study of a worker in a public organization. This new qualitative tool is developed on the basis of the Self-Construction Theory (Guichard, 2004, 2005) and the Life Construction Theory (Guichard, 2013). The results of the analysis using the QSEF coding system showed an increased awareness of the participant in relation to the functioning of her Subjective Identity Forms System (SIFS) supporting her career and life construction.

This book is a substantive contribution to scholarship that enhances reflection on the essential theme of accountability in post-modern guidance and career counseling narrative interventions. The book is a useful point of reference for practice, research, and teaching. The book's case studies, innovative qualitative interventions, and qualitative tools to evaluate interventions' effectiveness are invaluable resources. As a whole, this book advances counseling interventions for the twenty-first century in terms of narrative, dialogic interventions that facilitate clients' self-management in an unpredictable, liquid, and "under construction" world of work.

Florence, Italy Annamaria Di Fabio
Paris, France Jean-Luc Bernaud

References

Blustein, D.L., Kenna, A.C., Murphy, K.A., DeVoy, J.E., & DeWine, D.B. (2005). Qualitative research in career development: Exploring the center and margins of discourse about careers and working. *Journal of Career Assessment, 13*(4), 351–370.

Guichard, J. (2004). Se faire soi. *L'Orientation Scolaire et Professionnelle, 33*, 499–534.

Guichard, J. (2005). Life-long self-construction. *International Journal for Educational and Vocational Guidance, 5*, 111–124.

Guichard, J. (2013, September). *Which paradigm for career and life designing interventions contributing to the development of a fairer world during the 21st century*. Lecture presented at the IAEVG International Conference, Montpellier, France.

Rehfuss, M.C. (2009). The *Future Career Autobiography*: A narrative measure of career intervention effectiveness. *The Career Development Quarterly, 58*(1), 82–90.

Contents

Part I
Theoretical Perspectives and New Interventions in Different Contexts

Chapter 1
Introduction: Postmodern Guidance and Career Counseling Interventions—The New Scenario

Annamaria Di Fabio and Jean-Luc Bernaud

Abstract This chapter presents the new scenario in the twenty-first century characterized by insecurity, instability, and continuous change. In this scenario, postmodern guidance and career counseling interventions are based on a narrative paradigm. It introduces a narrative shift, and individuals are re-conceptualized as "storied" instead as composed of static traits. Career counselors are asked to help clients to give meaning to their personal and professional lives through the construction of their own self as story. In this framework, the chapter introduces the principles of accountability and the issue of the evaluation of the effectiveness of postmodern guidance and career counseling narrative interventions for the twenty-first century, focusing in particular on the necessity to create specific tools to fully capture the depth and nuances of changes after these narrative interventions. Furthermore, the guidelines for accountability in the twenty-first century are presented that also introduce a positive preventive perspective in postmodern guidance and career counseling narrative interventions.

1.1 The New Scenario in the Twenty-First Century

The world of work in the twenty-first century presents multiple complexities, being characterized by insecurity, instability, and continuous change (Blustein, 2006, 2011; Di Fabio & Bernaud, 2014; Guichard & Di Fabio, 2015, 2010; Savickas, 2011). In the twentieth century, workers develop their professional path within the stable organizational realities, whereas in the twenty-first century professional trajectories appear even more unpredictable and workers are called on not only to decide about their career but also to face the transitions even more frequently than

A. Di Fabio (✉)
Department of Education and Psychology (Psychology Section),
University of Florence, Florence, Italy
e-mail: adifabio@psico.unifi.it

J.-L. Bernaud
CNAM—Conservatoire National des Arts et Métiers, Paris, France

© Springer Nature Switzerland AG 2018
A. Di Fabio and J.-L. Bernaud (eds.), *Narrative Interventions in Post-modern Guidance and Career Counseling*, https://doi.org/10.1007/978-3-319-98300-4_1

in the past (Savickas, 2011). In this scenario, individuals are considered more responsible in delineating their own professional and life paths (Guichard & Di Fabio, 2015; Savickas, 2011): Career is no more related to organization but seems to belong even more to worker (Duffy et al., 2012; Duffy, Torrey, Bott, Allan, & Schlosser, 2013; Duarte, 2004). The personal success formula (Savickas, 2011) underlines the importance of awareness of one's own authentic values and life objectives to construct a professional and personal life fully significant for individual and not associated with a hetero-directed evaluation of success. Facilitating individuals in recognizing their own interests, values, and aims in line with the personal success formula by Savickas (2011) and with the awareness of one's own authentic self (Di Fabio, 2014c) is a key process to strengthen resources and thus to enhance resilience in the twenty-first century. Furthermore, workers are required to constantly develop knowledge and competences, be flexible, maintain high levels of employability, be open to change, and increase their adaptability (Di Fabio & Gori, 2016; Savickas, 2011). Individuals are called on to autonomously construct their own both professional and personal lives (Di Fabio, 2014c; Guichard & Di Fabio, 2015; Guichard, Bangali, Cohen Scali, Pouyaud, & Robinet, 2016; Savickas, 2011) in an increasingly liquid and hardly predictable context (Bauman, 2000). For this reason, it is no more possible to refer to career development but to career management (Savickas, 2011). In career management, it is essential not only to decide but above all to be able to become (Savickas, 2011). Moreover, it is fundamental the strict interrelation between working activities and aspects of personal life (Guichard, 2009), and thus between career management (Savickas, 2011) and life management (Guichard & Di Fabio, 2015). The aim for career counselors is also to help people to construct their own lives through work and relationships (Blustein, 2011; Blustein, Kenny, Di Fabio, & Guichard, in press; Di Fabio, 2016b; Di Fabio & Blustein, 2016; Duffy et al., 2017; Duffy, Blustein, Diemer, & Autin, 2016; Kenny, Blustein, & Meerkins, 2018; Maree & Di Fabio, 2015; Richardson, 2012), considering the principal social contexts for individuals with a focus on the construction of decent work for decent lives (Blustein et al., in press; Di Fabio & Blustein, 2016; Duffy et al., 2017).

In this century, the career counseling interventions evolved and it was first proposed to facilitate a deep reflection of individuals on themselves to develop a stable identity as an internal compass to deal with the difficulties and transitions of the postmodern world and successfully adapt to the professional and personal reality that it is unstable and constantly changing (Di Fabio, 2014a; Guichard, 2005; Guichard & Di Fabio, 2015; Savickas, 2005, 2011, 2015). Psychological narration is utilized as a paradigmatic practice in narrative counseling and in dialogic interaction to support individuals face the challenges of the fluid society (Bauman, 2000; Brott, 2004; Cochran, 1997; Guichard & Di Fabio, 2015; McMahon & Watson, 2010, 2011; Severy, 2002). The principal objective of narrative interventions is to facilitate the recognition of authentic meanings and aims of the life of clients (Allan, Duffy, & Douglass, 2015; Di Fabio, 2014a; Guichard, 2005; Guichard & Di Fabio, 2015; Savickas, 2005, 2011).

In this framework, career counselors are called on to help clients to attribute a meaning to their own personal and professional lives through the construction of their storied self (Savickas, 2005, 2011). Within this narrative perspective, career counseling for the twenty-first century is configured as a process in which career and life paths are constructed through psychological narration and stories representing instrument to construct one's own identity (Maree, 2013; Rehfuss, 2009; Rehfuss & Di Fabio, 2012; Savickas, 2011). The importance emerged to enhance the ability of individuals to project successful professional paths on the one side and on the other side the ability to manage adaptively one's own personal and professional lives, constructing well-being. It is considered not only as hedonic well-being (Diener, Emmons, Larsen, & Griffin, 1985; Douglass, Duffy, & Autin, 2016; Watson, Clark, & Tellegen, 1988), in terms of its effective components characterized by the prevalence of positive emotions on negative emotions and of its cognitive component of evaluation relative to life satisfaction, but particularly as eudaemonic well-being (Diener et al., 2010; Morgan & Farsides, 2009; Steger, Frazier, Oishi, & Kaler, 2006; Waterman et al., 2010) that is based on personal growth to reach the full functioning of an individual in terms of fulfillment, self-realization, authenticity, and meaningfulness to the benefit of both themselves and the community of belonging (Di Fabio, 2014a).

1.2 Accountability and Effectiveness of Postmodern Guidance and Career Counseling Narrative Interventions in the Twenty-First Century

The economic crisis that characterizes the twenty-first century has underlined the necessity to refer to accountability principles to offer effective career counseling interventions without loosing the available limited economic resources (Whiston, 1996, 2001). Accountability implies in particular an attention to service costs, to effectiveness of interventions, and to the best practices supported by research (Whiston, 2001). The study of the effectiveness of interventions is a traditional research theme in the field of career counseling (Di Fabio, Bernaud, & Kenny, 2013; Oliver & Spokane; 1988). To verify the effectiveness of interventions, the expertise (Whiston, 2008) suggests the use of different measures, using different perspectives. Traditionally, to verify the effectiveness of career counseling interventions, only quantitative tools were employed, but the current career counseling interventions are intrinsically narrative and for this intrinsically qualitative.

In fact in the twenty-first century, postmodern guidance and career counseling narrative interventions fundamentally aim to facilitate individuals to carefully reflect on themselves to develop a stable sense of their identity as a resource to successfully face the postmodern changing context (Brott, 2004; Cochran, 1997; Guichard, 2005; Guichard & Di Fabio, 2015; McMahon & Watson, 2010, 2011; Severy, 2002; Savickas, 2005, 2011, 2013, 2015). Thus, the current career counseling practice is based on the psychological narration (Savickas, 2001, 2005, 2011,

2013, 2015) as expressed in the narrative counseling (Savickas, 2011) and dialogue interaction (Guichard & Di Fabio, 2015) to help individuals to face the challenges of the fluid society (Bauman, 2000). The purpose of the narrative career counseling intervention is to facilitate the elaboration of individuals' issues, resulting in the reflexive process to construct meaningful aims for oneself and the society (Di Fabio, Maree, & Kenny, 2018; Guichard & Di Fabio, 2015; Savickas, 2011). This awareness needs a narrative shift in the approach to vocational behavior and re-conceptualizes individuals as "storied" instead of considering them as holders of static traits (Savickas, 2005). If in the twentieth century career counseling interventions have traditionally utilized a person–environment fit model as the dominant paradigm (Holland, 1997); in the twenty-first century, the postmodern paradigm calls for narrative interventions in a storied form (Savickas, 2011). Career counselors are asked to help clients to give a meaning to their own personal and professional lives through the construction of their own self as a story (Savickas, 2005, 2011). Clients narrate about their past and present, constructing their future career through an active approach that attends to how clients intentionally interact with the world and learn about it through these interactions (Cohran, 1997). Past experiences influence the present lives of individuals, and, together, past and present experiences influence the future of the individuals (McMahon & Watson, 2010, 2011). It is a storied approach that explores the client's world through story development as the client and counselor collaboratively co-construct, deconstruct, and construct life stories (Brott, 2004). This process of constructing life stories embraces all elements of self, including work and life outside of work, as well as multiple life roles such as family member, worker, student, and community member (Severy, 2002).

From this narrative perspective, career counseling in the twenty-first century is a process where career is constructed through narration and stories are the means to construct identity (Hartung, 2010a, 2013; Rehfuss, 2009; Rehfuss & Di Fabio, 2012; Savickas, 2011).

In this framework for career counseling in the twenty-first century in the literature, a gap emerged between the career counseling narrative interventions that are inherently qualitative (Blustein, Kenna, Murphy, Devoy, & DeWine, 2005; Hartung, 2010a, 2013; Rehfuss, 2009; Rehfuss & Di Fabio, 2012; Savickas, 2011) and the tools to evaluate them that are traditionally exclusively quantitative (Brown et al., 2003; Heppner & Heppner, 2003; Oliver & Spokane, 1988; Whiston, Brecheisen, & Stephens, 2003; Whiston, Sexton, & Lasoff, 1998). For this reason, the necessity to develop new qualitative tools to detect narrative change is highlighted (Blustein et al., 2005). This perspective stresses the passage from scores to stories (McMahon & Patton, 2002) in the evaluation of the effectiveness of career counseling interventions. This kind of approach is essential since the new narrative paradigm requires a qualitative evaluation of interventions (Di Fabio & Maree, 2013; Rehfuss, 2009; Rehfuss & Di Fabio, 2012) and traditional quantitative tools cannot detect qualitative changes in self-narrations (Rehfuss & Di Fabio, 2012). It was thus necessary to realize qualitative tools specifically developed to identify changes in the clients' narratives after career counseling narrative interventions. The first new tool available in the literature is the Future Career Autobiography

(FCA; Rehfuss, 2009; Rehfuss & Di Fabio, 2012). FCA permits to analyze the change themes but with vague directions and lack of specificity (capacity to discern only broad change themes), and this may hinder a full exploration of the impact of a counseling experience (Di Fabio, 2016a). Therefore, the necessity emerged to create more refined tools to fully capture the depth and nuance of changes after the narrative career counseling interventions (Busacca & Rehfuss, 2016; Di Fabio, 2015, 2016a, 2016c). Thus, other more specific narrative tools were developed: Life Adaptability Quality Assessment (LAQuA; Di Fabio, 2015) and Career Counseling Innovative Outcomes coding system (CCIO; Di Fabio, 2016a). These tools were described more in depth in the second part of this volume.

Furthermore, to complete the reflection regarding the evaluation of the effectiveness of career counseling interventions in the twenty-first century, it is possible to underline the recent introduction of a quali+ quanti perspective (Di Fabio & Maree, 2012, 2013) that combines the two different modalities of evaluation. This perspective underlines the subsequent passage from scores to scores and stories (Di Fabio & Maree, 2012, 2013) in the evaluation of career counseling interventions, basing on specific qualitative tools used together with quantitative tools (Di Fabio, 2014b; Di Fabio & Maree, 2012, 2013). Such approach underlines the importance of a quantitative modality of evaluation indissolubility joined to a qualitative modality of evaluation that permits to highlight the individual and subjective shades of change following the narrative career counseling interventions (Di Fabio & Maree, 2013; Rehfuss, 2009; Rehfuss & Di Fabio, 2012).

1.3 Guidelines for Accountability in the Twenty-First Century

To better evaluate the effectiveness of postmodern guidance and career counseling narrative interventions, guidelines for accountability in the twenty-first century have been developed (Di Fabio, 2014a, p. 199). The guidelines are as follows:

(1) The pillar of accountability (Di Fabio, 2014a; Whiston, 1996, 2001): in the twenty-first century, it is fundamental to attend to the principles of accountability, which give attention to service cost, intervention effectiveness, and best practices supported by research (Whiston, 1996, 2001).
(2) Attention to the choice of effective outcome criteria to evaluate effective career counseling in relation to different interventions: use of multiple measures from multiple perspectives (Di Fabio, 2014a; Whiston, 1996, 2008). It is essential to recognize the value of combining multiple perspectives, for example, subjective measures and more concrete objective measures (Whiston, 2008).
(3) A new paradigm and consequently new perspectives for the twenty-first century: the evolution of career intervention assessment from scores on psychometric tools to scores and stories (Di Fabio & Maree, 2012, 2013). This approach can be summarized as moving from "scores to stories" (McMahon &

Patton, 2011) to a more balanced approach characterized by the notion of moving from "scores" to "scores and stories" (Di Fabio & Maree, 2012, 2013).

(4) Moving forward from tradition to innovation in a quali + quanti perspective (Di Fabio, 2012, 2014a; Di Fabio & Maree, 2013; Maree, 2012): Since the qualitative modality is essential to assess career counseling narrative interventions (Rehfuss, 2009, Rehfuss & Di Fabio, 2012), its use is strongly desirable (Di Fabio, 2012; Di Fabio & Maree, 2012, 2013).

(5) The need of new qualitative measures to detect narrative change (Blustein et al., 2005; Hartung, 2010a, 2010b, 2013; Rehfuss, 2009; Rehfuss & Di Fabio, 2012): The widespread use of the narrative career counseling and new interventions has led to the need for new qualitative tools in order to effectively detect change after narrative interventions (Rehfuss, 2009; Rehfuss & Di Fabio, 2012).

(6) The need to consider new quantitative outcomes more congruent with new twenty-first-century career counseling narrative interventions (Di Fabio, 2015, 2016a): It is important to develop and to use quantitative assessment tools that detect the development of an authentic self and personal life meaningfulness, which are expected outcomes of postmodern narrative interventions (Bernaud, 2013, 2015; Di Fabio, 2015, 2016a).

(7) The need for new intervention methodologies that are compatible with accountability principles (less costs + effectiveness) (Di Fabio, 2012; Di Fabio & Maree, 2012, 2013; Whiston, 1996, 2001): Effective methodologies are needed to assess the balance between reducing career counseling costs and maintaining effectiveness (Di Fabio & Maree, 2012). One possible example is the power of the audience (Di Fabio & Maree, 2012). It is an innovative methodology: It is not a traditional workgroup, but it requires a specific theoretical and applicative framework. The group members are considered as participants of an individual career counseling, individually interacting in turn with a career counselor, but at the same time have the opportunity to constitute the audience who listen to the other participants without intervening. The intervention is divided into moments during which participants interact in turn individually with the career counselor for the process of facilitation, whereas the other participants listen as audience. Career counseling interventions that use the methodology of the power of the audience can be considered as individual interventions in group setting, thus permitting to reach more people in an effective way and with a cost containment. With this modality of intervention, it is realized the enhancement of the diffusion of career counseling interventions that also maintain an individual configuration, with a significant reduction in costs for a greater effectiveness and efficacy in line with the accountability principles (Whiston, 1996, 2001).

(8) Different outcome criteria are needed to assess intervention goals based on the new taxonomy (information, guidance, dialogue) of Guichard (2013) in order to assess the effectiveness of interventions (Di Fabio, 2014a). We have new goals suggested by the taxonomy of Guichard, which vary from traditional intervention goals. According to this taxonomy, information enables

individuals to locate significant and reliable information in relation to the world of work. Guidance develops employability skills so that clients can construct an adaptable vocational self-concept. Dialogue life construction intervention helps individuals to construct meaning of their own lives. Dialogue life construction intervention helps clients individualize future perspectives that currently give meaning to their life and consider what they want to achieve in various contexts of their lives (Guichard, 2013).

(9) The need for a positive psychology perspective in career management/life management is based on positive information, positive guidance, and positive dialogue to enhance individual strengths and self-attunement (Di Fabio, 2014a). The positive psychology framework emphasizes uniqueness, authenticness, and purposefulness of individuals (Di Fabio 2014c).

(10) Consequently, also the use of positive psychology goals to verify the effectiveness of the interventions (Di Fabio, 2014a) is needed. The use of outcomes according to both the hedonic approach (Watson et al., 1988) and the eudaemonic approach (Ryan & Deci, 2001; Ryff & Singer, 2008; Waterman et al., 2010) is fundamental (Blustein et al., in press; Kenny et al., 2018).

These guidelines should be used for evaluating postmodern guidance and career counseling narrative interventions in the twenty-first century, leading to accountability and to a positive prevention perspective (Hage et al., 2007; Kenny & Hage, 2009).

1.4 Conclusions

In the twenty-first century characterized by a changing world of work, it is underlined that individuals are considered as responsible of their lives both personal and professional (Bernaud, 2018; Bustein, 2006, 2011; Di Fabio, 2014c; Guichard & Di Fabio, 2015; Savickas, 2011) and thus are called on to maintain high levels of employability (Di Fabio, 2014c), to be open to change (Di Fabio & Gori, 2016), and to develop their adaptability (Savickas, 2011). In the twenty-first century, career counseling interventions use psychological narration to facilitate a careful reflection of individuals on themselves and on their authentic meanings and aim to develop a stable identity in a professional and personal context that instead is in constant change (Di Fabio, 2014a, 2014c). The economic crisis of the twenty-first century and the relative scarcity of resources introduce the importance to maximize the cost/benefit ratio in line with the principles of accountability (Whiston, 1996, 2001). The importance to reduce the costs of interventions, to evaluate their effectiveness, and to increase the best practice funded on empirical research emerges as fundamental (Whiston, 1996, 2001). It is essential to evaluate the postmodern guidance and career counseling narrative interventions for the twenty-first century that are essentially qualitative using new qualitative tools specifically developed to detect narrative change after these interventions (Di Fabio, 2015, 2016a; Rehfuss, 2009;

Di Fabio & Rehfuss, 2012). This is also a fundamental aspect of the guidelines of accountability for the twenty-first century (Di Fabio, 2014a) that introduce a positive preventive perspective for accountability in postmodern guidance and career counseling narrative interventions, answering to the challenge to help individuals to develop a professional and personal project anchored to one's own authentic self (Di Fabio, 2014c), contributing to both hedonic well-being and eudaemonic well-being of individuals and of the society on the whole (Blustein, 2006, 2011; Di Fabio & Kenny, 2016a, 2016b), closely basing on the results of empirical research (Di Fabio, 2014a, 2014c).

References

Allan, B. A., Duffy, R. D., & Douglass, R. (2015). Meaning in life and work: A developmental perspective. *The Journal of Positive Psychology, 10*(4), 323–331.

Bauman, Z. (2000). *Liquid modernity*. Cambridge, UK: Polity Press.

Bernaud, J. L. (2013). Career counseling and life meaning: A new perspective life designing for research and applications. In A. Di Fabio & K. Maree (Eds.), *Psychology of career counseling: New challenges for a new era*. New-York: Nova Science Publishers.

Bernaud, J.-L. (2015). *Psychologie de L'accompagnement: Concepts et Outils pour Développer le Sens de la vie et du Travail*. Paris: Dunod.

Bernaud, J.-L. (2018). *Introduction à la psychologie existentielle*. Paris: Dunod.

Blustein, D. L. (2006). *The psychology of working: A new perspective for career development, counseling and public policy*. NY: Routledge.

Blustein, D. L. (2011). A relational theory of working. *Journal of Vocational Behavior, 79,* 1–17.

Blustein, D. L., Kenna, A. C., Murphy, K. A., DeVoy, J. E., & DeWine, D. B. (2005). Qualitative research in career development: Exploring the center and margins of discourse about careers and working. *Journal of Career Assessment, 13*(4), 351–370.

Blustein, D. L., Kenny, M. E., Di Fabio, A., & Guichard, J. (in press). Expanding the impact of the psychology of working: Engaging psychology in the struggle for decent work and human rights. *Journal of Career Assessment*. https://doi.org/10.1177/1069072718774002.

Brott, P. E. (2004). Constructivist assessment in career counseling. *Journal of Career Development, 30*(3), 189–200.

Brown, S. D., Ryan Krane, N. E., Brecheisen, J., Castelino, P., Budisin, I., Miller, M., et al. (2003). Critical ingredients of career choice interventions: More analyses and new hypotheses. *Journal of Vocational Behaviour, 62,* 411–428.

Busacca, L., & Rehfuss, M. (Eds.). (2016). *Postmodern career counseling: A handbook of culture, contexts, and cases*. Alexandria: American Counseling Association.

Cochran, L. (1997). *Career counseling: A narrative approach*. London: Sage.

Di Fabio, A. (2012, July). *Narratability and career construction: Empirical evidence of intervention effectiveness*. State-of-the-Science Lecture, Invited keynote speaker in the field of Psychology of Counseling presented at the International Congress of Psychology (ICP) 2012, Cape Town, South Africa.

Di Fabio, A. (2014a). Career counseling and positive psychology in the 21st century: New constructs and measures for evaluating the effectiveness of intervention. *Journal of Counsellogy, 1,* 193–213.

Di Fabio, A. (2014b). Comparaison des approches qualitatives et quantitatives permettant d'évaluer l'efficacité de dispositifs du nouveau paradigme «construire sa vie». In D. Lhuilier (Ed.), *Qualité du travail, qualité au travail* (pp. 99–111). Toulouse, France: Octares.

Di Fabio, A. (2014c). The new purposeful identitarian awareness for the twenty-first century: Valorize themselves in the life construction from youth to adulthood and late adulthood. In A. Di Fabio & J.-L. Bernaud (Eds.), *The construction of the identity in 21st century: A Festschrift for Jean Guichard* (pp. 157–168). New York: Nova Science Publishers.

Di Fabio, A. (2015). Life adaptability qualitative assessment (LAQuA): A narrative instrument for evaluating counseling intervention effectiveness. In J. G. Maree & A. Di Fabio (Eds.), *Exploring new horizons in career counselling: Turning challenges into opportunities* (pp. 43–62). Rotterdam, The Netherlands: Sense Publishers.

Di Fabio, A. (2016a). Life design and career counseling innovative outcomes (CCIO). *The Career Development Quarterly, 64,* 35–48. https://doi.org/10.1002/cdq.12039.

Di Fabio, A. (2016b). Positive relational management for healthy organizations: Psychometric properties of a new scale for prevention for workers. In G. Giorgi, M. Shoss, & A. Di Fabio (Eds.), From organizational welfare to business success: Higher performance in healthy organizational environments. Research Topic in *Frontiers in Psychology. Organizational Psychology*, *7*, 1523. https://doi.org/10.3389/fpsyg.2016.01523.

Di Fabio, A. (2016c). The Life Design Genogram: A case study of an Italian female graduated student. In L. Busacca & M. Rehfuss (Eds.), *Postmodern career counseling: A handbook of culture, contexts, and cases* (pp. 229–244). Alexandria: American Counseling Association.

Di Fabio, A., & Bernaud, J.-L. (Eds.). (2014). *The construction of the identity in 21st century: A Festschrift for Jean Guichard*. New York: Nova Science Publishers.

Di Fabio, A., Bernaud, J.-L., & Kenny, M. E. (2013). Perceived career counselor relational and technical behaviors and outcomes among Italian university students. *Journal of Career Assessment, 21,* 190–199. https://doi.org/10.1177/1069072712466721.

Di Fabio, A., & Blustein, D. L. (Eds.). (2016). *From meaning of working to meaningful lives: The challenges of expanding decent work*. Lausanne: Frontiers Media. https://doi.org/10.3389/978-2-88919-970-9.

Di Fabio, A., & Kenny, M. E. (2016a). From decent work to decent lives: Positive self and relational management (PS&RM) in the twenty-first century. In A. Di Fabio & D. L. Blustein (Eds.), From meaning of working to meaningful lives: The challenges of expanding decent work. Research Topic in *Frontiers in Psychology. Section Organizational Psychology*, *7*, 361. https://doi.org/10.3389/fpsyg.2016.00361.

Di Fabio, A., & Kenny, M. E. (2016b). Promoting well-being: The contribution of emotional intelligence. In G. Giorgi, M. Shoss, & A. Di Fabio (Eds.), From organizational welfare to business success: Higher performance in healthy organizational environments. Research Topic in *Frontiers in Psychology. Organizational Psychology*, *7*, 1182. https://doi.org/10.3389/fpsyg.2016.01182.

Di Fabio, A., & Gori, A. (2016). Developing a new instrument for assessing acceptance of Change. *Frontiers in Psychology. Section Organizational Psychology*, *7*, 1182. https://doi.org/10.3389/fpsyg.2016.00802.

Di Fabio, A., & Maree, J. G. (2012). Group-based life design counselling in an Italian context. *Journal of Vocational Behaviour, 80,* 100–107.

Di Fabio, A., & Maree, J. G. (Eds.). (2013). *Psychology of career counseling: New challenges for a new era. Festschrift in honour of Prof. Mark Savickas*. New York: Nova Science Publishers.

Di Fabio, A., Maree, J. G., & Kenny, M. E. (2018). Development of the life project reflexivity scale: A new career intervention inventory. *Journal of Career Assessment, 12,* 1–13. https://doi.org/10.1177/1069072718758065.

Diener, E. D., Emmons, R. A., Larsen, R. J., & Griffin, S. (1985). The satisfaction with life scale. *Journal of Personality Assessment, 49*(1), 71–75.

Diener, E., Wirtz, D., Tov, W., Kim-Prieto, C., Choi, D. W., Oishi, S., et al. (2010). New well-being measures: Short scales to assess flourishing and positive and negative feelings. *Social Indicators Research, 97,* 143–156.

Douglass, R. P., Duffy, R. D., & Autin, K. L. (2016). Living a calling, nationality, and life satisfaction: A moderated, multiple mediator model. *Journal of Career Assessment, 24*(2), 253–269.

Duarte, M. E. (2004). O indivíduo e a organização: Perspectivas de desenvolvimento. [The individual and the organization: Perspectives of development]. *Psychologica (Extra-Série)*, 549–557.
Duffy, R. D., Allan, B. A., England, J. W., Blustein, D. L., Autin, K. L., Douglass, R. P. … Santos, E. J. (2017). The development and initial validation of the decent work scale. *Journal of counseling psychology*, *64*(2), 206.
Duffy, R. D., Blustein, D. L., Diemer, M. A., & Autin, K. L. (2016). The psychology of working theory. *Journal of Counseling Psychology, 63*(2), 127–148.
Duffy, R. D., Foley, P. F., Raque-Bodgan, T. L., Reid-Marks, L., Dik, B. J., Castano, M. C., et al. (2012). Counseling psychologists who view their careers as a calling: A qualitative study. *Journal of Career Assessment, 20*(3), 293–308.
Duffy, R. D., Torrey, C. L., Bott, E. M., Allan, B. A., & Schlosser, L. Z. (2013). Time management, passion, and collaboration: A qualitative study of highly research productive counseling psychologists. *The Counseling Psychologist, 41*(6), 881–917.
Guichard, J. (2005). Life-long self-construction. *International Journal for Educational and Vocational Guidance, 5,* 111–124.
Guichard, J. (2009). Self-constructing. *Journal of Vocational Behavior, 75,* 251–258.
Guichard, J. (2013, September). *Which paradigm for career and life designing interventions contributing to the development of a fairer world during the 21st century*. Lecture presented at the IAEVG International Conference, Montpellier, France.
Guichard, J., Bangali, M., Cohen Scali, V., Pouyaud, J., & Robinet, M. L. (2016). *Concevoir et orienter sa vie: Les dialogues de conseil en life design*. Paris: Editions Qui plus est.
Guichard, J., & Di Fabio, A. (2015, June). *How can career and life designing interventions contribute to a fair and sustainable development and to the implementation of decent work over the world?* Invited Keynote at the UNESCO Chair on Lifelong Guidance and Counseling International Conference "How can career and life designing interventions contribute to a fair and sustainable development and to the implementation of decent work over the world?" Florence 2015, University of Florence (Italy) and University of Wroclaw (Poland), Florence, Italy, 4–6 June 2015.
Guichard, J., & Di Fabio, A. (2010). Life-designing counseling: Specificità e integrazioni della teoria della costruzione di carriera e della teoria della costruzione di sé [Life-designing counseling: Specificities and integrations of career construction theory and self construction theory]. *Counseling Giornale Italiano di Ricerca e Applicazioni, 3,* 277–289.
Hage, S. M., Romano, J. L., Conyne, R. K., Kenny, M., Matthews, C., Schwartz, J. P., et al. (2007). Best practice guidelines on prevention practice, research, training, and social advocacy for psychologists. *The Counseling Psychologist, 35,* 493–566.
Hartung, P. J. (2010a). Career assessment: Using scores and stories in life designing. In J. K. Maree (Ed.), *Career counselling: Techniques that work* (pp. 1–10). Cape Town, South Africa: Juta & Company, Ltd.
Hartung, P. J. (2010b). Identifying life-career themes with the career story interview. In J. K. Maree (Ed.) *Career counselling: Techniques that work* (pp. 161–166). Cape Town, South Africa: Juta & Company, Ltd.
Hartung, P. J. (2013). Career as story: Making the narrative turn. In W. B. Walsh, M. L. Savickas, & P. J. Hartung (Eds.), *Handbook of vocational psychology* (4th ed.). New York: Routledge.
Heppner, M. J., & Heppner, P. P. (2003). Identifying process variables in career counselling: A research agenda. *Journal of Vocational Behaviour, 62,* 429–452.
Holland, J. L. (1997). *Making vocational choices: A theory of personalities and work environments* (3rd ed.). Odessa, FL: Psychological Assessment Resources.
Kenny, M. E., Blustein, D. L., & Meerkins, T. M. (2018). Integrating relational perspectives in career counseling practice. *The Career Development Quarterly, 66*(2), 135–148.
Kenny, M. E., & Hage, S. M. (2009). The next frontier: Prevention as an instrument of social justice. *The Journal of Primary Prevention, 30,* 1–10.

Maree, J. G. (2012). A (guided) meta-reflection theory of career counselling: A case study. *South African Journal of Higher Education, 26*(4), 661–669.
Maree, J. G. (2013). *Counselling for career construction: Connecting life themes to construct life portraits. Turning pain into hope*. Rotterdam, The Netherlands: Sense.
Maree, J. G., & Di Fabio, A. (Eds.). (2015). *Exploring new horizons in career counselling: Turning challenges into opportunities*. Rotterdam, The Netherlands: Sense Publishers.
McMahon, M., & Patton, W. (2002). Using qualitative assessment in career counselling. *International Journal for Educational and Vocational Guidance, 2,* 51–66.
McMahon, M., & Watson, M. (2010). Story telling: Moving from thin stories to thick and rich stories. In K. Maree (Ed.), *Career counselling: Methods that work* (pp. 53–63). Cape Town, South Africa: Yuta.
McMahon, M., & Watson, M. (2011). Career counselling: What's the story? In M. McMahon & M. Watson (Eds.), *Career counselling and constructivism: Elaboration of constructs* (pp. 13–24). New York: Nova Science.
Morgan, J., & Farsides, T. (2009). Measuring meaning in life. *Journal of happiness Studies, 10*(2), 197-214.
Oliver, L. W., & Spokane, A. R. (1988). Career-intervention outcome: What contributes to client gain? *Journal of Counselling Psychology, 35*, 447–462.
Rehfuss, M. C. (2009). The future career autobiography: A narrative measure of career intervention effectiveness. *The Career Development Quarterly, 58*(1), 82–90.
Rehfuss, M., & Di Fabio, A. (2012). Validating the future career autobiography as a measure of narrative change. *Journal of Career Assessment, 20,* 452–462.
Richardson, M. S. (2012). Counseling for work and relationship. *The Counseling Psychologist, 40* (2), 190–242.
Ryan, R. M., & Deci, E. L. (2001). On happiness and human potentials: A review of research on hedonic and eudaemonic well-being. *Annual Review in Psychology, 52,* 141–166.
Ryff, C. D., & Singer, B. H. (2008). Know thyself and become what you are: A eudaemonic approach to psychological well-being. *Journal of Happiness Studies, 9,* 13–39.
Savickas, M. L. (2001). Toward a comprehensive theory of career development: Disposition, concerns and narratives. In F. T. L. Leong & A. Barak (Eds.), *Contemporary models in vocational psychology: A volume in honor of Samuel H. Osipow* (pp. 295–320). Mahwah, NJ: Lawrence Erlbaum.
Savickas, M. L. (2005). The theory and practice of career construction. In S. D. Brown & R. W. Lent (Eds.), *Career development and counseling: Putting theory and research to work* (pp. 42–70). Hoboken, NJ: Wiley.
Savickas, M. L. (Ed.). (2011). *Career counseling*. Washington, DC: American Psychological Association.
Savickas, M. L. (2013). Life designing in 21st century. In *Closing Conference at the IAEVG International Conference*, Montpellier, France.
Savickas, M. L. (2015). *Life-design counseling manual*. Rootstown, OH: Author.
Severy, L. E. (2002). What's the story? Postmodern career counseling in student affairs. *Journal of College Student Development, 43*(1), 84–92.
Steger, M. F., Frazier, P., Oishi, S., & Kaler, M. (2006). The meaning in life questionnaire: Assessing the presence of and search for meaning in life. *Journal of counseling psychology, 53* (1), 80–93.
Watson, D., Clark, L. A., & Tellegen, A. (1988). Development and validation of brief measures of positive and negative affect: The PANAS Scales. *Journal of Personality and Social Psychology, 54,* 1063–1070.
Waterman, A. S., Schwartz, S. J., Zamboanga, B. L., Ravert, R. D., Williams, M. K., Bede Agocha, V. … Donnellan, M. B. (2010). The questionnaire for eudaemonic well-being: Psychometric properties, demographic comparisons, and evidence of validity. *The Journal of Positive Psychology*, *5*, 41–61.

Whiston, S. C. (1996). Accountability through action research: Research methods for practitioners. *Journal of Counseling and Development, 74,* 616–623.
Whiston, S. C. (2001). Selecting career outcome assessments: An organizational scheme. *Journal of Career Assessment, 9*(3), 215–228.
Whiston, S. C. (2008). *Principles and applications of assessment in counseling* (3rd ed.). Belmont, CA: Brooks/Cole.
Whiston, S. C., Brecheisen, B. K., & Stephens, J. (2003). Does treatment modality affect career counselling effectiveness? *Journal of Vocational Behaviour, 62,* 390–410.
Whiston, S. C., Sexton, T. L., & Lasoff, D. L. (1998). Career-intervention outcome: A replication and extension of Oliver and Spokane (1988). *Journal of Counselling Psychology, 45,* 150–165.

Chapter 2
Using Career Construction to Manage Career Choice-Related Transitions and Resolve Indecision: A Case Study

J. G. Maree

Abstract The chapter begins with a discussion of the link between career indecision (seen from a career construction point of view) and impending transformation. A change in viewpoint is discussed and a brief overview of research on career indecision is provided. Next, different conceptual frameworks that have been used in the past to investigate, interpret, and deal with the phenomenon of career indecision are elaborated briefly. In addition, key aspects of career construction that enable career counselors to help clients deal with career indecision are examined. The second part of the chapter is devoted to a case study that demonstrates the value of career construction counseling for a client battling with career indecision. It is concluded that this approach can help students in general deal with challenges experienced while they are studying.

2.1 Introduction

Many people, at various stages of their career lives, turn to career counselors for "advice." Stringer, Kerpelman, and Skorikov (2011), too, highlight the need to help clients plan their career journeys, reduce their career indecision (or hesitation before transformation (Savickas, 2015a), and enhance their decision-making capacity by equipping them with the skills required to manage career-related transitions. Savickas (2010) maintains that clients who show career indecision demonstrate a lack of the career control needed to make sound career-life decisions. Such clients have to explore their career-life themes by learning more about themselves.

This chapter is based on an article that has been previously published in the *South African Journal of Higher Education* (Maree, 2016). Permission was requested and granted by the Editor, Prof. Yusef Waghid, to rework the article for publication in this volume.

J. G. Maree (✉)
Department of Educational Psychology, University of Pretoria,
Pretoria 0001, South Africa
e-mail: kobus.maree@up.ac.za

© Springer Nature Switzerland AG 2018

A. Di Fabio and J.-L. Bernaud (eds.), *Narrative Interventions in Post-modern Guidance and Career Counseling*, https://doi.org/10.1007/978-3-319-98300-4_2

Moreover, career indecision (seen from a career construction point of view) denotes impending transformation and a change in viewpoint (Savickas, 1995; Severy, 2006).

Maree (2013) distinguishes between two broad groups of people facing points of transition that may result in career indecision, which can be defined as "an inability to make a decision about the vocation one wishes to pursue" (Guay, Senécal, Gauthier, & Fernet, 2003, p. 165). The first group of people experience career indecision when they are expected to make a "natural" transition or face a "natural" crossroads requiring career-related decisions. These decisions include having to choose particular subjects, a type of school, a field of study, a tertiary training institution, or a specific employment opportunity. The second group of people begin to question the choices they made in terms of, for instance, a school, a subject set, a field of study, a career, or an employer is the "right" (appropriate) choice. Various techniques, strategies, and interventions are at the disposal of career counselors to help both groups of clients resolve their career indecision. Career counselors can implement a predominantly "positivist" (quantitative), a predominantly narrative or storied approach, or an integrated approach (i.e., the combination and integration of quantitative and qualitative approaches) to help their clients, transition the impasse brought on by their career indecision.

Different conceptual frameworks that have been used in the past to investigate, interpret, and deal with the phenomenon of career indecision will now be discussed briefly.

2.2 Brief Overview of Research on Career Indecision

Guay et al. (2003) designed and tested a model of career indecision grounded in self-determination theory (SDT), which holds that healthy relationships between college students and their parents and peers impact positively on career indecision and vice versa. The researchers found in their study that the support of peers and parents in students' autonomy acquisition promoted the students' self-confidence with regard to their career decision making and enhanced their observed self-sufficiency. These findings correlate positively with those of Creed, Buys, Tilbury, and Crawford (2013) and Garcia, Restubog, Toledano, Tolentino, and Rafferty (2012) whose research showed that people who display a strong desire to become exceptionally skillful at tasks are more positive, give evidence of enhanced career-related ambitions, demonstrate enhanced self-efficacy levels, and, consequently, exhibit diminished levels of career indecision. Gianakos' (2001) research reveals that career decision self-efficacy mediates students' decision-making capacity and decreases career indecision. This all shows that enhanced self-efficacy levels, independence, a positive attitude, and autonomy contribute to a decrease in career indecision and counselors should therefore do all they can to promote these aspects.

Savickas (1995) explains that career indecision was initially considered an objective phenomenon. Early twentieth-century career counselors, influenced by the work of Parsons (2005), consequently based their efforts to help clients deal with career indecision on a "positivist" paradigm involving the theory and principles of logical positivism (also see Richardson, 1993), which stipulated the need for "reliable" and "valid" measuring instruments and techniques to assess career indecision. Career indecision was initially also considered a dichotomy (i.e., clients were categorized as either equipped to make viable career decisions or not equipped to do so). Over time, the belief grew that clients could be plotted on a one-dimensional continuum anchored by "undecided" and "decided." This view was in turn replaced by the belief that career indecision should be seen as a multidimensional phenomenon (i.e., clients with career indecision should be categorized into different subcategories of indecision).

In the following section, I elaborate on key aspects of career construction that enable career counselors to help clients deal with career indecision.

2.2.1 *A Constructivist Perspective on How to Deal with Career Indecision*

Arguing from a constructivist perspective, Savickas (1995) states that "[t]he career indecision experienced by adolescents and young adults may occur, in part, because they have not recognized their life themes" (p. 365). Savickas (2005) adds that career indecision frequently signifies hesitation before transformation occurs and presents oscillatory movement in search of meaning. When career indecision is at issue, career counselors working from a career construction perspective help their clients identify major life themes, choose careers, construct themselves, and, in the process, make meaning of their lives.

2.2.2 *Construction of the Self as Story*

To establish a clear sense of self and a stable self-concept, one first needs the ability to narrate one's career-life story (Di Fabio & Maree, 2013). Self-construction entails construction of the self as story and enhancement of the self as an inner compass to deal with transitions. Savickas (2011) blended the psychodynamic approach with differential and developmental approaches to create a meta-theoretical framework known as career construction counseling. This meta-theory explains the interpersonal processes people use to construct themselves; processes that direct their vocational behavior. It emphasizes the importance of meaning-making in and through their careers.

Facilitating narratability. Helping clients to say who they really are by getting them to enunciate and hear their career-life stories (autobiographical reasoning, Savickas, 2009a) lies at the heart of career construction counseling. Being able to narrate one's career-life story (narratability; Savickas, 2005; Savickas et al., 2009) facilitates the moderation and eventually the resolution of indecision because it helps clients locate career choice issues in the bigger pattern of lived meaning. Narratability involves the use of narratives to reduce confusion, end doubt, shed light on career-related choices, and, ultimately, promote clients' capacity to make decisions.

(Auto-)biographicity: re-construing past stories and encouraging (auto-) biographicity. Career-life stories, often characterized by numerous twists and turns in the storyline and sub-storylines, are elicited and used to deal with repeated transitions. These stories help to resolve indecision by shedding light on the digressions in people's career lives and by inspiring action and forward movement. In narrating the stories, clients are enabled to listen to themselves and helped to reconstruct their past. Biographicity (Alheit & Daussien, 1999) occurs when clients identify their central life themes (as revealed in their career-life stories) and become able to use work to heal themselves. Clients reinterpret and adapt their former stories so that they can draw on advice from within to help terminate career indecision and pave the way for forward movement (Savickas, 2011).

Creating a holding environment. When clients are helped by career counselors to make use of their elicited career-life stories (autobiographies) to negotiate repeated transitions (Savickas, 2009b), they often discover an existing but dormant ability to exploit their career stories. This enables them to take care of or "hold" (Winnicott, 1969) themselves if and when change happens and impacts on their career-life story—often resulting in the career indecision arising.

Constructing a biographical bridge. When biographicity occurs, clients are enabled to join micro-aspects of their lives into a "grand" story, thereby building a "biographical bridge" across the divide between indecision and sound decision making. Retrospective reflection (facilitated during career counseling) is transformed into prospective reflexivity and, eventually, life designing (Savickas, 2005, 2013, 2015a, 2015b, 2015c).

Self-authoring of the career-life story. Career construction counseling involves the search for a strategy to enable clients to author their career-life stories. Career construction counseling helps career counselors achieve this outcome by first enabling clients to recount (narrate) their career-life stories and then to enact these stories purposefully and intentionally.

Career construction counseling is thus a means of enhancing self-efficacy levels and independence, instilling a positive attitude, and fostering autonomy in clients—the very factors that can contribute to a decrease in career indecision.

Creating a "sacred space". Clients need a safe or "sacred" space where they can feel "safe" (at home) in the company of the career counselor—a place where he or she can ask them about their earliest recollections "deepest secrets." Asking the first four questions listed in Table 2 (Savickas, 2011, pp. 42–43) can help career counselors create such a safe space.

Using earliest recollections: theoretical background. Earliest recollections are used to clarify clients' fundamental preoccupations and major life themes. Adler (1932) maintains that clients draw on implicit messages from their subconscious—conveyed through their earliest recollections—to soothe, reprimand, caution, comfort, motivate, or inspire themselves. These outcomes are achieved by revisiting strategies and plans of action that worked for them in the past and using them to face current and future challenges. Career counselors refrain from "advising" clients and interpreting these fundamentally important stories. Instead, they gently and respectfully help clients recount and then reflect on and interpret these recollections themselves. The individual stories are eventually connected into an articulate and interrelated story that helps clients deal with impasses and discontinuation and inspires forward movement (Hartung, 2011a, 2011b). It enables clients to move from passive suffering to active mastery of pain/challenges (Savickas, 2011).

2.3 From Theory to Practice: Career Counseling as a Three-Act "Drama"

According to Savickas (2011, p. 42): "Similar to a three-act drama, career counseling has three parts. The three parts may be portions of a single interview or three separate interviews" (see Table 2.1). In career construction counseling, clients are introduced to their career counselors during the first act (comprising the administration of the *Career Construction Interview* (*CCI*)) (see the Methodology section). In the second act, the client's life portrait is discussed and related to why he or she sought career counseling in the first place. In the third act, the career counselor counsels the client on the reasons for seeking career counseling. Savickas (2011) states that "during the first act clients *construct* their careers through short stories, during the second act practitioners *re-construct* the small stories into a large story, and during the third act client and practitioner *co-construct* a revised identity narrative, new intentions, and possible actions" (Savickas, 2011, p. 43).

This process is summarized in Table 2.1.

The table shows that allowing clients' larger or grand career-life stories to emerge guides the career counseling process (even though career counselor and clients initially focus on the "smaller" stories that constitute the clients' career-life stories).

2.3.1 *Rationale for the Study*

While much has been written about the manifestation of career indecision at undergraduate level at university, very little has been reported on career indecision at postgraduate level. However, a substantial number of postgraduate students present with career indecision. Over time, I have moved from using a positivist approach to resolving postgraduate students' indecision to adopting an integrated, qualitative + quantitative approach to the problem.

Numerous publications over the past two or three decades have pointed to the value of a narrative approach to career counseling. Clients consistently report having

Table 2.1 Threefold organization of career construction counseling

Elements of three-act drama	Three aims of career construction counseling	Actions taken to realize the three aims	Part of career construction realized	Phases in crafting of life portrait
Act 1: Character is introduced	Part 1: Elicitation of clients' career stories	*CCI* and auxiliary instruments/ strategies are administered to introduce clients to counselors and to themselves	Clients *construct* their careers by narrating several short stories	Clients' small (micro-) narratives are elicited
Act 2: Basic conflict is presented. Insight is achieved and defining moments are uncovered	Part 2: Clients are asked to authorize their career	Counselor reads clients' life portraits, which are discussed and related to the reason for seeking counseling. New interpretation emerges	Counselor *deconstructs* and *reconstructs* (weaves) these micro-stories into a larger story	These narratives are *deconstructed, reconstructed,* and crafted into a preliminary draft of a larger narrative by counselor
Act 3: Change and revitalization are inspired by the new insights	Part 3: Counselor facilitates "movement" by clients	Actual counseling takes place, aimed at prompting clients to "move"	Clients and counselor *co-construct* a revised vision and mission statement (VMS). New aims and achievable actions are formulated. Intention is operationalized	"Final" life portrait is *co-constructed* with counselor and authorized by clients

Compiled from Savickas (2011, pp. 42–43)

experienced the strategy as respectful and useful, hence my decision to report on the implementation of a qualitative (storied) approach to this kind of counseling.

2.4 From Theory to Practice

2.4.1 Purpose of the Study

The study on which this article is based sought answers to the following questions.

a. What were the career counseling needs of a particular postgraduate student in psychology struggling with career indecision?

b. How did this student experience career construction counseling?
c. How did the counselor use the *CCI* to deal with the career indecision of the student?

2.5 Method

2.5.1 Participant and Context

The participant was a purposefully selected 26-year-old English-speaking white woman (Genevieve—a pseudonym). The selection criteria called for someone who had indicated a need for career counseling. Genevieve and a number of other participants volunteered to act as the "client" during a live demonstration that formed part of a workshop in career construction counseling in 2015.

Genevieve's parents divorced when she was very young—a traumatic experience for her. At the time of the interview, she had an honors degree in psychology and was enrolled for a master's degree, but she felt she had lost her passion for the subject. Superficially, Genevieve appeared undecided about what she should do after obtaining her master's degree, but, at a deeper level, her uncertainty seemed to be based on her not really knowing which subfield of psychology she actually wanted to pursue.

2.5.2 Mode of Inquiry

The study was based on naturalistic inquiry as the research methodology in the form of a single, explorative, descriptive, instrumental case study.

2.5.3 Data-Gathering Strategy

Career construction interview (CCI). The CCI comprises five questions in addition to the opening question, "How can I be useful to you …?" (Savickas, 2011). Clients' responses to this question reveal what they hope to get out of the career counseling. The first four career-life story questions (see the section entitled "Responses to Questions in the CCI") shed light on clients' career-life stories, after which their three earliest recollections are obtained.

The three acts of career construction counseling discussed earlier were carried out to elicit Genevieve's career-life story as part of the data-collecting process. Career construction (Savickas, 2005) and self-construction (Guichard, 2009) were facilitated. Genevieve's self-portrait was then completed by carrying out the eight steps recommended by Savickas (2011). Lastly, Genevieve's vision and mission statement was drafted.

Career-life story assessment and intervention (Savickas, 2011). The rationale proposed by Savickas served as the guideline for analyzing the client's responses to the questions in the CCI. For a discussion of the five steps followed in analyzing the three earliest recollections, see Maree (2013).

Noting repeated words or phrases. I carefully noted repeated words or expressions and made sure that Genevieve heard what she had told herself by repeating her own words and expressions to her. I authenticated her words by prompting her to say these words and expressions out loud (to make sure that she experienced them as real).

Observing Genevieve. I observed Genevieve closely and carefully noted her bodily movements, which were later integrated into the career counseling sessions (Savickas, 2009a).

Commencing feedback. I started the feedback with a discussion on the earliest recollections (Genevieve's "secrets") and drew her attention to the fact that they were filled with meaning, despite seeming superficial. I said that they reflected Genevieve's central life themes (Maree, 2015) and her advice to herself.

Creating a life portrait. Savickas' (2011) eight-step strategy was implemented in order to compose a life portrait or future scenario for Genevieve. I first considered her response to the first question in the *CCI* (which provided a strong indication of what she hoped to achieve during the career counseling sessions) when I crafted her life portrait.

2.5.4 Procedure

The intervention (individual narrative career counseling) comprised of two sessions. The *CCI* was completed during the first session (which lasted 70 min). In Session 2 (which lasted 100 min), I read Genevieve's career-life story back to her so that she could authorize it. She and I then co-constructed her life portrait, and we agreed on a number of action steps (see the Results section). Genevieve and I later communicated by e-mail on a number of occasions.

2.5.5 Ethical Issues

Informed consent was obtained from Genevieve, and confidentiality was maintained. Written permission was also obtained for the anonymous publication of the case study.

2.6 Findings

2.6.1 Responses to Questions in the CCI

In response to the question, "How can I be useful to you?", Genevieve responded[1]:

"*I have lost some of my passion for my field of study.*" She looks up, frowns lightly, and then resumes: "*Moreover, I am no longer sure if (and when) I should pursue a PhD after my initial studies, go into private practice immediately or work with somebody else in his or her practice first.*" She sighs and then continues: "*I want to learn more about myself that I did not know before.*"

1. Role models

"*The Spice Girls. They were kind, friendly, arty, sporty and beautiful, inside and outside. One of them had a cross tattoo on her arm to express her religious feelings. They just were themselves. I loved their Spice Girls scrap book, which was a way of exercising their creativity.*"

"*My mother*[2]*: She was very independent, caring, compassionate* (SMILES; MOVES HER LEGS). *The considerate way she interacts with others…she takes time getting to know people* (OPENS HER HANDS)*; always feels as if she is only speaking to you. She is kind and gracious.*"

(CLOSES AND SWIFTLY OPENS HER EYES) "*I admired a ballerina from the Bolshoi ballet group. She was disciplined, graceful, dedicated, passionate about dancing… took time to sign my book (the personal touch impressed me immensely).*"

"*My Grade 2 teacher. She was a petite, small woman* [Genevieve, too, is a beautiful, petite young woman]. *I admired her because of her creative teaching methods. She turned learning into fun. Class became fun. She took a personal interest in each child; made that child feel special.*"

2. Favorite magazine, television show, and Web site

(SMILES BRIGHTLY) "Elle. *The exciting pictures, the sense of creativity, the artistic themes, the fashion aspects, the striking, different colours.* (SMILES) *I, enjoy drawing, using creative fonts…I started compiling a quote book from an early age on. I love cooking for other people; exercising; reading; singing.*"

"The fixer. *It is about a woman who engages in problem-solving; works with people and their dilemmas. But also* The good wife: This is a*bout a female lawyer who started her own firm and pursued a professional career. Much of the story revolves around the many interactions with her family.*"

---

[1]The verbatim responses of the participant have been only lightly edited to preserve their authenticity.

[2]A guiding line rather than a role model.

"Pinterest. *A social media website. I love the creative approach. It is almost like an online pin board (a board where one can save for quotes, and notes on fashion and exercises).*"

3. Favorite book or movie

(SIGHS) "The language of flowers. *A beautiful, well-written book. I love the creative language! It is about an orphan girl who learns that different flowers have different meanings. So, when she gives flowers to others, they have different meanings. The story is about her life journey. It reveals how she goes through difficult circumstances and, as a result of that, grows as a person.*"

4. Favorite sayings or mottoes

"A Bible verse: 'She is clothed in strength and dignity and she laughs without fear of the future.'"

"CS Lewis: 'There are far better things ahead than any you have left behind.'"

"CS Lewis: 'Imagine yourself as a living house' (this is a religious quote). You are a house; God knocks down walls, etc. *and of course sooner or later it will start to hurt and you do not understand why God is acting in this manner.*"

5. Genevieve's earliest recollections

Elated youngster enjoys closeness of happy family

"*At the age of three, at my birthday party, the whole family joined in the fun. I remember the snow white birthday cake. I remember so well my young cousin (he was smaller than me). He drove around all the time while I curiously watched him participate in the fun and enjoyment. I enjoyed encouraging him and seeing his enjoyment. We were so happy.*"

Emotions associated with the story: joy, happiness, curiosity, love, and excitement.

Affectionate interaction with parent brings joy to creative child

"*When I was four years old, at our home in the city…mmmm* (LOOKS DOWN, SMILES) *…Daddy washed his car and involved me. Yes, he made a big effort to involve me in washing the car. He encouraged me to join in. We had lots of fun with the water and the sponges on that sunny day. I remember the driveway vividly; the green colour of the car.* (ILLUSTRATES WITH HER FINGER) *My parents and I always used to drive around and that was such fun.*"

Associated emotions: loving and being loved; joy; excitement.

Confused, heartbroken youngster turns separation into inspiring memory.

(SIGHS DEEPLY) "*I was five years at the time. I did not really understand what was happening or what had happened. I remember sitting at the front door, waiting for my father to come home (as I always did). On this day, he did not come home. After I had sat there for quite some time, Mommy came to me, crying, and said that he would not come home again ever.*"

Associated emotions: sadness, confusion.

Genevieve chose the following encompassing/inclusive heading for the three stories:

Excited and joyful child celebrates and cherishes family (life) despite separation.

2.6.2 Constructing a Life Portrait for Genevieve

Genevieve and I subsequently constructed the following life portrait for her (Savickas, 2011).

"Hopefully I will learn more about myself…about what I did not realise or thought about before. I am unsure as to whether I should go into private practice or link up with somebody else first. I am somewhat uncertain, too, about whether I should pursue my doctorate in psychology at a later stage."

"When I was very young, my parents divorced…for me, as a very young girl, that was a sad and devastating experience (a preoccupation; a central life theme). I cherished the togetherness and belongingness of Mommy, Daddy and me immensely. I realise how important it is for parents and their children to spend fun time together and have joy."

"That led to my developing a strong passion to encourage and inspire young children; especially to help children who have suffered trauma (such as seeing their parents get divorced). I believe that it is possible to remain excited and joyful; to celebrate and cherish family life…to ensure that families grow in spite of pain."

"I am a beautiful, graceful, caring, disciplined, dedicated, compassionate, friendly, arty, sporty and deeply religious young woman. It is important to me to take time to get to know people well, take a personal interest in them, make them feel special (children in particular—they deserve a personal touch). I am independent…arriving at decisions of my own accord is important to me. I want be the best person and psychologist I can be; a person that will be capable of helping people (children in particular) to construct themselves adequately, despite sometimes having to overcome personal trauma."

"I enjoy creative activities, exercising, reading, singing, and dressing in a stylish manner. Working with people in an environment where I can help people (children in particular) advise themselves by engaging them in problem solving; helping people deal with dilemmas has always been a great passion of mine. I just have to work with people and help them resolve personal issues."

"I guess part of me is also keenly interested in making sure that people are given the opportunity to be heard."

"I had to live through painful experiences on life's journey. A genuinely resilient woman, I have grown immensely as a result of this…I have acquired the skill to be kind to different people in different ways (depending on their idiosyncratic needs). I respect women who are courageous, who are willing to sacrifice independence in their work environment for a while if it is in their best, long-term interests; especially if that will help them to become independent, start their own business and be hugely successful."

"I am a strong and dignified woman. I enjoy life in a responsible manner and I do not fear the future. As the song goes: I know not what the future holds but I know Who holds the future. The best in my life is yet to come. Yes, I have suffered and experienced sadness but I know that God always knows what is best for me. God has challenged me but He also was always there to pick me up and hold me to His bosom when I was down. I trust my dear Saviour unconditionally and I always will."

I then asked her to compose her mission statement (MS), and this is what she and I decided on: "*I will complete my Master's degree, do my internship, link with an established person or entity to help me make a name for myself, fine tune my existing skills, learn how to run a private practice and, when the time is ripe, start my own business and become hugely successful...especially in the sense that I will be useful to many people who are in need of counseling.*"

"*I will put the decision as to whether I want to pursue my doctoral studies (including the topic that I want to work on) on hold for the time being. What has become clear to me is that there are many topics that I could possibly consider but that working with children who have suffered trauma and helping them to turn their pain into hope and a social contribution would probably form the basis of my choice.*"

"*In doing what I will be doing, I will be honouring the legacy of my beloved mother and father.*"

Genevieve and I used this MS to identify the resources she needed to devise a feasible action strategy to realize her stated aims. The plan of action was, first, to work as hard as she could to complete her studies. She could talk to people, volunteer to work in a private practice, investigate the possibility of starting her own practice as soon as she had completed her degree or perhaps work with someone she felt comfortable with for a while. I also advised her to attend short courses on how to start a private practice.

Lastly, I asked Genevieve to write a response to her original request for career counseling. She responded by saying: "*The interview was an amazing for me. It enabled me to see how the thread of my life was interwoven in my current choices and this was incredible to see. It made me think of things in depth; things that I would not usually have allowed myself to think of. It enabled me to reflect on my own life and to start to draw associations with my career choices and life history and reflect on who I am as a person. The penny dropped when I realized why I want to work with children—a culmination of my past experiences. I am looking forward to seeing how my future enfolds.*"

"*The life portrait has shown me just how valuable this process is; it is amazing how accurate this document is. I am looking forward to my future.*"

I then suggested she return home, consider possible options for dealing with the challenges confronting her, and report back to me if and when she wanted to.

2.6.3 *Limitations*

As a researcher in the social sciences, I was subjectively immersed in this study and interpreted the data from this perspective. Some researchers frown upon this style of analysis.

2.7 Discussion

This case study demonstrated the value of career construction counseling for a client battling with career indecision. The study also showed that this approach can help students in general deal with challenges experienced while they are studying. Their ability to narrate their stories and draw upon them in times of indecision will help them deal with transitions as and when they occur. The study confirmed Krieshok's (1998) view that decision making is not simply a linear, rational process but, rather, a complex process often involving subconscious motivations. The findings also reveal that career indecision may be brought about by (conscious and subconscious) emotional problems (Di Fabio & Kenny, 2011; Fouad et al., 2006). Hartung (2016), and Masdonati, Massoudi, and Rossier's (2009) findings, too, were substantiated as they indicated that individual career counseling reduced problems related to career decision making (also see Heppner, Multon, Gysbers, Ellis, & Zook, 1998).

The subconsciously induced central life themes (revealed by the three earliest recollections) of the participant in the present study suggest that the *CCI* could be used in addition to the administration of a career indecision scale to identify reasons for career indecision not identified by current career indecision questionnaires. Moreover, the "advice" offered by the participant to herself (through the responses to the first four questions) seemed extremely useful in finding ways to resolve her career indecision. The use of the *CCI* (in addition to career indecision scales) not only as an assessment instrument but, more importantly, as a therapeutic technique to resolve career indecision is therefore strongly recommended. Understanding their central life themes will help clients with career indecision appreciate the importance of not choosing a field of study solely on the basis of test results and expecting to be successful in the associated career.

2.8 Conclusion

The strategy advocated in this article presents an exciting opportunity to blend career counseling theory, research, and practice. Participation in the use of the CCI promoted the developing of and enhanced decision making in a participant who sought requested career counseling (the word "developing" here conveys the idea that people should play an active, ongoing role in authoring their career-life narrative) (Severy, 2006). It is preferred to the word "development," which suggests something that has been completed or finished. Drawing on career construction counseling by using the *CCI* and crafting life portraits turns career counseling assessment into a therapeutic strategy and should ideally be the right of every student. Career counselors working from a narrative framework are well situated and equipped to implement this strategy in contexts of indecision. This approach confirms Krieshok, Black, and Mckay's (2009) view that subconscious processes may well play a major role in career decision making.

Acknowledgements I would like to thank the client for participating in the study and Tim Steward for editing the text.

References

Adler, A. (1932). *What life should mean to you.* London, England: Allen & Unwin Ltd.

Alheit, P., & Daussien, B. (1999, February). *Biographicity as a basic resource of lifelong learning.* Paper presented at the Second European Conference on Lifelong Learning, Bremen, Germany.

Creed, P., Buys, N., Tilbury, C., & Crawford, M. (2013). The relationship between goal orientation and career striving in young adolescents. *Journal of Applied Social Psychology, 43,* 1480–1490.

Di Fabio, A., & Kenny, M. (2011). Promoting emotional intelligence and career decision making among Italian high school students. *Journal of Career Assessment, 19*(1), 21–34.

Di Fabio, A., & Maree, J. G. (2013). Career construction and life design: Heralding a new beginning to career counseling in the 21st century. In A. Di Fabio & J. G. Maree (Eds.), *Psychology of career counselling: New challenges for a new era* (pp. 1–15). Hauppauge, NY: Nova Science.

Fouad, N. A., Guillen, A., Harris-Hodge, E., Henry, C., Novakovic, A., Terry, S., et al. (2006). Need, awareness, and use of career services for college students. *Journal of Career Assessment, 14,* 407–420.

Garcia, P. R., Restubog, S. L., Toledano, L. S., Tolentino, L. R., & Rafferty, A. E. (2012). Differential moderating effects of student-and parent-rated support in the relationship between learning goal orientation and career decision-making self-efficacy. *Journal of Career Assessment, 20*(1), 22–33.

Gianakos, I. (2001). Predictors of career decision-making self-efficacy. *Journal of Career Assessment, 9,* 101–114.

Guay, F., Senécal, C., Gauthier, L., & Fernet, C. (2003). Predicting career indecision: a self-determination theory perspective. *Journal of Counseling Psychology, 50*(2), 165–177.

Guichard, J. (2009). Self -constructing. *Journal of Vocational Behavior, 78,* 251–258.

Hartung, P. J. (2011a). Career construction: Principles and practice. In K. Maree (Ed.), *Shaping the story: A guide to facilitating narrative career counselling* (pp. 103–120). Rotterdam, The Netherlands: Sense.

Hartung, P. J. (2011b, August). *Defining career services: Guidance, education, and counselling.* American Psychological Association 119th annual meeting. Washington, DC, USA.

Hartung, P. J. (2016). Career decidedness. *The Career Development Quarterly, 64*(1), 2–3.

Heppner, M. J., Multon, K. D., Gysbers, N. C., Ellis, C. A., & Zook, C. E. (1998). The relationship of trainee self-efficacy to the process and outcome of career counselling. *Journal of Counseling Psychology, 45,* 393–402.

Krieshok, T. S. (1998). An anti-introspectivist view of career decision making. *Journal of Career Development, 46,* 210–229.
Krieshok, T. S., Black, M. D., & Mckay, R. A. (2009). Career decision making: The limits of rationality and the abundance of non-conscious processes. *Journal of Vocational Behavior, 75,* 275–290.
Maree, J. G. (2013). *Counselling for career construction: Connecting life themes to construct life portraits. Turning pain into hope.* Rotterdam, The Netherlands: Sense.
Maree, J. G. (2015). Life themes and narratives. In P. J. Hartung, M. L. Savickas, & W. B. Walsh (Eds.), *APA handbook of career intervention. Vol. 2: Applications* (pp. 225–239). New York, NY: American Psychology Association. http://dx.doi.org/10.1037/14439-017.
Maree, J. G. (2016). Career construction as a way of resolving career indecision. *South African Journal of Higher Education, 30*(3), 5–13.
Masdonati, J., Massoudi, K., & Rossier, J. (2009). Effectiveness of career counselling and the impact of the working alliance. *Journal of Career Development, 36,* 183–203.
Parsons, F. (2005). *Choosing a vocation.* Broken Arrow, OK: National Career Development Association.
Richardson, M. S. (1993). Work in people's lives: A location for counseling psychologists. *Journal of Counseling Psychology, 40,* 425–433.
Savickas, M. L. (1995). Constructivist counselling for career indecision. *Career Development Quarterly, 43*(4), 363–375.
Savickas, M. L. (2005). The theory and practice of career construction. In S. D. Brown & R. W. Lent (Eds.), *Career development and counselling: Putting theory and research to work* (pp. 42–70). Hoboken, NJ: Wiley.
Savickas, M. L. (2009a). *The role of values in careers: Meaning and mattering in Life Design.* St Louis, MO, USA: Millennium Centre, University of St Louis.
Savickas, M. L. (2009b). Career-style counselling. In T. J. Sweeney (Ed.), *Adlerian counselling and psychotherapy: A practitioner's approach* (5th ed., pp. 183–207). New York, NY: Routledge.
Savickas, M. L. (2010). Vocational counselling. In I. B. Weiner & W. E. Craighead (Eds.), *Corsini's encyclopedia of psychology* (4th ed., pp. 1841–1844). Hoboken, NJ: Wiley.
Savickas, M. L. (2011). *Career counselling.* Washington, DC: APA.
Savickas, M. L. (2013). The theory and practice of career construction. In S. D. Brown & R. W. Lent (Eds.), *Career development and counselling: Putting theory and research to work* (2nd ed., pp. 147–186). Hoboken, NJ: Wiley.
Savickas, M. L. (2015a). *Life-design counseling manual.* Rootstown, OH: Author.
Savickas, M. L. (2015b). Designing projects for career construction. In R. A. Young, J. F. Domene, & L. Valach (Eds.), *Counseling and action: Toward life-enhancing work, relationships, and identity* (pp. 13–31). New York: Springer Science + Business Media.
Savickas, M. L. (2015c). Career counselling paradigms: Guiding, developing, and designing. In P. J. Hartung, M. L. Savickas, & W. B. Walsh (Eds.), *The APA handbook of career intervention* (Vol. 1, pp. 129–143)., Theory Washington, DC: APA Books.
Savickas, M. L., Nota, L., Rossier, J., Dauwalder, J.-P., Duarte, M. E., Guichard, J., et al. (2009). Life designing: A paradigm for career construction in the 21th century. *Journal of Vocational Behavior, 75,* 239–250.
Severy, L. E. (2006). What's my story? Narrative intervention in career counseling. *Doctoral Dissertation*, University of Florida, Gainesville, FL.
Stringer, K., Kerpelman, J., & Skorikov, V. (2011). Career preparation: A longitudinal, process-oriented examination. *Journal of Vocational Behavior, 79,* 158–169.
Winnicott, D. W. (1969). *The use of an object and relating through identifications in playing and reality.* London, England: Routledge.

Chapter 3
Individualized Counseling for Job Decency Analysis and Career Development—A New Approach

Jean-Luc Bernaud and Dominique Guédon

Abstract This chapter sets out a new approach for individual counseling to analyze work and consider career prospects. First, the importance of research into health at work is presented, and then a new method to analyze risks and resources at work is proposed. This method is based on a questionnaire of 156 items, measuring 29 scales and 3 factors: the QERPS. The outcomes are then presented in a stepwise process. A case study is used to demonstrate the relevance of the method to the analysis of work and career management. The conclusion addresses the theme of risks and labor resources in the context of individual counseling.

3.1 Introduction

Today, knowledge and methods to protect workers are available thanks to practitioners, researchers, and the studies they have conducted. It is known that work and working conditions have an effect on physical health; research studying psychological health, however, is more recent. In France, works by authors such as Aubert and De Gaulejac (1991), Hirigoyen (1998), Dejours (1999), Desrumaux (2011), and Vallery & Leduc (2012) underline the growing interest in psychosocial risks (PSR) and their importance. PSR studies mostly target stress and burnout; there are studies on work addiction, albeit rarer, a minority of which focus on improving our understanding of the phenomena (Burke, Matthiesen, & Pallesen, 2006; Guédon & Bernaud, 2015a).

Another concern is with the term PSR; it does not have a clear or unanimous definition (Lesage, Berjot, Amoura, Deschamps, & Grebot, 2012). Its definition depends on the field it is associated with and numerous additional individual and contextual variables. In addition, there is frequent confusion between the problems

J.-L. Bernaud (✉)
INETOP-CNAM, 41 rue Gay-lussac, 75005 Paris, France
e-mail: bernaud.jl@gmail.com

D. Guédon
Laboratoire CRFDP (EA7475), Université de Rouen-Normandie, Rue Lavoisier, 76821 Mont Saint Aignan, France

© Springer Nature Switzerland AG 2018

A. Di Fabio and J.-L. Bernaud (eds.), *Narrative Interventions in Post-modern Guidance and Career Counseling*, https://doi.org/10.1007/978-3-319-98300-4_3

themselves and the conditions causing them. Nevertheless, a consensus has surfaced indicating that PSR involves violence, harassment, addictive behaviors, and general suffering in the workplace (Douillet & Mary-Cheray, 2008). Gollac (2009, p. 31) points out "what constitutes a psychosocial risk is not the symptom of the problem, but what causes it."

There is consensus in the scientific literature about the six principal contextual determinants of PSRs; they are as follows: work overload, emotional expectations, decisional latitude, dysfunctional management, violence and harassment in the workplace, and career trajectory variables (Nasse & Légeron, 2008; Gollac, 2009). Dupret et al. (2012) tell us that none of the observed theoretical models can address the myriad of professional environments, nor are there many investigative tools based on these models to have been validated in the French language. As opposed to evaluating problems mainly associated with how people function, risk assessment is centered on a person's perception of their work environment and its limitations and is therefore becoming a subject of study.

3.2 A New Questionnaire: The QERPS

In order to assess PSRs with a new approach, a new psychometrically sound questionnaire called the QERPS[1] (Guédon & Bernaud, 2015b) was developed. The goal of this chapter is to present how results are restituted within the framework of the QERPS and individual counseling so employees are better able to understand the risks and resources in their workplace and put into place personalized strategies to overcome perceived difficulties. We will also examine a specific case of an employee experiencing difficulty in his job.

The QERPS is a French questionnaire designed to diagnose risks and resources within a given structure for its employees or for those who are transitioning careers. The QERPS has 29 themes[2] grouped into three general categories (social and managerial climate, professional pressure, and self-realization in the workplace), and 156 questions (e.g., "I handle heavy loads at work") answered on a four-level scale. It also evaluates stress and burnout levels as well as a client's tendency to acquiesce or give extreme answers.

---

[1]In French, the acronym QERPS stands for *Questionnaire d'Evaluation des Risques Psychosociaux*.

[2](1) Workload, (2) scheduling pressure, (3) work–family balance, (4) arduousness or drudgery of work tasks, (5) contact with suffering, (6) obligation to hide one's emotions, (7) fear at work, (8) stress in dealing with the public, (9) little or no autonomy, (10) absence of foreseeability, (11) underused skills, (12) requests ignored, (13) absence of colleague support, (14) absence of support from superiors, (15) absence of recognition, (16) general public recognition, (17) violence in the workplace, (18) conflicts in the workplace, (19) moral harassment, (20) sexual harassment, 21) conflicting roles, (22) conflicting values, (23) ambiguity of roles, (24) communication problems, (25) lacking materials and budgets, (26) professional instability, (27) little possibility of professional advancement, (28) lack of meaning at work, (29) boredom at work.

Two samples from a diverse variety of fields in public and private sectors were the testing ground for validating studies. Reliability studies show α medians of 0.74 and 0.76 for the scales and 0.86 and 0.88 for the factors (three categories). Exploratory and confirmatory factor analyses justify the three-category structure with satisfactory adjustment indices. In addition, correlational studies (Guédon & Bernaud, 2015b) have shown links between the scales and the numerous stress, burnout, personality, professional mobility, and health indicators.

The originality of the QERPS lies in its ability to analyze work-related risk factors as well as available resources. It allows participants to not only see various health-threatening risk factors in the workplace but also connect working conditions and career-related issues (professional mobility, success, and so on). It can be used with individuals as well as groups thanks to a 60-card game dealing with four themes (professional career, personal life, improving working conditions, and litigation). For example, one card reads "Ask for a review of professional objectives." This activity encourages reflection: envisioning long- and short-term possibilities, strategizing on how to prevent risk, and future career development.

It is important that the QERPS are not used for predictive diagnostics, but for informative purposes. Therefore, a particularly important part of our work was the aspect of giving results and feedback. More specifically, a client's questionnaire results are not to be used to direct them toward an outside view of their work but to help them analyze their current situation, ask themselves relevant questions, select pertinent information, look into what they can change, and increase their understanding of the work that may be perceived as unmanageable. Fundamentally, a client's results are just the beginning of a longer, more in-depth discussion. It is therefore preferable to adopt a protocol highlighting the importance of questioning and communicating with the client as opposed to using the results as an "absolute truth." The counselor has two elements at his disposal: the individualized report and the "actions, prevention, and remediation card game" and its accompanying worksheet. The introductory phase lasts at least ten to fifteen minutes in order to establish a rapport with the client as well as demonstrate the importance of their participation in their session. It is of critical importance that clients express themselves and lead the discussion. A recommended starting point is to talk about how they felt doing the questionnaire and what they thought about it. Were the questions amusing? Fascinating? Shocking? Did any of the questions make them want to dig deeper? This stage also leads to information about client attitudes and difficulties when the questionnaire was administered, their state of mind, and their work context. It is also a good time to ask them about their expectations. If it has not already been done, time should be devoted to what the client does professionally, their main responsibilities and activities, constraints and difficulties they face, how they manage, and the consequences that these factors can have on their well-being and stress levels.

Next, analyzing the control scales (tendency to acquiesce or give extreme answers) comes into play. If these results do not pose any specific problems, they are put aside. If this is not the case, it is important to talk with the client to understand their answers and strategies. At this point, it is also important to collaborate and agree on the following points: What the sessions will be about (the duration, materials to work with, results to achieve), the objectives (what is the goal of the session, what is not expected), and the overall framework (Where are we in the process? Who will see the results? How does the confidentiality policy work?).

After these preliminary steps and discussion, it is time for feedback and giving the client their results; this stage has seven steps. The first step is the auto-evaluation by the client of their results. Also during this phase, the counselor shares the protocol for giving the questionnaire results, comments on how the client answered (extreme answers or not), presents the significance of the factor scales (the three general categories) and the norms table (the four-level scale for answering), and then encourages the client to self-evaluate each category.

The second step is comparing results. Clients use a different color to indicate their scores; then, they find differentiations between their answers and the normed questionnaire results. They now share the discrepancies they find and explain them.

The third step is analyzing the factor scales. The counselor emphasizes that these three general categories show the broad, overarching nature of working conditions as they are subjectively experienced by an individual. The client is then invited to identify their dominant categories as well as the resources available and the limitations that exist. Next, they highlight in different colors their scores that are harmonious or very different from the questionnaire's normed scores. Once completed, an in-depth discussion ensues about the client's thoughts on their results. Are some points surprising? Does the client have a clearer view of the prominent elements in their current job? Now, each client should have defined the factors or elements that characterize their perception of their work.

The fourth step is handing back the results of the specific scales (the 29 themes). In this part of the session, the client proposes solutions to problems or identifies elements contributing to their well-being; the counselor is there to suggest additional ideas or facilitate more in-depth thinking; sometimes, help is needed to identify the scales having the highest and lowest values. Then, they give their opinion and develop ideas about how this came about, how they originated, and what their impact is.

The fifth step is analyzing the risk scales that reveal interpretations of stress and burnout levels. Commentary about and analysis of client results draw out protection strategies and identify causes of stress and burnout, ultimately, leading to prevention strategies or identification of the elements that can be changed.

The sixth step is summarizing; the best-case scenario is when clients write an overview of their observations so they can better outline main centers of interest and envision future courses of action (finding information, getting in contact with certain people, and so on.)

The last and seventh step is the card game; this helps a client to explore the different ways they relate to their work (either with concrete solutions for their environment or by developing stress management skills). The goal is to get clients directly involved with a fun activity which develops their power to act; second, to get clients to define their own solutions with their own words using their own interpretations; and finally, to move from an inactive to an active vision of their work. For this part of the consultation, the counselor should have a set of 60 "action, prevention, and improvement" cards and the corresponding handouts. There are several steps to using the cards. First, clients choose between 5 and 15 cards corresponding to the strategies they hope to use to better their situation at work. Next, the counselor encourages the client to talk about short-term (within 6 months) and long-term (6 months or longer) strategies. Now, the client presents and explains their choices all the while exploring alternatives and evaluating consequences. The discussion is of course not limited to the content of the cards, and other possible strategies helping the client to overcome limitations and difficulties at work can be brainstormed. Clients should now take stock of what they have learned by answering the following questions: Which aspects of my working environment do I want to change? Why is this important to me? What can I do to get results? For this psychoeducational exercise, actively asking themselves questions and summing up what they have learned is vital. Next, on the accompanying worksheet clients write down the cards they chose by filling out a two-way table: the long or short-term aspect and how many cards they chose in a particular category (career, personal live, improving work conditions, or legal recourse). The last step is for clients to write a few concluding words and strategies.

In order to illustrate more clearly the QERPS and its methodology, hereafter is an example of an employee experiencing difficulties at work and the different steps of analysis when the psychosocial risks questionnaire has been completed. His profile results are presented first and are followed by an analysis.

PSYCHOSOCIAL RISK IN THE WORKPLACE ASSESSMENT QUESTIONNAIRE
QERPS, editor Testallia
Client: YYYY - Counselor: XXX

The purpose of this questionnaire

The purpose of this questionnaire is to help you analyze your current job and its **resources** and **risk factors**. Your results will only be valid if you answer honestly. They can evolve throughout your career depending on the work you do, your professional environment, and your experiences.

Understanding your results

First, take the time to look at how to read your results.

Many resources	A few resources	Neutral : no resources / no risk	Moderate level of risk	Much ris

The above scale goes from resources to risk. Either your work offers you a few or many resources (meaning working conditions are advantageous), or your working conditions have risks that must be reduced or that require you to protect yourself.

The questionnaire is composed of the four following elements:

(A) **Control scales**: Indicating how you responded to the questionnaire—*see the two possibilities below*
(B) **General scales/categories**: Three categories relating to resources and risks at work, which are then broken down into specific themes
(C) **Specific scales/themes**: Relating to resources and risks at work
(D) **Risk scales/factors**: Stress and burnout scores.

(A) Control scales	*T*-Scores	Very weak	Weak	Moderate	Strong	Very strong
I. **Tendency to acquiesce** tendency to give consenting answers	41	-----------*				
II - **Answering in an extreme way** tendency to give reactionary answers	58	----------------------------*				

Assessing your results

First answer each of the three general scales/categories below. Indicate your answer by checking the box in the column of your choice. Then, compare your answers with the results on the next page and discuss what you observe with the counselor. Then, read through the totality of your answers and put together a summary of your observations and analyses.

Many resources	A few resources	Neutral : no resources / no risk	Moderate level of risk	High level of risk

General Scales

Category I. Managerial and social atmosphere				
General atmosphere / management style of my superiors is good			General atmosphere / the management style of my superiors generates problems	
☐	☐	☐	☐	☐

Category II. Professional stress				
Workload and deadlines are reasonable			Workload is overwhelming and deadlines are too short	
☐	☐	☐	☐	☐

Category III. Self-realization at work				
My work is interesting, important, and motivating			My work is not interesting enough, not important, and not motivating	
☐	☐	☐	☐	☐

Your results

B – General scales (relating to resources and risks)	*T*-scores	Many resources 0-34	A few resources 35 - 44	No resources / no risk **45 - 55**	Moderate level of risk 56 - 65	High level of risk 66 and above
I. Managerial and social atmosphere	56	--*				
II. Professional stress	53	----------------------------*				
III. Self-realization at work	47	----------------------------*				

T-scores read as follows:
0 – 34 points: Many resources are available / 35 – 44: A few resources are available
45 – 55: There are no resources but also no risks
56 – 65: There is a moderate level of risk / 66 and above: There is a high level of risk

NB: In the table the asterisk indicates your answer in relationship to the averaged score of all the people who have previously completed this questionnaire.

B – General: Category I	*T*-scores	Many resources	A few resources	Neutral : no resources / no risk	Moderate level of risk	High level of risk
I. Managerial and social atmosphere – the general atmosphere / management style of my superiors	56	--*				

C – Specific themes	*T*-scores	Many resources	A few resources	Neutral : no resources / no risk	Moderate level of risk	High level of risk
6. Obligation to hide one's emotions Outward expression of emotion at work is not allowed	*49*	----------------------------*				
12. Requests ignored Suggestions and propositions are hardly ever taken into account	*49*	----------------------------*				

13. Absence of colleague support - Colleagues don't listen, help or understand	*61*	--*
14. Absence of support from superiors Management doesn't listen, help or understand	*54*	----------------------------*
15. Absence of recognition There is no positive feedback or thanks	*63*	--*
18. Conflicts in the workplace - Work relationships are tense and conflictual and can lead to clashes	*71*	--*
19. Moral harassment There are behaviors aiming to isolate and belittle	*72*	--*
21. Conflicting roles Workload is confusing, contradictory or incongruous	*44*	----------------*
22. Conflicting values Your personal values are compromised by the work asked of you	*42*	----------------*
23. Ambiguity of roles Work tasks and professional objectives are ambiguous or vague	*54*	----------------------------*
24. Communication problems - Little information about policies, professional opportunities or company life exists or circulates	*51*	----------------------------*

B – General: Category II	*T*-scores	Many resources	A few resources	Neutral : no resources / no risk	Moderate level of risk	High level of risk
II. Professional stress Workload and deadlines	*53*	------------------------------*				

C – Specific themes	*T*-scores	Many resources	A few resources	Neutral : no resources / no risk	Moderate level of risk	High level of risk
1. Workload The number of tasks leads to an overload of work	*42*	-----------------*				
2. Scheduling pressure Work must be done quickly and urgently	*48*	------------------------------*				
3. Work-family balance Professional life infringes on personal life	*71*	---*				
10. Absence of foreseeability- My workload is frequently changed and is unforeseeable	*49*	------------------------------*				

B – General: Category III	*T*-scores	Many resources	A few resources	Neutral : no resources / no risk	Moderate level of risk	High level of risk
III. Self-realization at work Work is interesting, important, or motivating	*47*	------------------------------*				

C - Specific themes	*T*-scores	Many resources	A few resources	Neutral : no resources / no risk	Moderate level of risk	High level of risk
11. Underused skills My skills are underused at work	*74*	---*				
28. Lack of meaning at work The work I do doesn't make me feel useful or important	*39*	----------------*				
29. Boredom at work The work I do is boring, not motivating or is unpleasant	*47*	---------------------------*				

5. Contact with suffering I am exposed to suffering, emotional stress, aggressive people or people in distress	*66*	---*				
7. Fear at work I am afraid at work	*56*	---------------------------------------*				
8. Stress in dealing with the public I am open to criticism from people outside my workplace	*56*	---------------------------------------*				
16. General public recognition People outside of my workplace do not recognize the quality of my work	*43*	----------------*				
4. Arduousness or drudgery of work tasks My job requires significant physical abilities	*56*	---------------------------------------*				
9. Little or no autonomy I am not free to decide and have no autonomy in my work	*56*	---------------------------------------*				

17. Violence in the workplace I am exposed to strong language, threats or physical violence at work	*41*	----------------*
20. Sexual harassment I am exposed to words and acts that are sexually inappropriate	*42*	----------------*
25. Lacking materials and budgets Tools and materials are in disrepair and budgets aren't sufficient	*46*	----------------------------*
26. Professional instability Employment is not stable and could disappear	*42*	----------------*
27. Little possibility of professional advancement Few possibilities for career advancement and salary increase	*61*	--*

Your results – Risk factors

Risk Factors	*T*-scores	**Many resources**	**A few resources**	Neutral : no resources / no risk	**Moderate level of risk**	**High level of risk**
Stress score Likelihood of displaying nervousness or stress	*55*	----------------------------*				
Burnout score Likelihood of being burned out	*58*	---------------------------------------*				

In this case study, the client is a manager working in an establishment for the elderly; he is approximately 40 years old. At his workplace, several managers have come and gone in a short time. In addition to the issue of turnover, several types of problems are hindering his job as manager: Job sheets and descriptions are nonexistent, it is difficult to bring people in, there is "an abysmal atmosphere as if in the trenches" (or described as "heavy"), and workers are wary which leads to a permanent state of deception and dishonesty. His job description dictates that he lives on-site and works nights and weekends. He is frequently contacted during his off time, and 10-h days are common. His work situation is problematic due to a skewed work–life balance and not much room for maneuvering. Our case study client has asked for advice from a work-mandated doctor, human resources, and upper management in response to the deleterious and "barely acceptable" working conditions. He says, "I am asked to manage the unmanageable." Even if he feels he is being listened to, no concrete solution has been planned and it is indeed unlikely that his professional situation will evolve in his favor. In his case, his options are to either be promoted and transferred (highly unlikely) or change employers but stay within the human and care services field, because of this he has no intention of staying with the company. He feels that there is no "hidden agenda" on the part of upper management but is quite certain that the situation will not work itself out.

Data analysis of our example reveals the following points: The results of the control scales show no significant bias (there is no tendency to acquiesce); nevertheless, his answers are assertive. His self-evaluation reveals that the managerial and social atmosphere category presents a moderate risk. The second category of professional stress is seen neither as a resource nor as a risk, and the third category (self-realization at work) is seen as a moderate resource. Overall, for the three categories no professional resource has been pointed out. The second and third categories (professional stress and self-realization at work) show average scores, and the first category shows a moderate risk with a *T*-score of 56. If we compare these scores with his auto-evaluation, we see that two of the three categories have been correctly estimated and one is slightly off. The managerial and social atmosphere category has the highest score and the most variation in the eleven specific themes.

Two of these specific themes show a high level of risk; One shows a moderate risk, and two shows some resources. Of the eleven risk factors, the two highest are the presence of conflicts in the workplace ($T = 71$) and moral harassment ($T = 72$); these two points are aspects to keep watch of against the backdrop of already unfavorable working conditions. His answers also show the absence of colleague support and recognition at work, "even with basic things," with *T*-scores of 61 and 63, respectively. Our client evaluated conflicting values at 42 and conflicting roles at 44 which fall into some resources category. So for him, his job definition and objectives are clear and are compatible with his professional values; however, when he points out "It is beyond distrust, it is beyond conflict," we can see the problem with general atmosphere and upper management who is not proposing anything satisfactory.

If we now look at the second general category of professional stress, we see his assessment falls in the middle. Nevertheless, when broken down into specific themes, there are strong contrasts. There is a significant gap between a "bearable" workload (*T*-value 42) and his work–family balance (*T*-value 71 indicating high risk). During the interview, this last point was brought up when he spoke about his working hours being very constrictive and living on-site. When the third general category of self-realization at work is dealt with, we can see that the average evaluation given here hides the contrasting values given to specific themes in this category. He esteems that his work has meaning (*T*-value 39) because it involves taking care of people but he feels the job does not allow him to use all his skills (*T*-value 74); in particular, he says he would like to have a larger role when it comes to "innovating."

The specific themes we can list that fall into the resources end of the scale are general public recognition, the absence of violence and sexual harassment, and the job itself is stable. However, there is a considerably high risk observed with one question: The nature of his job dictates that he is exposed to suffering ($T = 66$). Then, there is moderate observable risk with several specific themes such as fear at work, stress in dealing with the public, arduous or drudgery of work tasks (some tasks requiring physical strength are listed), little or no autonomy ($T = 56$ for the four aforementioned themes), and finally the possibility of professional advancement with a T-value of 61.

Now, let us consider the stress and burnout factors. At 55, his stress score can be considered as median, and his burnout score of 58 shows moderate risk. These two factors are a long-term risk if his current working conditions do not improve or new deleterious conditions are added.

After the quantitative results had been dealt with, our card game allowed the participant to outline a plan for remedying the situation; for him, distinguishing between long-term and short-term plans was not easy. He pointed out that learning, doing things, and taking an active role in innovating are what is important to him. Our session leads to the idea of his creating a human services company. Legal solutions were explored but would only be put into place if his employer did not respect the pre-prescribed legal steps for a negotiated redundancy. On a more personal level, he recognized that he would like to find more time for himself.

To sum up, the analysis of his job converges with the psychosocial risk analysis questionnaire results. The social and managerial atmosphere is "heavy" and was described as problematic (even if this is not a high-risk factor). He is heard but not listened to, "I ask myself, who am I working for?" He comments about the QERPS questionnaire: "What's interesting is that I find a lot of myself in there", he goes on to say, "It's great to take a step back and say 'there are things that I'm not responsible for, the company is' and that gives me possible avenues to explore." From this point on his objective is not to be "locked into a system" but evolve toward starting his own company. He wants to "start fresh" and concludes by saying "I have learned what I needed to learn."

3.3 Conclusion

At the dawn of the twenty-first century, psychosocial risk has become a significant economic and social subject. As public health and company productivity are affected by new and evolving risks, the scientific community and public structures are working to find tangible legal, methodological, or theoretical solutions. Many structures have developed health and prevention strategies so as to render work environments more caring and human (Arnoux-Nicolas, Sovet, Lhotellier, Di Fabio, & Bernaud, 2016). Numerous tools and methods, some quantitative, have been put together (Beque, 2014; Chouanière, 2006; Dares, 2009; Gollac, 2009, 2011). Nevertheless, it is important to keep in mind that risk assessment tools and resources are not strictly quantitative. Leaders in the field insist on the importance of associating quantitative and qualitative, and using tools holistically, meaning using resources encompassing multiple aspects. They must also take into account what is at stake, the nature of the problems to be addressed, and study the available resources as well as the possibilities for change. That said, quantitative scales have two notable advantages. For research purposes, they contribute to databases allowing researchers to compare and clarify concepts as well as competing theoretical models and show their operational validity. Indeed, the field of health at work has a large scientific corpus of information largely thanks to assessment scales. And when a practitioner intervenes, they have a variety of measuring tools to use for individual diagnostics, supposing of course that they choose the best-adapted tool and most fitting method when intervening.

The choice of a scale or set of tools relies on pre-identified criteria (Bernaud, 2013).

1. It has undergone quality calibration (having been tested on a large, non-specialized, sample populations).
2. Metrologic studies are available showing the scientific soundness of the scales; in particular, they sufficiently satisfy reliability indices, confirmatory factor analyses as well as benefit from established links to health in the workplace and career development indicators.
3. When the tool is coherent with a client's issues or is at their company's request.
4. When the tool uses a diverse panel of methods which are complementary and not redundant.
5. Assessments are concurrent with ethics policies to protect client information.
6. There has been forethought about procedure and the goals of data feedback to clients and companies.

In addition to these six aforementioned criteria, there are also specific guidelines for using risk and resource assessment tools. The first guideline is to ensure sufficient communication between all the parties involved working up to the assessment. If clients are not convinced of the utility, reliability, or methods, client attitudes such as biased behaviors, unwillingness to participate, or answering haphazardly and overstating their positions can be observed. Unfortunately, and regrettably, some psychosocial risk studies are done only to respect legal requirements or are done with superficial intentions, meaning the company never intends to initiate change or improvement.

The second guideline deals with change. It is important to put into place all the steps (with each step involving the client) leading to concrete strategies that bring about change (Guédon & Bernaud, 2015b) in order to encourage the diagnostic be used within a social framework. These are often complex steps, which necessitate various types of scheduling, planning, and involvement on several levels. They rely on what is realistically possible for individuals and organizations and their specific needs.

The third and final point is the importance of not only doing the diagnostic work relating to risk but also doing the work of measuring (individual and company) resources. The keys to success are encouraging positive testing conditions and optimizing company strategy, as opposed to seeing the ordeal as an obligation.

Indeed, identifying resources gives companies avenues for exploration (Martin-Krumm, Tarquinio, & Shaar, 2013) and allows employees to put their situation into perspective and redefine their relationship to their job.

Finally, the method presented in this chapter is new in the field of individual career counseling in the postmodern period. Indeed, the analysis of risks and labor resources is often carried out at collective level, in companies. Here, the person's subjective interpretation of his work helps him determine what characteristics can be enriched or modified. This interpretation in individual counseling (Di Fabio & Bernaud, 2008, 2014) allows the building of a life-designing career by increasing the employee foresight and helping him to make career decisions independently. In summary, the method helps to develop skills to build the meaning of a career.

References

Arnoux-Nicolas, C., Sovet, L., Lhotellier, L., Di Fabio, A., & Bernaud, J.-L. (2016). Perceived work conditions and turnover intentions: The mediating role of meaning of life and meaning of work. In A. Di Fabio & D. L. Blustein (Eds.), From meaning of working to meaningful lives: The challenges of expanding decent work. Research Topic in Frontiers in Psychology. *Section Organizational Psychology*, *7*, 704.

Aubert, N., & de Gaulejac, V. (1991). *Le coût de l'excellence*. Paris: Editions du Seuil.

Beque, M. (2014). Les risques psychosociaux au travail - Un panorama d'après l'enquête Santé et itinéraire professionnel 2010. *Dares Analyses, 31,* 2–11.

Bernaud, J.-L. (2013). *Méthodes de tests et questionnaires en psychologie*. Paris: Dunod.

Burke, R. J., Matthiesen, S. B., & Pallesen, S. (2006). Personality correlates of workaholism. *Personality and Individual Differences, 40,* 1223–1233.

Chouanière, D. (2006). Stress et risques psychosociaux: concepts et prévention. *INRS: documents pour le médecin du travail, 106,* 169–186.

Dares (2009). http://www.travailler-mieux.gouv.fr/IMG/pdf/rapport_08_10.pdf.

Dejours, C. (1999). *La souffrance en France*. Paris: Editions du Seuil.

Desrumaux, P. (2011). *Le harcèlement moral au travail: réponses psychosociales, organisationnelles et cliniques*. Rennes: Presses Universitaires de Rennes.

Di Fabio, A., & Bernaud, J. (2008). The help-seeking in career counseling. *Journal of Vocational Behavior, 72*(1), 60–66.

Di Fabio, A., & Bernaud, J.-L. (Eds.). (2014). *The construction of the identity in 21st century: A festschrift for Jean Guichard*. New York: Nova Science Publishers.

Douillet, P., & Mary-Cheray, I. (2008). Agir sur le stress et les risques psychosociaux. *Travail et Changement, 318,* 1–4.

Dupret, E., Bocéréan, C., Téhérani, M., & Feltrin, M. (2012). Le COPSOQ: un nouveau questionnaire français d'évaluation des risques psychosociaux. *Santé Publique, 24,* 189–207.

Gollac, M. (2009). *Indicateurs provisoires de facteurs de risques psychosociaux au travail*. http://www.travailler-mieux.gouv.fr/IMG/pdf/rapport_08_10.pdf.

Gollac, M. (2011). Mesurer les facteurs psychosociaux de risque au travail pour les maîtriser. *Rapport du Collège d'expertise sur le suivi des risques psychosociaux au travail, faisant suite à la demande du Ministre du travail, de l'emploi et de la santé.* http://www.college-risquespsychosociaux-travail.fr/site/Rapport-College-SRPST.pdf.

Guédon, D., & Bernaud, J.-L. (2015a). Le Workaholisme dans une Université Française: une perspective transactionnelle. *Pratiques Psychologiques, 21,* 71–85. https://doi.org/10.1016/j.prps.2015.01.003.

Guédon, D., & Bernaud, J.-L. (2015b). *Questionnaire d'évaluation des risques psychosociaux au travail. Manuel de référence et d'interprétation*. Cergy: éditions Testallia.

Hirigoyen, M.-F. (1998). *Harcèlement moral, La violence perverse au quotidien*. Paris: Editions La Découverte & Syros.

Lesage, F.-X., Berjot, S., Amoura, C., Deschamps, F., & Grebot, E. (2012). Mesure du stress en milieu de travail par auto-questionnaires validés en français: revue de la littérature. *Archives des Maladies Professionnelles et de l'Environnement, 73,* 596–606. https://doi.org/10.1016/j.admp.2012.06.003.

Martin-Krumm, C., Tarquinio, C., & Shaar, M.-J. (2013). *Psychologie positive en environnement professionnel*. Bruxelles: De Boeck.

Nasse, P., & Légeron, P. (2008). *Rapport sur la détermination, la mesure et le suivi des risques psychosociaux au travail*. Rapport remis le 12 mars 2008 au ministre du travail, des relations sociales et de la solidarité. http://www.dgdr.cnrs.fr/drh/protect-soc/documents/fiches_rps/rapport_légeron.pdf.

Vallréy, G., & Leduc, S. (2012). *Les risques psychosociaux*. Paris : Presses Universitaires de France, coll. «Que sais-je».

Chapter 4
A Meaning-Centered Career Intervention: A Case Study

Lin Lhotellier, Caroline Arnoux-Nicolas and Laurent Sovet

Abstract An innovative framework for career intervention focused on meaning was developed on the basis of a joint research project carried out over several years (Bernaud et al., 2015). This framework includes seven to eight 2-hour sessions held approximately once a week. The purpose of the present chapter is to introduce a case study with a focus on analyzing the interactions between counselor and client, as well as the qualitative effectiveness of the career intervention. The importance of exploring both the quantitative and qualitative effects of a meaning-centered career intervention is discussed with respect to the challenges of career counseling in a postmodern context.

4.1 Introduction

The purpose of the present chapter is to conduct a case study concerning the outcomes of an innovative meaning-centered career intervention. This intervention is the result of work by a French research group (Bernaud, Lhotellier, Sovet, Arnoux-Nicolas, & Pelayo, 2015) at the *Conservatoire National des Arts et Métiers* (National Conservatory of Applied Technology).

The first section of the chapter introduces the relevance of meaning of life and meaning of work for career counseling practices in a changing socioeconomic

---

L. Lhotellier (✉)
Centre de Recherche sur le Travail et le Développement, Conservatoire National des Arts et Métiers, 41, rue Gay Lussac, 75005 Paris, France
e-mail: lin.lhotellier@lecnam.net

C. Arnoux-Nicolas
Centre de Recherche sur la Formation et Centre de Recherche sur le Travail et le Développement, Conservatoire National des Arts et Métiers, 41, rue Gay Lussac, Paris, France

L. Sovet
Laboratoire Adaptations Travail-Individu, Université Paris Descartes, 71, avenue EdouardVaillant, Boulogne-Billancourt, France

© Springer Nature Switzerland AG 2018
A. Di Fabio and J.-L. Bernaud (eds.), *Narrative Interventions in Post-modern Guidance and Career Counseling*, https://doi.org/10.1007/978-3-319-98300-4_4

context. The theoretical foundation of these two concepts is also explored. The second section presents the different sessions of our meaning-centered career intervention with a focus on analyzing the effects on our client. The last section discusses the importance of examining both the quantitative and qualitative effects of meaning-related career interventions.

4.1.1 Meaning of Life, Meaning of Work: New Directions for Career Counseling Practices

In the current socioeconomic context characterized by uncertainty and unpredictability, meaning of life and meaning of work are increasingly becoming central in career issues (Bernaud, 2016; Savickas et al., 2009). In the face of rapidly accelerating societal changes, Savickas et al. (2009) suggested the need to switch toward a new paradigm for career counseling practices. Indeed, individuals are looking for meaning in their lives and in their work. The new type of career intervention that was used for our case study was designed to help our clients explore their own meaning of life and meaning of work.

Accordingly, it is important to introduce the concepts of meaning of life and meaning of work from a theoretical point of view. Two main epistemological approaches have been used to study the psychology of meaning: existentialist psychology and positive psychology. Meaning of life and meaning of work are the most important concepts to have been explored through the psychology of meaning (Bernaud et al., 2015). For Auhagen (2000), meaning of life can be defined as "denot[ing] reflections on, and/or ways of experiencing, contexts of meanings in relation to human life in general, to one's own individual life, or to parts of the latter" (p. 38). Moreover, Frankl (1959), who was deported to a Nazi concentration camp during the Second World War, considered that meaning of life was a vital aspect for human beings, one that helped them to function better.

Quantitative studies have also made it possible to highlight the determinants of the meaning of life. Thus, Schnell (2009, 2011) has developed a Sources of Meaning and Meaning in Life Questionnaire (SoMe) inventory, identifying 26 sources of meaning that she then reduced to four higher-order dimensions on the basis of a factor analysis: (1) self-transcendence (setting goals beyond one's own needs), (2) self-realization (challenging one's own abilities), (3) order (holding one's own values), and (4) personal and social well-being (increasing one's hedonistic joy).

Some authors have shown a strong correlation between the level of meaningful life and meaningful work (Steger, Dik, & Duffy, 2012). The concept of "meaningful work" covers a variety of definitions. It is usually understood as a subjective experience that has personal meaning for the individual (Rosso, Dekas, & Wrzesniewski, 2010). The meaning of work covers both the content of the meaning and the level of meaning that the individual experiences in his or her work. Recently, a new model of the meaningful work was validated among a large sample of French employees (Arnoux-Nicolas, Sovet, Lhotellier, & Bernaud, 2017).

This new model is based on four dimensions: the importance of work in one's existence, the understanding of one's work, the directing of work, and the purpose of work.

4.2 Method

4.2.1 Participant

The client is named Ariane.[1] She is 43 years old and is single with no children. She had attended or completed a graduate degree program. She is currently a job-seeker and is undergoing a transition in both her career and life.

4.2.2 Principles of Our Meaning-Centered Career Intervention

The intervention framework is based on seven to eight 2-h sessions held approximately once a week (see Fig. 4.1). It is open to all committed persons in transition situations with a psychological state that is compatible with reflection on their existence and future—persons who are in the process of exploring the question of meaning, regardless of their age, sex, level of training, professional field, or status. The framework is based on the following principles: respect for ethical rules and a commitment to complete all relevant assignments before each session. Sessions are supervised by a counselor who helps the client identify the most salient aspects of the process through a co-construction approach.

4.3 Our Meaning-Centered Career Intervention

4.3.1 Preliminary Interview and Clarification of the Request

4.3.1.1 Purpose of the Preliminary Interview

The representation of the framework (see Fig. 4.1) does not include a reference to the preliminary interview which is aimed, first, at introducing the framework to the client and, second, at analyzing his or her expectations. It should also ensure that such support is tailored to the client's situation.

[1]The name of our client was changed for reasons of confidentiality.

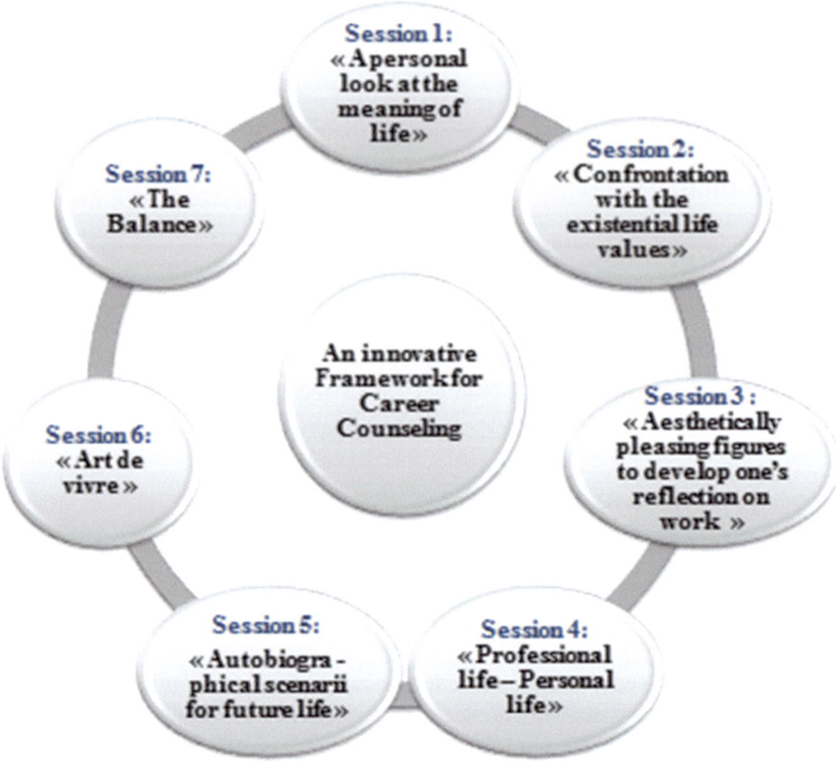

Fig. 4.1 Framework of our meaning-centered career intervention

4.3.1.2 The Preliminary Interview: Ariane Needs to Take a Step Back

When Ariane embarked on the meaning-centered career intervention, she had been retrenched after six months in a position. She interpreted this as the result of an insufficiently precise definition of the position to which she was recruited, which was presented as a position of commercial director. Her experience demonstrated that her employer actually required a development director, a position that did not match her professional profile. Before this six-month period, Ariane had remained for 14 years with the same employer. She wanted to take some time out before embarking on a new job abroad.

She agreed to commit to a framework that we presented to her as being psychologically demanding and requiring sustained personal work. She had already undergone a skills assessment seven years earlier. At that time, she was not looking for a career change but for the benefit of an external perspective on her work. That assessment was demanding in emotional terms but she stated that it was a good experience.

4.3.1.3 Our Analysis

Our exchange with Ariane highlighted her need to take a step back as she turned a page in her existence. The meaning of life was thus a central concern for her at this point in time. In any case, it is up to the recipient to assess the appropriateness of the proposed career intervention for their purposes. Hence, the importance of this preliminary exchange emerged: the participant should be advised that they will be expected to perform sustained work, both in quantitative terms (the time commitment is at least equal to time spent in meetings with the counselor) and in qualitative terms (to the extent that this process is demanding in emotional terms).

4.3.2 First Session: Where Is Ariane in Terms of Her Reflection on the Meaning of Life and Work?

4.3.2.1 Objectives and Aims of the First Session

The objective of the first meeting is, on the one hand, to build a working relationship between the counselor and the client based on an agreement on the objectives to be pursued and the activities to be implemented (Bernaud & Bideault, 2005). On the other hand, the objective is to take stock with the recipient of the state of his or her own reflection on the meaning of life and the meaning of work.

4.3.2.2 A First Assessment

In the past, Ariane had had an important opportunity to reflect on the meaning of her life and work during the skills assessment referred to above. Her participation in that assessment had been motivated, first, by the fact that Ariane had taken on a genuine leadership position for the first time in her career. Second, she had worked under the same manager for a considerable period of time and in three different companies, a person described by Ariane as having difficult relations with his staff. He was reluctant to support Ariane and her co-workers by providing positive assessments of their work. Ariane stated that, in that context, she was keen to obtain an objective assessment of her work.

This first exchange led Ariane to talk about her experience. She had worked for a long time in a communications agency, where she was responsible for the promotion of her clients' products. Specifically, Ariane explained that she was the agency's sole contact with the customer. She was therefore required to understand her clients' requests, make presentations to the agency's creative teams, and identify the "voice" of the client. Her work required a high level of diplomacy, especially when working with creative professionals. She was also required to perform managerial duties.

Ariane pointed to the difficulties she experienced in separating her private life from her professional life. These difficulties were due to a strong sense of duty and a strong commitment to customer service, resulting in a very significant investment in the professional sphere of her existence. She described a tendency to take on all requests that were made to her, a situation that sometimes led to her "exploding," which was difficult to understand by other employees. She also referred to her tendency to mollycoddle the members of her team, for example, by doing their work for them when they were on leave. Before undertaking her skills assessment, Ariane had also been through a period where she was severely overworked. She struggled to talk about this with her director, and she eventually resigned. Her director requested her return, and she accepted. Following this episode, she reduced the amount of time spent in her job, including by refraining from doing the work of absent employees. Ariane felt that these difficulties arose from an issue of meaning, insofar as they reflected the importance she attaches to duty. They also reflected one of the main points to emerge from the assessment conducted seven years earlier: the illusory nature of a robust distinction between one's private and professional life.

In addition, this preliminary assessment enabled her to build up confidence in herself. As a result, over the next three to four years, Ariane enjoyed more peaceful relations with her manager and in her private relations.

4.3.2.3 Ariane's Expectations Regarding the Career Intervention

Six months ago, Ariane felt she was stagnating and becoming bored in her professional and personal life. She wished to make a change, both in her career and in terms of looking for a new apartment. Her main expectation with respect to the career intervention was to put things in perspective and develop a guideline for her life.

Our first session also led us to question Ariane with respect to her early career. After a first 12-month experience in a humanitarian organization, Ariane worked in a communications agency with no particular specialization for a period of 18 months. Following a redefinition of her position, Ariane regrettably left this organization for financial reasons.

Our interview led her to discuss her understanding of the concept of career. Several years ago, "career" meant "sacrificing everything to her work," a definition that she now rejected. Today, her concept of career involves notions of development and progress, indicating a real change in her perspective.

4.3.2.4 The Exercise of the Funeral Eulogy

During the exercise of the funeral eulogy, Ariane highlighted the idea of her presence vis-à-vis others. She described herself as someone who strives to be close to others at particular times in their lives, and she associates difficult periods in her life with chance. However, she expressed this idea in an exaggerated manner: It resulted in her sense of sacrifice to others and combined the idea of her presence to others with the idea of creativity in the professional context. Associating that presence to others with creativity, Ariane described herself as accompanying the creative teams and others in general.

4.3.2.5 Summary

The summary of this first meeting led us to discuss the following elements. First, Ariane highlighted her need to help others do their best, especially in the professional context. She described her career path as the result of chance meetings. Nevertheless, she distrusted the professional world of business, in which she trained initially, where she described relationships between people as based on self-interest and manipulation. She also talked about her interest in the arts. Reflecting on her experience in humanitarian communications, Ariane noted that she hesitated between the professional fields of communications and of humanitarian aid. She stated that she opted for communications because she felt she was not sufficiently "robust" to take on humanitarian work. Given the uncertain nature of the current work environment, we suggested that she should reflect on the different ways in which she could express her desire to accompany others. Following this first meeting, it became clear that most of her views and beliefs were drawn from her experience in the communications agency where she worked for 14 years. We asked her to talk about her first professional experiences, but little reference was made to her early private and family life.

4.3.2.6 Our Analysis

The presentation of this first session illustrates a number of aspects of our career intervention, as well as a number of life characteristics we regularly find among our clients. The people we receive frequently refer to their difficult relationships in the workplace. Similarly, they have difficulty striking the right balance between their personal and professional lives, confirming the value of further exploration of this point. Regarding the session itself, the funeral eulogy represents a delicate moment: The relationship between counselor and client is still fragile, because we are still at the very beginning of our career intervention, and this exercise may appear as quite confronting. It is therefore appropriate to explain that the aim is to create the conditions from which to embark on a reflection on the direction and priorities of one's life. We will see that Ariane was prepared to take up that challenge. She continued to work on this alone after the meeting, and during the last session she described the "funeral eulogy" exercise as a key moment in the career intervention. We also note that the discussions made it possible to refer to subjects that were not explicitly planned for in the intervention—for example, Ariane's description of the content of her work. The framework of subjects covered in the career intervention includes some flexibility, further enriching the material available for reflection. The question of her predominant values provides a guiding thread here, with Ariane referring to her sense of duty and rejection of opportunistic behavior in the first session. We stressed the importance of a firm commitment to the subject in the working sessions and in personal preparation. Concerning Ariane in particular, we asked her to reflect on possible ways that she could express her desire to support others.

4.3.3 Second Session: A Dialogue on Existential Values

4.3.3.1 Objectives and Aims of the Second Session

The purpose of the second session was to identify the client's priorities in life (Schnell & Becker, 2006). A participatory restitution of the French version of the Existential Values Questionnaire of Life (Schnell, 2009) was performed, and it was completed by the client between the two sessions. Note that the use of a *participatory* restitution facilitates the appropriation of the results by the client (Hanson, Claiborne, & Kerr, 1997).

4.3.3.2 A First Informal Exchange

We began the second session with an informal dialogue on the client's latest news, and the thinking generated by the previous session. Ariane again worked on the funeral eulogy and confirmed the elements that emerged in the previous session: Those who knew her would remember her as someone who was a good listener and liked to help others.

She also added a new characteristic to the results of the first session: her taste for concrete action. In addition, she noted the difficulties she faces in strategic thinking: She likes strategic thinking but it was also a source of anxiety for her. This has a professional impact, and discussing it allows Ariane to talk about the work processes that she implemented in the communications agency. As the principal contact point for the client, Ariane's work took place in three stages: a summary of the client's request, a strategic recommendation, and implementation. This last phase was not problematic for her. However, she tended not to ask certain key questions with respect to the client's demands. As a result, the strategic recommendation phase, when she was supposed to raise the customer's awareness of certain sensitive matters, was sometimes difficult for her.

Following our suggestion at the end of the previous session, Ariane reflected on the different ways in which she could express her desire to help others: communication, relationships with others, and human contact.

Finally, the overview of recent news, prior to entry into the specific content of the second session, provided Ariane with an opportunity to talk about her taste for international matters and, related to this, her desire to improve her English. She planned to leave for New Zealand in two months' time and wanted to work in a sector that was very different from communications. However, she had not yet established any contacts in connection with this project. She saw New Zealand in terms of sports, linked to her love of sailing and skiing, and in terms of authenticity.

4.3.3.3 Presentation of the First Video

The actual content of the second session began with a first video presenting an individual in the process of changing jobs. Compared to the person in the video, Ariane stated that she always felt helpful and autonomous in her work, and had no difficulties in this area. What was lacking in her work was of a different nature: a guide and a sense of being valued, which was related to her tendency to doubt and even assess herself negatively. Ariane found it interesting that the person filmed discussed the importance of the purpose of his work. On this point, her interpretation of the person featured in the video was incorrect. He was pleased to focus more on the path to reaching a given goal than he did in the past, in a professional environment that he ultimately rejected.

4.3.3.4 Ariane's Response to the Existential Values Questionnaire

Generally speaking, Ariane's responses to the Existential Values Questionnaire achieved an average score. In particular:

- She expressed a desire for daily commitment to the people around her and a certain mistrust concerning the defense of major causes that she described "noisy" and "bombastic."
- She described herself as sensitive to nature, which she considered in terms of a return to simplicity and authenticity.
- She was very much interested in personal development, which she defined as an intellectual openness to new learning rather than a question of personal power
- She also valued freedom and felt the need to be accompanied rather than directed. On this point, she noted that she had lacked parental authority.
- Moral values, respect for others, tolerance, authenticity, and kindness are important to Ariane. She described herself as empathetic but authoritarian, while being open to revising her opinions.
- She expressed a tendency to pragmatism and organization, resulting, for example, in the use of sleep schedules, "she does not lie in bed all morning."
- She had worked on the value of hedonism, fighting against a tendency to mull over on the subject of her negative self-image.
- Harmony was important to her, and she often tried to smooth out conflicts between people.
- She gave importance to the company of others and stated that she had many very good friends.

- She also attached importance to love, conceived of as friendship, and recognized that she would like to be in a relationship, while having some difficulty in admitting this. (With respect to love, the sharp contrast between the score obtained in the questionnaire and her self-evaluation was raised, enabling us to question Ariane about this aspect of her life.)

We were then able to dive further into the details of Ariane's values by raising a number of different items.

- She saw her life as an opportunity for continuous improvement, which was related to her progress in personal development.
- The item "Examining me in a critical manner is important to me," which she agreed with, was said to involve a less severe perspective on herself than in the past, and comprehension rather than judgment.
- Generativity was undervalued by Ariane, who did not see how she could hope to leave a trace of her time in this world. However, the item "I try to create things whose value is sustainable" was still credited with the maximum score: In reality, this corresponds for her to a respect for commitments made, to loyalty.
- She described herself as being more a concrete and pragmatic person than a "thinker."
- She gave the maximum score to the proposition "I think there is a meaning to what I do," but her comment on this response indicated that she felt a need for meaning that was currently unmet.
- She agreed with the statement "I feel like I belong to something larger than myself," which corresponds to her conviction that there is something beyond the human mind: She said that she believes in god.

During the dialogue on values, Ariane referred to some of her hobbies such as tennis, jogging, and her interest in art history. She also discussed a private aspect of her life, her conception of the couple and the family. According to her, the idea of the couple has long been inseparable from that of a household with children. Today, the idea of a couple without children is possible, as is the idea of adoption.

4.3.3.5 Ariane's Main Values

The most important values for Ariane are personal development, freedom, moral values, pragmatism, harmony, the well-being of others, love, and contact with the community. In contrast, she rejected the values of generativity, power, success, and challenge.

4.3.3.6 Summary

The summary of values also led Ariane to assert the centrality of dialogue with others, to express her need to achieve, but also her lack of confidence and compassion toward herself. She perceived her project to live and work abroad as a means of cementing her preferred values. She was not simply running away but opening herself up to new career choices, meeting new people, and entering into new dialogues. Her poor command of the English language, far from being seen as an obstacle, released her from performance pressure and accordingly offered her the prospect of new experiences. Finally, Ariane considered that this second session had allowed her to clarify what was really important for her. She, nevertheless, felt unable to connect with her new project and break with a path that had been determined on the basis of chance encounters only.

4.3.3.7 Our Analysis

We can note several learnings from this session, which is aimed at giving our clients a moment of "free" expression, before embarking on our work properly. In addition to providing additional elements of dialogue, the session makes it possible to link the work done to the rest of the subject's life: Keeping the two separate would in fact be in contradiction to the very nature of the intervention. The workshop provides the time and place for a free expression of the subject's weaknesses. These "hot spots" are common among our clients, as demonstrated by Ariane's self-depreciation that came up often during the sessions even though she was fully aware of it. Beyond the obtained scores, we consider the values questionnaire as a valuable tool for the interview. Self-evaluation serves this purpose, as does the discussion of certain items, clarifying the person's preferences and allowing us to understand the meaning given to certain sentences. For example, the person who designed the test considers that the statement "I try to create things whose value is sustainable" is related to the value of "generativity." Ariane, however, understood this as the respect for commitments made, which is more linked to "moral values." As an accompaniment to reflection, our workshop also aims to be a lever for change for the client, who is repeatedly prompted to action. Thus, at the end of the second session, Ariane was asked to consider the practical implementation of her key values. We noted that, in Ariane's case, she was already deeply committed to an implementation of concrete actions as she planned to leave for the antipodes. Finally, Ariane stated how important dialogue with others was in her life. We will see that this element was largely confirmed later on.

4.3.4 Third Session: Coming Out of Oneself

4.3.4.1 Objectives and Aims of the Third Session

In the third session, the recipient is invited to look at the bigger picture of their own situation through an artistic work (film, book, painting, photos, etc.) and a quotation of their choice (Bernaud et al., 2015). This is aimed at enhancing the reflection on the meaning of life and the meaning of work, a practice based on the principles of bibliotherapy (Jackson, 2001).

4.3.4.2 A First Informal Exchange

During the initial, informal conversation, Ariane referred to her pleasure in preparing the session, as well as the anxiety related to the necessity to look for job offers. While this was conducted in a very different spirit from that of a job search, it nevertheless plunged her into an uncomfortable reflection. Since the last session, Ariane was offered a one-month mission by a friend in the internal communications department of a large company. Her role would be to raise employee awareness about security. Ariane's first reaction was one of fear: Would she really be able to carry out this work? This type of first reaction is familiar to her. In a second step, she was more reassuring, knowing that she will receive professional help when needed, in the same way that she helps others. She does, however, note that she is not a real source of help for herself as she feels the need of a "screen," a reward for the quality of her own work to counterbalance her negative self-depreciation. When considering the previous session, she had no difficulty in identifying the meaning of each of her actions, but felt a general lack of direction in her life. She also expressed her negative perception of her current unemployment situation, referring to a fear of laziness and of the pressure she was under. The existence of people who benefit from our help often leads to a perception of emotional tension. Ariane does not appear to be depressed but she does express negative effects and beliefs in various forms. After remembering a number of work conflicts in the first session, and expressing her lack of self-compassion during the second, she highlighted her perceived ambivalence with respect to her situation of unemployment during the third session: She felt she was at a crossroads in her life; while this was a welcome break on the one hand, she still had difficulty in benefiting from it on the other.

4.3.4.3 "Keeping Corner" (Un sari couleur de boue) by Kashmira Sheth

In preparation for the third session, Ariane chose to read the work of Kashmira Sheth "Keeping Corner" (Sheth, 2010). With respect to her reflection on the meaning of life, she noted the idea of acceptance of failure and "rebound" after failure. She also referred to the need to remain unaffected by the fears of others, and the need to trust oneself and be one's own guide. With respect to the meaning of work, the book refers to resuming one's studies as providing a second chance, a rebirth if you will. It also highlighted the importance for Ariane of building up her project progressively, of preparing and anticipating in advance—something that she had always struggled to do in the field of communications. The book also illustrated the possibility of learning activities anew—skills that were once mastered but had not been exercised for a long time. However, while the possibility of relearning existed, Ariane preferred to remain in a known field as this would be less difficult than having to relearn a skill. Ariane also noted the parallel between the main character's life and the evolution of Indian society. We drew her attention to the possibility that this aspect of the book could be seen as contradictory to her lack of appetite for a commitment to great causes, which she had expressed in the previous session. However, Ariane stated that the heroine took concrete actions that corresponded to her own inclinations. This illustrates the role in this process of the career advisor. The advisor's attention to the mental universe of the recipient, through the words of the latter, allows him or her to relate to statements that have been made at different times in the process. The possible effects are diverse. In this case, Ariane confirmed a value to which she was attached: concrete implementation. In this way, meaning is built up during the different sessions in a joint approach between counselor and client. The development of dialogue around the chosen work brought Ariane to reconsider the idea of the general sense of her life. Founding a home had long been her most important desire, one that she had not realized. Ariane now described looking for general direction in one's life as ambiguous: One searches for such direction but is also afraid to find it. Feedback on the selected novel appeared to encourage Ariane to be more "proactive" (which she defines as the action to "initiate self-reflection to the original action") and to clarify the meaning of work and life. For Ariane, the other has a role to play in encouraging this proactivity; it is a "gateway" idea to which we shall return below. She sees the heroine as being more reactive than proactive and, from this point of view, she felt close to the character. Ariane believes that better defining one's way makes it possible to be more proactive. However, she is not there yet, she stated, as demonstrated by the difficulties she encountered in writing her resume: She is unable to define a guiding principle for the resume, just as she is unable to identify a meaning for her life. In addition, it was important for us to clarify the meaning of the words used by the client. In this case, Ariane's use of the term "proactive" did not seem clear enough to us. At times, we therefore asked Ariane to complete her sentences beyond the point where she would spontaneously stop. This helped her push her thinking beyond the usual limits and helped her clarify her own thoughts.

4.3.4.4 The Other as a "Bridge"

Ariane chose the following quotation from Brassaï: "We sometimes wonder if life has meaning… and then we encounter beings that give meaning to life." This posits the idea of the other as a "bridge," not as a mirror. The other is a "gateway" in expressing the words that engender confidence. (However, taking advantage of the other as a "gateway" does not mean being carried by that other.) The "mirror" is the idea of the other as a model to follow, which Ariane stated she was not looking for. She rejected Alain Prochiantz's idea that "Life has no meaning, only each individual life has meaning, given by one who lives this life. The individual traces his line and disappears." Ariane disagreed with this vision, which "includes the idea of loneliness."

The comments inspired by citing Brassaï illustrate the possibilities offered by using such excerpts as part of the session. Their brevity and a certain ambiguity in the terms used make for a rich and fertile reflection as part of the career intervention.

4.3.4.5 Summary

Ariane's main takeaway from this session was the importance of others. She must keep this in mind when building up her own project in order to make it more proactive than reactive. It is important that her relationship with the other takes the form of a *mutual* contribution. Ariane had previously expressed the view that she felt better able to help others than herself. We suggested that she should think about the reasons for that, and how she could become more capable of helping herself.

4.3.5 Fourth Session: On the Meaning of Work

4.3.5.1 Objectives and Aims of the Fourth Session

The fourth session allows the recipient to identify the important values in their professional activity (Létourneau, Christian, & Lecine, 2012) and to focus reflection on the notions of satisfaction, the centrality of work, and its reconciliation with other spheres of life (Rosso et al., 2010). The recipient is required to undertake work in the form of selecting attractive job offers and filling out a questionnaire on work values.

4.3.5.2 A First Informal Exchange

Ariane stated that the third session had an emotional dimension for her in that she became aware of the importance to her of the idea of balance in relation to the other. This led to a clear understanding of management, which includes the idea of accompanying the development of others. She also felt capable of reassuring others.

Ariane's words in this first informal exchange testify to the special role played by the meaning of work as an object of thought and a source of effects for recipients during the career intervention. If Ariane thinks back on what she felt during the previous session, it is probably a sign that the content discussed led to recollections from the past, in a "metabolic" manner, so to speak. For our participants, daily life and work intertwine with the ideas that are generated over the duration of the workshop. Ariane had further detailed her project since the last meeting. On the advice of a New Zealander she met, she tried to highlight her strengths in the resume she would use when seeking employment in this country. We asked her to clarify, and she stated the following.

- Her ability to adapt to change, as demonstrated by the variety of functions she had exercised and the situations she had encountered in the agency.
- Her ability to design and achieve practical implementation, two very important aspects in her opinion.
- Relational skills that allow her to nurture harmony and be a "gateway" to the other, in the sense that she gave to this term in the previous session.
- Her ability to manage teams and various aspects of project implementation: design, budget management, management.

On our side, while skills are not the central focus of this work, we allowed a small detour in this case for two reasons. First, the scope of discussions held during the workshop is vast. It is therefore difficult to determine with geometrical precision when one is in a position to advise. Separating the human into isolated components is an approach that, in our situation, would create artificiality. Second, we believe that such an exercise can lead to an improvement in self-confidence. Our clients often lack a belief in their own worth, and asking them to reflect on their knowledge and attitudes is a way of improving that. Ariane actively continued her job search in New Zealand and built up her contacts in that country.

4.3.5.3 A Video About Work Values

We entered the program for the fourth session by watching a video on the value of work. Ariane was surprised to learn that two-thirds of French people say they are happy at work. She also noted the importance, in the value of work, of having the employee's voice heard. That was something that she did not experience in 14 years of work, where she was only able to express herself through her achievements. She also stated that she sought to foster harmony between her employees and promote an atmosphere of *healthy* competition and not competition per se. Another point that was raised was the fact that Ariane perceived work as a preferred means of socialization. Her temporary feeling of anxiety when she stopped working was probably a consequence of that belief. However, Ariane gradually felt more and more free. The fact that she had stopped working allowed her to recover and realize that she had been pulled under by her work for many years. This thought had arisen in her mind in the past, but she rejected it, lying to herself, she thinks today. She realized the exaggerated place she gave to work in her life, a situation that had contributed to her current celibacy. The problem of reconciling life and work is often central to our beneficiaries, and this case is further evidence of that.

4.3.5.4 Work as a Synonym of Flourishing, Freedom, and Social Inclusion

Ariane's representation of work was based on three terms: flourishing, freedom, and social inclusion. Two points can be made here, first, the positive value of work for our beneficiary. Next, and more specifically, it is possible to note the remarkable convergence for Ariane of the meanings of work with the values of life she highlighted in the meetings: personal development, freedom, moral values, pragmatism, harmony, well-being of others, love, contact with the community and, in summary, dialogue with the other.

4.3.5.5 The Job Offers She Selected

The first job offer selected related to an internal communications service in a New Zealand export company, where her position would provide support to management in the definition of a communications plan. For Ariane, the most pleasing aspects of the proposed job lay in the fact that the communications plan would be built jointly, creating a sense of belonging within the business. The major limitation of this job was Ariane's overall ignorance about the company.

The second selected job offer was an executive communications position for a famous French brand. The position was of interest because it would involve working for a quality French brand, with an international reputation. She would be addressing an audience of children and adults, would have various modes of action, and would be required to implement a guideline. A restriction, however, Ariane did not want to limit her work to pure design, something that led to difficulties during her years in the communications agency. The relationships and behavior built up in the agency allowed her to compensate for those difficulties, but they remain an obstacle to her. This led us to work with Ariane on the possibilities that would enable her to overcome these difficulties. We discussed the existence of training courses for creativity, and the idea that, as a communications professional, she should be able to ask others how they deal with design-related issues. This idea is similar to that of a practical analysis: We were aware of the interest in and development of the practical analysis in the social, health and education sectors, in particular, but we knew nothing of its use in the field of communications. It was a possible track of reflection for Ariane.

It should be noted that the objective of the fourth session was not to build a short-term career plan. The use of job offers is consistent with the general orientation or "spirit" of the career intervention. Our workshop is therefore complementary to other actions and services available in the field of counseling, for example, the "Cité des métiers" of Paris, which we advised her to visit. Ariane would go on to discuss this matter in her assessment of the career intervention.

The third job offer selected was not a "real" job but something that she created. It concerned a concept store—a hybrid space that brings together a bookshop, tea salon, clothing store, and events organization—allowing visitors to live different experiences. Ariane was enthusiastic about the prospect of such a variety of actions, as well as the opportunity of linking people together. The areas that required attention primarily concerned the importance for Ariane of not working alone. For her, managing this kind of space requires a team effort. In addition, she wanted to participate in design work and not be limited to the business development function. This idea of the concept store is a fictitious job. In that sense, Ariane has partially sidestepped our instructions. However, by imagining this activity and explaining its pros and cons, Ariane respects the objectives of this session. In accepting her choice to reflect on an "ideal" job, we demonstrated our flexibility in the intervention process.

4.3.5.6 Ariane's Work Values as Perceived by Others

Late in the session, we came to the question of how one of her relatives, a childhood friend, epitomized important work values for Ariane. According to this friend, Ariane's preferred work values were a diversity of activities, intellectual stimulation, self-realization, autonomy, opportunities for development, and learning opportunities—values with which Ariane was in agreement. In contrast, being able to work quickly to tight deadlines was not an important value for Ariane, according to her friend. Ariane agreed, but noted that it was nevertheless one of the characteristics of her working conditions over 14 years. She was able to survive in such a context thanks to the support of other co-workers.

4.3.5.7 Summary

Ariane highlighted three principal elements from this session. First, the video shed light on her lack of detachment from work. Second, the session highlighted her difficulties with pure design tasks. Finally, it demonstrated her need for diversified activities in her work.

4.3.6 Fifth Session: Two Future Scenarios of Life in New Zealand

4.3.6.1 Objectives and Aims of the Fifth Session

During the fifth meeting, we embarked the recipient on a true autobiography of the future, according to the methodology proposed by Rehfuss (2009). She was asked to indicate, year after year in unrestricted terms, possible personal and professional events in two different scenarios. The scenarios are meant to be realistic, reflect the values of the person, and include both positive and negative events. Discussions during the session enabled us to highlight, in particular, the core values, potential resources, obstacles, and key drivers of change for the individual.

4.3.6.2 A First Informal Exchange

Initially, Ariane advised that she had reworked her resume in the spirit of the English-speaking world, with a greater emphasis on her achievements, her positive experiences, and the personal added value she could bring to a position. It should be noted that the fifth session came after two postponements by Ariane who went away on weekends. This delay marked a distancing process in her relation to work, a step back from her situation. It is difficult to assess to what extent our intervention was responsible for this change. The mere fact of not being in a job clearly had an impact beyond any of the work carried out in the workshop. We can, however, simply note that Ariane's life was evolving, and we were accompanying that evolution.

4.3.6.3 First Imaginary Scenario

Both scenarios start when Ariane left the agency where she worked for 14 years. She begins by taking one-month vacation. In the first scenario, Ariane imagines the beginning of a relationship in France. She, nevertheless, leave France for New Zealand, where a job is waiting for her and where she spends one year making contacts. She then returns to France where her career may include an international dimension, and where she once again meets up with her partner. Later, she returns to New Zealand for 20 years and then comes back to France without completely cutting ties with New Zealand. Her time in New Zealand excludes her from certain events in France, in spite of the communications technology, such as video conferencing, that is available. However, in her opinion, the French labor market does not sufficiently integrate the international dimension, which she defines as openness to others and to different viewpoints. New Zealand is a challenge, because of the distance (although she has a family contact in New Caledonia). The downside of this scenario lies primarily in the fact that she will not be present for the death of certain relatives. However, those deaths are unavoidable in the order of things; they do not ultimately represent a real obstacle to the realization of this scenario.

4.3.6.4 Second Imaginary Scenario

The second scenario includes a start in New Zealand a few months later than in the first. She travels to New Zealand without a solid expectation of finding work there, which is clearly a less stable situation for her. With people she meets in the country, she sets up a multi-activity project, a type of concept store as discussed at the previous meeting. She receives visits from friends and family, and she could enter into a relationship in New Zealand. As in the first scenario, she plans to move back and forth between France and New Zealand. As in the first scenario, she also notes the negative issue of not being present at the death of certain relatives.

4.3.6.5 Differences and Similarities Between the Two Scenarios

The major difference between the two scenarios is that she sees herself working in a company for the next 20 years in the first case and not in the second. The common point is that, in both cases, she sees herself working in a field different from "pure" communications. She envisages exporting her 20 years of experience in this field to a new one, which will allow her to continue learning. In particular, she wishes to carry out projects in a new professional position that will open her up to more perspectives than communications only, resulting in a broader view and more varied activities. An improved self-confidence should allow her greater openness in her professional activities.

4.3.6.6 Obstacles to Be Overcome

When she talked about possible obstacles to these projects, Ariane referred to the need to obtain visas. To overcome this difficulty, she actively used her network to increase her contacts in New Zealand, and she completed her resume. She also referred to the steps she needs to carry out in France, in particular the need to rent out her apartment. Going to an unknown country was not a source of anxiety for her: She can bounce back when necessary as she has already been to England twice to work for several months. She can rely on her French network to establish contacts abroad. In short, she clearly faces a number of potential problems, one of which is the fact that she will leave her relatives behind in France. However, trying to do something despite the obstacles it entails is better than not trying at all. From these two possible scenarios, she expects to improve her quality of life, and the wealth of her experiences and encounters.

4.3.6.7 Positive Consequences of Events Generally Considered Negative

We addressed the issue of the possible positive consequences of events that are generally considered negative. Ariane has already experienced job loss. It forced her to explore what she really wants from life and work—in that it can be considered a stepping stone. In addition, it allowed her to take a break and have a welcome rest. Finally, it provided the opportunity to take care of herself in a guilt-free manner. For Ariane, failure is in this sense inconceivable; it can only be seen as a challenge. Ariane is not concerned by a radical change in working hours, with weeks of four 10-h days partly carried out on the weekend. Her only concern is to ensure that the framework is respected: That will ensure she is not totally submerged by work and that she maintains a level of freedom. According to Ariane, the net reduction in her salary would force her to focus on the essentials: For her, going out on the weekend rather than shopping or going to restaurants, for example.

4.3.6.8 Summary

At the end of the fifth session, Ariane concluded that the two proposed scenarios were enriching and positive experiences. Even if there were obstacles along the way, there would also be opportunities to rebound. The main obstacles seemed to her to be of an immediate material nature.

4.3.6.9 Our Analysis

The fifth session led Ariane to elaborate a general attitude to life characterized by a consistently positive experience. We will see that she will later push this idea even further; questioning the very idea that failure is possible in life. For now, we can note that the future autobiography exercise was probably a real incentive for Ariane to reflect on her perception of the challenges of life that come with the major changes in her future life.

4.3.7 *Sixth Session: The "art de vivre"*

4.3.7.1 Objectives and Aims of the Sixth Session

During the sixth meeting, we suggested a number of lifestyle ideas inspired by various psychological and philosophical traditions. The recipient selects the ideas that are dear to them—ones that they are committed to put into practice through various concrete actions at the end of the session. In this context, it should be noted that a number of studies have shown the influence of our actions on our cognitions (Weiss & Girandola, 2009).

4.3.7.2 A First Informal Exchange

Ariane's new communications mission has begun. She notes that she has fallen back into her tendency to go beyond her working hours, as was the case in her previous agency. This point should be emphasized: The career intervention enables individuals to identify their priorities in life and their values. In other words, it allows the individuals to take stock of certain matters, which leads them to make actual changes in their lives. However, the inclusion of this practice in one's everyday life is never easy, and this is undoubtedly one of the limitations of our contribution to the people we accompany. Ariane also indicated that she had gone through a phase of depression when embarking on this task—a feeling that she would not be able to successfully complete it. That experience was familiar to her whenever she embarked on a task: She had a painful sensation of not knowing "where to start," which she clearly distinguished from her lack of confidence in her ability to fulfill a given mission. We questioned Ariane about something that surprised us in the previous session: The early starting point of her two autobiographies had led to "forget" her last professional year. She responded that the New Zealand project should be seen as the pursuit of a process initiated with her employer subsequent to his departure from the agency where she worked for 14 years: She considered her six-month experience as Commercial Director, that had just ended, as a mere interlude.

4.3.7.3 "Le sel de la vie"

Ariane was positive about the audiovisual materials used in preparation of the meeting. Her comments on the video entitled "The salt of life" [Le sel de la vie] showed that she was now fully capable of letting go. That was not the case in the past, except when she was jogging or walking (activities during which she took advantage of her environment, looking at the landscape, and so on). Ariane noted her particular use of physical exercise: It enabled her to solve problems by allowing her to take a step back. However, its effectiveness depended on a prior reflection on the problem in question. The use of physical activity was therefore the end of the process, and it was mainly confined to the decision in question. Finally, Ariane stated it was now time for running and walking in order to reduce tension and become calmer.

4.3.7.4 The Importance of "Concrete" Actions

From the paper "Impossible wisdom," Ariane stressed the importance of being concrete. She cited the character, Zorba, who preferred to live his life writing books. For her, wisdom lies in having the audacity to reach fulfillment. Unless we live things out, they can be falsified, which is, for example, the case if one sees life through reading. To achieve wisdom, it is necessary to confront reality, with its share of mistakes and successes.

4.3.7.5 The Idea of Relative Happiness

Ariane appreciated the ideas expounded by André Comte-Sponville, in that they expressed a design philosophy that excluded a pure use of thought. In particular, she noted the idea of accepting a *relative* happiness. She also noted the argument that one should not expect happiness from others and that it was important to be concerned only with things over which one has control. Ariane noted two ideas from the three documents used.

- The importance of letting go rather than seeking control. In the past, she had been overwhelmed by a sense of duty. Ariane therefore had trouble with this idea initially, but she progressively managed to adopt it for herself.
- The value of experience, which means that failure does not exist.

4.3.7.6 Ariane's "Art de vivre" Themes

Ariane holds with the three following lifestyle themes.

- "Being faithful to one's values": This is a fundamental basis of life, implying respect for oneself and for others.
- "Developing positive relationships with others": For Ariane, this means developing a dynamic. Indeed, she has always maintained the quality of her relationships. However, she is now more interested in respect and appreciation. In the past, she perceived the other as having more value than herself, considering people lucky if they were able to arouse the interests of others.
- "Enjoy the present and letting go": Ariane's current period of non-employment is positive in her eyes; she would not want a full-time job for the time being. She envisages being taken up by many activities in New Zealand, including the need to communicate in English, which should keep her away from the pressures of work.

The first two topics chosen reflect Ariane's desire for a balanced relationship between the other and herself. That was already one of the conclusions of the third session. It is therefore not surprising that Ariane wants to give this element an important place in the actuation of her life. She envisages the practical application of these themes as follows.

- "Being faithful to one's values" is a principle that will guide her in her job search. She will not accept any job proposals without this principle in mind.
- "Developing positive relationships with others" means that Ariane wants to continue to network with others in a sincere and honest manner. She wants to be open to others in her projects, *explaining* her positions without needing to *justify* them. Ariane distinguishes clearly between explanation and justification, the latter being a defensive attitude that she does not wish to adopt.
- "Enjoy the present and letting go," where Ariane proposes to pursue the development of this new trend in her life, for example, by continuing to visit exhibitions in the middle of the day.

4.3.7.7 Summary

Ariane highlighted two major elements from this session: the importance of letting go, and the idea that everything can be seen as an experience—as such, there are no failures. Thus, according to Ariane, life systematically excludes the possibility of failure, a belief that resonates with the previous session.

4.3.7.8 Our Analysis

Even if our career intervention prompts actions and changes in the client, we can see that, in the case of Ariane, it relies on a process that began prior to and independently of our interviews: The three mentioned themes have already been put into action.

4.3.8 *Seventh Session: The Evaluation*

4.3.8.1 Objectives and Aims of the Seventh Session

The seventh session represents an opportunity for the client to draw up an evaluation or appraisal of the concrete actions undertaken since the last session. It also allows clients to assess the progression of their thoughts about the meaning of life and work (Savickas et al., 2009) since the beginning of the intervention. The recipient is asked to write a personal evaluation before the session.

4.3.8.2 A First Informal Exchange: Some Concerns

At the beginning of the session, Ariane referred to the period of doubt that she had just come through, due to financial difficulties. She recently felt the need to once again "put aside" the New Zealand project and identify the steps necessary for its implementation. At the same time, the number of her contacts in New Zealand was increasing.

4.3.8.3 Implementation of the "art de vivre": Letting Go Proves to Be Somewhat Difficult

The level of implementation of the "art de vivre" varied from one subject to the next. In particular, "enjoying the present time and letting go" remained a difficult exercise for Ariane. She found it quite easy to go jogging but was still not able to go to the cinema in the middle of the afternoon. We previously highlighted the difficulty of putting the ideas that emerged from the intervention into concrete actions in a sustainable manner. After avoiding professional over-investment, "letting go" was still sometimes difficult for Ariane. We can, however, consider as positive Ariane's awareness of the relevance but also the fragility of her progress in this area. Therefore, while our career intervention provides favorable conditions for launching the change process, it may be supplemented by other counseling work with other types of counselors. Ariane practiced a more retrospective (rather than daily) use of the monitoring grid of "putting *art de vivre* into concrete actions." That is also the case with other clients. Stating that achieved actions are consistent with desired changes in one's life maintains a clear awareness of the changes to be implemented. However, we assume that this is a preliminary step to a more sustained implementation of change. In our opinion, the person should go beyond this retrospective statement and reach a more prospective willingness, revealing a clear "ownership" of his or her own life.

Finally, Ariane drew three notable elements from the implementation of a certain "art de vivre":

- She wants to be the initiator of events. Instead of reducing her career path to chance encounters, she wants to be more "proactive," as she stated at the end of the third session.
- She is committed to sharing with others in a spirit of explanation rather than justification.
- It is important for her to promote herself while remaining within reasonable limits.

4.3.8.4 Evaluation of Ariane's Reflection Since the Beginning of the Career Intervention

We then discussed her written evaluation of the 2.5-month reflection in the framework of the intervention. In particular, she described the outlines of her "credo" that she compared to a "compass guiding her career and her life": *being her own creator, sharing and explaining her anxiety and uncertainty, promoting herself, developing her skills, and finally letting go.*

4.3.8.5 Proposal of an Additional Meeting

Ariane welcomed the proposal for an eighth session. She would like it to take place shortly before her departure, to review her project and see if she has remained aligned with the direction that emerged in the seventh session.

4.3.9 Eighth Session: Additional Session or Epilogue

4.3.9.1 Objectives and Aims of the Eighth Session

The objectives of the eighth session can vary, according to the counselor's feedback on an experience or a decision made. The key point here is that the content of this final session is defined in agreement with the client (Bernaud et al., 2015).

4.3.9.2 Change of Course, from New Zealand to London

Our final meeting with Ariane took place four months later. The impossibility of obtaining a work visa led her to give up her project of going to New Zealand, but not of going abroad immediately: Ariane has decided to move to London one week later. Initially, she plans to stay a few days with a friend and arrange job interviews in situ. After one year, she will reconsider the New Zealand project.

4.3.9.3 Four Key Points

Ariane highlighted four key points in the final session.

- "Being her own creator": This corresponded to her idea of proactivity, which is not consistent with the fact of working in a company.
- "Better sharing with others what she thinks or feels" without having to justify herself or become aggressive.
- "Letting go."
- Developing her skills and promoting herself.

During our exchange, Ariane highlighted a key idea to emerge from her evaluation: her desire to participate in the development of others in an educational manner.

We note that these four key points are constituent parts of her "credo," which emerged at the end of the seventh session.

4.3.9.4 Epilogue

In her final evaluation, Ariane discussed the idea of moving toward jobs that involve social and cultural facets. Looking back, she considers this a fantasy. However, she adopted a firm position on the following points: the refusal to accept casual jobs or work in a generalist communications agency. Instead, she wants to work in communications for a specific company, which will allow her to develop a longer-term vision of her work. (This is in contrast to her career over the years where she provided one-off services to clients based on short-term contracts.) It will also allow her to diversify the media used in her work (events, digital, etc.). Ariane would also be favorable to working in an international events agency. In terms of her preferred fields, she was interested in luxury goods and cosmetics, areas in which she had some experience and that had long been a personal dream. She would also be attracted to humanitarian projects conducted by non-profit organizations. Ariane has, however, put to one side the idea of a concept store.

We also discussed the balance between her professional and personal spheres. In the future, Ariane wishes to put aside more time for her private life. She was still keen to discover another culture. In terms of the "art de vivre," she continued to abide by the three elements that emerged in the sixth session—for example, the fact of expressing what she feels. While her long-term objectives remained clear, she recognized that their implementation was more difficult. She would therefore proceed step by step. We also referred to a technical aspect: The difficulties she said she had experienced in her work with respect to strategic reflection. She was able to discuss this issue with other communications specialists who indicated that they never worked on strategic issues alone. Ariane accepted that she would be less comfortable in the initiation of actions in her professional life than in the tasks that followed. Overall, she felt that the sessions had helped her to clarify her beliefs, even though the progress made as a result of the intervention was very gradual.

4.3.9.5 Our Analysis

Our career intervention recommends that clients use all available resources to help develop their sense of well-being. In this, social support clearly plays a particularly important role, and this is illustrated by a rather technical professional issue which is discussed with other communication specialists. The role of social support corresponds to Ariane's key conviction: the importance of others. Her last remark allows us to conclude by returning to an essential aspect. The intervention is aimed at bringing the client an increased understanding of what matters most to him or her, autonomy and harmony in both one's inner and social life. Such a program certainly does not lack ambition. Therefore, it is necessary to recognize that regardless of the value of the proposed exercises, the efforts of the participants in performing the required work, and the advisor's skills, "time" appears to be a necessary component in one's development: that is, what we want to encourage among our clients who honor us with their trust.

4.3.10 Assessment of the Effects of the Intervention

We obtained the elements of a qualitative assessment from the participant herself during the seventh session. We asked her what she would say if she had to present the intervention to a third party. She stated that she was very satisfied with the results of the intervention: It brought her balance by allowing her to take some distance and think about the quality of her choices; it enabled her to develop her own thoughts on the matter. She stressed the importance of the "funeral eulogy" exercise and the autobiography scenarios that lead her to anticipate the future. She also referred to the value brought by the opportunity to reflect on other experiences. Ariane also confirmed that writing a personal evaluation formed a good basis for a reflection on her career choices. Accordingly, she now plans to seek coaching based on a method of career guidance. We mentioned earlier the complementarity between our work and other counseling approaches. According to Ariane, the intervention enabled her to come up with new ideas and complete her reflection. She also appreciated the fact that we constantly asked her to finish her sentences during the interviews, as this forced her to develop her thoughts. *We therefore stress the importance of dialogue between the client and the counselor in the implementation of the intervention. This requires a solid training in counseling from the professional.*

Four months after the end of the intervention, during the eighth session, Ariane still thought that the intervention had clarified her beliefs. We observed a stabilization of the effects on the participant.

Moreover, the following evolution emerged from a comparison of the results of a pre- and post-test consisting of 16 items assessing the meaning of life (The Meaning in Life Questionnaire, Steger et al., 2006), the meaning of work and the career choices made: increased scores for 10 items in the post-test, and stable scores for three other items. These results support Ariane's positive evolution in terms of the level of meaning and of career choices.

4.4 Discussion

Clearly, in this exploratory case study, the assessment of the counseling intervention is primarily based on qualitative elements and self-reported data by the participant. Nevertheless, these elements support a positive evolution in Ariane's life in general, and in the professional sphere in particular, which characterizes our career intervention as very promising. While considering it as a lever of change, we observe that, in Ariane's case, the implementation of concrete actions had already begun as she expected to depart for the antipodes within a short period of time. Nevertheless, the intervention allowed her to realize to what extent her project to live abroad was not only a headlong rush but also a means to expressing her preferred values. She was actively looking for a job in New Zealand and rapidly made new contacts in this country in order to foster her professional transition. She also gathered more general information about the country. In particular, she carried out a number of actions since the beginning of the intervention, for example, adapting her resume to an English-speaking environment.

Her comments also demonstrated her positive development: She stated that she now realizes the exaggerated place she used to give to work in her life. Going forward, she wants to devote more time to her inner life. She also compares her new "credo" to a "compass to guide her career and her life," which is a further sign of a progress.

Four months later, the change process is tangible as she moves abroad to London, where she plans to reconsider her New Zealand project in a year's time. Similarly, her career plan has emerged with the project of working in the communications department of a company and diversifying the range of media used. She stated that she felt better at the end of the intervention as she was more aware of her long-term objectives. Ultimately, all of these elements, as well as the results of the pre- and post-test, provide some evidence for the effectiveness of our meaning-centered career counseling intervention and of a positive change in the person undergoing the intervention.

4.4.1 Limits and Future Research

The subjective and self-reported nature of the assessment of our career counseling intervention may be considered a limit. Nevertheless, the interview conducted four months later shows that Ariane has undertaken new actions.

It would be of interest to pursue the assessment of the produced effects, on the one hand one year later to confirm their stabilization, and on the other hand on a larger number of participants to compare the results obtained from a quantitative perspective.

4.5 Conclusion

As described throughout this case study, the present meaning-centered framework relies on the quality of the relationship established. In particular, it is based on a co-construction of meaning between the counselor and the client, aimed at equipping individuals with the skills they need to manage their professional and personal lives (Bernaud et al., 2015). On the client side, the reflection process continues beyond the intervention period. Going forward, the challenge will be to develop new meaning-centered career counseling interventions adapted to specific audiences such as the long-term unemployed for whom meaning is a central issue.

Thus, the comparison of the results of the pre- and post-test measuring the meaning of life (The Meaning in Life Questionnaire, Steger et al., 2006), the meaning of work and career choices on a larger number of persons is in process. Further research will be devoted to these aspects, which are clearly of great interest. In the future, it is indeed important to identify new tools that can be used to assess the effectiveness of the qualitative counseling intervention (Di Fabio, 2016).

References

Arnoux-Nicolas, C., Sovet, L., Lhotellier, L., & Bernaud, J.-L. (2017). Development and validation of the meaning of work inventory among French workers. *International Journal for Educational and Vocational Guidance, 17*, 165–185. https://doi.org/10.1007/s10775-016-9323-0.

Auhagen, A. E. (2000). On the psychology of meaning of life. *Swiss Journal of Psychology, 59,* 34–48. http://doi.org/10.1024//1421-0185.59.1.34.

Bernaud, J.-L. (2016). Le «sens de la vie» comme paradigme pour le conseil en orientation [Meaning of life as a paradigm for career counseling]. *Psychologie Française, 61,* 61–72. https://doi.org/10.1016/j.psfr.2013.06.004.

Bernaud, J.-L., & Bideault, A. (2005). Les déterminants de l'attractivité face à une démarche de conseil en orientation [Determinants of attractivity in vocational guidance]. *Carriériologie, 10,* 289–303.

Bernaud, J.-L., Lhotellier, L., Sovet, L., Arnoux-Nicolas, C., & Pelayo, F. (2015). *Psychologie de l'accompagnement: Concepts et outils pour développer le «sens» de la vie et du travail [Psychology of coaching: Concepts and tools to develop meaning of life and of work].* Paris: Dunod.

Di Fabio, A. (2016). Life design and career counseling innovative outcomes. *The Career Development Quarterly, 64,* 35–48. http://doi.org/10.1002/cdq.12039.

Frankl, V. E. (1959). *Man's search for meaning*. Boston, MA: Beacon Press.

Hanson, W. E., Claiborn, C. D., & Kerr, B. (1997). Differential effects of two test interpretation styles in counseling: A field study. *Journal of Counseling Psychology, 44,* 400–405. http://doi.org/10.1037/0022-0167.44.4.400.

Jackson, S. A. (2001). Using bibliotherapy with clients. *The Journal of Individual Psychology, 57,* 289–297.

Létourneau, I., Chrétien, L., & Lécine, M.-E. (2012). L'évaluation de la formation à l'harmonisation travail-vie personnelle: Bilan et perspectives de recherche [Assessment of training to harmonize work and of personal life: Review and research perspectives]. *Psychologie du Travail et des Organisations, 18,* 102–120. http://doi.org/10.1016/S1420-2530(16)30088-7.

Rehfuss, M. C. (2009). The future career autobiography: A narrative measure of career intervention effectiveness. *The Career Development Quarterly, 58,* 82–90. http://doi.org/10.1177/1069072712450005.

Rosso, B. D., Dekas, K. H., & Wrzesniewski, A. (2010). On the meaning of work: A theoretical integration and review. *Research in Organizational Behavior, 30,* 91–127. http://doi.org/10.1016/j.riob.2010.09.001

Savickas, M. L., Nota, L., Rossier, J., Dauwalder, J.-P., Duarte, M. E., Guichard, J., et al. (2009). Life designing: A paradigm for career construction in the 21st century. *Journal of Vocational Behavior, 75,* 239–250. https://doi.org/10.1016/j.jvb.2009.04.004.

Schnell, T. (2009). The sources of meaning and meaning in life questionnaire (SoMe): Relations to demographics and well-being. *The Journal of Positive Psychology, 6*(4), 483–499. http://doi.org/10.1080/17439760903271074

Schnell, T. (2011). Individual differences in meaning-making: considering the variety of sources of meaning, their density and diversity. *Personality and Individual Differences, 51,* 667–673. http://doi.org/10.1016/j.paid.2011.06.006

Schnell, T., & Becker, P. (2006). Personality and meaning in life. *Personality and Individual Differences, 41,* 117–129. http://doi.org/10.1016/j.paid.2005.11.030

Sheth, K. (2010). *Un sari couleur de boue*. Paris. Poche.

Steger, M. F., Dik, B. J., & Duffy, R. D. (2012). Measuring meaningful work: The work and meaning inventory (WAMI). *Journal of Career Assessment, 20,* 322–337. http://doi.org/10.1177/1069072711436160

Steger, M. F., Frazier, P., Oishi, S., & Kaler, M. (2006). The meaning in life questionnaire: Assessing the presence of and search for meaning in life. *Journal of Counseling Psychology, 53,* 80–93. http://doi.org/10.1037/0022-0167.53.1.80

Weiss, K., & Girandola, F. (2009). Qualité environnementale et comportements écocitoyens. In J. Lecomte (Ed.), *Introduction à la psychologie positive* (pp. 243–255). Paris: Dunod.

Chapter 5
Counseling Case Formulation as Metaphor

Peter McIlveen and Allison Creed

Abstract Case formulation is the rhetorical centerpiece of counseling. Case formulation arises from empirical assessment and directs evidence-based intervention. Case formulation emanates from an epistemology that is enlivened in an arcane rhetoric. Case formulation speaks to the ontology of life and an axiology for living a good life. Case formulation is defined by and concomitantly defines the counselor. In the interpersonal dynamic of counseling, the counselor cannot be any other than the one who conceptualizes the life of the other—the client. The counselor's rhetoric is an aesthetic form found within a very specific discourse that construes the mental life of the client and ipso facto, the counselor. It is in the conceptualization of the case that the counselor is revealed, consciously or unconsciously, through the rhetoric used to objectify the life of another. Here, we focus on the professional practice of *case formulation* as a highly specialized aesthetic of counseling practice.

5.1 Introduction

There are different definitions and models of case formulation. In a practical sense, case formulation is a selective summary of the data gleaned during interviews with a client. It is a selective process in the sense that the practitioner decides—consciously or unconsciously—which data are more relevant amidst the volumes that may issue forth as the narrative of a life. Case formulation is more than a selective summary; it is a proto-theory of the person and presenting problem before the counselor. It is *pragmatic* theorization in the sense that its explanatory power is assumed truthful and useful until reformulated in light of new evidence (James, 1907/2000). A case formulation is "proto" because it can never assume the status of a scientific theory per se with all of the attendant capacity for generalization beyond the case in and of itself as an $N = 1$ study; however, it is redeemed by the quality of

P. McIlveen (✉) · A. Creed
School of Linguistics Adult and Specialist Education, University of Southern Queensland, Toowoomba, QLD 4350, Australia
e-mail: peter.mcilveen@usq.edu.au

© Springer Nature Switzerland AG 2018

A. Di Fabio and J.-L. Bernaud (eds.), *Narrative Interventions in Post-modern Guidance and Career Counseling*, https://doi.org/10.1007/978-3-319-98300-4_5

falsifiability (Popper, 1935/2005) because it can be subject to logically derived empirical tests and be found demonstrably incorrect.

What is produced as a proto-theory for any one client's presenting problem, by way of case formulation, is a working model for the practitioner's actions in counseling.

> Psychotherapy case formulation is a process for developing a hypothesis about, and a plan to address, the causes, precipitants, and maintaining influences of a person's psychological, inter-personal, and behavioral problems in the context of that individual's culture and environment. As a hypothesis, a case formulation is the therapist's best account of the client's problems: why the client is experiencing them, what precipitates symptom onset, and why symptoms continue to occur instead of resolving (Eells, 2015, p. 16).

Eell's definition captures the notion of formulation as both a process (i.e., developing hypotheses and plans) and product (i.e., a hypothesis per se). It is more than a diagnostic account, however; it is a plan for action presumably designed on the basis of some foregoing expert knowledge and skill as to what is the most effective thing to do to resolve the client's presenting problem.

The term *hypothesis* used here reveals case formulation's roots in the logic of a scientific method (Popper, 1935/2005), whereby the hypotheses drawn from the proto-theory are put to empirical test by a trial-and-error process of engaging in actions played out by the counselor and the client so as to bring about change—cognitive, behavioral, or emotional. Where the counseling actions fall flat without effect, the hypothesis is abandoned (or, more formally put: rejected); where the actions produce change that is positive, the proto-theory is affirmed by retaining the hypothesis as a veridical assumption. This logic is a variant of the hypothetico-deductive method associated with the doctrine of falsifiability. Although there are different expressions of this scientific thinking in the *scientist–practitioner* and *practitioner–scholar* models (Stoltenberg et al., 2000), both retain a pragmatic (James, 1907/1907) empirical attitude toward intervention and regard for evidence-based practice. Thus, the mind-set of the counselor is empirical—or at least it is meant to be so.

Counseling would not be counseling without the counselor having some conceptualization of the case in front of him. Beyond each case, counselors construct their own personal epistemology that facilitates the construction of proto-theories. Their epistemologies accrete what is deemed evidence, case by case, experience by experience, reflection by reflection, and treat their own unique ways of knowing, doing—an *epistemology of the practitioner* (Polkinghorne, 1992). Where the practitioner's epistemology loses its scientific quality is when the practitioner inducts conclusions on the basis of the evidence before him that are consistent with his proto-theory, rather than deducting conclusions that are derived from a genuine attempt to falsify the theory. In this way, counselors are susceptible to *confirmation bias* (Nickerson, 1998) and may become trapped in their own rhetoric in attempts to prove a proto-theory true. Thus, counselor's rhetoric must be subject to analysis to determine how its logic and vocabulary constrain their thinking into an inductive defense of a proto-theory.

5.2 Where There Is Rhetoric There Is Metaphor

The very first words uttered between the counselor and client at upon that moment of meeting in psychological space between them are the first in the narrative stream that is rendered into a case formulation. Yet, even before words are spoken, the counselor is already primed to hear and speak words, key phrases, idioms, and expressions that are to be deployed in the process of formulation because he is already informed by his proto-theory.

When formulating a case, a counselor is ineluctably inhered in his own discourse and cannot think about his client outside vocabulary and conventions of that discourse. A case cannot be formulated in any other discourse than that which is specific to case formulation, namely psychology, psychotherapy, and counseling. This discourse comes with its vocabulary that is meaningful only to those who speak it with the facility of an expert. Any given word of that discourse is most meaningful within the parameters of that discourse and changes when used in any other. The word "obsession," for example, means something quite knowable and known to a psychologist as dysfunctional cognition, whereas it may mean something quite different to another profession or person not privy to the connotative meanings taken for granted by those on the inside of a discourse.

To the uninformed layperson, the experience of reading a case conceptualization may be similar to that of a first-year student reading an advanced textbook about statistics. They will comprehend enough of the headline material to guess what is being conveyed in the narrative, but there are specifically meaningful parts that are impenetrable. Case conceptualizations can be peppered with key terms meaningful only to the informed reader (e.g., obsession).

Thus, the rhetoric of case conceptualization is an articulation of an exclusive language of a closed/discourse community (Swales, 1990) that assumes certain epistemological perspectives, such as post-positivist, social constructionist, or critical/ideological (McIlveen, 2009). The key to unlock the codex of their language is *conceptual metaphor* (Lakoff & Johnson, 1980), which we introduce here as the foundation of a new research method for research into case conceptualization.

Consider Freud's (1915/1991) classical model of mind and its three components: conscious, preconscious, and unconscious. One may better comprehend this model through a conceptual metaphor: Mind is an iceberg. The top of the iceberg is seen clearly rising above the surface of the water, the bulk remains beneath the surface of the water, deep below, and unseen in the dark watery depths. Rather than eluding to qualities of an iceberg that may be comparable to the human mind through simile, here, the metaphor juxtaposes the two concepts to evoke something quite emphatic using knowledge of the target domain of the mind with that of the source domain of an iceberg. Rather than comprehending the mind in abstruse terms, conceptual metaphor better enables thinking about and talking about the conscious, subconscious, and unconscious minds using words associated with the iceberg (e.g., "above the surface," "deep below," "dark," and "depths").

Consider the language used to formulate the Case K, the 17-year-olds who had just graduated from high school and decided to enroll in college because "a friend of mine thought it would be a good idea" (Brown, 2002, p. 25). This young man has no clear goals for a career apart from something that involves computers, lots of money, perhaps architecture, and professional skateboarding. Below is an excerpt from the case formulation by Savickas (2002):

> K evinces the *avoidant* style in his emotional *approach to* coping, … The career theme interview *reveals* a vocational self-concept that portrays someone who is *on the move* and likes to learn. His *line of movement* seems *to go from* being scared *to* being excited. His choice of role models indicates that he wants to *develop from* procrastinating and *moving hesitantly to* being an *initiator of* activity. He wants *to launch* new projects and even *lead*, yet also wants a partner available to provide reassurance and structure. His competence at self-knowledge and occupational information appears weak, and he now uses an intuitive decision-making style. In counseling, I would invite K *to stop skating* across the top of life. I would encourage him *to take hold*, *to explore* other ways *to move*—ways that use his talents and gratify his needs. The first *goal* would be to help him *take initiative*… [italic font added] (pp. 194–195).

The words in italic font shown in this excerpt have meaningfulness in figurative notions of change and motion (e.g., "Purposes are Destinations," and "Difficulties are Impediments to Motion") that represent the therapists aims for K to use literal movement efficiently and effectively, so that he is "more courageous in moving forward in life" (p. 196).

Let us hear from Savickas once again when he formulates the Case E, a 20-year-old student at the university where she is studying history and religion, and wanting to refine her career plan to focus on specific occupations. Savickas (2002) states

> She wants *to move from* her preoccupation with feeling sad about *being left out* of "a man's world" to *moving to* an occupation in which she can enact her compassionate vision, be a pioneer, work for change, and yet *balance* other life roles and keep stress low. To do so she needs *to turn* her tension into intention. She is conflicted about *staying versus going*. *Staying put in* a traditional role makes her depressed, but *running off* in a pioneer role scares the people who care for her, so for now *she stays put* (p. 196).

In both cases, Savickas uses words, specifically verb part-of-speech, associated with motion reflecting a source-path-goal image schema or pre-conceptual structuring (Johnson, 1987).

Motion is very much associated with the metaphorical conceptualization of a journey, a prototypical example of a conceptual metaphor from Lakoff (1987, p. 275), that is representative of the conceptualization of a career. Lakoff and Johnson (1980) argue for the pervasiveness of the journey metaphor in people's everyday communication:

> Our understanding of life as a journey uses our knowledge about journeys. All journeys involve travellers, paths travelled, places where we start, and places where we have been. Some journeys are purposeful and have destinations that we set out for, while others may involve wandering without any destination in mind, consciously or more likely

> unconsciously, a correspondence between a traveler and person living life, the road traveled and the 'course' of a lifetime, a starting point and a time of birth, and so on (p. 66).

Are the words used by Savickas in his case formulation representative of a schema he used to understand the data about the case and then communicate that understanding in terms readily understood by the reader? We suggest that the use of these words is not the mere convenience of expression; instead, we suggest that these words hold much greater import that pertains to thinking through conceptual metaphor.

A definitive feature of conceptual metaphor is that it allows for the comprehension of one object in terms of another, such as an iceberg for mind. In their conceptual metaphor theory (CMT), Lakoff and Johnson (1980) categorize two important features of conceptual metaphor as the SOURCE domain and TARGET domain. The source domain of knowledge is used as the referent object (e.g., iceberg) in order to understand the target object (e.g., mind). It is commonplace for people to think of one thing in terms of another, and the notion of transfer between SOURCE domain and TARGET domain captures this natural thinking in natural language-in-use.

In CMT, Lakoff and Johnson argue that people think and talk in metaphors that are representative of concepts. Moreover, metaphors enable people to communicate abstract ideas with one another, to share knowledge and experiences, and arrive at common understandings. Accordingly, the conceptual metaphors and vocabulary of case conceptualizations enable the discourse community of career practitioners to efficiently communicate quite specific and meaningful ideas with one another without recourse to long and complicated explanations. In this way, conceptual metaphor acts as a special code that is expressed and understood in clinical shorthand.

We hasten to clarify the distinction between conceptual metaphor and the linguistic device, simile. Conceptual metaphor and simile are ostensibly similar in that one object is used to comprehend another object; however, the definitive difference is that simile involves a comparison (e.g., career is *like* a journey; mind is *like* an iceberg) that serves to describe affordances of an object much where one descriptively complements the other, but one is not given as the other (e.g., career is a journey; mind is an iceberg). The literal difference in words—"is like" and "is"—is not so relevant. What matters most is that the words of conceptual metaphor are presented as if the relation between the two words is unequivocal and absolute: Mind is an iceberg is an emphatic statement. Thus, it may be more meaningful to state that "Freud is a giant" as distinct from the simile and "Freud is like a giant," to conceptualize his profound impact on intellectual disciplines and clinical professions.

As a framework for case conceptualization, conceptual metaphor is also a limitation. Just as we assert that counselor conceptualizations are limited to the discourse in which clinical vocabulary and conventions are deemed meaningful, it is likewise constraining to contemplate and talk about a case through any given conceptual metaphor. If mind is an iceberg, then all one can ever know about mind is its watery world of hydraulic dynamics. If, however, one uses an alternative conceptual metaphor, then new vistas are opened. For example, Inkson's (2004) nine metaphors of career (as inheritance, construction, cycle, matching, journey, encounters and relationships, roles, resource, and story) are potentially productive as conceptual metaphors.

What is unknown is to what extent conceptual metaphors are typically used in counseling practice and, moreover, how their application to case formulation enhances, yet concomitantly limits, the meaningfulness of any given case formulation.

5.3 Metaphor Identification Procedure

The retrospective analysis of case material and experts' case formulations is accepted in the field as a research method to discern theoretical and technical developments (e.g., Blustein et al., 2001; Whiston, Lindeman, Rahardja, & Reed, 2005). Using consensual qualitative research, Whiston et al. identified themes within the experts' opinions: theoretical orientation, helping skills, assessment, career-specific intervention, information and resources, social-contextual factors, and relational aspects. We extend this line of research by demonstrating a research method that uses similar data sources as these methods but one that provides an entirely different perspective on the rhetoric of case formulation.

Case formulation is a structured narrative of description and evaluation that is motivated and likewise constrained by the frequent use of metaphor. Metaphoric language acts as a framework for interaction between practitioner and client because it makes more complex or abstract phenomena more tangible or concrete. Significantly, metaphor is a socially situated phenomenon that is expressed through cultural, educational, and historical contexts of understanding (Bowdle & Gentner, 2005; Gibbs, 2008; Kövecses, 2005). The identification of key metaphors used in career counseling can reveal the personal lens of interlocutors and their predilection for or image of career that structure their understanding ultimately derived from their theoretical orientation. To identify linguistic instantiations of metaphor, the Metaphor Identification Procedure Vrije Universiteit (MIPVU) (Steen et al., 2010) is put forward in this paper. MIPVU is an extension of the MIP procedure developed by the Pragglejaz Group (2007) who, as a group of metaphor scholars, came together over a period of years to construct a systematic and explicit method of annotation that would reliably identify potentially metaphoric expressions in talk and text. Situated conceptualizations (i.e., discourse situation-specific occurrences) of linguistic units are analyzed for meaning assisted by their behavior in the context of natural language data. Surface realizations can in turn be examined for possible mappings from SOURCE to TARGET domains or blending of conceptual domains. The claim made by Steen et al. (2010) is that "all words that can be related to metaphor in this way could in theory be candidates for the cognitive cross-domain mapping by language users when they produce or comprehend language" (p. 13).

MIPVU provides an effective tool for determining the metaphoricity of a word, or phrasal verb, in its linguistic context of use. Most metaphorical language use constitutes indirect meaning by comparison with discourse. For instance, take the first sentence in the Savickas' (2002) vignette: "K evinces the avoidant style in his emotional *approach to* coping, …." Here, the noun part-of-speech (POS) *approach* can be argued to be metaphorical language use in this situated context because the basic meaning taken from the McMillan dictionary of a path or road that leads to a place can be compared and contrasted with the contextual meaning of a particular way of thinking about or dealing with something. The word *approach* involves indirect meaning by comparison and would be marked as a metaphor-related word (MRW) according to MIPVU.

Although most metaphorically used words are typically indirectly used (Steen et al., 2010), cross-domain mappings can surface or be triggered by an alien referent. Consider, for example, the sentence taken from the Savickas (2002) vignette 1: "In, counseling, I would invite K to stop *skating across the top of life*. The italics highlight a topic shift from the domain of career to that of sport, specifically skating." Because one can imagine the process of skating on blades across ice or perhaps on wheels along a path, one can understand the experiential comparison with the approach of K to life and more specifically career. The comparison of K with a skater and life/career to a surface of ice invites a mapping between these two contrastive domains of knowledge. Although the mapping encompasses a length of text rather than a single linguistic unit, the MIPVU procedure facilitates the annotation of the more common indirect conceptualizations along with the less frequent topically incongruous instances that are expressed directly or even deliberately afford conscious metaphorical cognition.

MIPVU involves six procedural phrases for manual annotation: (1) Read the whole text, (2) establish lexical units, (3) establish contextual meaning of the lexical unit, (4) determine if there is a more basic meaning, (5) decide if the basic and the contextual meaning can be contrasted but understood by comparison, and (6) mark the lexical unit as metaphoric if the answer is affirmative. Basic and contextual meaning are determined through the prescribed use of a corpus-based dictionary based on the World English Corpus such as the Macmillan dictionary. Identification of linguistic instantiations is the goal of the procedure and the abstinence from "precise conceptual analysis is in fact a sound and productive methodological strategy that yields better linguistic data, which, in turn, can be used for relatively independent conceptual research" (Steen et al., 2010, p. 10).

For purposes of demonstration, the MIPVU was applied to two vignettes taken from Savickas (2002). The results show that conventional, non-deliberate metaphor is most often used in the case conceptualizations with manner-of-motion or agentive verbs evidenced in the figurative motivation of the JOURNEY metaphor for a cognitive schema of source-path-goal. Motion refers to the direction of movement (e.g., go from, to, across, into) and in a satellite-framed language such as English, and particles are used to indicate the path of motion, for instance, in vignette (1): His line of movement seems to *go from* being scared *to* being excited, and (2): to do so, she needs *to turn* her tension *into* intention. Composing the case formulation, the practitioner most frequently used verb POS MRW semantically related to the notion of movement be that location, travel, or transport in the linguistic forms of *explore, go, launch, move* and *moving,* and *turn* as well as the prepositions *in, into, on, out,* and *to.* Other MRW with less explicit semantic relations to movement in the context of the text was *develop, help, lead, makes, reveals, take,* and *balance.* The identified MRW analyzed in the vignettes invites an association of a physical sense meaning (i.e., a journey) to frame a more abstract idea of career conceptualization, as in examples (1)–(4):

(1) I would encourage him *to take* hold, *to explore* other ways *to move*—ways that use his talents and gratify his needs.
(2) He wants to *launch* new projects and even *lead* …
(3) She wants *to move from* her preoccupation with feeling sad about being left *out* of "a man's world" to *moving to* an occupation …
(4) To do so she needs *to turn* her tension *into* intention.

Albeit a brief example of MIPVU, it is evident that it reveals a more informative analysis of metaphoric language in case conceptualization.

5.4 Applications to Teaching

The pedagogical utility of the MIPVU is significant. Current approaches to training in counseling, such as audiovisual recording sessions, reflections on what transpired in sessions, and supervision, are valuable teaching methods. We suggest that MIPVU can be used as a new teaching method whereby counselors explore their transcripts in search for metaphors that both enhance and limit their conceptualization of the cases and recommendations for interventions. Reformulating cases using different metaphors may not only widen a student's perspective of a case, so as to minimize cognitive bias, but also improve the specificity of interventions needed by the client. Furthermore, addressing countertransference may be somewhat less confronting for a student when reflections are discussed in terms of metaphors. Entering into difficult conversations about past experiences or patterns of behavior that seem to unconsciously influence a student's counseling may be eased somewhat if the conversation is initially focused on the metaphors that the student consistently uses in counseling.

5.5 Conceptual Implications and Future Research

Here, we express a critical point that extends from the stance that counselors who perform career counseling and life designing must engage in an ethic of reflexivity (McIlveen, 2015b) and that the distance between psychotherapy and career counseling, both conceptually and pragmatically, is not so far (McIlveen, 2015a). For example, qualitative analyses of career counseling case formulations reveal experts' emphasis on counseling activities traditionally associated with psychotherapy (Whiston et al., 2005), such as the dynamics of relationships (Blustein et al., 2001). Common to both psychotherapy and career counseling is the practice of case conceptualization, which may vary in form and terminology; but, ultimately, they share common root metaphors (Lyddon, 1989) that guide their practitioners' conceptualization of cases. Using metaphor analysis may well prove an informative approach to investigate the presumed differences between psychotherapy and career counseling by focusing on the language of counseling and case conceptualization.

5.6 Conclusion

Here, we have reformulated case formulation in terms of metaphor. Producing an authentic and credible story about a person within the limits of a few pages seems like an impossibility, especially given the many and varied biographies that may capture myriad stories about a person's life. There is a need for a conceptual shorthand that, like a picture, says a thousand words. From the perspective of conceptual metaphor theory, counselors think about and talk about their clients using metaphoric language. In counseling to capture a person's life may necessitate thinking metaphorically because literal description may not suffice as a way to meaningfully render a life in words. Moreover, it may not be possible to do otherwise for metaphor represents thinking itself. Thus, we recommend that metaphor is given greater prominence in counseling theory and practice, to make it explicitly known and utilized. Doing so will enhance empathic communication between counselor and client, and among counselors sharing their case formulations with one another.

References

Blustein, D. L., Fama, L. D., White, S. F., Ketterson, T. U., Schaefer, B. M., Schwam, M. F., … Skau, M. (2001). A qualitative analysis of counseling case material: Listening to our clients. *The Counseling Psychologist, 29*(2), 242–260. https://doi.org/10.1177/0011000001292004.

Bowdle, B. F., & Gentner, D. (2005). The career of metaphor. *Psychological Review, 112*(1), 193. https://doi.org/10.1037/0033-295X.112.1.193.

Brown, D. (2002). Case studies. In D. A. Brown (Ed.), *Career choice and development* (4th ed., pp. 24–34). San Francisco, CA: Jossey-Bass.

Eells, T. D. (2015). *Psychotherapy case formulation* (1st ed.). Washington, DC: American Psychological Association.

Freud, S. (1915/1991). The unconscious *The essentials of psycho-analysis. The definitive collection of Sigmund Freud's writing* (pp. 142–183). London, UK: Penguin Books.

Gibbs, R. W., Jr. (2008). *The Cambridge handbook of metaphor and thought*. Cambridge, UK: Cambridge University Press.

Inkson, K. (2004). Images of career: Nine key metaphors. *Journal of Vocational Behavior, 65*(1), 96–111. https://doi.org/10.1016/S0001-8791(03)00053-8.
James, W. (1907/2000). *Pragmatism and other writings*. New York, NY: Penguin.
Johnson, M. (1987). *The body in the mind: The bodily basis of meaning, imagination, and reason*. Chicago: University of Chicago Press.
Kövecses, Z. (2005). *Metaphor in culture: Universality and variation*. New York, NY: Oxford University Press.
Lakoff, G. (1987). *Women, fire, and dangerous things: What categories reveal about the mind*. Chicago, IL: University of Chicago.
Lakoff, G., & Johnson, M. (1980). *Metaphors we live by*. Chicago, IL: University of Chicago Press.
Lyddon, W. J. (1989). Root metaphor theory: A philosophical framework for counseling and psychotherapy. *Journal of Counseling & Development, 67*(8), 442.
McIlveen, P. (2009). Career development, management, and planning from the vocational psychology perspective. In A. Collin & W. Patton (Eds.), *Vocational psychological and organisational perspectives on career: Towards a multidisciplinary dialogue* (pp. 63–89). Rotterdam, The Netherlands: Sense Publishers.
McIlveen, P. (2015a). Psychotherapy, counseling, and career counseling. In P. J. Hartung, M. L. Savickas, & W. B. Walsh (Eds.), *APA handbook of career intervention, Volume 1: Foundations* (Vol. 1, pp. 403–417). Washington, DC: American Psychological Association.
McIlveen, P. (2015b). A reflexive research approach to professional competencies for life designing. In L. Nota & J. Rossier (Eds.), *Handbook of life design: From practice to theory and from theory to practice* (pp. 269–281). Boston, MA: Hogrefe Publishing.
Nickerson, R. S. (1998). Confirmation bias: A ubiquitous phenomenon in many guises. *Review of General Psychology, 2*(2), 175–220. https://doi.org/10.1037/1089-2680.2.2.175.
Polkinghorne, D. E. (1992). Postmodern epistemology of practice. In S. Kvale (Ed.), *Psychology and postmodernism* (pp. 146–165). London: Sage.
Popper, K. (1935/2005). *The logic of scientific discovery*. London, UK: Routledge.
Pragglejaz Group. (2007). MIP: A method for identifying metaphorically used words in discourse. *Metaphor and Symbol, 22*(1), 1–39. https://doi.org/10.1207/s15327868ms2201_1.
Savickas, M. L. (2002). Career construction: A developmental theory of vocational behavior. In D. Brown & Associates (Eds.), *Career choice and development* (4th ed., pp. 149–205). San Francisco, CA: Jossey-Bass.
Steen, G. J., Dorst, A. G., Herrmann, J. B., Kaal, A. A., Krennmayr, T., & Pasma, T. (2010). *A method for linguistic metaphor identification: From MIP to MIPVU* (Vol. 14). Amsterdam, The Netherlands: John Benjamins Publishing.
Stoltenberg, C. D., Pace, T. M., Kashubeck-West, S., Biever, J. L., Patterson, T., & Welch, I. D. (2000). Training models in counseling psychology: Scientist-practitioner versus practitioner-scholar. *The Counseling Psychologist, 28*(5), 622–640. https://doi.org/10.1177/0011000000285002.
Swales, J. (1990). *Genre analysis: English in academic and research settings*. Cambridge, UK: Cambridge University Press.
Whiston, S. C., Lindeman, D., Rahardja, D., & Reed, J. H. (2005). Career counseling process: A qualitative analysis of experts' cases. *Journal of Career Assessment, 13*(2), 169–187.

Chapter 6
Impacts of a Group-Based Career Counseling Model for Unskilled Adults in Crisis: A Case Study

Marcelo Afonso Ribeiro, Guilherme de Oliveira Silva Fonçatti and Maria da Conceição Coropos Uvaldo

Abstract The career counseling field has been challenged by the current working world marked by heterogeneity and flexibility which have generated a disembedding experience associated with an identity crisis in most workers all over the world. This new working world frame led to the increase of mature people in search of career counseling, because of the continuum experience of non-expected crises, which do not qualify as expected transitions. To this extent, the objective of this chapter is to investigate and discriminate social and personal determinants that are present in search of career counseling, and what the impacts and effectiveness of a group-based career counseling model for adults are, regarding their specificity, as well as the possibility of psychosocial intervention that considers the inextricable relation between social and personal determinants. With this goal, we describe a case study of a group-based career counseling with unskilled adults in crisis. The proposed group-based career counseling model for adults is based on research and practices systematically developed in the Brazilian context in the recent decades, grounded on a psychodynamic approach inspired by the South American critical psychoanalysis and by the traditional psychodynamic approach in the career counseling field, which are articulated with the theories that have been produced around the world with similar and related purposes, as Life Design and Psychology of Working. This is a contextualized model of career counseling focused on the radicalization of the reflexivity and on the possibility of offer, at the same time, a subjective instrumentation (clinical function) and an objective instrumentation (operative function). On the one hand, this model enables clinical space of holding, identity reconstruction, and deconstruction of preconceived stereotyped ideas about

---

This chapter is based on a systematic research developed by the authors, which has begun with the Doctoral Dissertation developed by Uvaldo (2002). It has been supported by CNPq—Conselho Nacional de Desenvolvimento Científico e Tecnológico, Brasil (National Council for Scientific and Technological Development—Brazil) by means of a regular research grant (308786/2013-0)

M. A. Ribeiro (✉) · G. de Oliveira Silva Fonçatti · M. da Conceição Coropos Uvaldo
Instituto de Psicologia da Universidade de São Paulo, Av. Prof. Mello Moraes, 1721, São Paulo CEP 05508-030, Brazil
e-mail: marcelopsi@usp.br

© Springer Nature Switzerland AG 2018

A. Di Fabio and J.-L. Bernaud (eds.), *Narrative Interventions in Post-modern Guidance and Career Counseling*, https://doi.org/10.1007/978-3-319-98300-4_6

themselves and the working world (societal metanarratives) for a subjective instrumentation, aiming the deconstruction, reconstruction, and co-construction of the working life project. On the other hand, it enables operative space for the construction of the career projects or action plans within a relational context through the constant negotiation with the working world. The effectiveness of the intervention was qualitatively evaluated by a non-structured method based on the participants' life and working narrative changes throughout the group process, and the main results indicated an increased reflexivity and a clear process of narrative changes during the counseling. In conclusion, career counseling has much to contribute with unskilled adults in crisis and the qualitative non-structured method based on narrative changes has shown to be a reliable method to assess counseling effectiveness.

6.1 Introduction

The predominant attended public in career counseling and career guidance in the Brazilian context in general and in the Career Counseling Service of Psychology Institute of the University of São Paulo, Brazil (SOP-IPUSP), where the model to be presented here has been developed, was traditionally composed of middle- and high-class youths in search of help to choose a profession (Melo-Silva, Leal, & Fracalozzi, 2010; Rascován, 2013; Ribeiro, 2014). However, since the late 1990s, a slightly different population has been looking for SOP services, including: unemployed adults, workers without university education, people with disabilities, retirees, housewives, believing that the university should offer them some kind of work, which has led to a scenario change in the interventions offer in career counseling. They are workers of both genders and various ages, looking for SOP with problems related to their occupation, working activity, working experience, or entering the labor market, usually without a profession or defined working activity.

This is not the public who usually attended in career guidance and career counseling in the Brazilian context, as showed in the researches of Melo-Silva et al. (2010), Teixeira, Silva and Bardagi (2007) and Lassance, Levenfus and Melo-Silva (2015), which indicate that less than 10% of the publications about intervention concerning various populations were not formed by teenagers in a moment of choice, and there were no publications on career counseling for adults without a university degree or doing informal jobs at all.

Social and political issues emerge from the interviews and counseling at SOP with greater emphasis and concern about the working world, changing the scenario of the choice dynamics.

> According to Hobsbawm (1984), the working world was traditionally represented by labor market, which is formed by those who need the working activity from the others to produce goods (employers) and those who have their labor power to offer (workers). This market sets the price and terms of achievement of this exchange through the employment contract. Therefore, the labor market has been traditionally considered the official place to work.

> Nevertheless, some people that works, do not do such activity in the labor market, but in an extended version of the labor market named as working world. The working world encompasses the labor market, because it is determined by the various forms of possible relationships with the world through the means of work, including not only the paid productive work of the labor market, but also the unpaid productive work and the reproductive work and maintenance (Ribeiro, 2016, pp. 80–81).

Therefore, the changing of the scenario of the choice dynamics in the contemporary working world has raised some questions: such as, will there be room for me? How can I survive in this new working world? What can be done if the known models no longer serve anymore?

The model of choice based on personal definition, in which inclinations and values come in the first place and are combined with working activities, seems not to be so relevant in the face of new issues brought by advanced capitalism (Blustein, 2006; Savickas, 2011, 2015a) marked by instability, insecurity, and flexibility, as pointed by Duarte (2015), Guichard (2015), Metz and Guichard (2009), and Savickas (2011).

From the late twentieth century to the present, the characteristics of instability, previously reserved for workers with lower level of vocational training, have become marks of almost all the working world. The uncertain and unpredictable employment, in which risks are mainly taken by the employees, and not by their employers or the government (Sá, 2010), has become the working world paradigm, receiving the denomination of boundaryless career (Arthur, 1994).

Thus, certain dimensions that generate fear prevail on insecurity and uncertainty in adults: fear that their occupation ceases to exist, fear of losing their source of income, fear of having their knowledge become obsolete, fear of the loss of social space and of an identity as a worker and citizen, as a result of the current working world (Auer, 2007).

In the last four decades, much has been written about the growing complexity of the working world with a lot of workers' living situations of unemployment, underemployment, more flexible and insecure employment contracts, and informality. In the world, there are about 200 million unemployed and 1.5 billion people in vulnerable employment (over 46% of total employed people), according to the data by the International Labour Office (ILO, 2015).

The abandonment of highly predictable routines, previously linked to the professional activity, causes people to feel bewildered in the midst of a permanent transformation period in the definition of occupations and occupational roles. The future disappears as dimension of time that guides human action, and it is more difficult to plan or expect something. Anguish and non-understanding take care of workers (Sennett, 1998).

In addition, the requirement to have a lot of qualifications increases the need for undergraduate degree and puts those who do not have it in a disadvantaged and vulnerable situation, meaning they will be in predetermined low-quality jobs, underemployment, informal jobs, and, ultimately, unemployment (Antunes, 2015; Barbier, 2004).

Therefore, significant changes, transitions, and movements in the working world have been happening. The career counseling has been deeply affected by these situations. It is this new reality of the working world that has caused the growth in search of a career counseling by more mature people, mainly due to unscheduled continuous crisis experiences, not characterized as expected transitions, as postulated by Schlössberg, Goodman and Anderson (2006). They seek a support to understand and reconstruct their bond with work, affected by this new context. How do these changes affect the bond of the person with his/her work? How to design their life project? What are the consequences for their working identity?

In line with Mark Savickas' idea (personal communication, July 9, 2014), we also think about the identity at work as a working identity for its dual interpretation: as an identity of those who work and as the working of identity.

Many authors have pointed out that, due to contemporary phenomena such as flexible working (Grote & Raeder, 2009) and disembedding (Giddens, 1991), the identity has been suffering from frequent and successive disintegration processes with a consequent weakening described as anti-identity (Sveningsson & Alvesson, 2003), de-identification (Touraine, 2007), or diffusion of identities (Dubar, 2000), which constituted an identity crisis in contemporary times.

Based on the assumption that the activity and working experience would allow the self-construction in the social world, via identity, Duarte (2009), Guichard (2009), Richardson (2012), and Savickas et al. (2009) point out the importance of identity as a central axis to a career counseling process, because of the need or radicalization of reflexivity indicated by Giddens (1991). For Savickas et al. (2009), a contemporary issue is the question of identity, not of personality, because the identity is a co-construction and the current paradigm must be contextual, not subjective.

This paradigm change is essential for the analysis of the career construction in contexts strongly marked by social inequality factors (inequality on income, gender, and access to basic rights), such as Latin America, and contexts of increasing racial and cultural plurality, as it has been happening in Western Europe.

By making the proposition of Life Design model in career counseling intervention, Savickas (2015b) points out: (a) the replacement of career development idea for the design of life trajectories, because the working life would be a constant negotiation with the working world; (b) the importance of building contextualized models of career counseling; (c) the importance of radical reflexivity, as advocated by Giddens (1991) because the only way out for people nowadays is to determine what life means to them in a continuous and changing process; and (d) the need to engage in an ongoing process of Life Design.

The search for theoretical references to support possible interventions refers to the need of knowing and researching this universe, that is, the career counseling of adults in this new context (Savickas, 1995), as has been internationally performed in the past decade by authors such as Bimrose and Hearne (2012), Guichard, Pouyaud, De Calan and Dumora (2012), Nota, Soresi, Ferrari and Ginevra (2014), Savickas (2015b), Schlössberg et al. (2006), and Whiston and Rose (2013).

In this respect, based on research and practices systematically developed in the Brazilian context in the recent decades, grounded on the psychodynamic approach inspired by the South American critical psychoanalysis (Bohoslavsky 1977; Rascován, 2005, 2013) and by the traditional psychodynamic approach in the career counseling field (Bordin, 1968, 1980a, b), which are articulated with the theories that have been produced around the world with these similar and related purposes (Dubar, 2000; Blustein, 2006, 2011; Guichard, 2009, 2015; Savickas, 2011, 2015a, b, c), this chapter aims to raise and discriminate social and personal determinants that are present in this search for career counseling and what the impacts and effectiveness of a group-based career counseling model for adults are, respecting its specificity, as a possibility of psychosocial intervention that considers the inextricable relation between social and personal determinants.

A group of unskilled adults in crisis will be taken as a case study. Why unskilled adults in crisis? Because they present some central features that lead us to think about the contemporary workers, namely: (a) They are workers without an undergraduate degree, working in a world that is increasingly demanding qualification and specialization through continuing learning; (b) they are adults, which is an emerging public who has been seeking career counseling interventions; and (c) they are in crisis in the face of instability and flexibility of the current working world, which is a career crisis, but mainly an identity crisis, and can assist the counseling field in the theoretical understanding of the choices, working life projects, and working life trajectories in the contemporaneity.

6.1.1 Challenges at the Working World

L., 46, attended a career counseling group and says on the first meeting that, after high school, she started to work as an office assistant in a real estate company. About a year and a half later, she was transferred into a big company and little by little climbed positions, getting to be head of the Human Resources department. In the early 1990s, she began to realize that things had been changing, such as layoffs and restructuring had been happening. Then, she went to college to "ensure her employment," and she ended up enrolling in a law school. She spent a great part of her salary on monthly installments and finally graduated in 1998, but this was not enough. Early in 2000, she ended up being fired on the grounds of the need or staff downsizing, and since then, she has lived in a working trajectory of discontinuity, and she does not know what to do to change the situation.

> You know, sometimes I stop to think and feel like an actress of a sitcom. They do not know what will happen to the character, those whose roles are not the leading ones. Only the man who writes knows. I don't think that even he knows, because I read that the characters grow in the plot or disappear whether the public identifies with them or not. I feel that I observe and try to understand the scenario, I learn to interpret the roles they want, much in improvisation, because they don't give us the script. Still (…) I can't make it. I was born in a world that worked in a way, I did everything right, I tried to follow the changes, but (…).

Like so many other people, L. realizes that there have been major changes in the world, specifically in the productive sphere. She tried, even without understanding why and how, to adapt to the new reality. As a more immediate, more visible consequence, we have unemployment. The whole world speaks of unemployment (Elsby, Hobijn, & Ahin, 2013; ILO, 2015), which includes proposals that come from the career counseling field (Bobek & Robbins, 2005; Ribeiro, 2010; van Vianen, Koen, & Klehe, 2015).

Increasingly, we experience a dualization of society: those who have and those who do not have a working activity. Such a scenario of exclusion and social tension puts at risk the future of social relations and the own person, making recurrent the reference to fragmentation, embrittlement, and career crisis. But what scenario is this?

This situation has caused outcomes such as: the growth of the unemployment and the living in the flexicurity experiences, the need for developing skills and lifelong learning, and, mainly, the necessity to fight against vulnerability and exclusion from the working world with the intellectual working exploitation, market flexibility, knowledge devaluation, and illegible rules of changes (Ribeiro, 2009, 2016).

It is demanded from the worker, even the most qualified one, to adapt to all circumstances, having for motivation the economic and individual success. Recognition is always ephemeral, success is never considered sufficient, and every day a new test takes place and a winner can become a loser.

"In the postmodern working world, individuals must respond to and interact with ambiguous social opportunities and complex societal offerings" (Savickas, 2015a, p. 137).

In this scenario, failure is not understood as an effect of the structure, but as a strictly personal failure, even with most workers experiencing it. In the general working world, the integration of workers has become increasingly precarious and unstable, setting up a new structure formed by three social cohesion zones: disaffiliation, vulnerability, and integration as Castel (2000) stated.

> (…) to be in the zone of integration means that one has the guarantees provided by a permanent job and can mobilize solid supports from relationships; the zone of vulnerability involves both insecure work and fragile relationships; the zone of disaffiliation combines absence of work and social isolation (pp. 524–525).

Therefore, we have a state of tension on both ends, those excluded from the working world, struggling to survive, and those who work and worry all the time about becoming disposable, in a new morphology of the working class or class that live from their working activity as Antunes (2015) postulated.

As pointed by Ribeiro (2016, p. 83):

> In sum, this psychosocial situation has marked a breakdown of the categories that serves to define itself and others, for the past is no longer the most relevant, and the future has not taken place, therefore, it cannot be stabilized. This is the contemporary ongoing transition in which the social contexts are changing and the people are rebuilding their references. In addition, they are accomplishing a constant movement that goes from the inner references to the outer references and vice versa. This process has built the new ways of being a person in social contexts in the current world (Blustein, 2011; Savickas, 2015a; Savickas et al., 2009).

The psychosocial is defined, based on Frosh (2012), "as a process that is neither 'psychological' nor 'social,' but transcends the separation of these elements to create something new—the psychosocial" (Ribeiro, 2015, p. 20).

This way, the career construction, which used to be an internal and psychological process performed from external and social references, has had to be realized from the intermediation between people and contexts, making the identity to become one of the operational concepts nowadays, as indicated by Castells (2000), Dubar (2000), Giddens (1991), Guichard (2009), Savickas et al. (2009), as well as stressing the importance of networks and social relations for the self-construction process in the world (Blustein, 2011; Castells, 2000; Guichard, 2009; Ribeiro, Silva, & Figueiredo, 2016; Richardson, 2012).

Regarding this, Ribeiro (2014) points out that:

> (…) in a world with more fragile and heterogeneous social and institutional references, the idea of constructing a working life and therefore a working life project and identity constructions, having as reference the social network, seems to be an analytical path to be considered, as advocated by Castells (2000) in his writings on the network society and the conception of identity project. That is, which is made in the trying of negotiating one's identity in the network of social relations seeking possible and temporary syntheses that take into account both the person and the society, and produce meaning and continuity to the person. Social networks would be an important reference for the contemporary process of identity construction (pp. 35–36).

As pointed by Savickas et al. (2009): "If there exist multiple ways to interpret one's own diverse life experiences, different life perspectives and designs become possible" (p. 243).

In that sense, what would the contemporary challenges for the career counseling field be?

6.1.2 Contemporary Challenges for the Career Counseling Field

Guichard (2003) said that "emerging contexts produce new questions and the need to update interventions and research in career counseling" (p. 308) because the career counseling field has been questioned by the constant and deep changes in the working world.

According to the scenario formerly presented, what would the main challenges for the career counseling field be?

Ribeiro (2016), from a summary of the main authors who discuss the main challenges for the career counseling field, pointed out seven central challenges that interventions in career counseling should deal with in today's contemporary contexts, namely (1) contexts of uncertainty, instability, flexibility, and discontinuity; (2) the absence of relativized truths or societal metanarratives (Rossier et al., 2015) as hegemonic models; (3) the need to be a contextualized process of intervention; (4) the plural, heterogeneous, complex, and discontinuous person's life experiences;

(5) the offer of stable and unstable opportunities in the working world; (6) the impossibility of knowing the social and professional reality as a whole; and (7) people and contexts are constantly changing.

Based on these contemporary challenges, Savickas et al. (2009), by proposing the paradigm of Life Design process, state that a contemporary model in career counseling should be based on dynamic, procedural, and transitional concepts and strategies, with emphasis on how people fit working into their lives and the meaning attributed by themselves to their working trajectory, co-constructed based on a constant negotiation with the working world. In other words, the self-construction in the social world, via identity, by the radicalization of the reflexivity and by the construction of life, held in the procedural relationship between human agency and social structure.

For this task, there are five basic principles: focus on (1) contextual possibilities, (2) dynamic processes, (3) nonlinear dynamics, (4) multiple narrative realities, and (5) co-construction as a core operation for an intervention in career counseling. Rossier et al. (2015) reinforce these ideas by saying that the career is now constructed in the dialogue between the self and the others and the representations generated in this dialogue, because:

> The interaction of different representations may take the form of a negotiation, a dialogue, between the individual and his or her environment, which, may, in turn, lead to changes at the level of both the individual and the environment (…) Moreover, interactions between the counselee and counselor might take the form of a life design dialogue that is aimed at increasing and promoting narratability (p. 287).

Savickas et al. (2009) pointed out that, in a flexible and changing world, career counseling should help a person construct his/her working life, because society no longer provides stable, generic, and predefined working life trajectories, which puts all workers as potential counselees.

Nota et al. (2014) complement these ideas indicating that interventions in career counseling, in order to attend contemporary demands, should "help a wide range of people—not only the highly educated—and to examining people's careers in terms of their entire life spans," moreover, "working with small and large groups" (p. 253), "not only to the individuals typically privileged in career counseling, but also to the weaker segments of society" (p. 254) by the development of "personalized career counseling activities that make it possible to approach clients by giving them voice, respecting their uniqueness, establishing a counseling relationship, based on working alliance where both client and counselor actively participate" (p. 255). That is, we see the need to increase both the intervention models and the conceptual understanding on which career counseling should be based to attend people from all segments of society.

Having been aware of these facts for some time, this proposal constitutes a group-based career counseling model with psychodynamic basis intended for adults, whether qualified or not. Let us make the presentation of the model, to discuss a career counseling group case in action later on.

6.2 A Group-Based Career Counseling Model

The model that will be presented was discussed in a preliminary way in Lehman, Ribeiro, Uvaldo and Silva (2015), Ribeiro, Uvaldo and Silva (2015), and Ribeiro (2016). The main novelty in this chapter is a case study of group-based career counseling with unskilled adults and the evaluation of its effectiveness by the investigation of the short-term impacts of the career counseling intervention by means of a qualitative non-structured method based on narrative changes.

6.2.1 Theoretical Underpinning: A Psychodynamic Approach

Currently, narrative theoretical approaches have been highlighted in the career counseling field, mainly on constructivist and constructionist bases (Young & Collin, 2004; Savickas, 2015b). Our proposal aims to rescue a less traditional theoretical approach in career counseling, which is the psychodynamic approach, having in mind that it is also a narrative approach and works with construction, deconstruction, and reconstruction of meanings and narratives (Rascován, 2005), as contemporary proposals in career counseling have been pointing, as the previously mentioned Life Design paradigm (Savickas et al., 2009; Nota & Rossier, 2015), and models such as Psychology of Working (Blustein, 2006; Duffy, Blustein, Diemer, & Autin, 2016), Counseling for Life and Relationships (Richardson, 2012), and Contextual-Action approach (Young, Valach, & Collin, 2002).

Watkins and Savickas (1990) explain what a psychodynamic approach would be like:

> The term *psychodynamic* refers to psychological systems that use motives, drives, and related covert variables to explain behavior. *Psychodynamic career counseling* refers to counseling approaches that are guided by attempts to understand, make meaning of, and utilize individual motives, purposes, and drives to facilitated career exploration. Psychodynamic theories include both Freudian and neo-Freudian theories (p. 79).

A psychodynamic approach, then, allows the understanding of the processes and meanings generated by the person's career construction, not in a prescriptive way but in a procedural, and thus more a subjective career counseling than an objective career guidance model (Watkins & Savickas, 1990), based on an interpretative method realized by the relation between counselor and counselee (or group of counselees). The counselor acts more like an intermediary than a counselor, because he/she has a nondirective function and intermediates actions and processes needed for the construction, deconstruction, and reconstruction of working life projects, working identity, and working life trajectories (Rascován, 2013; Ribeiro, 2014, 2016; Savickas et al., 2009).

Bohoslavsky (1977), who wrote a book called "Career counseling—A clinical strategy," grounded on the British psychoanalytical theory, mainly Klein (1984) and Pichon-Riviére's bond theories (Tubert-Oaklander & Tubert, 2004), is a reference to Brazilian career counseling and points out that the proposed psychodynamic approach focuses on the unconscious dimension and makes it possible to consider the existing interrelationships between potential and unconscious demands (called vocational identity) and socioeconomic demands (called occupational identity) through the building of a dialectical way from psychological to social and vice versa. This focus on the unconscious conceives the counselee as:

> (…) a subject of choices that occur through identification processes as well as current, past, and potential links established with the world, that define not only what must be done, but also who to be, who not to be, and what not to do (Lehman et al., 2015, p. 26).

Identification is a defense process, that is, a set of protection demonstrations against internal attacks (unconscious impulses) and external, that can provoke excitations and tensions that lead to unpleasantness (Laplanche & Pontalis, 1988). However, it is also a process "in the individual's lifelong effort to differentiate himself while retaining a unity with others" (Bordin, 1957, p. 5), constructing, step by step, an identity—the central axis for contemporary interventions in career counseling.

The basic career conflict is the "conflict involved in choosing a way to be through something to do (an occupation)" (Bohoslavsky, 1977, p. 66), which makes the counselee's working identity to be generated in the relationship between vocational identity [or biographical process for Dubar (2000) and cognitive dimension to Guichard (2009)] and occupational identity [or relational process for Dubar (2000) and sociological dimension to Guichard (2009)].

"Moreover, choosing the future is, at the same time, designing a project" (Bohoslavsky, 1983, p. 11), meaning that, before anything else, the chosen career is a career project. Therefore, Bohoslavsky (1977) said that, "every choice undertakes a project and a project is no more than a strategy within time" (p. 99), because "the moment of choice is a pre-rehearsal of this future behavior" (p. 79), which is called a career. "The vocational (being) needs a project (strategy within time) so that it can become a trajectory (career), whereas the occupational (doing) needs an object to accomplish the vocational" (Ribeiro et al., 2015, p. 199).

"In other words, the vocational counseling has become a personal counseling" (Bordin, 1968, p. 426). Bordin (1980a) draws attention to the fact that taking occupations in terms of intrinsic motivation does not eliminate the existence of extrinsic motivations and conformations and that they should take place in the counseling process.

It presents two ethical and political contributions while giving more autonomy and power to the counselees and the right to their choices and to their own projects (subject of choices for Bohoslavsky, 1977) and when, traditionally, attempting to realize vocational counseling works with all people, with not only a select group of young people from the best schools but a larger population, aiming the fight against the dehumanization generated by working and the ability to help people express their humanity through working activity, mainly to empower the working activity as a means of expressing themselves (Bordin, 1980b).

6.2.2 Intervention Model: Group-Based Model

Career counseling has traditionally been conducted in an individualized way, and it has focused on the counselor–counselee relationship. Therefore, it justifies what Di Fabio and Maree (2012) have recently said: "for a number of reasons, little has been written on ways career counselling can be provided in group contexts" (p. 100). However, in Brazil, 61% of the career counselors have used group counseling (Lehman et al., 2015).

A possible explanation for this predominance of group-based work is that Brazil is mostly formed by more collectivistic than individualistic contexts, according to the ideas proposed by Brewer and Chen (2007), which leads us to conclude that "the collectivistic tradition of the social embeddedness is more meaningful to the people's experience than the individualistic tradition of the self-esteem" (Ribeiro, 2016, p. 94). Besides that, a considerable part of the Brazilian everyday activities usually occurs collectively. It is worth noticing that, in order to exist, careers currently depend on social networks, mainly in contexts marked by collectivistic cultures.

According to Savickas (2002), "individuals construct their careers in a particular social ecology (…) while the context shapes the individual, the individual shapes the context" (pp. 157–158), and the understanding of career would only be known if you know the web of social roles that connect the person to society. Thus, identity, relationships, intermediation, networks, and processes should be the theoretical framework for the career counseling intervention.

Consequently, if the career construction has been going through the process of relations between people and contexts, having as structural axis the identity and social networks as the basis for this construction, and if career counseling interventions should be contextualized, we can say that a proposal of group-based career counseling model will be in line with the demands and current opportunities for workers, mainly based on the idea that the group device artificially reproduces the social relations prevailing in a given social context and it would be a privileged space for experimentation of oneself in the world before its concrete realization.

Hence, in a group, you can work the issue of identity and not only the issue of personality traits. The psychosocial co-construction, which constitutes the identity process, can be experienced in a group in a realistic and productive way. This is because a group has the advantage of being the relational space where it is possible to analyze the personal, the intersubjective, and the institutional dimensions, or the verticality, the horizontality, and the transversality of the functioning of a group and of the people in the group. It is the interpersonal space marked by individual needs that must be suited through a collective task, with the central focus on the bond, which is the matrix of human relations (Tubert-Oaklander & Tubert, 2004).

According to Lehman et al. (2015), a group work has several advantages as "the sensation of relief created by the socialization of singular problems [that] ends isolation" (p. 27), the existent common denominators have the power to strengthen and contextualize each person's projects and decisions, the stimulation of cooperation instead of competition allows the counselee the opportunity to learn from the experience of others as well as to receive help from those who are in the same career crisis, counselees are encouraged to assume responsibility for their projects and decisions (Di Fabio & Maree, 2012), and, finally, based on Klivlighan (1990), "the instrumentation for the construction of projects within a relational context allows this process to create characteristics and forms that are similar to what could emerge in concrete social relations" (Lehman et al., 2015, p. 27).

> The group represents a micro society that gives each person a global view of the situation in which he or she is inserted. [It] facilitates the exploration of existing possibilities, the individuals' potential, and his or her environment, experimentation with future roles, the construction of career projects, and the social-historic contextualization shared via group relations (Lehman et al., 2015, p. 27).

Conceptually inspired by the psychodynamic approach, mainly by psychoanalysis, Winnicott (1965) views a group as a potential space and an intermediate area of experience where some group processes, named as intermediate formations (Käes & Kirshner, 2006), work as bridges connecting three distinct and simultaneously interlinked psychic spaces: the intrapsychic space, the attached space, and the group's own space.

> Intermediate formations are those that allow one to articulate, re-articulate, turn on, turn off, and mobilize contrary forces in conflict. These processes articulate the intra-psychic space and the group. Intermediate formations are shaken by crises and traumas that shattered the once continuous area between spaces. The group technique favours the presence of these intermediate formations, which are worked on and used to deal with these various spaces, their articulations, and disjunctions (Lehman et al., 2015, pp. 28–29).

The group may work as a transitional object, sustaining and supporting the holding, and providing a shared experience between the group members that provides a holding environment (Winnicott, 1965). It helps counselees to deal with their crisis, mainly identity crisis, share it with the others, and expose themselves to a life with the demands of external reality. Moreover, it is able to break the counselees' preconceived stereotyped ideas about themselves and the working world, allowing space for doubts about social and work truths making them more flexible and also for new questions and issues.

The group process allows counselees to:

> (…) reorganize and articulate his or her intra-psychic, intersubjective, and social relationships. Nevertheless, s/he may find it hard to do so if this process is carried out directly in the social world. The group technique whose basic configuration forms temporary space of external sustenance, holding, and transition can help clients build their projects for a professional life (Lehman et al., 2015, p. 29).

A group-based career counseling based on a psychodynamic approach can be conceived as a non-structured intervention modality with a therapeutic and operative functions that cope with career crisis understood as "the individual difficulty to project himself/herself into the future and construct his or her self and the relations with the working world" (Ribeiro et al., 2015, p. 200). It can be defined as a clinical-operative method, because it deals with identity reconstruction (clinical method) as well as it supports the process of career construction, deconstruction, and reconstruction (operative method).

This view is corroborated by Bordin (1954), who said that counseling should be a non-structured intervention, "which is the key to making relationships therapeutic" (p. 195).

Furthermore, this proposal has been used with people of different ages, socioeconomic status, gender, level of education, and life stage.

Therefore, for all the several reasons pointed out, a group device is configured as a pertinent, relevant, and current strategy for career counseling interventions in contemporary times.

6.2.3 *Specific Target Audience: Unskilled Adults in Crisis*

In general, interventions in career counseling used to be mainly for young people or young adults in the expected life-cycle transitions, and the adults have never constituted the largest group of people attended in career counseling in the Brazilian context, as it has already been stated, which seems to happen around the world, as said by Savickas (2015b).

The expansion of the scope of activity in the career counseling field is necessary, because the reality of the working world, as discussed earlier in this chapter, has been generating frequent transitions underlying identity crises. "Today, adults repeatedly have the need to make choices during their 40-year working life" (Savickas, 2015b, p. 135).

Assisting adults is a fundamental task for career counseling in the twenty-first century.

If the help for adults in general is crucial, the assistance to adults without a college degree is even more important since this group represents a significant portion of the economically active population (EAP) worldwide. Recent data by the Organization for Economic Co-operation and Development (2016) indicate that an average of 32% of the population in the Member States have an undergraduate degree. The Institute of Applied Economic Research (Instituto de Pesquisa Econômica Aplicada, 2015) shows that, in Brazil, approximately 82% of the EAP have no college degree which leads them to difficulties in their working trajectories. The improvement of their socioeconomic status and also the access of the population to the basic rights, in general, have increased the demand for helping career construction; however, there are not many strategies developed, especially during crisis time. It is worth mentioning that economic instability has always been a constant reality in Brazil, facilitating the establishment of the culture of immediatism and of the difficulty in thinking about the future and in the medium- and long-term planning.

6.2.4 Technical Underpinnings

As it has already been described in Lehman et al. (2015), the proposed group-based career counseling has been developed all over the last 40 years through research and interventions with this counseling modality conducted by a specialized service at the Institute of Psychology of the University of São Paulo, Brazil. This service assists about 600 counselees a year, of whom 80% attended group-based career counseling with a psychodynamic approach. About 40% of the counselees are composed of male and female workers, at the age of 25–50 years, coming from the middle and lower social classes, interested in developing their careers; about 15% of these people are unemployed, unqualified, and vulnerable. The intervention model has some important assumptions.

Firstly, the career counselor leaves the guiding position and assumes a position of intermediary (Käes & Kirshner, 2006), because he or she does not have the control over the process of counseling, sharing this responsibility with the group of counselees in order to create a dialogue between the counselor's scientific knowledge and the counselees' everyday-life knowledge. This process is named by Santos (2002) *diatopical hermeneutics,* and it generates an intercultural dialogue which requires a collective and interactive production of knowledge.

Secondly, this issue highlights the significance of both personal narratives from the group of counselees and societal metanarratives from the counselors in order to be able to produce identity and career reconstructions.

In third place, the counselor "uses words as mediating objects and his or her interventions are based on the interpretations of the transferential elements (contradictions, not explicit feelings, unknown relationships between facts)" (Lehman et al., 2015, p. 28). According to Freud (1920), transference is a psychoanalytical concept comprehended as a phenomenon of the unconscious redirection of feelings from the client to the therapist or, in the career counseling field, from the counselee (or group of counselees) to the counselors. These unconscious projections should be worked through in the group. The group-based career counseling always has two counselors, one being responsible for coordinating the group process and the other responsible for the participant observation of the process, both acting jointly and in a complementary way.

Next to that, as it has already been stated, the career counseling, as a clinical-operative method, allows the subjective instrumentation (identity and life project reconstruction) and the objective instrumentation (construction of operational strategies to build action plans in the world) (Ribeiro, 2014, 2016).

> In this sense, the career counseling provides protected potential space for co-construction of contextualized narratives in group, which needs the legitimacy of the others to be able to exist as a narrative reality. This process is guaranteed through diatopical hermeneutics, which (...) problematizes the world and the dominant social discourse. Also, it turns continuous career construction into possible conditions. This takes place through a negotiation process with the context represented by the members of the group and mediated by the counselor (Ribeiro, 2016, p. 98).

The speeches and the group dialogues are the basis for psychodynamic career counseling as a listening model, "intended to assist people in developing the reflexivity they need to design their lives" (Guichard, 2015, p. 18)—named by the author as a dialogue kind of intervention. "Additionally, there are some playful group techniques, collages, and games that facilitate access to the speech, exposing internal contents or unexplored contents in a non-threatening manner" (Lehman et al., 2015, p. 32). It aims to reconstruct the working life project and the working identity.

Nevertheless, the career counseling can be complemented by the provision of some information about the working world or additional training requirements, and by the development of a working action plan, as Guichard (2015) recommended.

The group is composed of people in similar moments of life and in similar career crisis. On the one hand, there is a group homogeneity represented by age and educational level, and, on the other hand, the group heterogeneity is represented by different aspects such as gender, professional interest, race, and social class. The number of participants ranges from 5 to 15, and this is justified by the maintenance of group integration dynamics and for a wealth of contributions (Lehman et al., 2015).

In operational terms, there are six meetings of three hours each, divided into three stages: The first moment focuses on the subjective instrumentation, the second moment is an intermediary moment of transition, and the third moment focuses on the objective instrumentation. There is no predefined content sequence for the group's functioning, but an initial proposal for the group process trajectory can be outlined.

The first moment aims to shelter and construct, deconstruct, and reconstruct narratives for the subjective instrumentation, and it happens in three meetings (first to third meeting).

The first meeting is dedicated to the group formation and to the binding process through the counselees' introduction of themselves, the rescue of working histories, and the survey of the issues to be worked with during the group process.

In the second meeting, a discussion on the transformation of the working world and its implications for the group members is held.

In the third meeting, research reports and more realistic views about the working world of oneself take place, aiming the narrative reconstruction about him or her in terms of identity and life project.

In the fourth meeting, an intermediary moment of transition and the beginning of the second stage of the process, which aims the objective instrumentation, present themselves.

The third moment aims to prepare the working action plan for the objective instrumentation of the working life project and lasts two meetings (fifth to sixth meeting).

In the fifth and sixth meetings, an individualized working project is co-constructed based on the identity and life project reconstruction that has been done in the first moment of the group process, which is not an individual project, because it is built in a relational context. Moreover, a working action plan is also co-constructed. The last meeting also addresses the presentation of the projects co-constructed by each counselee, mourning the end of the group and evaluating the counseling process.

Finally, periodic follow-up meetings are proposed to each counselee.

6.2.5 The Effectiveness Evaluation of Career Counseling: A Qualitative Non-structured Method Based on Narrative Changes

The effectiveness of the intervention was qualitatively evaluated by a non-structured method based on the changes of the participants' working life narratives throughout the counseling process.

The main goal is to identify the first narratives from each counselee regarding his/her current career situation and follow up the narrative changes that are being created. However, it is worth noting that the proposed method does not provide a pre- and post-assessment (Bimrose, 2008; Di Fabio, 2015; Di Fabio & Palazzeschi, 2016) or proposes previously defined categories (Di Fabio, 2015; Di Fabio & Palazzeschi, 2016). Instead of that, the method is non-structured, mainly because it works with counselee's own narrative production that arises from the group relations through the diatopical hermeneutics. In this sense, it is a processual and relational method without a pre- and post-assessment previously defined by the counselors.

The analysis base for the effectiveness evaluation of counseling is therefore the narrative changes produced by the counselees during the group process, toward the understanding of their career crisis, the deconstruction of the current career issues and ineffective strategies, and the reconstruction of new career issues and new strategies for dealing with these career issues by means of a co-construction process.

6.2.6 A Case Study: The Proposed Group-Based Career Counseling Model in Action

As a way to illustrate the proposed model, we report a brief excerpt of the career counseling group process and an analysis of the methodological aspects involved with its outcomes and impacts over each counselee, as well as the effectiveness evaluation of the intervention.

The group was attended at the Career Counseling Service at Psychology Institute of the University of São Paulo, Brazil (SOP-IPUSP), which is the most important university in the country, where most people would like to study because of its quality and its recognition. This note is necessary, because sometimes there is a strong transference between counselees and the pair of counselors, which are identified as objects of desire for being in a desired social and educational space for all.

The group was composed of seven workers, who were adults with high school degree, which makes them unskilled for the working world, as it has already been discussed; 29–39 years old; four men and three women; coming from the middle and lower social classes; interested in developing their careers, which began when they were around 16 years old; three of them were employed (a radio station employee, a secretary, and a prison guard); three were unemployed; and one of them had a small candy sales business. From now on, the counselees will be called E. (man), J. (man), M. (woman), R. (man), S. (woman), A. (man), and T. (woman).

The two coordinators were psychologists (one woman and one man) and career counselors, trained in the psychodynamic model, and, as stated previously, one had the coordinating role and the other the participant observation role.

The first moment of the group process aims to shelter and construct, deconstruct, and reconstruct narratives for the subjective instrumentation and lasts three meetings (first to third meeting).

6.2.7 *First Meeting*

The group began with the introduction of each counselee, and the main complaints were the difficulty to get a better job because of their age, outdating and lack of qualification. Those who have been working in mid-level occupations and without having made a choice of a working activity, felt unhappy and unmotivated and without chances of career advancement, while the unemployed ones felt stuck in time. Everyone lived a sense that "falling behind" as pointed by R.

The presentations are complainants, resentful, and they report not having received support to study in adolescence, either by their parents or by their teachers; the women had to leave their professional development to raise their children or due to their husbands' careers. In other words, they talked about feeling stuck and blamed the circumstances and significant others, which is expressed in the speech of T.: "We are wasting time not studying and coming to the SOP is an attempt to recover it." Not even once they pointed the influence of socioeconomic and historical aspects of this process.

They bring as a solution to their issues enrolling in universities, and it is illustrated in M.'s comment: "I need to study to see if I can improve"; they seek assistance for this task in the career counseling, as pointed by E.: "I want to return to the college project but I do not know in which course."

Some initial questions seem to limit the possibilities of the group of counselees.

First, there is an operational issue of not knowing how and where to look for information to perform their entry projects at the university. R. states that he has no information on how to continue studying and says he is embarrassed to ask friends about it. The group answers R. questions and also reports their difficulties in obtaining information. This movement indicates a difficulty to get resources and information for future projects and indicates the underlying dynamics to a career counseling group that welcomes the demand of each person and returns this demand to the group to be reflected collectively, to ultimately assist the initial applicants to reconstruct their projects. Zimerman (1993) named this kind of intervention the in-group interventions, because they focus on group relationships as well as on the individuals in the group.

Second, a gender issue question appears, specifically for women. The access to the undergraduate education, for people like S., depends on the realization of family projects, indicating a moment of identity reconstruction by the possibility of focusing on the construction of a working identity, as pointed by S.'s speech: "Now that my husband is finishing graduate school and our daughters are grown, I can go to college." Here appears the issue of gender through the influence of motherhood in women's careers as a societal metanarrative (Rossier et al., 2015) as a hegemonic model for women.

Third, there is an issue once again based on a societal metanarrative (Rossier et al., 2015) that "the labor market does not accept older people," as pointed by R., and going to college at their age would not be a valid action.

Finally, they talk about how they despise themselves and the fear they feel about making plans.

It clearly expresses an experience of crises marked by the rupture in the process of continuity among the old working life projects, the illusions about the future (new projects) and certainties for such an achievement, especially based on societal metanarratives (Rossier et al., 2015) of the reduction of working life project opportunities for adults, and of the disqualification and also the entry into universities as the only possibility of career advancement.

In terms of the technical effectiveness of the intervention, two points should be highlighted.

The effectiveness of psychodynamic career counseling as a listening model emerged in a spontaneous comment by T.: "Thanks for the conversation because this alone made me reflect on these issues," ensuring the entry into the reflexivity process that is needed to design people's lives, according to Guichard (2015).

The beginning of the group formation and the feeling of belonging that the group space generated are explained in E.'s and S.'s speeches, who said, respectively: "I realize that we can exchange a lot in the group" and "We will not let each other give up their projects" showing the possibility of addressing individual issues and thinking about the construction of the personal project into a collective, where there is the network function in which occurs the process of self-construction (Castells, 2000). That is, the personal task in a group situation becomes a group task established by the bond, fulfilling the main task of the first meeting.

In terms of the effectiveness evaluation of career counseling, the first narratives presented the issues and demands of counselees, namely the difficulty of getting a better job because of their age, their outdating and lack of skills associated with demotivation and dissatisfaction with the current work activity focused on mid-level occupations that were not chosen and did not offer them chances to grow in their careers, while the unemployed felt stuck in time.

"Falling behind" (R.) is the synthesis of the central issue of counselees, and "We are wasting time not studying" (T.), and "I need to study to see if I can improve my career" (M.) are the main solutions to the issue raised. Everyone looks at his/her issues as an individual matter on which the counselors will indicate how to solve.

They have constructed their narratives by reproducing societal discourses, such as: Older people have fewer opportunities in the working world, the woman has no right to construct a career, they are unskilled for not having a college degree, and the only possibility to have a career progress is pursuing college-level studies.

6.2.8 Second and Third Meetings

After a resume of the previous meeting, A. said:

> The more time passes, the less you can make mistakes. We see 19, 20-year-old people already entering college. At the age of 25, they take a post-graduate course in any area. And I do not know which way to go. It seems that I've only got one shot to hit the target.

Again, we see emerging the basic experience of career crisis of this group of counselees: people that are "falling behind," locating also an identity crisis because they perceive themselves as people with a self-reference that was lost in the past and in search of an identity reconstruction to assign a new meaning to their lives—subjective demand for career counseling that reveals its clinical dimension, namely the identity reconstruction task, as shown by Rascován (2005), Ribeiro (2014, 2016), and Savickas et al. (2009).

After that, they wonder if the output to their questions would really be starting a university college, because they do not know if "going to college will guarantee their job"—objective demand for career counseling that reveals its operative dimension, namely the construction of an action plan to implement the new identity construction (Ribeiro, 2014, 2016; Savickas et al., 2009).

The action of the pair of counselors, at this moment, was to try to help them out of generic complaints and to make them start to think about their own unique difficulties. Then, some appeared, such as: "I am not able to grow in my career" (J.), "I consider my current job repetitive" (E.), "I have a tiring routine and a sense that I cannot change anything" (M.), and "I have a very limited career" (S.).

Given this, the counselors ask how they think about taking forward their new projects, aiming to deconstruct the *discourse of limit* (current working situation or unemployment), and they encourage the co-construction of the *discourse of possibility* (construction of the working life projects). This remark makes the counselees point, once again, the limits of their new projects, expressed in their talking about the difficulties of studying in Brazil as J. says: "I feel unprepared to compete in the market," yet it makes room for the narrative that studying would be "a chance to have a global view of the world not only to work" (A.), and indicating appreciation of cultural growth that can be obtained and generate new career opportunities, showing a process of narrative deconstruction and reconstruction that fulfills the objective of this meeting: the discussion on the transformation of the working world and its implications for the group members.

The project to be constructed in the group takes another status, college can be a form of cultural growth, a way not to feel inferior to the others, in short, they could add other senses, establishing the constant movement of identification to an ideal and the openness to the news, all built inside the protected space of the group, without the immediacy and standardize social pressures. That is why we conceive the group space as potential space characterized as a simultaneous area of illusion and constitutive reality of privileged space to try and put into action identity reconstruction processes (Anzieu, 1984; Winnicott, 1965).

The pair of counselors do not assume the group the role of experts, who have the absolute knowledge, to be consulted, even if they have studied more than the counselees. Instead, they assume the role of *intermediaries* between counselees and the issue of studying at a college, providing thus the expansion movement of speech possibilities on the subject.

J. remembers that he gave up a good job because he believed in which he heard, about the necessity to be an entrepreneur, but he failed as a business owner and had to return to his previous activity elsewhere, when he was outdated technologically. That is, the group began to establish a deconstruction process of societal meta-narratives (Rossier et al., 2015) as hegemonic models, a process reinforced by the redemption of their working life trajectories in which they had already achieved good positions in the working world and have once been very pleased, which gradually made the feeling of being delayed fade away.

In terms of technical effectiveness of the intervention, the group clearly starts feeling relieved by the socialization of singular problems which ends in isolation, receiving the group continence stimulated by the interventions of the pair of counselors, the dependency models begin to be shattered by the questioning of societal metanarratives (Rossier et al., 2015) as hegemonic models, mainly due to the opportunity to learn from the experience of others as well as to receive help from those who are in the same career crisis. They intuitively realize that a choice is different from a project: For the latter, several objective and subjective information, strategies, and evaluating the probability of achievement are required, that is why this model has the characteristic of a clinical-operative intervention. The career counseling for them is not only a choice, but the reconstruction of objectives and strategies.

In the last part of the meeting, they show displeasure and talk about the difficulty of joining a university such as USP, a clear transference movement with the counselors that represented, in that moment, the impossibility of getting a quality undergraduate degree.

In terms of the effectiveness evaluation of career counseling, the narratives produced in the second and third meetings outlined a difficulty of changing career, as well as stagnation in working life and reproduction of personal narratives based on societal discourses, for example, "I am not able to grow in my career" (J.),

"I consider my current job repetitive" (E.), "I have a tiring routine and a sense that I cannot change anything" (M.), and "I have a very limited career" (S.). They remained constructing their narratives based on reproducing societal discourses, and the next step should be the deconstruction of these narratives and an openness to reconstruct them by questioning the societal discourses.

6.2.9 Fourth Meeting

This is the second moment of the group process or the intermediary moment of transition, in which the work of identity reconstruction and of life project begins to materialize through the objective instrumentation for its realization through a career project or working action plan, that is, an instrumentation for the construction of action plans within a relational context that is protected, although with similarities "to what emerges in concrete social relations" (Lehman et al., 2015, p. 27).

The counselees are encouraged to assume responsibility for their projects and decisions (Di Fabio & Maree, 2012).

They bring through the whole meeting their inability to seek information and to get to know about the possibilities of the working world and also the fear of the view that the working world would have about their new chosen working activities. They report several attempts to change their career and all the difficulties inherent to them, but a search for stereotyped alternatives is denoted and, often, unrealistically opportunities available for them, for example, taking a helicopter pilot course, studying at a very expensive university, or opening an unviable business.

At this time, the intervention of the pair of counselors was essential in order to deconstruct stereotypical impossibilities, which generate more paralysis than movement, once again pointing their career crisis, and to establish a diatopical hermeneutics (Santos, 2002), in which a new collective and interactive form of production of knowledge could emerge, breaking stereotypes and causing the group to search according to their reality and to see the possibilities existing therein or expected to be created.

To this end, an intermediate strategy was used, called RO (*roles ocupacionales* or working roles), described by Bohoslavsky (1977) and systematized by Leite (2015), consisting of a series of cards, each one with the name of a possible career. This material was offered to the group, with the request that they could separate the known and the unknown courses. Excitedly, they begin to handle the cards, exchange information, and try to learn more about them. However, gradually the exploration of the cards gives way to a dialogue. That is, the RO strategy, as a mediating object, allowed the passage of paralysis in the stereotypical outputs to the establishment of a dialogue, or Life Design dialogues, aiming to develop "the reflexivity they need to design their lives" (Guichard, 2015, p. 18). Moreover, it made possible for the counselees to break their preconceived stereotyped ideas about themselves and the working world.

They comment on their financial difficulties, on how they could conciliate college studies with work and kids, and talk about how spouses are resistant to this idea. J. summarizes the discussion by speaking of the need to plan, starting from the desires and concrete reality, to create something possible. T. agrees, adding "it is not only a personal decision; in our recent story, we have a lot of people, whom we didn't have when we were 17 years old." He adds: "The best college is the one that best suits our needs and possibilities."

The use of RO strategy allowed the gradual deconstruction of stereotypes and building of a dialogue in which the reflexivity could operate in order to think about alternatives for the future, allowing the space for doubts about social and work truths, making them more flexible and opening space for new questions and issues. At this moment, the counselors talk about the need to think and structure a project and an action plan to overcome the existing career crisis.

M. enthusiastically comments on the lack of reflexivity in her life, saying: "I never did this. I find it interesting; I'm always doing things without much thinking."

T. says she does not have a working life project, but discovered she had a "family project, having children and a husband, and this is just as important"; that is, she notes that identity is multidimensional and that there is a significant part of her identity dedicated to the family and now she needs to think about the part focused on working.

E., thinking about the importance of constructing a working life project associated with a working action plan, said: "I see that every cloud has a silver lining."

In short, the RO's strategy seems to have been effective, as the group of counselees talk about their desires and real difficulties. They went from idealization to the thought and reflection on how a college course or any other course could be included in the life of each of them and still they could get good things from it, view the difficulties, profits and losses, approaching to the idea of the project, and realizing the need to rebuild their identity. They realize there is no perfect profession, without problems or with an eternally heated labor market. They approach their socioeconomic determinations, their "failures," the valuation they give to people with an undergraduate degree. Despite the tough talk, they cannot return to the past and choose as if they were 17 years old, and they realize that even then they chose which was possible, spent their lives adapting, and now they can plan a new way, trying to predict the difficulties and ways to deal with them. That is, to have greater autonomy is possible, realizing the need to construct a working action plan to accomplish the working life project and an identity reconstruction process.

In terms of the effectiveness evaluation of career counseling, the narratives produced in the fourth meeting suggested a start of a career transition that can be evidenced by the improvement of reflexivity and by the breaking up of prescriptive and inflexible societal discourses, as indicated by narratives about planning the future: "I never did this. I find it interesting; I'm always doing things without much thinking" (M.), and "the best college is the one that best suits our needs and possibilities" (T.). E. summarized this group movement, saying: "I see that every cloud has a silver lining."

The third moment of the group process aims to prepare the working action plan for the objective instrumentation of the working life project and, it lasts two meetings (fifth to sixth meeting).

6.2.10 *Fifth Meeting*

During the fifth meeting, the group of counselees takes up the issue of having obtained a lot of information about opportunities in the working world and clearly tells that they realized the need to think of their working action plan to make it viable, always based on their identity.

The group as a whole presents the limits and possibilities of the working action plans they are reflecting about, indicating the difficulty of paying an undergraduate course, as E. said: "We run into the financial issue. The wage increases do not follow the colleges' installments"; the difficulty of entering the labor market from the working action plan they are building; and the importance of having guarantees of accomplishment, so they can leave their stable job, demanding a security in the career transition they want.

The group answers that an ideal profession does not exist, like a profession which does not present problems, there are no plans without difficulties when leaving the paralyzed situation, as in the beginning of the group, and entering a movement of reflexivity in which they think about the difficulties and possibilities of the process, and mainly they seek ways and strategies to implement a working action plan that is feasible and makes sense itself.

In this sense, as a spokesman of the group, S. says: "I notice that things are changing and that life only makes sense when we have goals." E. adds: "It is hard to recognize that we are guilty. We keep putting the blame on everyone else. The fact is that we need to see the reality, go and really see it and not to think that it is fine the way it is."

They retake the projects, which have to be based on reality and not on what they think or want to believe, integrating desire and reality, as Bohoslavsky (1977) indicated.

The group could now get in touch with reality, seek information, and question themselves, and this gives a new face to the group. They talk more, exchange more information, and give each other hints. They seem to be more comfortable not only in the group but also with their own projects.

In terms of the effectiveness evaluation of career counseling, counselees produced some narratives integrating desire and reality, as pointed by S.: "Life only makes sense when we have goals." At the same time, they gradually have been deconstructing the early narratives that have blamed others for their own career stagnation, as indicated by E.: "It is hard to recognize that we are guilty. We keep putting the blame on everyone else." It has paved the way therefore for the gradual emergence of constructed narratives, which seemed to be a clear narrative change movement.

6.2.11 Sixth Meeting

This meeting begins with each counselee reporting his/her research, projects, and plans.

Part of the counselees decided to enter a university as his/her working action plan, including A., S., E., and J.

A. is determined to take a degree in Advertising. He researched and, through his wife who is a journalist, got a stage in the area. He talked with advertising professionals and realized that experience comes to be more important than the course itself. His wife can pay the bills for some time.

S. says the group helped a lot in order for her to come down to earth. “I thought it was going to happen. Suddenly everything was going to change. I put the blame on others for not doing what I wanted.” She talked with her husband who will finish his graduate course, and then she can take the money to enroll in a preparatory course and pay for the psychology course. She says: “My daughters are already grown and they found it would be good that I study.”

J. and E. are researching, but they will enroll in an undergraduate course only after they have researched a lot.

The story of these four counselees demonstrates awareness of the need or a career transition that involves the immediate social network in the working life project, meaning that the project is co-constructed in relation to others and that the career group counseling experience, as a protected relational space, allowed to the counselees the possibility to deal with their crisis, mainly their identity crisis, to share it with the others, rehearsal new possibilities, and, finally, expose themselves to live with the demands of external reality, negotiating their projects with immediate social network, for example, the family, which led a joint project, not an individualized one.

The other part of counselees group (M., T. and R.) have constructed working action plans that did not include the entrance to a university, which shows a deconstruction of societal metanarratives (Rossier et al., 2015) as a model of hegemonic according to which the professional training would be the only way for the career success, and points out an important finding for counselors who want to work with unskilled workers: We must perform a movement of diatopical hermeneutics to enable working life projects and working action plans contextualized in the reality of counselees and not in the societal metanarratives.

M. comments that she has learned a lot in the group. She hopes to take a technical course in nursing, because she thinks that going to college is still far for her reality. And R. wants to invest in his current job. They know, however, that this is not just a personal choice, and there are social determinants. They were joyful because with this group they could understand what happens in their current job, marking the importance of reflexivity (Guichard, 2015), and the need of coordination between the subjective and the socioeconomic demands to enable contextualized working life projects and working action plans (Bohoslavsky, 1977).

T. has discovered the location of the *Brazilian Service of Support to Micro and Small Business* (*Sebrae*) nearby her home, and on a telephone conversation, they informed her about the course which the pair of counselors had suggested in the previous meeting: Small Business Management. She thinks that this way she can further expand her business. T. makes some money making chocolate mousses to a pizzeria. She had never thought about the possibility of investing on it, turning it into a business and how it could be done without disturbing the family dynamics. She pointed out that the failed experiment of J. was very important for her to realize that she had to properly organize this new phase that, in the beginning, would be the course. She also realized that her priority project was her motherhood, especially because one of her children has some difficulties. She exits the group-based career counseling with identity issues clarified; that is, for her the family identity dimension is more important than the working identity dimension.

At the end, they talk about the expectations they had of the group-based career counseling: a magic answer to indicate a glorious way without any setback. They realized that, in fact, it does not exist and so they could rescue the responsibility of each one with his/her project, life, and perspectives, that is, the induction of reflexivity with consequent deconstruction of societal metanarratives (Rossier et al., 2015) as a hegemonic model, based on a diatopical hermeneutics in a protected potential space group (Winnicott, 1965), where the relationship between subjective demands and socioeconomic demands may occur, resulting in an identity reconstruction and co-construction of contextualized working life projects and working action plans.

This sets the central feature of the group-based career counseling model as a clinical-operative strategy, that is, a strategy that aims both identity reconstruction (clinical dimension) and the co-construction of contextualized working life projects and working action plans (operative dimension). In both constructions, the counselees take part actively, as they assume the role of authors of their working life projects and working action plans, casting off the role of the counselor as the professional that, from scientific assessment instruments, would clarify the best solution for each counselee.

In terms of the effectiveness evaluation of career counseling, the narratives created during the last meeting have made clear a gradual transition from career stagnation (sense that they are "falling behind") to a movement, which encompassed a wider vision of reality, a deconstruction of the societal discourses understood as the only available career narratives ("the labor market does not accept older people," "I need to study to see if I can improve," and "I feel unprepared to compete in the market"), and a great potential to reconstruct working life projects ("I notice that things are changing and that life only makes sense when we have goals").

In other words, a narrative change took place during the counseling process, and it could be assessed by the qualitative non-structured method based on narrative changes that were here proposed.

6.3 Conclusion

The career counseling field has been challenged by the current working world marked by heterogeneity and flexibility which has generated a disembedding experience (Giddens, 1991) associated with an identity crisis of most workers worldwide.

Therefore, it must construct contextualized models of career counseling (Savickas, 2015b) focused on the radicalization of reflexivity (Giddens, 1991) and the possibility of offering at the same time, a subjective instrumentation (clinical function) and an objective instrumentation (operational function), as shown by Bohoslavsky (1977) and Ribeiro (2016).

The group-based career counseling proposal that was presented here is an attempt to meet at least part of these conditions imposed by the contemporary working world.

On the one hand, it provides a clinical space continence, identity reconstruction and deconstruction of preconceived stereotyped ideas about themselves and the working world, named societal metanarratives by Rossier et al. (2015), to the subjective instrumentation (Ribeiro, 2016), aiming the deconstruction, reconstruction, and co-construction of working life project. And, on the other hand, it generates the operating space of construction of projects or working career action plans within the relational context (Klivlighan, 1990) through a constant negotiation with the working world (Savickas, 2015b).

Its effectiveness can be evaluated through the study of the case shown by means of a qualitative non-structured method based on narrative changes during the group process. First, the effectiveness evaluation of career counseling was focused on the narrative produced about the situation and the demands brought by the group in the first meeting, which made their career crisis emerge as an identity crisis, as well as the solution thought to this crisis and the request for the counselors' help.

The main complaints were the difficulty of getting a better job because of their age, their outdating and lack of skills associated with demotivation and dissatisfaction with the current work activity focused on mid-level occupations that were not chosen and did not offer them chances to grow in their careers, while the unemployed felt stuck in time. They summarized their career crisis into the experience of feeling "falling behind" as pointed by R.

They saw their crisis as an individual problem and elected as output for the same the entrance in undergraduate courses. In this sense, they demand from the career counseling intervention the explanation of how to enter a college and how to succeed in the working world.

They bring as central elements some societal metanarratives that guide their lives, among them: a gender issue generated by the bipolarity of women's working, that is, the social convention of having to choose between productive work outside the home and the role of taking care of home and family; a prejudice against the age, because "the labor market does not accept older people" (J.); and the college education as the only alternative to grow and have satisfaction at work.

The group-based career counseling proposed aimed to help the counselees' group through continuous encouragement of reflexivity (Guichard, 2015), the group continence, the break of stereotypical and idealized outputs, represented in societal metanarratives (Rossier et al., 2015), and the possibility of the opening to relational and contextualized constructions (Savickas, 2015b).

To this end, the group generated space for a reflection on identity, possibility of identity reconstruction and de-idealization movements through diatopical hermeneutics (Santos, 2002) and the use of intermediate strategies; the awareness of the importance of constructing a project; learning strategies to realize their projects, via working action plan; the perception that the personal project is collective, because it involves their immediate social network and the understanding that the career can be only implemented when you know the web of social roles that connect the person to the society (Savickas, 2002); and, finally, the construction of a career project or working life project and working action plan in the articulation between psychological desire and socioeconomic demands, as proposed by Bohoslavsky (1977).

This group movement can be tracked down through the narrative changes during the career counseling process. First, the counselees presented an early stagnation position ("falling behind"). Second, they went to an intermediate stage with increased reflexivity and sense of reality ("The fact is that we need to see the reality, go and really see it and not to think that it is fine the way it is"). And, finally, they were able to deconstruct the predominant societal discourses ("the labor market does not accept older people," "I need to study to see if I can improve," and "I feel unprepared to compete in the market") and reconstruct their working life projects ("I notice that things are changing and that life only makes sense when we have goals"). The main results indicated therefore an increased reflexivity and a clear process of narrative changes during the counseling.

All this was provided by the group device that artificially reproduces the social relations prevailing in a given social context and can be a privileged space for self-experimentation in the world before the concrete realization, in a relational experience of learning from the experience of others as well as of receiving help from those who are in the same career crisis, which makes counselees be encouraged to assume responsibility for their projects and decisions. The experimentation with future roles, the construction of career projects, and the social—historical contextualization shared via group relations that are similar to what could emerge in concrete social relations allowed the group of counselees to leave the paralysis position and the stereotyping of complaints and outputs that were initially presented and to expand their universe of experiences and meanings, via reflexivity, creating an articulated identity reconstruction with a working life project (Lehman et al., 2015).

The partial results presented in this chapter are very promising; however, a longitudinal follow-up of the participants is necessary for the actual confirmation of the validity of the process through long-term effectiveness of the intervention (Bimrose, 2008). We take as a hypothesis, to be verified in future researches, the idea that the group-based career counseling can provide, in addition to the construction of a working life project, another effect: the learning of the ability to design a project, which counselees may use at other times in their life when going through other crises, expected or not.

This proposal is, therefore, an attempt to help people understand the current critical situation of working and develop possible relational strategies, without denying the need or social, political, and economic solutions, required to reverse the current scenario of exclusion and precariousness, because as Chanlat (1996, p. 20) points so well "a society cannot be allowed to produce the exclusion in high dose without paying the price, sooner or later."

In conclusion, career counseling has much to contribute with unskilled adults in crisis and the qualitative non-structured method based on narrative changes has shown to be a reliable method to assess counseling effectiveness.

References

Antunes, R. (2015). The new morphology of the working class in contemporary Brazil. *Socialist Register, 51,* 178–198.

Anzieu, D. (1984). *The group and the unconscious*. London, UK: Routledge.

Arthur, M. B. (1994). The boundaryless career: A new perspective for organizational inquiry. *Journal of Organizational Behavior, 15,* 295–306. https://doi.org/10.1002/job.4030150402.

Auer, P. (2007). *Security in labour markets: Combining flexibility with security for decent work.* Geneva, Switzerland: International Labour Office - ILO.

Barbier, J.-C. (2004). *Precarious employment in Europe*. Luxembourg: European Commission.

Bimrose, J. (2008). *Adult career progression and advancement: A five-year study of the effectiveness of guidance*. London/Coventry, UK: Warwick Institute for Employment Research/ Department for Innovation, Universities and Skills. Retrieved from http://www2.warwick.ac.uk/fac/soc/ier/research/eg/.

Bimrose, J., & Hearne, L. (2012). Resilience and career adaptability: Qualitative studies of adult career counseling. *Journal of Vocational Behavior, 81*(3), 338–344. https://doi.org/10.1016/j.jvb.2012.08.002.

Blustein, D. L. (2006). *The psychology of working: A new perspective for career development, counseling, and public policy*. New York, NY: Routledge.

Blustein, D. L. (2011). A relational theory of working. *Journal of Vocational Behavior, 79*(1), 1–17. https://doi.org/10.1016/j.jvb.2010.10.004.

Bobek, B. L., & Robbins, S. B. (2005). Counseling for career transition: Career pathing, job loss, and reentry. In S. D. Brown & R. W. Lent (Eds.), *Career development and counseling: Putting theory and research to work* (pp. 625–650). Hoboken, NJ: Wiley.

Bohoslavsky, R. (1977). *Orientação vocacional: A estratégia clínica* [Vocational counseling: A clinical strategy]. São Paulo, Brazil: Martins Fontes.

Bohoslavsky, R. (1983). *Vocacional: teoria, técnica e ideologia* [The vocational: Theory, technique and ideology]. São Paulo, Brazil: Cortez.

Bordin, E. S. (1954). Student personnel work and personality development. *The Personnel and Guidance Journal, 33*(4), 194–198. https://doi.org/10.1002/j.2164-4918.1954.tb01566.x.

Bordin, E. S. (1957). A counseling psychologist views personality development. *Journal of Counseling Psychology, 4*(1), 3–8. https://doi.org/10.1037/h0040596.

Bordin, E. S. (1968). *Psychological counseling* (2nd ed.). New York, NY: Appleton-Century.

Bordin, E. S. (1980a). A psychodynamic view of counseling psychology. *The Counseling Psychologist, 9*(1), 62–70. https://doi.org/10.1177/001100008000900114.

Bordin, E. S. (1980b). Counseling psychology in the year 2000: Prophecy of wish fulfillment? *The Counseling Psychologist, 8*(4), 24–26. https://doi.org/10.1177/001100008000800410.
Brewer, M. B., & Chen, Y. R. (2007). Where (who) are collectives in collectivism? Toward conceptual clarification of individualism and collectivism. *Psychological Review, 114*(1), 133–151. https://doi.org/10.1037/0033-295X.114.1.133.
Castel, R. (2000). The roads to disaffiliation: Insecure work and vulnerable relationships. *International Journal of Urban and Regional Research, 24*(3), 519–535. https://doi.org/10.1111/1468-2427.00262.
Castells, M. (2000). *The rise of the network society*. New York, NY: Wiley.
Chanlat, J. F. (1996). Quais carreiras e para qual sociedade? (II) [Which careers and for which society? (II)]. *Revista de Administração de Empresas, 36*(1), 13–20.
Di Fabio, A. (2015). Life Adaptability Qualitative Assessment (Laqua). In J. G. Maree & A. Di Fabio (Eds.), *Exploring new horizons in career counseling: Turning challenge into opportunities* (pp. 43–61). Rotterdam, The Netherlands: Sense Publishers.
Di Fabio, A., & Maree, J. G. (2012). Group-based life design counseling in an Italian context. *Journal of Vocational Behavior, 80,* 100–107. http://dx.doi.org: https://doi.org/10.1016/j.jvb.2011.06.001.
Di Fabio, A., & Palazzeschi, L. (2016). Marginalization and precariat: The challenge of intensifying life construction intervention. *Frontiers in Psychology, 7*(444). http://dx.doi.org/10.3389/fpsyg.2016.00444.
Duarte, M. E. (2009). The psychology of life construction. *Journal of Vocational Behavior, 75*(3), 259–266. https://doi.org/10.1016/j.jvb.2009.06.009.
Duarte, M. E. (2015). Some reflections on guidance and career counselling in the 21st century. In A. Di Fabio & J.-L. Bernaud (Eds.), *The construction of the identity in 21st century* (pp. 59–72). New York, NY: Nova Science Publishers.
Dubar, C. (2000). *La crise des identités: l'interprétation d'une mutation [Crisis of identity: The interpretation of a mutation]*. Paris, France: PUF.
Duffy, R. D., Blustein, D. L., Diemer, M. A., & Autin, K. L. (2016). The psychology of working theory. *Journal of Counseling Psychology, 63*(2), 127–148. https://doi.org/10.1037/cou0000140.
Elsby, M., Hobijn, B., & Ahin, A. (2013). Unemployment dynamics in the OECD. *Review of Economics and Statistics, 95*(2), 530–548.
Freud, S. (1920). Transference. *A general introduction to psychoanalysis* (pp. 372–387). Horace Liveright: New York, NY.
Frosh, S. (2012). Psychosocial theory. In T. Teo (Ed.), *Encyclopedia of critical psychology* (pp. 144–149). New York, NY: Springer.
Giddens, A. (1991). *Modernity and self-identity*. Stanford, CA: Stanford University.
Grote, G., & Raeder, S. (2009). Careers and identity in flexible working. *Human Relations, 62*(2), 219–244. https://doi.org/10.1177/0018726708100358.
Guichard, J. (2003). Career counseling for human development: An international perspective. *The Career Development Quarterly, 51,* 306–321. https://doi.org/10.1002/j.2161-0045.2003.tb00612.x.
Guichard, J. (2009). Self-constructing. *Journal of Vocational Behavior, 75,* 251–258. https://doi.org/10.1016/j.jvb.2009.03.004.
Guichard, J. (2015). From vocational guidance to life design dialogues. In L. Nota & J. Rossier (Eds.), *Handbook of life design: From practice to theory and from theory to practice* (pp. 11–26). Boston, MA: Hogrefe.
Guichard, J., Pouyaud, J., De Calan, C., & Dumora, B. (2012). Identity construction and career development interventions with emerging adults. *Journal of Vocational Behavior, 81*(1), 52–58. https://doi.org/10.1016/j.jvb.2012.04.004.
Hobsbawm, E. J. (1984). *Worlds of labour*. London, UK: Weidenfeld & Nicolson.
International Labour Office. (2015). *World employment and social outlook: Trends 2015*. Geneva, Switzerland: International Labour Office - ILO.

Instituto de Pesquisa Econômica Aplicada [IPEA] (2015). Análise do mercado de trabalho [Labour market analysis]. *Mercado de Trabalho,* 58, 9–16.

Käes, R., & Kirshner, L. A. (2006). *Linking, alliances, and shared space*. London, UK: International Psychoanalytic Association.

Klein, M. (1984). *Writings of Melanie Klein: Love, guilt and reparation and other works 1921–1945*. New York, NY: Free Press.

Klivlighan, D. M. (1990). Career group therapy. *The Counseling Psychologist, 18,* 64–79. https://doi.org/10.1177/0011000090181003.

Laplanche, J., & Pontalis, J. B. (1988). *The language of psychoanalysis*. Karnac Books.

Lassance, M. C. P., Levenfus, R. S., & Melo-Silva, L. L. (2015). *Orientação de carreira: investigação e práticas* [Career counseling: Research and practices]. Porto Alegre, Brazil: Associação Brasileira de Orientação Profissional.

Lehman, Y. P., Ribeiro, M. A., Uvaldo, M. C. C., & Silva, F. F. (2015). A psychodynamic approach on group career counseling: A Brazilian experience of 40 years. *International Journal for Educational and Vocational Guidance, 15*(1), 23–36. https://doi.org/10.1007/s10775-014-9276-0.

Leite, M. S. (2015). O RO como instrumento diagnóstico [RO as a diagnostic tool]. In: *Orientação profissional* [Career counseling] (pp. 172–188). São Paulo, Brazil: Casa do Psicólogo.

Melo-Silva, L. L., Leal, M. S., & Fracalozzi, N. M. N. (2010). Produção científica em congressos brasileiros de orientação vocacional e profissional: Período 1999–2009 [Analysis of Brazilian scientific production in vocational and career guidance: 1999–2009 Congresses]. *Revista Brasileira de Orientação Profissional, 11*(1), 107–120.

Metz, A. J., & Guichard, J. (2009). Vocational psychology and new challenges. *The Career Development Quarterly, 57,* 310–318. https://doi.org/10.1002/j.2161-0045.2009.tb00116.x.

Nota, L., & Rossier, J. (Eds.). (2015). *Handbook of life design: From practice to theory and from theory to practice*. Boston, MA: Hogrefe.

Nota, L., Soresi, S., Ferrari, L., & Ginevra, M. C. (2014). Vocational designing and career counseling in Europe. *European Psychologist, 19*(4), 248–259. https://doi.org/10.1027/1016-9040/a000189.

Organization for Economic Co-operation and Development. (2016). *Skills matter: Further results from the survey of adult skills*. Paris, France: OECD Publishing.

Rascován, S. E. (2005). *Orientación vocacional: Una perspectiva crítica* [Career counseling: A critical perspective]. Buenos Aires, Argentina: Paidós.

Rascován, S. E. (2013). Orientación vocacional: Las tensiones vigentes [Career counseling: The existing tensions]. *Revista Mexicana de Orientación Educativa, 10*(25), 47–54.

Ribeiro, M. A. (2009). *Psicologia e gestão de pessoas: Reflexões críticas e temas afins (ética, competência e carreira)* [Psychology and human management: Critical thinking and related topics (ethics, competence and career)]. São Paulo, Brazil: Vetor.

Ribeiro, M. A. (2010). Estratégias micropolíticas para lidar com o desemprego: contribuições da psicologia social do trabalho [Micro-political strategies to deal with unemployment: Contributions of social psychology of work]. *Revista Psicologia Política, 9*(18), 331–346.

Ribeiro, M. A. (2014). *Carreiras: Novo olhar socioconstrucionista para um mundo flexibilizado [Careers: A new social constructionist view for a flexible world]*. Curitiba, Brazil: Juruá.

Ribeiro, M. A. (2015). Contemporary patterns of career construction of a group of urban workers in São Paulo (Brazil). *Journal of Vocational Behavior, 88,* 19–27. https://doi.org/10.1016/j.jvb.2015.02.008.

Ribeiro, M. A. (2016). Career counseling for people in psychosocial situations of vulnerability and flexicurity: A social constructionist proposal. In T. V. Martin (Ed.), *Career development: Theories, practices and challenges* (pp. 79–110). New York, NY: Nova Science Publishers.

Ribeiro M. A., Silva, F. F., & Figueiredo, P. M. (2016). Discussing the notion of decent work: Senses of working for a group of Brazilian workers without college education. *Frontiers in Psychology, 7*(207). http://dx.doi.org/10.3389/fpsyg.2016.00207.

Ribeiro, M. A., Uvaldo, M. C. C., & Silva, F. F. (2015). Some contributions from Latin American career counselling for dealing with situations of psychosocial vulnerability. *International Journal for Educational and Vocational Guidance, 15*(3), 193–204. https://doi.org/10.1007/s10775-015-9285-7.
Richardson, M. S. (2012). Counseling for work and relationship. *The Counseling Psychologist, 40*(2), 190–242. https://doi.org/10.1177/0011000011406452.
Rossier, J., Nota, L., Dauwalder, J. P., Duarte, M. E., Guichard, J., Savickas, M. L., et al. (2015). Conclusion. In L. Nota & J. Rossier (Eds.), *Handbook of life design: From practice to theory and from theory to practice* (pp. 285–290). Boston, MA: Hogrefe.
Sá, T. (2010). Precariedade e trabalho precário: consequências sociais da precarização laboral [Precariousness and precarious work: Social consequences of labor casualization]. *Configurações, 7,* 91–105.
Santos, B. S. (2002). Toward a multicultural conception of human rights. In B. Hernandez-Truyol (Ed.), *Moral imperialism: A critical anthology* (pp. 39–60). New York, NY: New York University Press.
Savickas, M. L. (1995). Current theoretical issues in vocacional psychology: Convergence, divergence and schism. In W. B. Walsh, M. L. Savickas, & P. J. Hartung (Eds.), *Handbook of vocational psychology: Theory, research and practice* (2nd ed.). New Jersey, NJ. Lawrence Erlbaum Associates.
Savickas, M. L. (2002). Career construction: A developmental theory of vocational behavior. In D. Brown & Associates (Eds.), *Career choice and development* (4th ed., pp. 149–205). San Francisco, CA: Jossey-Bass.
Savickas, M. L. (2011). New questions for vocational psychology: Premises, paradigms, and practices. *Journal of Career Assessment, 19*(3), 251–258. https://doi.org/10.1177/1069072710395532.
Savickas, M. L. (2015a). Life designing with adults. In L. Nota & J. Rossier (Eds.), *Handbook of life design: From practice to theory and from theory to practice* (pp. 135–149). Boston, MA: Hogrefe.
Savickas, M. L. (2015b). Career counseling paradigms: Guiding, developing, and designing. In P. J. Hartung, M. L. Savickas, & W. B. Walsh (Eds.), *APA handbook of career intervention: Vol. 1. Foundations* (pp. 129–143). Washington, DC: American Psychological Association.
Savickas, M. L. (2015c). *Life-Design counseling manual*. Retrieved from www.vocopher.com/LifeDesign/LifeDesign.pdf.
Savickas, M. L., Nota, L., Rossier, J., Dauwalder, J. P., Duarte, M. E., Guichard, J., et al. (2009). Life designing: A paradigm for career construction in the 21st century. *Journal of Vocational Behavior, 75,* 239–250. https://doi.org/10.1016/j.jvb.2009.04.004.
Schlössberg, N. K., Goodman, J., & Anderson, M. L. (2006). *Counseling adults in transitions—Linking practice with theory* (3rd ed.). New York, NY: Springer.
Sennett, R. (1998). *The corrosion of character: The personal consequences of work in the new capitalism*. New York, NY: Norton.
Sveningsson, S., & Alvesson, M. (2003). Managing managerial identities: Organizational fragmentation, discourse and identity struggle. *Human Relations, 56,* 1163–1193. https://doi.org/10.1177/00187267035610001.
Teixeira, M. A. P., Silva, B. M. B., & Bardagi, M. P. (2007). Produção científica em orientação profissional [Scientific production in career guidance and counseling]. *Revista Brasileira de Orientação Profissional, 8*(2), 25–40.
Touraine, A. (2007). *A new paradigm for understanding today's world*. Cambridge, UK: Polity.
Tubert-Oaklander, J., & Tubert, R. H. (2004). *Operative groups: The Latin-American approach to group analysis*. London, UK: Jessica Kingsley.
Uvaldo, M. C. C. (2002). *Impacto das mudanças no mundo do trabalho sobre a subjetividade: em busca de um modelo de orientação profissional para adultos* [Impact of changes in the working world in subjectivity: In the search of a career counseling model for adults]. Tese de Doutorado não-publicada, Instituto de Psicologia, Universidade de São Paulo, São Paulo.

van Vianen, A. E. M., Koen, J., & Klehe, U.-C. (2015). Unemployment—Creating and conserving resources for career self-regulation. In L. Nota & J. Rossier (Eds.), *Handbook of life design: From practice to theory and from theory to practice* (pp. 201–218). Boston, MA: Hogrefe.

Watkins, C. E., Jr., & Savickas, M. L. (1990). Psychodynamic career counseling. In W. B. Walsh & S. H. Osipow (Eds.), *Career counseling: Contemporary topics in vocational psychology* (pp. 79–115). New York, NY: Routledge.

Whiston, S. C., & Rose, C. S. (2013). Career counseling with emerging adults. In W. B. Walsh, M. L. Savickas, & P. J. Hartung (Eds.), *Handbook of vocational psychology: Theory, research and practice* (4th ed., pp. 249–272). New Jersey, NJ: Lawrence Erlbaum Associates.

Winnicott, D. W. (1965). *Maturational processes and the facilitating environment.* London, UK: Hogarth.

Young, R. A., & Collin, A. (2004). Introduction: Constructivism and social constructionism in the career field. *Journal of Vocational Behavior, 64,* 373–388. https://doi.org/10.1016/j.jvb.2003.12.005.

Young, R. A., Valach, L., & Collin, A. (2002). A contextualist explanation of career. In D. Brown & Associates (Ed.), *Career choice and development* (4th ed., pp. 206–252). San Francisco, CA: Jossey-Bass.

Zimerman, D. (1993). *Fundamentos básicos das grupoterapias [Basics of group therapies].* Porto Alegre, Brazil: Artmed.

Part II
Expanding the Horizons Using the Lenses of Accountability: New Qualitative Tools for Evaluating the Effectiveness of Post-modern Guidance and Career Interventions in the Twenty-First Century

Chapter 7
Postmodern Guidance and Career Counseling: The Need for New Qualitative Tools for Evaluating Intervention Effectiveness

Maureen E. Kenny and Annamaria Di Fabio

Abstract This chapter presents an argument for the development of new qualitative tools to evaluate the effectiveness of guidance and career counseling interventions in the postmodern age. The vast changes that have and are continuing to take place in the world of work (e.g., globalization, rapid spread of technology, instability, unpredictability, liquidity, acceleration) across the twenty-first century have contributed to innovations in the paradigms and interventions that guide the fields of vocational psychology and career counseling. The psychological skills and resources that are needed to effectively manage one's life and career in this context have changed. Constructs, such as adaptability, purposeful identitarian awareness, grounded reflexivity, and fluidity management, represent some of the important psychological abilities that are now needed to effectively navigate and manage one's life and career. New theories and career counseling interventions have emerged that reflect shifts in the field from an emphasis on career development to a concern for career and self and relational management. This chapter describes the evolving understanding of important individual psychological competencies, the emergence of conceptual paradigms, and the creation of new interventions that demand innovative instruments that will qualitatively assess the outcomes and effectiveness of these interventions.

M. E. Kenny
Lynch School of Education, Boston College, Chestnut Hill, MA, USA

A. Di Fabio (✉)
Department of Education and Psychology (Psychology Section),
University of Florence, Florence, Italy
e-mail: adifabio@psico.unifi.it

© Springer Nature Switzerland AG 2018

A. Di Fabio and J.-L. Bernaud (eds.), *Narrative Interventions in Post-modern Guidance and Career Counseling*, https://doi.org/10.1007/978-3-319-98300-4_7

7.1 The Work-Related Characteristics in the Twenty-First Century and the Abilities for the Future

Globalization, rapid transformations in information and communication technology (Guichard, 2013; Savickas, 2013, 2015), growing economic disparities (Standing, 2014), and accelerated levels of social change (Di Fabio, 2017a, 2017b; Rosa, 2015) are contributing to vast changes in the world of work and to life in general. In response to these changes, workers need to continuously renew their skills to deal with more frequent and sometimes unexpected work-related transitions (Di Fabio, 2017a, 2017b; Di Fabio & Maree, 2016) and to take increased responsibility for their both professional and personal lives (Di Fabio & Bernaud, 2014; Di Fabio & Maree, 2013; Guichard, 2013; Savickas, 2011a, 2015).

In this context, scholars have begun to conceptualize, measure, and study an array of psychological competencies that could equip individuals in effectively navigating these changes. While this list is continuing to evolve, we provide examples of several important constructs, including adaptability, purposeful identitarian awareness, grounded reflexivity, and fluidity management that have been noted in the literature (Di Fabio, 2014e, 2017a, 2017b; Di Fabio & Maree, 2016; Di Fabio, Maree, & Kenny, 2018).

Adaptability represents the degree to which individuals are equipped with resources for facing current and anticipated developmental vocational tasks and occupational transitions (Savickas & Porfeli, 2012). The construct encompasses four dimensions: *Concern* (an interest in), *Control* (taking control or responsibility), *Curiosity* (showing an active desire to discover more), and *Confidence* (in oneself) (Savickas, 2001; Savickas & Porfeli, 2012). *Concern* pertains to interest in one's own future including the ability to plan and foresee possibilities with a sense of optimism and consciously analyzing one's own situation. *Control* concerns the degree to which people feel responsible for their future and are able to autonomously make decisions regarding themselves. *Curiosity* regards the ability to explore possible selves and future alternative scenarios. *Confidence* pertains to confidence in the ability to pursue one's goals and to overcome difficulties and barriers (Savickas, 2001; Savickas & Porfeli, 2012). A growing body of research has documented the relationship of career adaptability with adaptive career progress across age-groups and national contexts (Duffy, Blustein, Diemer, & Autin, 2016).

Purposeful identitarian awareness (Di Fabio, 2014e) was conceptualized in response to the challenges posed to one's sense of identity and self-coherence in the context of uncertainty and rapid change. In order to maintain a sense of meaning, authenticity, and autonomous self-direction, individuals need to be aware of the most authentic aspects of their selves and professional purposes, and to unifying the plural identities that emerge in an unstable and liquid society (Bauman, 2000; Di Fabio, 2014e; Guichard, Bangali, Cohen Scali, Pouyaud, & Robinet, 2016). Purposeful identitarian awareness is rooted in the concepts of narrative identity (Savickas, 2011a, 2013) and plural identities (Guichard, 2008, 2010, 2013). Narrative identity refers to the development of self as a story, contributing to one's adaptability (Savickas, 2011a, 2013). By producing stories about themselves and their varied life experiences, individuals can shape their sense of self and develop intentionality in their lives (Savickas, 2011a, 2013, 2015), find meaning and define future projects (Di Fabio, 2014b), and integrate their plural identities in designing future possible selves (Guichard, 2008, 2010, 2013). Plural identities (Guichard, 2008, 2010, 2013) encompass the individuals' Subjective Identity Forms (SIF), their System of Subjective Identity Forms (SSIF), and the aspired SIF that individuals desire to achieve and that have real meaning for them in designing possible future selves. Awareness of one's own identity is therefore important for the discovery of individual authenticity and meaning. In sum, purposeful identitarian awareness (Di Fabio, 2014c, 2014e) entails two key narrative meta-competencies of the twenty-first century, adaptability (Savickas, 2001; Savickas & Porfeli, 2012), and identity (Guichard, 2004, 2010) and is formed through the process of narration (Savickas, 2011a, 2013) and the construction of the possible future self and life (Guichard, 2008, 2010, 2013).

Grounded reflexivity represents another crucial skill in responding to the increasingly unstable world of work (Di Fabio, 2014e; Di Fabio & Maree, 2016; Di Fabio et al., 2018; Guichard, 2004, 2005; Maree, 2012a, 2012b). Grounded reflexivity pertains to the ability of the person to analyze the present and to reconsider the past, recognizing the dimensions that matter and are most meaningful for building a bridge toward the future (Di Fabio & Maree, 2016). Grounded reflexivity integrates two key elements: *reflecting* (Maree, 2012a, 2012b; Polkinghorne, 2005; Savickas, 2005) and *reflexivity* (Kuenzli, 2006; Schön, 1987). *Reflecting* refers to thinking about something that has already occurred (Finlay & Gough, 2003), whereas *reflexivity* refers to the active and continuous process of reaching self-awareness (Finlay & Gough, 2003) by balancing aspects of one's present, past, and future (Di Fabio & Maree, 2016; Maree, 2012a, 2012b). *Meta-reflection* is also essential (Maree, 2012a, 2012b) and entails three different aspects of reflection (Farrell, 2004; Killion & Todnew, 1991, Maree, 2012a, 2012b): *reflection-in-action,* namely reflection in the context of action; *reflection-on-action*, namely examining an action after it has occurred, and *reflection-for-action*, namely proactive reflection (thinking about past actions in order to make a connection with certain future actions). Reflection and meta-reflection are two processes that allow people to discover authentic aspects of themselves and to think about their future self-projects. When considering the self as an evolving story, rather than as an array of stable personality traits (Savickas, 2011a), it is important to develop and implement narrative interventions that afford individuals with the opportunity to reflect on themselves in the construction of authentic and comprehensive selves as life projects (Brott, 2004; Cochran, 1997; Di Fabio & Maree, 2016; Guichard, 2013; Maree, 2012a, 2012b; McMahon & Watson, 2010, 2011; Savickas, 2011a; Severy, 2002). By creating narratives of their personal and professional stories (Brott, 2004; Cochran, 1997; McMahon & Watson, 2010, 2011; Savickas, 2011a, 2014, 2015; Severy, 2002), individuals can anticipate and build their future according to a purposeful projectuality (Di Fabio, 2014b, 2014e).

Managing fluidity in the workplace represents another valuable skill that can enable individuals to deal successfully with the challenges, ongoing changes, and transitions that characterize the twenty-first century (Di Fabio & Maree, 2016). Individuals are expected to be able to anticipate and achieve their personal and professional paths, while managing the increasing fluidity in the world of work (Di Fabio & Maree, 2016) and taking responsibility for the directions of their life and careers (Guichard, 2013; Savickas, 2011a, 2015).

It is important thereby to design and implement preventive interventions that respond to the demand for repeated changes in the workplace (Di Fabio, 2017a) and to develop individuals' abilities to design successful careers and adequately manage their career lives (Di Fabio, 2017a, 2017b; Di Fabio & Maree, 2016). In that regard, the development of adaptability, purposeful identitarian awareness, reflexivity, and fluidity management (Di Fabio, 2014e, 2017a, 2017b; Di Fabio & Maree, 2016) has received increased attention, with their value in constructing the self as a sustainable life project emerging as a central focus (Di Fabio & Blustein, 2016; Di Fabio & Kenny, 2016a) for decent work for decent lives (Blustein, Kenny, Di Fabio, & Guichard, in press). The uncertainty of the current era has undermined traditional sources of motivation and meaning in the workplace and suggests that people need to focus their life project on rediscovering meaning in their lives, which entails a shift in the field of vocational psychology from the paradigm of motivation to the paradigm of meaning (Di Fabio & Blustein, 2016).

7.2 Constructing Life and Career: From Career Development to Career Management Through Self and Relational Management

In the twentieth century, career development was conceptualized as a predictable evolution of steps in a stable organization (Super, 1957, 1980) or a sequence of vocational activities across the life span (Osipow, 2012). In the twenty-first century, with increasing work flexibility, instability, and fluidity in organizations, this conceptualization is no longer applicable (Hartung, 2012; Savickas, 2011a).

The traditional understanding of career development (Savickas, 2001) has been replaced by the notions of career management (Savickas, 2011a) and life management (Guichard, 2013); the goals of career and life management have become the foundations for contemporary vocational theory and practice. In a liquid society (Bauman, 2000; Guichard, 2013), the process of career management focuses on the person, rather than the organization (Duffy et al., 2012; Duffy, Torrey, Bott, Allan, & Schlosser, 2013; Duarte, 2004). People are actively responsible for gathering relevant information concerning their internal (interests, values, talents, lifestyle) and external worlds (opportunities, resources, obstacles) and need to intentionally plan their activities in order to achieve their personal (Guichard, 2013) and professional objectives (Greenhaus, Callanan, & Goodshalk, 2010; Savickas, 2011a).

Individuals need to implement and monitor diverse strategies to effectively achieve their life (Guichard, 2013) and career aspirations (Greenhaus et al., 2010; Savickas, 2011a). Career and life management represent fundamental challenges for the successful implementation of one's future vision or complex projectuality (Di Fabio, 2014b, 2014e) in which work and other personal activities are strongly interconnected (Guichard, 2004, 2005, 2008, 2009). Adaptability, intentionality, lifelong learning, autobiographical reasoning and meaning (Savickas, 2011a, 2013), grounded reflexivity, purposeful identitarian awareness, and fluidity management (Di Fabio, 2014e, 2017a, 2017b; Di Fabio & Maree, 2016) are among the personal skills that can enable individuals to balance and reshape varied aspects of their lives as they strive to realize the authentic self (Di Fabio, 2014b, 2014e).

Furthermore, in an era characterized by a multiplicity of life and career shifts and directions, the complexity and importance of relationships for career and life management are increasing (Blustein, 2011; Di Fabio & Gori, 2016b; Di Fabio, Kenny, & Claudius, 2016; Duffy et al., 2016, 2017; Kenny, Blustein, & Meerkins, 2018; Maree & Di Fabio, 2015). The Relational Theory of Working (Blustein, 2011) builds on the tenet highlighted in the Psychology-of-Working Perspective (Blustein, 2006) that work is an intrinsically relational act, with every decision, experience, and interaction in the work context being influenced and shaped at some level by relationships. The degree to which work and relationships within and outside of the workplace interface and are reciprocally impacted by broad changes in work and society emphasizes the need to go beyond the *career project* to the *life project* (Di Fabio, 2014a, 2014e). With regard to intervention, the focus expands from shaping careers to helping people to construct their lives with work and relationships considered as integrated frameworks (Richardson, 2012). Given the central role of relationships across multiple life spheres and the workplace, self and relational management are inevitably related to career and life management. This premise underlies the Relational Theory of Working (Blustein, 2011) and is a direct focus of the Positive *Self and Relational Management* model (Di Fabio, 2014a; Di Fabio & Kenny, 2016a). Accordingly, intervention should also attend to both self and relational management (Di Fabio, 2016), with the model of *Positive Self and Relational Management* (PS&RM, Di Fabio & Kenny, 2016a) highlighting the development of individual strengths, potential, and talents across the life span (Blustein, 2011; Di Fabio & Kenny, 2016a; Di Fabio & Maree, 2013).

The PS&RM model (Di Fabio & Kenny, 2016a) emphasizes the promotion of individual and relational strengths. In this way, it is aligned with developments in positive psychology (Seligman, 2002; Seligman & Csikszentmihalyi 2000) and prevention and wellness promotion (Di Fabio, 2014a; Di Fabio & Kenny, 2016b; Di Fabio, Kenny, & Minor, 2014; Di Fabio et al., 2016; Kenny & Di Fabio, 2009; Kenny & Hage, 2009; Kenny, Horne, Orpinas, & Reese, 2009; Hage et al., 2007). Rather than focusing on individual and relational weaknesses, the model highlights the "the development of individuals' strengths, potentials, and varied talents from a lifespan perspective" (Di Fabio & Kenny, 2016a, p. 3) that will help individuals to successfully adapt to life and career changes and thrive in the world (Di Fabio & Kenny, 2016a; Di Fabio et al., 2016). Rather than intervening after problems emerge, the model highlights a prevention perspective by emphasizing the development of personal and relational resources as protective factors that can serve to sustain personal and social well-being by welcoming change as opportunity for growth (Di Fabio & Gori, 2016a; Di Fabio & Kenny, 2016a). Equipped with these resources, individuals will be better able to manage the economic, structural, and social transitions of the postmodern era (Di Fabio, 2015a; Di Fabio & Blustein, 2010; Di Fabio & Kenny, 2016a; Di Fabio & Saklofske, 2014a, 2014b) in constructing their careers and lives (Guichard, 2013).

7.3 Fundamental Theories for Postmodern Guidance and Career Counseling Intervention

A number of vocational theories have emerged that take into account the challenges of the twenty-first century and the individual skills important for navigating these challenges to inform vocational guidance and career counseling. While we have referenced some of these in previous sections, we now offer a more comprehensive discussion.

Career Construction Theory (CCT, Savickas, 2001, 2005, 2011a) has been one of the central frameworks informing new directions in guidance and career counseling. In recognition of the importance of the construction of self, CCT focuses centrally on the vision of the *self as a project*, attending to objective and a subjective perspective on the self and the self in relationships (Savickas, 2011b). Self-construction is not an individual process, but a social construction that is co-constructed in collaboration with close social groups and the larger community (Savickas, 2011a). The construction of self occurs through the narration of self as story, which places problems in the broader context of lived meaning, identifies life patterns and the constellation of choices, and uses storytelling to reduce confusion, resolve doubts, and clarify choices (Savickas, 2001, 2005, 2011a). Stories not only can be a tool for resolving indecision and increasing capacity to decision making but also can foster action as the individual builds a vision of future possibilities (Savickas, 2011a). Through narration and biographicity, the individual gives personal meaning to past memories, present experiences, and future aspirations, making them flow into a life theme. The meaning discovered in these biographical themes can enable individuals to adapt to changes in their career paths (Savickas, 2011a).

Self-Construction Theory (SCT, Guichard, 2004, 2005) adds to the focus on the career project in *Career Construction Theory* (Savickas, 2001, 2005) with a focus on the life project. SCT recognizes people as plural identities associated with a dynamic system of Subjective Identity Forms (SIF). In the postmodern society, people act across varied career life domains and their behavior depends at any given time on their plan and expectations (Guichard & Dauwalder, 2010). Plural identities or self-images develop as individuals engage in different contexts, have varied experiences, take on many roles, and implement different selves (Guichard, 2004, 2005). It is thus vital to take into account the way in which people interact with themselves and with varied contexts in specific moments in time in specific societies (Guichard & Lenz, 2005; Zunker, 1998).

SCT recognizes furthermore the need to achieve a unified self that integrates varied experiences and shapes future expectations. As proactive agents, individuals strive for self-organization to uphold stability and continuity in their lives (Guichard, 2004, 2005).

In the evolution of SCT (Guichard, 2004, 2005), *Life Construction Theory* (LCT, Guichard, 2013) attends to individuals' ability to unify their plural selves associated with different life experiences in order to provide a sense of meaning to their lives. Given the interconnection of life and career (Guichard, 2004, 2009), the design and realization of the life project need to address and integrate individuals' plural selves and the multiple directions of their personal and professional paths (Guichard, 2013). Through this process, they can delineate and realize their life projects in a postmodern era characterized by a deregulated life path (Guichard, 2013).

As the challenges of achieving decent work and decent lives are growing in the twenty-first century (Di Fabio & Blustein, 2016), the discovery of a sense of meaning in work and other types of activities is increasingly important (Allan, Duffy, & Douglass, 2015; Bernaud, 2013; Bernaud, Lhotellier, Sovet, Arnoux-Nicolas, & Pelayo, 2016; Di Fabio & Blustein, 2016). We must go beyond a concern for work motivation to consider how people can obtain meaning in a world where access to decent work is diminishing (Di Fabio & Blustein, 2016). Work and life meaning are vital as human beings consider the nature of their existence, its value, and scope (Frankl, 1963). The identification of objectives based on the authentic self permits and brings order, coherence, and consistency to life (Reker, 2000). Accordingly, vocational scholars are now seeking to better understand how people find meaning, how interventions can help people to construct meaning that leads to fulfilling work and life, and how to anchor the decent life project in a sustainable and meaningful construction (Di Fabio & Blustein, 2016).

Life Meaning Theory (Bernaud, 2013; Bernaud et al., 2016) focuses on life meaning as both a product and a process. Meaning as a product occurs as the result of existential reflection; meaning emerges from process that includes the exploration of past, present, and future to identify worthwhile and meaningful directions for one's life. Work meaning is not objective, but follows from the subjective appraisal of the individual and varies by context (Rosso, Dekas, & Wrzesniewski, 2010). Work meaning offers coherence, direction, significance, and belonging (Di Fabio & Maree, 2016; Schnell, Höge, & Pollet, 2013), thereby supporting the sustainability of one's personal project (Di Fabio, 2017b) across life, career, and time. The construction of the *self as a sustainable project* matters not only for individuals but also for the organizations and contexts of which they are part (Di Fabio, 2017b; Di Fabio & Maree, 2016). Grounded reflexivity can be an important tool for individuals in discovering the personal meaning in their narratives that guides the development of the sustainable self and life project. The subjective exploration of one's narratives to identify themes and individuals' meanings aids individuals in writing the next chapters of their life stories, building bridges for individuals, organizations, communities, and societies from the present, back to the past, and toward the future.

7.4 The Need for New Postmodern Guidance and Career Counseling Interventions

According to a taxonomy developed by Guichard (2013), guidance and career counseling interventions can be classified as offering information, guidance, or dialogue. Information interventions are directed toward improving the skills of individuals for gathering pertinent and consistent information in relation to the world of work (Guichard, 2013). Guidance interventions aim at increasing clients' employability by encouraging the construction of an adaptable and vocational self-concept. Dialogue interventions seek to help clients clarify their future perspectives and find personal life meaning for constructing their lives in an ever-changing life context. Clients are inspired to construct their own lives through narratability, biographicity, and reflexivity (Guichard, 2013).

The narrative/dialogic approach to counseling is central for twenty-first-century guidance and career interventions (Maree, 2007; McMahon, 2010; Savickas, 2005, 2007, 2011a, 2013, 2015). The role of the career counselor in this approach is to help clients identify meaning in their personal and professional lives through the construction of their self as a story (Guichard, 2013; Savickas, 2005, 2011a). The critical meta-competencies of adaptability and identity are developed in this process (Savickas, 2013), as the understanding and meaning that individuals gain through their stories can guide them in dealing with new events and transitions and in making decisions about their future (Savickas, 2011a). Central to the narrative approach based on Career Construction (Savickas, 2001, 2005, 2011a), Life Construction (Guichard, 2013), and Life Meaning Theories (Bernaud, 2013; Bernaud et al., 2016) is the process of making meaning through the narration of stories that help them advance their career and life projects (Savickas, 2001, 2005).

While quantitative instruments have traditionally been used exclusively for assessing the effectiveness of career counseling interventions (Brown et al., 2003; Heppner & Heppner, 2003; Oliver & Spokane, 1988; Whiston, Brecheisen, & Stephens, 2003; Whiston, Sexton, & Lasoff, 1998), postmodern guidance and career counseling interventions are inherently qualitative (Hartung, 2010, 2012, 2013; Maree, 2007; McMahon & Patton, 2002; Rehfuss, 2009; Rehfuss & Di Fabio, 2012). This misalignment between intervention and assessment is noted in the literature as a limitation, along with a call for developing qualitative instruments that can detect changes in narratives (Blustein, Kenna, Murphy, Devoy, & DeWine, 2005). The assessment of meaningful change in self-narrative would serve as an indicator of enhanced comprehension in conceptualization of the self (Savickas, 2010) and an indicator for successful life and career construction.

7.5 Specific Examples of Some Postmodern Guidance and Career Counseling Interventions

The narrative approach to postmodern guidance and career counseling interventions was developed in response to the need for innovative modalities to meet the changes of the twenty-first century. The following dialogue interventions are currently implemented within the narrative or life story (storied) counseling approach (Busacca & Rehfuss, 2016; Guichard & Di Fabio, 2010; Maree, 2007; McMahon, 2010; Savickas, 2007, 2010): Career Construction Interview (Savickas, 2010), Life Meaning Counseling (Bernaud, 2013; Bernaud et al., 2016), Constructing My Future Purposeful Life (Di Fabio, 2014b), Career Interest Profile (Maree, 2010, 2016), and Intrapreneurial Self-Capital Training (Di Fabio, 2014d; Di Fabio & Van Esbroeck, 2016).

The *Career Construction Interview* (CCI, Savickas, 2010) was developed as a means of facilitating life design. Since stories play a fundamental role in empowering clients to design a successful personal and professional life (Savickas, 2010), the CCI was created as a tool to assist professionals in facilitating their client's inner exploration and dialogue as a basis self-construction. The CCI dialogue intervention encourages clients to explore and gain understanding of the main issues of their life, through an increased ability to self-reflect and to implement effective actions within a significant and meaningful framework (Savickas, 2011a). In responding to the CCI, clients become an audience for themselves and are encouraged to listen to their stories and to reconsider their past objectives, their present experiences, and their future projects. Counselors also represent an audience for their clients with the role of highlighting and calling attention to key aspects of their clients' stories. In this way, clients are helped to express and clarify their narratives and to listen indirectly through the voice of the counselor (Di Fabio & Maree, 2012). The dialogue intervention also focuses on recognizing inconsistencies in the clients' occupational story plots and relating them to the principal themes of the life story. The intervention seeks to balance the occupational plot and the career themes in the narrative to uncover new pathways. The attainment of this new equilibrium allows clients to move forward with their life project with greater awareness and intentionality (Savickas, 2010).

In order to recognize past and present experiences that are crucial for their lives, and the realization of their life projects, clients are asked to reflect on questions that are relevant to their presenting life concerns (Guichard, 2010, 2013; Savickas, 2005, 2011a, 2013). The questions of the CCI explore the following basic areas (Savickas, 2011a).

(1) *Role models*. The first core area concerns clients' self-concept or the kind of persons they see themselves as, their principal goals in life and their solutions to their main life problems. Role models represent ego ideals, with a focus on what is admired rather than who is admired and how they offer solutions to a central life problem.

(2) *Favorite magazines/television shows/Web sites*. The second core area elicits client's preferred educational (e.g., classes) and occupational (job) contexts.
(3) *Movies/books*. The third core area elicits a life script that discloses a pathway for reaching one's goals and resolving one's problems. Books can reveal a major character who copes with the same problem as the client and can offer examples of how that character dealt with the problem.
(4) *Mottos*. The motto can represent a source of self-advice (clients' own best advice for themselves) and titles for their life story.
(5) *Earliest memories*. An exploration of early memories can uncover clients' main life problems—the central problems they face at present.

Life Meaning Counseling (Bernaud et al., 2016) is an intervention rooted in a meaning-centered framework that includes seven to eight 2-h sessions held approximately 1 week apart (Bernaud et al., 2016). This approach can be useful for people who are facing transitions, have the ability to reflect on their existence and their future, and can ask themselves questions about meaning, regardless of age, sex, level of training, professional field, and status. Each session includes reflection supervised by the counselor, who helps the client to identify the main themes through a co-construction process. A preliminary interview presents the framework to the client, responds to client questions and requests, and focuses on how the interventions will be tailored to their specific needs. The sessions proceed in the following manner.

(1) *Implicit theories of meaning*. The objective of the first session is on building a working alliance with agreement on the aims to be pursued in counseling and the activities and level of reflection that will be implemented (Bernaud & Bideault, 2005).
(2) *Analysis of values*. The objective of the second session is to identify priorities in life, reflect upon existential values, and consider how those values will be applied in action, behavior, and commitments.
(3) *Analysis of models and life paths*. The objective of the third session is to help clients to distance themselves from their immediate situations and consider the paths and the strategies used by others. Through a process of bibliotherapy and analysis of other media (e.g., film, paintings, photographs), clients are encouraged to reflect on the meaning of their lives and careers and consider next stages of their lives.
(4) *Relationship with work*. The objective of the fourth session is to identify values that are important in the individual's professional activity (Létourneau, Christian, & Lecine, 2012), to attend to the notion of satisfaction and importance of work, and to understand how to integrate work with other life domains (Rosso et al., 2010).
(5) *Autobiography of the future scenarios of life and career*. The objective of the fifth session is to write a future autobiography (Rehfuss, 2009). Clients are asked to accurately indicate what they did in the past, what they can do in the present, and what they will do in the future, on the basis of their life priorities.

This session allows clients to identify their core values, potential resources, and the skills that they can use to successfully overcome frequent transitions.

(6) *Development of "art of living."* During the sixth session, topics of lifestyle inspired by various psychological and philosophical traditions and research are introduced. Clients are asked to identify those that can help them to define their "art of living" and how they can be applied in their lives after the session. Clients are then invited to write a synthesis.

(7) *A 360-degree view of life and work meaning*. The seventh session provides the opportunity for clients to reflect on their actions since the sixth meeting and how their thoughts about meaning of life and work and priorities have changed since the beginning of the intervention.

(8) *Additional session or epilogue*. The objective of the (possible) eighth session varies depending on the goals agreed upon by the client and counselor (Bernaud et al., 2016).

The session might focus on a specific decision or experience or counselor feedback.

An innovative life construction dialogue intervention, entitled *Constructing My Future Purposeful Life*, was developed by Di Fabio (2014b) with the aim of fostering a purposeful identitarian awareness (Di Fabio, 2014e) as career and life management competence (Di Fabio, 2014e) through the enhancement of the two key meta-competencies of adaptability for an ever-changing environment (Savickas, 2001) and identity (Guichard, 2004, 2010). The intervention (Di Fabio, 2014b) seeks to help clients increase their sense of authentic intentionality (Di Fabio, 2014e) that will guide them in dealing with the challenges of "becoming" in a changing world. Enhanced purposeful identitarian awareness enables individuals in writing the next chapters of their lives with greater clarity (Guichard, 2013; Savickas, 2013, 2015) and well-being (Di Fabio & Blustein, 2016).

Constructing My Future Purposeful Life was developed as a life construction dialogue and is structured in three modules offering advancing levels of reflexion (Di Fabio, 2014b) in relation to the complexity of working (Blustein, 2006, 2011). The basic stages of this intervention are rooted in postmodern narrative career theories (Guichard & Di Fabio, 2010). The first module is based principally on Career Construction (Savickas, 2001, 2005, 2011a) and Life Construction (Guichard, 2013) Theories. The second module focuses on self-reflection, self-advising (Guichard, 2013), guided meta-reflection (Maree, 2013), and reflexivity (Di Fabio & Maree, 2013; Di Fabio et al., 2018; Guichard, 2009; Maree, 2013). The third module aims "To make oneself self" (Guichard, 2004) as further level of exploration that aims to enhance reflexivity.

More specifically, the first module includes two genogram activities: the Career Construction Genogram (Di Fabio, 2010, 2012) and the Life Construction Genogram (Di Fabio, 2015c, 2016b). At the end of these two genogram exercises, clients are asked to reflect, respectively, on the career motto and the life motto of their mother and father in formulating "My career motto" and "My life motto." The second activity, "Me and the future," seeks to foster the meta-competence of adaptability in revising the personal mottos produced in the first part (Savickas, 2001; Savickas & Porfeli, 2012).

The second module, entitled "Self-advising the Future Self," seeks to foster reflection on past and current life roles (Guichard, 2004, 2013), to identify the most authentic aspects to inform the development of the future self (Di Fabio, 2014b). After reflecting on their life roles, clients are asked to give good advice to the future self according to the authentic self (Di Fabio, 2014e).

The third module, entitled "Constructing the Purposeful Self," focuses on the process "To make oneself self" (Guichard, 2004). Individuals are encouraged to unify their plural selves by connecting their different life experiences through narration. Based on a guided meta-reflection (Maree, 2013), clients are encouraged to extend this reflection to their future projects on the basis of their authentic intentionality (Di Fabio, 2014e), Overall, the construction of a *Purposeful Self* (Di Fabio, 2014e) is facilitated through a series of guided meta-reflections that foster the identification of authentic project intentionality as basis for the construction of a meaningful life (Di Fabio & Blustein, 2016).

The *Career Interest Profile* (CIP, Maree, 2010) is a narrative career counseling tool articulated in four parts: biographical details, family influences, and work-related information (Part 1); career category preferences/dislikes (Part 2); career choice questions (Part 3); and career life story narratives (Part 4). Participants are required to complete Part 1, Part 2, and Part 3 and, eventually, Part 4. At the beginning of Part 2, clients are asked to select the five categories they prefer most and the five they like least from a total of 19 comprehensive career categories. The selection of a small number of categories activates a process for identifying, analyzing, and elaborating careers and career-related issues in greater depth with the career counselor.

The CIP helps clients to become actively engaged in the process of self- and career construction by narrating, listening to, and revising their career stories. The CIP has demonstrated good psychometric properties in a South African context (Maree, 2006; Maree & Sommerville, 2008) in terms of test–retest reliability, content, and criterion-related validity in relation to the Rothwell Miller Interest Blank (Hall, Halstead, & Taylor, 1986). The Italian version (Di Fabio & Maree, 2013; Maree, 2016) of the CIP (Maree, 2010) also demonstrated good criterion validity in relation to the *Self-Directed Search* (*SDS*) (Holland, Powell, & Fritzsche, 1994) with significant Spearman's rank correlations between the *CIP* and *SDS*.

The construct of *Intrapreneurial Self-Capital* and the corresponding Intrapreneurial Self-Capital Scale (ISC, Di Fabio, 2014d) was developed from a prevention and promotion perspective (Di Fabio, 2014a; Di Fabio et al., 2014, 2016; Kenny & Di Fabio, 2009; Kenny & Hage, 2009; Kenny et al., 2009; Hage et al., 2007) as a *core set* of individual attributes for dealing proactively with career and life construction challenges. ISC is aligned with a prevention perspective as it represents a set of personal strengths or core resources that could be promoted to help individuals cope adaptively with the stressors of change and foster successful career and life management (Di Fabio, 2014d). The construct and the scale aim at identifying and detecting individual characteristics considered as *intrapreneurial* that produce innovative solutions to complex situations and transform constraints into resources (Di Fabio, 2014d). The ISC is a higher-order construct composed of seven specific constructs (i.e., core self-evaluation, hardiness, creative self-efficacy, resilience, goal mastery, decisiveness, and vigilance) (Di Fabio, 2014d) that encompass positive self-evaluation (core self-evaluation); perceived commitment, control, and challenge in one's own life (hardiness); perceived ability to creatively solve problems (creative self-efficacy); perceived ability to cope adaptively with adversity (resilience); pursuit of the development of one's own skills (goal mastery); perceived ability to use decision-making skills in all the contexts (decisiveness); and the ability to make decisions carefully and adaptively (vigilance) (Di Fabio, 2014d).

Following from the positive promotion and prevention perspective, a training program in two versions was developed for enhancing ISC (Di Fabio & Van Esbroeck, 2016). The shorter program is structured across five weekly sessions of four hours each. The longer program is articulated in five weekly sessions of eight hours each. The first part of the sessions in both versions of the training is the same, but some specific exercises are added in the longer version to strengthen each of the ISC components.

At the beginning of the training, participants are involved in the exercise "the book of my life story" that encourages reflection on one's life up to this point and "the future chapter of my life story." The next three sessions address the components of the ISC, with the second session focusing on positive self-concept and hardiness, the third session on creative self-efficacy and resilience, and the fourth session on goal mastery, decisiveness, and vigilance. The exercises for each session are presented in three steps, focusing first on self-evaluation for the specific ISC component, followed by the recognition of positive elements or benefits of the specific ISC component and finally to recognize how positive elements of that component are evident across the past, present, and future chapter/s in the individuals' life story. The future chapter of the participants' life story is depicted graphically, followed by thought and discussion about how that ISC component can best be developed and applied in one's future life story. The three steps of each exercise build on each other to foster an in-depth reflection on each ISC component and their relative importance for the present and future. Specific exercises to strengthen each component are presented and practiced. The final fifth session focuses on the commitment to the role as author in building the next chapter of their life story, along with the development of personal strategies for developing and sustaining ISC.

In sum, ISC training is an innovative dialogue intervention (Di Fabio & Van Esbroeck, 2016) that promotes reflection on individuals' career and life stories through narration. Individuals are stimulated to develop and apply their skills and talents to face the complexity of the twenty-first century with success (Di Fabio & Van Esbroeck, 2016).

7.6 New Qualitative Instruments for the Evaluation of the Effectiveness of Postmodern Guidance and Career Counseling Interventions

As previously discussed, the narrative approach typical of the postmodern guidance and career counseling requires a different mean for assessing the effectiveness of the interventions, moving from the traditional reliance on quantitative measures to the design of qualitative instruments specifically aligned with the goals of the intervention (Busacca & Rehfuss, 2016; Di Fabio, 2015b, 2016a; Di Fabio & Maree, 2012; Rehfuss, 2009). A number of new qualitative evaluation instruments are emerging in the field, which we describe below.

The *Future Career Autobiography* (FCA, Rehfuss, 2009) is the first method that emerged in the literature for evaluating narrative change outcomes. The FCA is administered before and after narrative interventions and allows for the detection of qualitative change in personal and career motives, values, and future goals. The FCA presents clients with a written exercise before and after the intervention with the following instructions: "Please use this page to write a brief paragraph about where you hope to be in life and what you hope to be doing occupationally five years from now" (Rehfuss, 2009; Rehfuss & Di Fabio, 2012). Clients are instructed to complete the exercise in 10 min. The length of the FCA administration is deliberately limited as the desired outcome is a focused and brief narrative (Rehfuss, 2009). A concise narrative helps the professional to develop a quick portrait of the clients' life and occupational themes and goals, and then facilitates comparison between the narratives produced before and after the intervention to assess change or lack of change (Rehfuss, 2009). The comparison of the initial and subsequent FCAs focuses on the following Eight Degrees of Change identified by Rehfuss (2009).

(1) General Fields and Desires to Specification and Exploration, which describe a shift from general fields and desires to specific themes;
(2) General Interests to More Specificity, in which clients begin with multiple general interests, but over time refine their FCAs;
(3) Non-description to Specificity, where clients' initial FCAs start with general themes and then move to more specific personal and professional themes;
(4) Disregard to Direction, where clients ignore the life and career parts of their initial FCAs and are apparently unable to finish the task. In their subsequent FCAs, nonetheless, they tackle the same task with specificity and direction;
(5) Vagueness to Focus, in which the clients' FCAs moved from an initial perception of insecurity about their personal and professional life to a more detailed and focused narrative;
(6) Hindered to Hopeful, where an initial perception of worry or indifference toward work is substituted with specificity;

(7) Fixation to Openness, where clients have hastily ignored a personal situation or an occupation and are surprised by the incongruence between their life/career goals and their skills. In subsequent FCAs, they attempt to overcome this dilemma;
(8) Stagnation, when there are no changes from initial to subsequent FCAs.

Although the FCA represents important progress in assessing the effectiveness of narrative interventions, it assesses only broad changes due to imprecise categories that are difficult to score with reliability. As a result, more refined instruments are needed for an in-depth exploration of the effects of postmodern career counseling interventions (Di Fabio, 2016a). The *Life Adaptability Qualitative Assessment* (LAQuA, Di Fabio, 2015b) and the Career Counseling Innovative Outcomes (CCIO, Di Fabio, 2016a) were developed to address this need.

The *Life Adaptability Qualitative Assessment* (LAQuA, Di Fabio, 2015b) is a promising narrative instrument developed to assess the change or lack thereof in individuals' narratives in relation to adaptability before and after intervention. The LAQuA consists of 12 questions with three questions corresponding to each of the four dimensions (Concern, Control, Curiosity, and Confidence) of the Career Adapt-Abilities Inventory-International Version 2.0 (Savickas & Porfeli, 2012). The LAQuA 12 questions to which the client responds in writing are:

Concern: (1a) What does it mean to you to be oriented toward your future? (1b) Do you think you are oriented toward your future? (1c) Why?

Control: (2a) What does it mean to you to take responsibility for your future? (2b) Do you think you do take responsibility for your future? (2c) Why?

Curiosity: (3a) What does it mean to you to be curious about your own future? (3b) Do you think you are curious about your future? (3c) Why?

Confidence: (4a) What does it mean to you to have confidence in your ability to build your future? (4b) Do you think you have confidence in your ability to build your future? (4c) Why?

The responses to the 12 questions are compared before and after the intervention in relation to 24 qualitative indicators for each of the four dimensions (Concern, Control, Curiosity, and Confidence) of the Career Adapt-Abilities Inventory-International Version 2.0 (Savickas & Porfeli, 2012). The comparison and analysis of the narratives based on these qualitative indicators were organized into a coding system, of five qualitative analysis change categories. The LAQuA coding system addresses change or lack of change for each dimension of adaptability with regard to level of reflexivity (Increased Reflexivity, Revised Reflexivity, Open Reflexivity, Enhanced Reflexivity, and No Change) (Di Fabio, 2015b).

The *Career Counseling Innovative Outcomes* (CCIO, Di Fabio, 2016a) represents another promising narrative instrument inspired by the psychotherapeutic Innovative Moment Coding System (IMCS, Gonçalves, Ribeiro, Mendes, Matos, & Santos, 2011) and its application in career construction counseling (Cardoso, Silva, Gonçalves, & Duarte, 2014). The IMCS is used to observe the process of change during psychotherapeutic intervention (Gonçalves et al., 2011) and during career construction counseling intervention (Cardoso et al., 2014) through an examination of transcripts, audio recordings, or video recordings to detect narrative changes after each session. In comparison with the IMCS, the CCIO was designed to be easier to use, eliciting, examining, and comparing specific narratives produced before and after life construction interventions. The CCIO includes the following seven questions, developed on the basis of the narrative paradigm (Savickas, 2011a). These questions are administered both before and after the intervention.

(1) In which ways can/was this intervention (be) useful to you? (2) What resources are most useful to you? (3) What are the main obstacles you encounter? (4) Who do you think can be useful to you in addressing these obstacles? (5) What do you think can be useful to you? (6) What are the main challenges you face? (7) What are the main objectives you are hoping to achieve?

The narratives elicited by these seven questions are coded using the CCIO coding system that includes the following five categories: Action, regarding actions or specific behaviors to facilitate problem-solving; Reflection, concerning thought processes that indicate an understanding of something new which creates a different point of view with regard to the problem (type I creates distance from the problem (s); type II centered on change); Protest concerns the act of criticism (type I criticizes problems; type II entails the emergence of new points of view), Reconceptualization regards to the description of the process at a meta-cognitive level; and Performing Change relates to the individuals' subsequent new aims, experiences, activities, or projects, anticipated or at hand.

The emergence of these qualitative instruments to detect change in individual narratives reflects the response to the need for new qualitative approaches for the evaluation of postmodern guidance and career counseling interventions. These instruments were designed to assess interventions based on Career Construction (Savickas, 2001, 2005), Life Construction (Guichard, 2004, 2005), and Life Meaning (Bernaud, 2013; Bernaud et al., 2016) Theories and thus represent important progress in developing new instruments to assess narrative change in postmodern guidance and career counseling. Clearly, there is a need for additional work in this area, including research to more fully appraise the reliability and validity of these and other new instruments across varied populations. Indeed, what is reliable and valid in terms of intervention and assessment may vary across populations based on age, gender, race and ethnicity, social class, and other individual and contextual factors, and may need to be tailored more specifically to match their needs. Such instruments contribute to the accountability of our field and are critical in assessing the effectiveness of our interventions for clients and for the schools, agencies, and other organizations that sponsor guidance and counseling programs. The knowledge gained from these assessments is also important in providing feedback for further refining current interventions and for designing additional interventions to more effectively build client resources and develop individual career and life management skills to meet the challenges of the twenty-first century in specific contexts. The chapters and case studies that follow in this section are an important start in advancing this agenda.

References

Allan, B. A., Duffy, R. D., & Douglass, R. (2015). Meaning in life and work: A developmental perspective. *The Journal of Positive Psychology, 10*(4), 323–331.

Bauman, Z. (2000). *Liquid modernity*. Cambridge, UK: Polity Press.

Bernaud, J.-L. (2013). Career counseling and life meaning: A new perspective life designing for research and applications. In A. Di Fabio & K. Maree (Eds.), *Psychology of career counseling: New challenges for a new era*. New-York: Nova Science Publishers.

Bernaud, J., & Bideault, A. (2005). Le déterminants de l'attractivité face à une démarche de conseil en orientation. *Carriérologie, 10*(2), 289–303.

Bernaud, J.-L., Lhotellier, L., Sovet, L., Arnoux-Nicolas, C., & Pelayo, F. (2016). *Psicologia dell'accompagnamento. Il senso della vita e del lavoro nell'orientamento professionale* [*Psychologie de l'accompagnement. Concepts et outils pour développer le sens de la vie et du travail*]. (Italian version edited by A. Di Fabio). Trento: Erickson.

Blustein, D. L. (2006). *The psychology of working: A new perspective for career development, counseling and public policy*. NY: Routledge.

Blustein, D. L. (2011). A relational theory of working. *Journal of Vocational Behavior, 79*(1), 1–17.

Blustein, D. L., Kenna, A. C., Murphy, K. A., DeVoy, J. E., & DeWine, D. B. (2005). Qualitative research in career development: Exploring the center and margins of discourse about careers and working. *Journal of Career Assessment, 13,* 351–370.

Blustein, D. L., Kenny, M. E., Di Fabio, A., & Guichard, J. (in press). Expanding the impact of the psychology of working: Engaging psychology in the struggle for decent work and human rights. *Journal of Career Assessment.* https://doi.org/10.1177/1069072718774002.

Brott, P. E. (2004). Constructivist assessment in career counseling. *Journal of Career Development, 30*(3), 189–200.

Brown, S. D., Ryan Krane, N. E., Brecheisen, J., Castelino, P., Budisin, I., Miller, M., et al. (2003). Critical ingredients of career choice interventions: More analyses and new hypotheses. *Journal of Vocational Behavior, 62,* 411–428.

Busacca, L., & Rehfuss, M. (Eds.). (2016). *Postmodern career counseling: A handbook of culture, contexts, and cases*. American Counseling Association.

Cardoso, P., Silva, J. R., Gonçalves, M. M., & Duarte, M. E. (2014). Innovative moments and change in career construction counseling. *Journal of Vocational Behavior, 84,* 11–20.

Cochran, L. (1997). *Career counseling: A narrative approach*. London: Sage Publications.

Di Fabio, A. (2010). Life designing in 21st century: Using a new, strengthened career genogram. *Journal of Psychology in Africa*, *20*(3), 381–384.

Di Fabio, A. (2012). Evaluation of the effectiveness of the new career construction genogram. *Cypriot Journal of Educational Sciences*, *7*(4), 287–297.

Di Fabio, A. (2014a). Career counseling and positive psychology in the 21st century: New constructs and measures for evaluating the effectiveness of intervention. *Journal of Counsellogy*, *1*, 193–213.

Di Fabio, A. (2014b). "Constructing my future purposeful life": A new life construction intervention. In A. Di Fabio & J.-L. Bernaud (Eds.), *The construction of the identity in 21st century: A Festschrift for Jean Guichard* (pp. 219–239). New York: Nova Science Publishers.

Di Fabio, A. (2014c). Due meta-competenze chiave narrative per la nuova consapevolezza identitaria purposeful nel XXI secolo. *Counseling. Giornale Italiano di Ricerca e Applicazioni*, *7*, 133–141.

Di Fabio, A. (2014d). Intrapreneurial self-capital: A new construct for the 21st century. *Journal of Employment Counseling*, *51*, 98–111.

Di Fabio, A. (2014e). The new purposeful identitarian awareness for the twenty-first century: Valorize themselves in the life construction from youth to adulthood and late adulthood. In A. Di Fabio & J.-L. Bernaud (Eds.), *The construction of the identity in 21st century: A Festschrift for Jean Guichard* (pp. 157–168). New York: Nova Science Publishers.

Di Fabio, A. (2015a). Beyond fluid intelligence and personality traits in social support: The role of ability based emotional intelligence. *Frontiers in Psychology*, *6*, 395. https://doi:10.3389/fpsyg.2015.00395.

Di Fabio, A. (2015b). Life adaptability qualitative assessment (LAQuA): A narrative instrument for evaluating counseling intervention effectiveness. In J. G. Maree & A. Di Fabio (Eds.), *Exploring new horizons in career counselling: Turning challenges into opportunities* (pp. 43–62). Rotterdam, The Netherlands: Sense Publishers.

Di Fabio, A. (2015c). The life design genogram. In M. McMahon & M. Watson. (Eds.), *Career assessment: Qualitative approaches* (pp. 97–103). Rotterdam, The Netherlands: Sense Publishers.

Di Fabio, A. (2016a). Life design and career counseling innovative outcomes (CCIO): A case study. *The Career Development Quarterly, 64*, 35–48.

Di Fabio, A. (2016b). The life design genogram: A case study of an Italian female graduated student. In L. Busacca & M. Rehfuss (Eds.), *Postmodern career counseling: A handbook of culture, contexts, and cases* (pp. 229–244). American Counseling Association.

Di Fabio, A. (2017a). Positive healthy organizations: Promoting well-being, meaningfulness, and sustainability in organizations. In G. Arcangeli, G. Giorgi, N. Mucci, J.-L. Bernaud, & A. Di Fabio (Eds.), Emerging and re-emerging organizational features, work transitions and occupational risk factors: The good, the bad, the right. An interdisciplinary perspective. Research Topic in *Frontiers in Psychology. Organizational Psychology*, *8*, 1938. https://doi.org/10.3389/fpsyg.2017.01938.

Di Fabio, A. (2017b). The psychology of sustainability and sustainable development for well-being in organizations. In G. Arcangeli, G. Giorgi, N. Mucci, J.-L. Bernaud, & A. Di Fabio (Eds.), Emerging and re-emerging organizational features, work transitions and occupational risk factors: The good, the bad, the right. An interdisciplinary perspective. Research Topic in *Frontiers in Psychology. Organizational Psychology*, *8*, 1534. https://doi.org/10.3389/fpsyg.2017.01534.

Di Fabio, A., & Bernaud, J.-L. (Eds.). (2014). *The construction of the identity in 21st century: A Festschrift for Jean Guichard.* New York: Nova Science Publishers.

Di Fabio, A., & Blustein, D. L. (2010). Emotional intelligence and decisional conflict styles: Some empirical evidence among Italian high school students. *Journal of Career Assessment*, *18*(1), 71–81.

Di Fabio, A., & Blustein, D. L. (Eds). (2016). *From meaning of working to meaningful lives: The challenges of expanding decent work.* Lausanne: Frontiers Media. https://doi.org/10.3389/978-2-88919-970-9.

Di Fabio, A., & Gori, A. (2016a). Assessing workplace relational civility (WRC) with a new multidimensional "mirror" measure. In A. Di Fabio & D. L. Blustein (Eds.), From meaning of working to meaningful lives: The challenges of expanding decent work. Research Topic in *Frontiers in Psychology. Section Organizational Psychology*, *7*, 890. https://doi:10.3389/fpsyg.2016.00890.

Di Fabio, A., & Gori, A. (2016b). Developing a new instrument for assessing acceptance of change. *Frontiers in Psychology. Section Organizational Psychology*, *7*, 802. https://doi:10.3389/fpsyg.2016.00802

Di Fabio, A., & Kenny, M. E. (2016a). From decent work to decent lives: Positive self and relational management (PS&RM) in the twenty-first century. In A. Di Fabio & D. L. Blustein (Eds.), From meaning of working to meaningful lives: The challenges of expanding decent work. Research Topic in *Frontiers in Psychology. Section Organizational Psychology*, *7*, 361. https:// doi:10.3389/fpsyg.2016.00361

Di Fabio, A., & Kenny, M. E. (2016b). Promoting well-being: The contribution of emotional intelligence. In G. Giorgi, M. Shoss, & A. Di Fabio (Eds.), From organizational welfare to business success: Higher performance in healthy organizational environments. Research Topic in *Frontiers in Psychology. Organizational Psychology*, *7*, 1182. https://doi:10.3389/fpsyg.2016.01182

Di Fabio, A., Kenny, M. E., & Minor, K. (2014). Emotional intelligence. School-based research andpractice in Italy. In M. J. Furlong, R. Gilman, & E. S. Huebner (Eds.), Handbook of positive psychologyin the schools (2nd ed., pp. 450-464). New York: Routledge, Taylor and Francis.

Di Fabio, A., Kenny, M. E., & Claudius, M. (2016). Preventing distress and promoting psychological well-being in uncertain times through career management intervention. In M. Israelashvili & J. L. Romano (Eds.), *The Cambridge handbook of international prevention science* (pp. 233–254). Cambridge: Cambridge University Press.

Di Fabio, A., & Maree, J. G. (2012). Group-based Life Design Counseling in an Italian context. *Journal of Vocational Behavior, 80*, 100–107.

Di Fabio, A., & Maree, J. G. (Eds.). (2013). *Psychology of career counseling: New challenges for a new era. Festschrift in honour of Prof. Mark Savickas*. New York: Nova Science Publishers.

Di Fabio, A. & Maree, J. G. (2016). A psychological perspective on the future of work: promoting sustainable projects and meaning-making through grounded reflexivity. *Counseling. Giornale Italiano di Ricerca e Applicazioni, 9*(3).

Di Fabio, A., Maree, J. G., & Kenny, M. E. (2018). Development of the life project reflexivity scale: A new career intervention inventory. *Journal of Career Assessment*, 1–13. https://doi.org/10.1177/1069072718758065.

Di Fabio, A., & Saklofske, D. H. (2014a). Comparing ability and self-report trait emotional intelligence, fluid intelligence, and personality traits in career decision. *Personality and Individual Differences, 64*, 174–178.

Di Fabio, A., & Saklofske, D. H. (2014b). Promoting individual resources: The challenge of trait emotional intelligence. *Personality and Individual Differences, 65*, 19–23.

Di Fabio, A., & Van Esbroeck, R. (2016). Intrapreneurial self-capital: A concept fitting a life-designing intervention. *Counseling. Giornale Italiano di Ricerca e Applicazioni, 9*(2).

Di Fabio, A., Giannini, M., Loscalzo, Y., Palazzeschi, L., Bucci, O., Guazzini, A., & Gori, A. (2016). The challenge of fostering healthy organizations: An empirical study on the role of workplace relational civility in acceptance of change, and well-being. In G. Giorgi, M. Shoss, & A. Di Fabio (Eds.), From organizational welfare to business success: Higher performance in healthy organizational environments. Research Topic in *Frontiers in Psychology. Organizational Psychology, 7*, 1748. doi: https://doi.org/10.3389/fpsyg.2016.01748

Duarte, M. E. (2004). O indivíduo e a organização: Perspectivas de desenvolvimento. [The individual and the organization: Perspectives of development]. *Psychologica (Extra-Série)*, 549–557

Duffy, R. D., Allan, B. A., England, J. W., Blustein, D. L., Autin, K. L., Douglass, R. P., … Santos, E. J. (2017). The development and initial validation of the decent work scale. *Journal of Counseling Psychology, 64*(2), 206.

Duffy, R. D., Blustein, D. L., Diemer, M. A., & Autin, K. L. (2016). The psychology of working theory. *Journal of Counseling Psychology, 63*(2), 127–148.

Duffy, R. D., Foley, P. F., Raque-Bodgan, T. L., Reid-Marks, L., Dik, B. J., Castano, M. C., et al. (2012). Counseling psychologists who view their careers as a calling: A qualitative study. *Journal of Career Assessment, 20*(3), 293–308.

Duffy, R. D., Torrey, C. L., Bott, E. M., Allan, B. A., & Schlosser, L. Z. (2013). Time management, passion, and collaboration: A qualitative study of highly research productive counseling psychologists. *The Counseling Psychologist, 41*(6), 881–917.

Farrell, T. S. C. (2004). *Reflective practice in action*. Palo Alto, CA: Corwin Press Inc.

Finlay, L., & Gough, B. (Eds.). (2003). *Reflexivity: A practical guide for researchers in health and social sciences*. Oxford, UK: Blackwell Science.

Frankl, V. (1963). *Man's search for meaning* (Rev ed.). London, UK: Hodder & Stoughton.

Gonçalves, M. M., Ribeiro, A. P., Mendes, I., Matos, M., & Santos, A. (2011). Tracking novelties in psychotherapy process research: The innovative moments coding system. *Psychotherapy Research, 21*, 497–509.

Greenhaus, J. H., Callanan, G. A., & Godshalk, V. M. (2010). *Career management* (4th ed.). SAGE Publications, Inc.

Guichard, J. (2004). Se faire soi. *L'Orientation Scolaire et Professionnelle, 33,* 499–534.
Guichard, J. (2005). Life-long self-construction. *International Journal of Education and Vocational Guidance, 5,* 111–124.
Guichard, J. (2008). Proposition d'un schéma d'entretien constructiviste de conseil en orientation pour des adolescents ou de jeunes adultes. *L'Orientation Scolaire et Professionnelle, 37,* 413–440.
Guichard, J. (2009). Self-constructing. *Journal of Vocational Behavior, 75,* 251–258.
Guichard, J. (2010, March). *Les théories de la construction des parcours professionnels et de la construction de soi: Deux approches de la construction de la vie individuelle.* Paper presented at Colloque International INETOP, Paris, France.
Guichard, J. (2013, September). *Which paradigm for career and life designing interventions contributing to the development of a fairer world during the 21st century.* Lecture presented at the IAEVG International Conference, Montpellier, France.
Guichard, J., Bangali, M., Cohen Scali, V., Pouyaud, J., & Robinet, M. L. (2016). *Concevoir et orienter sa vie: Les dialogues de conseil en life design.* Paris: Editions Qui plus est.
Guichard, J., & Dauwalder, J. (2010). The role of the theories of career construction and self-constructing in life designing. Paper presented at the 27th International Congress of Applied Psychology Symposium on Life design: A Paradigm for Career Construction in the 21st century, Berlin.
Guichard, J., & Di Fabio, A. (2010). Life-designing counseling: Specificità e integrazioni della teoria della costruzione di carriera e della teoria della costruzione di sé. *Counseling. Giornale Italiano di Ricerca e Applicazioni, 3,* 277–289.
Guichard, J., & Lenz, J. (2005). Career theory from an international perspective. *Career Development Quarterly, 54,* 17–28.
Hage, S. M., Romano, J. L., Conyne, R. K., Kenny, M., Matthews, C., Schwartz, J. P., et al. (2007). Best practice guidelines on prevention practice, research, training, and social advocacy for psychologists. *The Counseling Psychologist, 35,* 493–566.
Hall, B. A., Halstead, M. E., & Taylor, T. R. (1986). *Test administrator's manual for the Rothwell-Miller Interest Blank.* Pretoria, South Africa: Human Sciences Research Council.
Hartung, P. J. (2010). Practice and research in career counseling and development-2009. *Career Development Quarterly, 59,* 98–142.
Hartung, P. J. (2012). Career development in global context: History, status, and prospects. In M. Watson & M. McMahon (Eds.), *Career development: Global issues and challenges* (pp. 11–26). Hauppauge, NY: Nova Science.
Hartung, P. J. (2013). Career as story: Making the narrative turn. In W. B. Walsh, M. L. Savickas, & P. J. Hartung (Eds.), *Handbook of vocational psychology* (4th ed., pp. 33–52). New York: Routledge.
Heppner, M. J., & Heppner, P. P. (2003). Identifying process variables in career counseling: A research agenda. *Journal of Vocational Behavior, 62,* 429–452.
Holland, J. L., Powell, A. B., & Fritzsche, B. A. (1994). *The self-directed search professional user's guide* (4th ed.). Odessa, FL: Psychological Assessment Resources.
Kenny, M. E., Blustein, D. L., & Meerkins, T. M. (2018). Integrating relational perspectives in career counseling practice. *The Career Development Quarterly, 66*(2), 135–148.
Kenny, M., & Di Fabio, A. (2009). Prevention and career development. *Risorsa Uomo. Rivista di Psicologia del Lavoro e dell'Organizzazione, 15,* 361–374.
Kenny, M. E., & Hage, S. M. (2009). The next frontier: Prevention as an instrument of social justice. *The Journal of Primary Prevention, 30,* 1–10.
Kenny, M. E., Horne, A. M., Orpinas, P., & Reese, L. E. (2009). Social justice and the challenge of preventive interventions: An introduction. In M. E. Kenny, A. M. Horne, P. Orpinas, & L. E. Reese (Eds.), *Realizing social justice: The challenge of preventive interventions* (pp. 3–14). Washington, DC: American Psychological Association.
Killion, J., & Todnew, G. (1991). A process of personal theory building. *Educational Leadership, 48,* 14–16.

Kuenzli, F. (2006). *Inviting reflexivity into the therapy room: How therapists think in action*. Lanham, MD: University Press of America.

Létourneau, I., Chrétien, L., e Lécine, M.-E. (2012). L'évaluation de la formation à l'harmonisation travail-vie personnelle: Bilan et perspectives de recherche. *Psychologie du travail et des organisations, 18*, 102–120.

Maree, J. G. (2006). *Manual for the career interest profile*. Randburg, South Africa: Jopie van Rooyen & Partners.

Maree, J. G. (Ed.). (2007). *Shaping the story: A guide to facilitating narrative career counseling*. Pretoria: Van Schaik.

Maree, J. G. (2010). *The career interest profile* (3rd ed.). Randburg, South Africa: Jopie van Rooyen & Partners.

Maree, J. G. (2012a). Editorial. promoting children's rights: Rekindling respectivity. *South African Journal of Psychology, 42*(3), 295–300.

Maree, J. G. (2012b). A (guided) meta-reflection theory of career counselling: A case study. *South African Journal of Higher Education, 26*(4), 661–669.

Maree, J. G. (2013). *Counselling for career construction: Connecting life themes to construct life portraits. Turning pain into hope*. Rotterdam, The Netherlands: Sense.

Maree, J. G. (2016). *Intervista CIP - Career interest profile. Valutare e rilevare gli interessi professionali per la carriera* [*Career interest profile. Evaluate and detect professional interests for career*] (Italian version edited by A. Di Fabio). Trento: Erickson.

Maree, J. G., & Di Fabio, A. (Eds.). (2015). *Exploring new horizons in career counselling: Turning challenges into opportunities*. Rotterdam, The Netherlands: Sense Publishers.

Maree, J. G., & Sommerville, J. (2008). Development of a post-modern career interest questionnaire for South-African school settings. *Journal for Psychology in Africa, 18*, 125–132.

McMahon, M. (2010). Career counseling and storytelling: Constructing a 21st narrative for practice. In H. Ohlsson & H. Borg (Eds.), *Career development* (pp. 1–23). New York, NY: Nova Science.

McMahon, M., & Patton, W. (2002). Using qualitative assessment in career counseling. *International Journal for Educational and Vocational Guidance, 2*, 51–66.

McMahon, M., & Watson, M. (2010). Story telling: Moving from thin stories to thick and rich stories. In K. Maree (Ed.), *Career counselling: Methods that work* (pp. 53–63). Cape Town, South Africa: Yuta.

McMahon, M., & Watson, M. (2011). Career counselling: What's the story? In M. McMahon & M. Watson (Eds.), *Career counselling and constructivism: Elaboration of constructs* (pp. 13–24). New York: Nova Science.

Oliver, L. W., & Spokane, A. R. (1988). Career-intervention outcome: What contributes to client gain? *Journal of Counseling Psychology, 35*, 447–462.

Osipow, S. H. (2012). Career development. *Encyclopedia Human Behaviour*, 430–433.

Polkinghorne, D. E. (2005). Language and meaning: Data collection in qualitative research. *Journal of Counseling Psychology, 52*(2), 137–145.

Rehfuss, M. C. (2009). The *future career autobiography*: A narrative measure of career intervention effectiveness. *The Career Development Quarterly, 58*(1), 82–90.

Rehfuss, M., & Di Fabio, A. (2012). Validating the future career autobiography as a measure of narrative change. *Journal of Career Assessment, 20*, 452–462.

Reker, G. T. (2000). Theoretical perspectives, dimensions and measurement of existential meaning. In G. T. Reker & K. Chamberlain (Eds.), *Exploring existential meaning: Optimising human development across the life span* (pp. 39–55). Thousand Oaks, CA: Sage.

Richardson, M. S. (2012). Counseling for work and relationship. *The Counseling Psychologist, 40* (2), 190–242.

Rosa, H. (2015). *Accelerazione e alienazione. Per una teoria critica del tempo nella tarda modernità* [*Acceleration and alienation. For a critical theory of time in late modernity*] (Trad. it. E. Leonzio). Torino: Einaudi.

Rosso, B. D., Dekas, K. H., & Wrzesniewski, A. (2010). On the meaning of work: A theoretical integration and review. *Research in Organizational Behavior, 30,* 91–127.
Savickas, M. L. (2001). Toward a comprehensive theory of career development: Disposition, concerns and narratives. In F. T. L. Leong & A. Barak (Eds.), *Contemporary models in vocational psychology: A volume in honor of Samuel H. Osipow* (pp. 295–320). Mahwah, NJ: Lawrence Erlbaum.
Savickas, M. L. (2005). The theory and practice of career construction. In S. D. Brown & R. W. Lent (Eds.), *Career development and counseling: Putting theory and research to work* (pp. 42–70). Hoboken, NJ: Wiley.
Savickas, M. L. (2007). Prologue: Reshaping the story of career counseling. In K. Maree (Ed.), *Shaping the story. A guide to facilitating narrative counseling* (pp. 1–3). Pretoria, South Africa: Van Schaik Publishers.
Savickas, M. L. (2010, July). *Life designing: Framework and introduction.* Paper presented at the 27th International Congress of Applied Psychology, Melbourne, Australia.
Savickas, M. L. (Ed.). (2011a). *Career counseling.* Washington, DC: American Psychological Association.
Savickas, M. L. (2011b). New questions for vocational psychology: Premises, paradigms, and practices. *Journal of Career Assessment, 19,* 251–258.
Savickas, M. L. (2013). *Life designing in 21st century.* Closing Conference at the IAEVG International Conference, Montpellier, France.
Savickas, M. (2014). *Career counseling: Guida teorica e metodologica per il XXI secolo* [*Career counseling: Theoretical and methodological guide for the 21st century*]. (Italian version edited by A. Di Fabio). Trento: Erickson.
Savickas, M. L. (2015). *Life-design counseling manual.* Rootstown, OH: Author.
Savickas, M. L., & Porfeli, E. J. (2012). Career adapt-abilities scale: Construction, reliability, and measurement equivalence across 13 countries. *Journal of Vocational Behavior, 80,* 661–673.
Schnell, T., Höge, T., & Pollet, E. (2013). Predicting meaning in work: Theory, data, implications. *The Journal of Positive Psychology, 8*(6), 543–554.
Schön, D. (1987). *Educating the reflective practitioner.* San Francisco, CA: Jossey-Bass.
Seligman, M. E. P. (2002). Positive psychology, positive prevention, and positive therapy. In C. R. Snyder & S. J. Lopez (Eds.), *Handbook of Positive Psychology* (pp. 3–9). New York: Oxford University Press.
Seligman, M. E., & Csikszentmihalyi, M. (2000). *Positive psychology: An introduction.* Washington, DC: American Psychological Association.
Severy, L. E. (2002). What's the story? Postmodern career counseling in student affairs. *Journal of College Student Development, 43*(1), 84–92.
Standing, G. (2014). *A precariat charter: From denizens to citizens.* New York: Bloomsbury.
Super, D. E. (1957). *The psychology of career.* New York: Harper.
Super, D. (1980). A life-span, life-space approach to career development. *Journal of Vocational Behavior, 16,* 282–298.
Whiston, S. C., Brecheisen, B. K., & Stephens, J. (2003). Does treatment modality affect career counseling effectiveness? *Journal of Vocational Behavior, 62,* 390–410.
Whiston, S. C., Sexton, T. L., & Lasoff, D. L. (1998). Career intervention outcome: A replication and extension of Oliver and Spokane (1988). *Journal of Counseling Psychology, 45,* 150–165.
Zunker, V. G. (1998). *Career counselling: Applied concepts of life planning* (5th ed.). Pacific Grove, CA: Brooks/Cole.

Chapter 8
Career Interest Profile (CIP) as a Life Design Counseling Intervention: A Case Study on an Italian PhD Student Using Both FCA and LAQuA as Qualitative Evaluation Tools

Ornella Bucci, Allison Creed and Annamaria Di Fabio

Abstract This chapter describes the case study of a graduate student who, at the time of the research, was undertaking the first year of a PhD course. The young man participated in a life design counseling intervention through the Career Interest Profile (CIP) and completed two narrative instruments before and after the intervention: the Future Career Autobiography (FCA), a more traditional narrative instrument, and the Life Adaptability Qualitative Assessment (LAQuA), a promising innovative narrative instrument. The effectiveness of the life design counseling intervention using the CIP, evaluated through the FCA and the LAQuA, is discussed in the chapter. The results of the study revealed more specific life and occupational goals after the intervention as well as narrative changes in the adaptability dimensions. The life design counseling intervention using the CIP helped the participant to increase the awareness of himself and to develop his career and life paths.

8.1 Introduction

The postmodern world of work is characterized by instability, uncertainty, fluidity, and increasing demands of new and updated knowledge and skills such as flexibility, communication, and digital competences (Guichard, 2013; Savickas, 2011). These competences are important for workers enabling them to deal successfully

O. Bucci · A. Di Fabio (✉)
Department of Education and Psychology (Psychology Section),
University of Florence, Florence, Italy
e-mail: adifabio@psico.unifi.it

A. Creed
School of Linguistics, Adult and Specialist Education,
University of Southern Queensland, Toowoomba, Australia

© Springer Nature Switzerland AG 2018

A. Di Fabio and J.-L. Bernaud (eds.), *Narrative Interventions in Post-modern Guidance and Career Counseling*, https://doi.org/10.1007/978-3-319-98300-4_8

with an ever-changing world of work (Blustein, 2006, 2011; Guichard & Di Fabio, 2015; Savickas, 2011). People are confronting many work challenges because they cannot envision only one job in the same organization for their working life. Career belongs to the person and no longer to the organization (Duffy et al., 2012, 2017; Duffy, Blustein, Diemer, & Autin, 2016; Duffy, Torrey, Bott, Allan, & Schlosser, 2013; Duarte, 2004). Individuals' career and life could have different trajectories, and people should be prepared to face many transitions (Savickas, 2007, 2011). Career is thus seen as a story (Brott, 2004; Cochran, 1997; McMahon & Watson, 2010; Savickas, 2011; Severy 2002).

In this new scenario of career, there are three main challenges in guidance and career counseling (Di Fabio, 2016): (1) to design and realize novel psychological narrative interventions; (2) to address the evaluation of the effectiveness of the intervention; and (3) to develop novel instruments to evaluate the effectiveness of the interventions.

Firstly, new theoretical approaches in guidance and career counseling based on a psychological narrative storied approach (Hartung, 2010, 2012, 2013; Hartung & Subich, 2011; Maree, 2007, 2013; McMahon, 2010; McMahon & Watson, 2011; Rehfuss, 2009; Rehfuss & Di Fabio, 2012; Savickas, 2005, 2011, 2013) for the twenty-first century are required to help people to cope with the challenges of the current fluid society. In contrast to the modern era in which career interventions and career counseling traditionally were based on the principal person–environment fit paradigm (Holland, 1997), the postmodern era comprises a paradigm related to the concept of the self as a story requiring a narrative approach and story-based interventions (Savickas, 2011). According to the life design paradigm (Savickas et al., 2009), counselors are assumed to help clients discover a meaning to their own personal and professional lives through the narrative construction of their own selves as stories (Busacca & Rehfuss, 2016; Guichard & Di Fabio, 2015; Savickas, 2005, 2011; Savickas et al., 2009), considering stories as the instruments to construct identity (Hartung, 2010, 2013; Hartung & Subich, 2011; Rehfuss, 2009; Savickas, 2011; Savickas et al., 2009). Thus, counselors need an approach that dynamically helps clients to think and explore different possible selves (Guichard, 2004, 2005; Oyserman, Bybee, & Terry, 2006; Savickas, 2005, 2011), to unify them by connecting their various experiences and to build a bridge toward their future (Guichard, 2009; Savickas, 2011). Guidance and career counseling interventions for career construction (Savickas, 2005, 2011) and life construction (Guichard, 2013) focus on facilitating self-reflection and reflexivity (Di Fabio, Maree, & Kenny, 2018; Maree, 2013).

In line with the Career Construction Theory (Savickas, 2005, 2011), clients should be involved in a process of construction, deconstruction, reconstruction, and co-construction of their life story (Maree, 2014; Savickas, 2011). It calls for an active perspective including clients in a reinterpretation of their past memories, present experiences, and future ambitions. Through narration, individuals can find meaningful life themes and construct their identity in biographical terms, ready to understand and overcome work problems and movements (Savickas, 2001).

According to the Life Construction Theory (Guichard, 2013), clients have plural identities through the production of stories about different life experiences and the association of these experiences to possible future projects. This process enables individuals to obtain a unified sense of identity, find authenticity and meaning in their career lives, toward the design of future selves (Allan, Duffy, & Douglass, 2015; Douglass, Duffy, & Autin, 2016; Guichard, 2005, 2013). In doing so, people can acquire a new, purposeful identitarian mindfulness (Di Fabio, 2014b)—a key requisite for success in the twenty-first century occupational and personal contexts.

In light of these two basic career theories, life design interventions today aims at facilitating an accurate reflection by individuals to develop a stable sense of identity and the adaptability in order to have success in the ever-changing life and uncertain workplaces (Guichard, 2005, 2013; Guichard et al., 2016; Maree & Di Fabio, 2015; Savickas, 2005, 2013, 2015). The focus is on helping clients to work narratively through their problems, refining their reflexive ability to identify meaningful purposes and to be able to productively contribute to the larger society (Guichard & Di Fabio, 2015; Savickas, 2011).

In keeping with this new narrative perspective (Hartung, 2010, 2012, 2013; Maree, 2007; McMahon & Patton, 2002; Rehfuss, 2009; Savickas, 1995, 1997), other fundamental challenges in guidance and career counseling are the evaluation of the effectiveness of the guidance and career counseling interventions through the development of adequate novel qualitative instruments (Di Fabio & Maree, 2012). Traditional quantitative instruments are limited in terms of their capacity to measure and understand the nature of qualitative changes in individuals' self-narratives (Rehfuss, 2009; Rehfuss & Di Fabio, 2012). On the contrary, qualitative instruments can help clients to tell their story and counselors to listen, elaborate, and clarify individuals' stories (Rehfuss, 2009). Contemporary and innovative narrative approaches to life design interventions, which comprise qualitative instruments (Blustein, Kenna, Murphy, Devoy, & DeWine, 2005), can be useful for satisfying the needs of the twenty-first century people and strengthening personal and professional resources (Di Fabio, 2014b). Thus, the necessity for researchers and practitioners to establish and verify the rigor and the efficiency of life design interventions can be addressed through qualitative narrative instruments congruent with narrative intervention to detect narrative change (Hartung, 2010, 2013; Rehfuss, 2009; Rehfuss & Di Fabio, 2012).

Until recently, the only trustworthy qualitative instrument in the literature for assessing life design counseling outcomes is the Future Career Autobiography (FCA, Rehfuss, 2009; see below). Although the FCA represents a valuable instrument for evaluating the effectiveness of life design interventions, it can only detect broad change themes hindering a deep exploration of the impact of a counseling experience. A less vague and more refined instrument is the Life Adaptability Qualitative Assessment (LAQuA, Di Fabio, 2015). This is a new instrument specifically designed to detect qualitative changes in the four career adaptability dimensions (Savickas, 2001; Savickas & Porfeli, 2012).

The present study examined the value of life design counseling realized by applying the Career Interest Profile (CIP, Maree, 2010), using a more traditional narrative instrument, the Future Career Autobiography (FCA, Rehfuss, 2009), and in addition a promising innovative narrative instrument, the Life Adaptability Qualitative

Assessment (LAQuA, Di Fabio, 2015). This chapter presented the case study of a young PhD architectural student who participated in a life design counseling intervention using the CIP. It also discusses the effectiveness of the life design counseling intervention evaluated through qualitative instruments (FCA and LAQuA).

8.2 Aim of the Case Study

This chapter aims at presenting the process and usefulness of a life design counseling intervention through the use of the CIP (Maree, 2010) in helping the participant to better understand himself by identifying, analyzing, and discussing career and life themes. This case study underlines the participant's involvement in his process of career and life construction, enabling him to listen to himself and authorizing the writing of a new chapter of his life.

The study is guided by the following two research questions.

- How was the life design counseling intervention using the CIP administered to a young PhD architectural student?
- How did the life design counseling intervention using the CIP help the participant to increase the awareness of himself and to develop his career and life paths?

8.3 Materials and Methods

8.3.1 Participant and Context

David (a pseudonym) was a 26-year-old man who had a master's degree in architecture obtained at the University of Florence. He had commenced the first year of a PhD course in architecture at the University of Florence. He asked to participate in a life design counseling intervention at the career counseling center of the university. David requested the intervention because he was not sure about the choice of the PhD course with reference to a possible research career. He did not really know whether he should start another career path as an independent professional or a consultant for an architectural firm.

8.3.2 Qualitative Instruments

8.3.2.1 Qualitative Instrument for Intervention

The Career Interest Profile (CIP)

The CIP (Maree, 2010) is a narrative career counseling instrument consisting in four parts: biographical details, family influences, and work-related information

(Part 1); career category preferences/dislikes (Part 2); career-choice questions (Part 3); and career-life story narratives (Part 4). Participants are asked to sequentially complete Part 1 followed by Part 2 and Part 3 and, eventually, Part 4. In Part 2, clients are required first to select the five categories they prefer most and the five they like least from a total of 19 broad career categories. The clients' selections among these 19 career categories in the CIP represent a starting point for recognizing, examining, and elaborating careers and career-related question in greater depth with the career counselor. The CIP aims at helping clients narrate their career stories and become actively involved in the process of career and life construction. The CIP showed adequate psychometric properties in a South African context (Maree, 2006; Maree & Sommerville, 2008) in terms of test–retest reliability, content, and criterion-related validity in relation to the Rothwell Miller Interest Blank (Hall, Halstead, & Taylor, 1992). The Italian version (Di Fabio & Maree, 2013) of the CIP (Maree, 2010) and its narrative supplement were used in the present study to facilitate data collection. The Italian version of the CIP demonstrated good criterion validity in relation to the *Self-Directed Search* (*SDS*) (Holland, Powell, & Fritzsche, 1994).

8.3.2.2 Qualitative Instrument for the Evaluation of the Effectiveness Intervention

The Future Career Autobiography (FCA)

The FCA is a founding novel narrative tool developed to assess the effectiveness of narrative career counseling interventions. The FCA consists of a sheet of paper entitled "Future Career Autobiography" which gives these specific instructions: Please use this page to write a brief paragraph about where you hope to be in life and what you hope to be doing occupationally five years from now (Rehfuss, 2009, Rehfuss & Di Fabio, 2012). The narratives produced in FCAs administered before and after the career counseling intervention are compared, and the presence or lack of change is examined with respect to eight degrees of change themes identified by Rehfuss (2009). These eight change themes are: (1) General Fields and Desires to Specification and Exploration, which indicate a movement from general fields and desires toward specific themes; (2) General Interests to More Specification, where individuals start with a variety of general interests, but over time, their FCAs are refined; (3) Non-Description to Specification, where individuals' initial FCAs begin with general themes and then focus on personal and occupational themes; (4) Disregard to Direction, where individuals disregard the personal and occupational aspects in their initial FCAs and seem unable to accomplish the task; nonetheless, in their subsequent FCAs, they address the same task with specificity and direction; (5) Vagueness to Focus, where the participants' FCAs move from an initial sense of uncertainty and vagueness about their life or career to a narrative with a clearer direction and focus; (6) Hindered to Hopeful, where an initial sense of fear or indifference toward work is substituted with specificity in subsequent FCAs;

(7) Fixation to Openness, where individuals have prematurely excluded a life situation or an occupation and are caught off-guard by the incongruence between their personal and occupational goals and their abilities; nonetheless, in their subsequent FCAs, they try to respond to this dilemma; and (8) Stagnation, where there are not any changes from initial to subsequent FCAs.

8.3.2.3 Life Adaptability Qualitative Assessment (LAQuA)

The LAQuA (Di Fabio, 2015) is a promising innovative qualitative instrument developed to evaluate the effectiveness of life design counseling interventions. This instrument aims at qualitatively assessing career adaptability, evaluating change or lack of change in individuals' narratives after life design counseling interventions (Savickas, 2011). The LAQuA comprises 12 written questions with three questions for each dimension (Concern, Control, Curiosity, and Confidence) of the Career Adapt-Abilities Inventory—International Version 2.0 (Savickas & Porfeli, 2012), and it is administered before and after life design counseling interventions. The LAQuA 12 written questions (Di Fabio, 2015) are:

Concern: (1a) What does it mean to you to be oriented toward your future? (1b) Do you think you are oriented toward your future? (1c) Why?
Control: (2a) What does it mean to you to take responsibility for your future? (2b) Do you think you do take responsibility for your future? (2c) Why?
Curiosity: (3a) What does it mean to you to be curious about your own future? (3b) Do you think you are curious about your future? (3c) Why?
Confidence: (4a) What does it mean to you to have confidence in your own ability to build your future? (4b) Do you think you have confidence in your ability to build your future? (4c) Why?

The LAQuA allows to compare the narratives produced by the individuals before and after the life design counseling intervention. Responses to the 12 questions are analyzed with respect to 24 qualitative indicators for each of the four dimensions of career adaptability (Concern, Control, Curiosity, and Confidence). These indicators are the following:

Anticipating, Predicting, Equipping, Involved, Strategic, Aware (of choices and transitions to be made) for the Concern dimension of Career Adaptability.

Positive attitude, Autonomous, Conscientious, Assertive, Responsible, and Honest for the Control dimension of Career Adaptability.

Investigative, Developing, Inquisitive, Recognizing/Discovering, Inquiring, and Searching for the Curiosity dimension of Career Adaptability.

Productive, Mindful, Innovative, Capable, Resilient, and Able to work out answers for the Confidence dimension of Career Adaptability.

These qualitative indicators are structured in the LAQuA coding system (Di Fabio, 2015). The LAQuA coding system entails five qualitative analysis change categories, permitting the detection of change or no change for each dimension of career adaptability in relation to different levels of reflexivity (Increased Reflexivity, Revised Reflexivity, Open Reflexivity, Enhanced Reflexivity, and No Change).

1. Increased reflexivity: there are two different forms (Type I and Type II). Type I: in narratives produced post-intervention, we have the identical descriptor/s present in narratives produced pre-intervention but with more in-depth reflexivity. Type II: in narratives produced pre-intervention, there is an absence of descriptors, whereas in narratives produced post-intervention, a descriptor appears. So, we have a depth increase in reflexivity in the same descriptor/s (Type I) or an increase in reflexivity with the appearance of a descriptor/s (Type II).
2. Revised reflexivity: in narratives produced post-intervention, we see the disappearance of the previous descriptor/s present in narratives produced pre-intervention and the appearance of new different descriptor/s. So, we now have a new focus on a different facet/s of the specific Career Adaptability dimension.
3. Open reflexivity: in narratives produced post-intervention, we see the same identical descriptor/s present in narratives produced pre-intervention and with the same level of reflexivity, but new descriptor/s also appear in addition. So, the previous focus is maintained, and there is also new awareness of a different facet/s of the specific Career Adaptability dimension.
4. Enhanced reflexivity: in narratives produced post-intervention, we have the identical descriptor/s present in narratives produced pre-intervention but with more in-depth reflexivity, and a new descriptor/s also appears in addition. So, we have an expansion in the complexity regarding the dimension because we have both a depth increase in reflexivity in the same descriptor/s and also a diversification of a different facet/s of the specific Career Adaptability dimension.
5. No change: it appears in two different forms (Type I and Type II). Type I: in the narratives produced post-intervention, we have the same identical descriptor/s present as in the narratives produced pre-intervention and with the same level of reflexivity related to the descriptor/s. Type II: in the narratives produced pre-intervention, there is an absence of a descriptor/s and in the narratives produced post-intervention; we continue to have an absence of descriptors regarding the specific Career Adaptability dimension. The *LAQuA* is, therefore, an innovative instrument that permits the detection of change in narratives pre- and post-intervention in a specific manner for the four Career Adaptability dimensions (Concern, Control, Curiosity, and Confidence) and with a division of change into different levels of reflexivity.

8.3.3 Procedure

The FCA and the LAQuA were administered before and after the intervention by a psychologist specialized in life design counseling and in the administration of these qualitative instruments. The participant's initial and final responses to the written questions of these narrative instruments were compared by three independent, trained expert reviewers (raters). An interrater reliability analysis using the Kappa statistic was calculated to indicate the level of consistency among the raters.

The study was realized observing the requests of privacy and informed consent in Italian law (Law Decree DL-196/2003) and the ethical standards for research of the Declaration of Helsinki revised in Fortaleza (World Medical Association [WMA], 2013), followed and approved by the Department of Education and Psychology of the University of Florence (Italy).

David participated in an intervention that comprised group-based narrative career counseling. The intervention was divided into two 1-day sessions (8 h a day, 7 days apart). The participants filled individually all four parts of the CIP but in group contexts on the first day. Intervention on the second day comprised a group-based career counseling session (Di Fabio & Maree, 2012) using the methodology of the power of an audience (Di Fabio & Maree, 2012). During the intervention, the participants (in a circular arrangement) interacted with the career counselor one at a time (individually). The professional discussed the participant's *CIP* outcomes with the participant, while the other group members constituted the audience having the possibility to elaborate personal aspects elicited by the career counselor. They participate in the process without addressing other participants directly. In other words, the group members were considered as clients of an individual counseling session while at the same time self-reflecting on the issues examined by the other participants. The career counselor helped the participants discover a) core themes that emerged from the answers to the CIP, b) their principal career-related questions, and c) find autonomously a way to turn these questions into themes of hope that could improve their individual career and life projects. The participants were given stimuli to reflect and obtain a greater self-awareness as well as awareness of their career and life projects (Di Fabio & Maree, 2012).

8.3.4 Criteria for Quality Assurance

Quality assurance criteria are needed to determine the trustworthiness of the case study results with regard to the strategies used for gathering and analyzing the data. Credibility, confirmability, transferability, and dependability of the data are central to quality assurance (Maree, 2012). Credibility refers to "the significance of results and their credibility for participants and readers" (Maree, 2012, p. 141). Credibility was ensured in the present study through verification of the results by researchers external to the study. Confirmability regards "the objectivity of the data and the absence of research errors. Results can be regarded as confirmable when they are derived from the participants and the research conditions rather than from the (subjective) opinion of the researcher" (Maree, 2012, p. 142). Confirmability was realized through an assessment by external and independent researchers regarding the clarity and detail of the methods and general procedures of the study that would allow data verification and replication. Transferability regards "the extent to which the results can be 'exported' and generalised to other contexts" (Maree, 2012, p. 142). Transferability was ensured through the thorough and accurate description of the participant's personal situation and the methodologies used to obtain the narratives. Detailed information on the case context was included to enable other readers to judge the applicability of the results to other settings. The research was based on a comprehensive description of the specific case study without any endeavors at generalization, but sufficient detail was provided so that the potential for generalizability could be assessed. Dependability regards "the stability and consistency of the research process and methods over time and influences the degree of control in a study" (Maree, 2012, p. 141). Dependability was ensured through the independent analysis of the participant's narratives by three expert raters to strengthen the accuracy of the deductive process and to guarantee that the identified themes precisely represented the data.

8.4 Results

The participant's responses to the written questions of the FCA and the LAQuA before and after the life design counseling intervention are described in the next paragraph. The life and occupational themes of the narratives produced by David through the FCA, administered before and after the intervention, are presented.

Regarding life themes, the participant's answer to the FCA question before the life design counseling intervention was: "*I don't know exactly where I live. I'm uncertain if I live abroad or in Italy. Perhaps I could be live in North-Europe where I will have more opportunities to be a researcher in my field or perhaps in the United States where the Italian architect are very appreciated and in this case I could work in a study as a professional. I could also remain in Italy and I will become a researches or a professional*"; and after the life design counseling intervention, it was: "*I hope to live in the North-Europe where my PhD supervisor said me that there are more opportunities for a Post doc in my field of study*" (General Interests to More Specification: the initial client's FCA began with a variety of general interests, but over the time, his FCA elaborated this interests).

With regard to occupational themes, the participant's answer to the FCA question before the life design counseling intervention was: "*I hope to have a job permitting me to continue to study*"; and after the life design counseling intervention, it was: "*I hope to be a researcher in the architectural field after obtaining the title of PhD and to live and work outside Italy*" (Non-Description to Specification: the initial client's FCA began with general themes, and then, client focused on personal and occupational themes).

In relation to the LAQuA, the answers to the four questions by David are reported as well as the results of the analysis obtained through the LAQuA qualitative indicators and the different levels of reflexivity (Increased Reflexivity, Revised Reflexivity, Open Reflexivity, Enhanced Reflexivity, and No Change).

The participant's response to the first LAQuA question before the life design counseling intervention was: "*To me, to be oriented toward my future means to have clear objectives and plan how to achieve them using personal resources. Unfortunately, now I don't know what I really want to do in my future. I wish to recognize a path to follow between the research career or a career being a professional*" (qualitative descriptor: Strategic); and after the life design counseling intervention, it was: "*To me, to be oriented toward my future means have a greater awareness of myself, especially of my strengths also in terms of emotions that I can use for building my future and satisfying my objectives*" (new, different qualitative descriptor: Equipping). (Revised reflexivity (R): in the narratives produced after the life design counseling intervention, the previous descriptor/s has disappeared, and a new, different descriptor/s has emerged.)

The participant's response to the second LAQuA question before the life design counseling intervention was: "*To me, to take responsibility for my future means being autonomous and responsible in accomplishing my tasks and obtaining my objectives. Now I'm confused about the choice I've made beginning a PhD course because I don't know if it is a mistake*" (qualitative descriptor: Responsible); after the life design counseling intervention, it was: "*To me, to take responsibility for my future means counting on myself and being able to autonomously realize the necessary steps for satisfying my objective to remain in the research field. For me it is important to acquire all the necessary resources to carry out my project without depending on others.*" (identical qualitative descriptor but more in-depth reflexivity: Responsible). (Increased reflexivity: in the narratives produced after the life design counseling intervention, there were identical descriptors, but they were presented with more in-depth reflexivity.)

The participant's answer to the third LAQuA question before the life design counseling intervention was: "*To me, to be curious about my future means welcoming my future, trying to experience different ways of doing things, for example both in the academic environment and in a professional environment like an architectural study, before made a definitive choice.*" (qualitative descriptor: Recognizing/Discovering); after the life design counseling intervention, it was: "*To me, to be curious about my future means do multiple professional experiences in the future. For example, before finally choosing an academic career, I would like to have an experience in an architectural study to gain experience of different ways of being an architect.*" (identical qualitative descriptor: Recognizing/Discovering); "*For me be curious means also to deeply analyse issues related not only with my work or my research topics but also with my life outside the work. How to balance my professional and personal life is a question that I have*" (new, different qualitative descriptor: Inquiring). (Open reflexivity (O): in the narratives produced after the life design counseling intervention, there is an identical descriptor/s—with the same level of reflexivity in presenting the descriptor—plus a new, different descriptor/s.)

The participant's response to the fourth LAQuA question before the life design counseling intervention was: "*To me, to have confidence in my own abilities to build my future means using my willpower and in my decision-making abilities*" (qualitative descriptor: Capable); after the life design counseling intervention, it was: "*To have confidence in my own abilities to build my future means to use my willpower and my decision-making abilities specifically to be able to do meaningful choices for my career. My motivation to became a researcher could help me in individuating the better path for developing my career*" (identical qualitative descriptor but more in-depth reflexivity: Capable); "*To have confidence in my own abilities to build my future means also having realized that the choice of enrolling in a PhD course is the best choice for me, in line with my desire to do research in architectural field. It is also important to have confidence to be able to do things well during my PhD to shape my future*" (new, different qualitative descriptor: Mindful). (Enhanced reflexivity (E): in the narratives produced after the life construction intervention, there is an identical descriptor/s but presented with more in-depth reflexivity plus a new, different descriptor/s).

8.5 Discussions

The case study in the present chapter showed the value of the life design counseling intervention using the Career Interest Profile (Maree, 2010) for a PhD student who is undecided about his career and life paths. He expresses uncertainty about his future because he does not know if he wants to become a researcher or a professional in architectural field. The life design counseling intervention using the Career Interest Profile (Maree, 2010) can help clients to discover the real career and life issues, interests, meaning and then to construct desirable career and life (Maree, 2010).

In this case study, the results achieved by David can be verified through the analysis of the narratives before and after the life design counseling intervention (Maree, 2010) detected with the FCA (Rehfuss, 2009; Rehfuss & Di Fabio, 2012) and the LAQuA (Di Fabio, 2015).

The analysis of the participant's response to the FCA questions indicated changes in life and occupational themes. These modifications are relative to the following Degrees of Change (Rehfuss, 2009): General Interests to More Specification and Non-Description to Specification. Regarding General Interests to More Specification, the initial client's FCA began with a variety of general interests but over the time his FCA elaborated this interest. He understood that he wanted to live in the North Europe where his PhD supervisor has indicated that there are more opportunities to continue to do research in architectural field. Regarding Non-Description to Specification, the initial client's FCA began with general themes and then he focused on specific occupational themes. David realized that he wanted to become a researcher in the architectural field and to live and work outside Italy.

The FCA analysis allowed to narratively detect David's personal and career themes in relation to his future life and occupational directions. The results reflect the development of his self and his life and career objectives.

The analysis of the answers to the LAQuA questions, administered before and after the life construction intervention, indicated changes in the participant's ability to reflect on his life and career, increasing his adaptability. The level of reflexivity improved in the four dimensions of adaptability (Concern, Control, Confidence, and Curiosity). Regarding Concern, the participant showed a greater awareness of the importance to have clear objective and to plan how to achieve them using his personal resources. Regarding Control, the participant highlighted the importance of counting on himself to realize his aim to remain in the research field. Regarding Curiosity, the participant realized the importance for him of creating many experiences to see different ways of doing things. Regarding Confidence, the participant expressed greater confidence in his abilities in terms of willpower and decision-making to make satisfying choices.

The less vague and more refined LAQuA analysis allowed to narratively detect David's adaptability in terms of his ability to comprehend challenges and anticipating his future (Savickas, 2001), envisioning also some useful steps to obtain his objectives through the complexities of the ever-changing world of work.

8.6 Conclusion

Generally, the results of the analysis of the narratives before and after the life design counseling intervention using the CIP, through a more traditional qualitative instrument (the FCA) and a more innovative one (the LAQuA), revealed changes in the narratives of the participant, showing that this kind of intervention enabled David to increase the self-awareness useful to identify the next steps for the construction of his career and life. The recognition of his values and interests, strongly connected with his occupational and life themes, seemed to help him to construct the next phase of his life.

The case study also underscored that through life design counseling intervention using the CIP (Maree, 2010), a vulnerable condition can be transformed in a moment of reflection on his personal elements, real objectives, and current opportunities in the world of work. This kind of reflection allowed David to understand better which is his authentic project.

Nonetheless, the results of this case study showed changes in the narratives produced by the participant before and after the life design counseling intervention using the CIP, the effectiveness of the intervention needs to be confirmed by further studies. The trustworthiness and credibility of the study were ensured, but a limitation could be the subjective interpretation of the scholar. A follow-up session 6 weeks after the intervention underscored that the participant was more involved in the tasks due to the PhD course in which he was enrolled, began to write scientific articles, and worked a lot to attend national conferences. Nevertheless, a follow-up assessment 6–12 months after the life design counseling intervention would be important to confirm the findings achieved in the study.

Notwithstanding the above limitations, the study indicated that through the life design counseling intervention using the CIP (Maree, 2010), the participant was enabled to better design his life and career (Guichard & Di Fabio, 2015; Savickas, 2011, 2015), focusing on individual resources (Di Fabio, 2014a; Di Fabio & Kenny, 2012a, 2012b, 2015; Di Fabio & Palazzeschi, 2016; Di Fabio, Palazzeschi, & Bucci, 2017; Di Fabio & Saklofske, 2014a, 2014b). The greater self-awareness reached by the participant relating to his occupational and life themes, thanks to the CIP (Maree, 2010), and the increased adaptability (Savickas, 2001; Savickas & Porfeli, 2012) pointed to more adequate career and life construction in the current complex times (Blustein, Kenny, Di Fabio, & Guichard, in press; Di Fabio & Kenny, 2016; Guichard & Di Fabio, 2015; Kenny, Blustein, & Meerkins, 2018; Maree & Di Fabio, 2015; Savickas, 2005, 2011, 2015).

References

Allan, B. A., Duffy, R. D., & Douglass, R. (2015). Meaning in life and work: A developmental perspective. *The Journal of Positive Psychology, 10*(4), 323–331.

Blustein, D. L. (2006). *The psychology of working: A new perspective for career development, counseling and public policy*. New York: Routledge.

Blustein, D. L. (2011). A relational theory of working. *Journal of Vocational Behavior, 79,* 1–17.

Blustein, D. L., Kenna, A. C., Murphy, K. A., DeVoy, J. E., & DeWine, D. B. (2005). Qualitative research in career development: Exploring the center and margins of discourse about careers and working. *Journal of Career Assessment, 13*(4), 351–370.

Blustein, D. L., Kenny, M. E., Di Fabio, A., & Guichard, J. (in press). Expanding the impact of the psychology of working: Engaging psychology in the struggle for decent work and human rights. *Journal of Career Assessment.* https://doi.org/10.1177/1069072718774002.

Brott, P. E. (2004). Constructivist assessment in career counseling. *Journal of Career Development, 30*(3), 189–200.

Busacca, L., & Rehfuss, M. (Eds.). (2016). *Postmodern career counseling: A handbook of culture, contexts, and cases*. American Counseling Association.

Cochran, L. (1997). *Career counseling: A narrative approach*. London: Sage publications.

Di Fabio, A. (2014a). Intrapreneurial self-capital: A new construct for the 21st century. *Journal of Employment Counseling, 51,* 98–111.

Di Fabio, A. (2014b). The new purposeful identitarian awareness for the twenty-first century: Valorize themselves in the life construction from youth to adulthood and late adulthood. In A. Di Fabio & J.-L. Bernaud (Eds.), *The construction of the identity in 21st century: A Festschrift for Jean Guichard* (pp. 157–168). New York: Nova Science Publishers.

Di Fabio, A. (2015). Life adaptability qualitative assessment (LAQuA): A narrative instrument for evaluating counseling intervention effectiveness. In J. G. Maree & A. Di Fabio (Eds.), *Exploring new horizons in career counselling: Turning challenges into opportunities* (pp. 43–62). Rotterdam, The Netherlands: Sense Publishers.

Di Fabio, A. (2016). Life design and career counseling innovative outcomes (CCIO): A case study. *The Career Development Quarterly, 64,* 35–48.

Di Fabio, A., & Kenny, M. E. (2012a). The contribution of emotional intelligence to decisional styles among Italian high school students. *Journal of Career Assessment, 20,* 404–414.

Di Fabio, A., & Kenny, M. E. (2012b). Emotional intelligence and perceived social support among Italian high school students. *Journal of Career Development, 39,* 461–475.

Di Fabio, A., & Kenny, M. E. (2015). The contributions of emotional intelligence and social support for adaptive career progress among Italian youth. *Journal of Career Development, 42,* 48–49.

Di Fabio, A., & Kenny, M. E. (2016). From decent work to decent lives: Positive Self and Relational Management (PS&RM) in the twenty-first century. In A. Di Fabio & D. L. Blustein (Eds.), From meaning of working to meaningful lives: The challenges of expanding decent work. Research Topic in *Frontiers in Psychology. Section Organizational Psychology*, *7*, 361. https://doi:10.3389/fpsyg.2016.00361.

Di Fabio, A., & Maree, J. G. (2012). Group-based life design counseling in an Italian context. *Journal of Vocational Behavior, 80,* 100–107.

Di Fabio, A., & Maree, J. G. (2013). Career counseling: The usefulness of the career interest profile (CIP). *Journal of Psychology in Africa, 23,* 41–50.

Di Fabio, A., & Palazzeschi, L. (2016). Marginalization and precariat: The challenge of intensifying life construction intervention. In A. Di Fabio & D. L. Blustein (Eds.), *From meaning of working to meaningful lives: The challenges of expanding decent work.* Research topic in *Frontiers in Psychology. Section Organizational Psychology*, *7*, 444. https://doi:10.3389/fpsyg.2016.00444

Di Fabio, A., & Saklofske, D. H. (2014a). Comparing ability and self-report trait emotional intelligence, fluid intelligence, and personality traits in career decision. *Personality and Individual Differences, 64,* 174–178.

Di Fabio, A., & Saklofske, D. H. (2014b). Promoting individual resources: The challenge of trait emotional intelligence. *Personality and Individual Differences, 65,* 19–23.

Di Fabio, A., Maree, J. G., & Kenny, M. E. (2018). Development of the life project reflexivity scale: A new career intervention inventory. *Journal of Career Assessment*, 1–13. https://doi.org/10.1177/1069072718758065.

Di Fabio, A., Palazzeschi, L., & Bucci, O. (2017). In an unpredictable and changing environment: Intrapreneurial self-capital as a key resource for life satisfaction and flourishing. In G. Arcangeli, G. Giorgi, N. Mucci, J.-L. Bernaud, & A. Di Fabio (Eds.), Emerging and re-emerging organizational features, work transitions and occupational risk factors: The good, the bad, the right. An interdisciplinary perspective. Research Topic in *Frontiers in Psychology. Organizational Psychology*, *8*, 1819. https://doi:10.3389/fpsyg.2017.01819.

Douglass, R. P., Duffy, R. D., & Autin, K. L. (2016). Living a calling, nationality, and life satisfaction: A moderated, multiple mediator model. *Journal of Career Assessment, 24*(2), 253–269.

Duarte, M. E. (2004). O indivíduo e a organização: Perspectivas de desenvolvimento. [The individual and the organization: Perspectives of development]. *Psychologica (Extra-Série),* 549–557.

Duffy, R. D., Allan, B. A., England, J. W., Blustein, D. L., Autin, K. L., Douglass, R. P., … & Santos, E. J. (2017). The development and initial validation of the decent work scale. *Journal of counseling psychology*, *64*(2), 206.

Duffy, R. D., Blustein, D. L., Diemer, M. A., & Autin, K. L. (2016). The psychology of working theory. *Journal of Counseling Psychology, 63*(2), 127–148.

Duffy, R. D., Foley, P. F., Raque-Bodgan, T. L., Reid-Marks, L., Dik, B. J., Castano, M. C., et al. (2012). Counseling psychologists who view their careers as a calling: A qualitative study. *Journal of Career Assessment, 20*(3), 293–308.

Duffy, R. D., Torrey, C. L., Bott, E. M., Allan, B. A., & Schlosser, L. Z. (2013). Time management, passion, and collaboration: A qualitative study of highly research productive counseling psychologists. *The Counseling Psychologist, 41*(6), 881–917.

Guichard, J. (2004). Se faire soi. *L'Orientation Scolaire et Professionnelle, 33*(4), 499–533.

Guichard, J. (2005). Life-long self-construction. *International Journal for Educational and Vocational Guidance, 5,* 111–124.

Guichard, J. (2009). Self-constructing. *Journal of Vocational Behavior, 75,* 251–258.

Guichard, J. (2013, September). *Which paradigm for career and life designing interventions contributing to the development of a fairer world during the 21st century*. Lecture presented at the IAEVG International Conference, Montpellier, France.

Guichard, J., & Di Fabio, A. (2015, June). *How can career and life designing interventions contribute to a fair and sustainable development and to the implementation of decent work over the world?* Invited Keynote at the UNESCO Chair on Lifelong Guidance and Counseling International Conference "How can career and life designing interventions contribute to a fair and sustainable development and to the implementation of decent work over the world?" Florence 2015, University of Florence (Italy) and University of Wroclaw (Poland), Florence, Italy, 4–6 June 2015.

Guichard, J., Bangali, M., Cohen Scali, V., Pouyaud, J., & Robinet, M. L. (2016). *Concevoir et orienter sa vie: Les dialogues de conseil en life design*. Paris: Editions Qui plus est.

Hall, B. A., Halstead, M. E., & Taylor, T. R. (1992). *Manual for the administration of the Rothwell-Miller Interest Blank*. Pretoria, South Africa: HSRC.

Hartung, P. J. (2010). Practice and research in career counseling and development-2009. *Career Development Quarterly, 59,* 98–142.

Hartung, P. J. (2012). Career development in global context: History, status, and prospects. In M. Watson & M. McMahon (Eds.), *Career development: Global issues and challenges* (pp. 11–26). Hauppauge, NY: Nova Science.

Hartung, P. J. (2013). Career as story: Making the narrative turn. In W. B. Walsh, M. L. Savickas, & P. J. Hartung (Eds.), *Handbook of vocational psychology* (4th ed., pp. 33–52). New York, NY: Routledge.

Hartung, P. J., & Subich, L. M. (Eds.). (2011). *Developing self in work and career: Concepts, cases, and contexts*. Washington, DC: APA Books.

Holland, J. L. (1997). *Making vocational choices* (3rd ed.). Odessa, FL: Psychological Assessment Resources.

Holland, J. L., Powell, A. B., & Fritzsche, B. A. (1994). *The Self-directed search professional user's guide* (4th ed.). Odessa, FL: Psychological Assessment Resources.

Kenny, M. E., Blustein, D. L., & Meerkins, T. M. (2018). Integrating relational perspectives in career counseling practice. *The Career Development Quarterly, 66*(2), 135–148.

Maree, J. G. (2006). *Manual for the Career interest profile*. Randburg, South Africa: JvR Psychometrics.

Maree, J. G. (2010). *The Career Interest Profile* (3rd ed.). Randburg, South Africa: JvR Psychometrics.

Maree, J. G. (2013). *Counselling for career construction: Connecting life themes to construct life portraits. Turning pain into hope*. Rotterdam, The Netherlands: Sense.

Maree, J. G. (2014). Using life construction XE "Life Construction" counseling to harness reflexivity with a mid-career woman: a case study. In A. Di Fabio & J.-L. Bernaud (Eds.), *The construction of the identity in 21st century: A Festschrift for Jean Guichard* (pp. 157–168), New York, NY: Nova Science Publishers.

Maree, J. G. (Ed.). (2007). *Shaping the story: A guide to facilitating narrative career counseling*. Pretoria: Van Schaik.

Maree, J. G., & Di Fabio, A. (Eds.). (2015). *Exploring new horizons in career counselling: Turning challenges into opportunities*. Rotterdam, The Netherlands: Sense Publishers.

Maree, J. G., & Sommerville, J. (2008). Development of a post-modern career interest questionnaire. *Journal for Psychology in Africa, 17,* 125–130.

Maree, J. G. (2012). A (guided) meta-reflection theory of career counselling: A case study. *South African Journal of Higher Education, 26*(4), 661–669.

McMahon, M. (2010). Career counseling and storytelling: Constructing a 21st narrative for practice. In H. Ohlsson & H. Borg (Eds.), *Career development* (pp. 1–23). New York, NY: Nova Science.

McMahon, M., & Patton, W. (2002). Using qualitative assessment in career counseling. *International Journal for Educational and Vocational Guidance, 2,* 51–66.

McMahon, M., & Watson, M. (2010). Story telling: Moving from thin stories to thick and rich stories. In K. Maree (Ed.), *Career counselling: Methods that work* (pp. 53–63). Cape Town, South Africa: Yuta.

McMahon, M., & Watson, M. (2011). Career counselling: What's the story? In M. McMahon & M. Watson (Eds.), *Career counselling and constructivism: Elaboration of constructs* (pp. 13–24). New York: Nova Science.

Oyserman, D., Bybee, D., & Terry, K. (2006). Possible selves and academic outcomes: How and when possible selves impel action. *Journal of Personality and Social Psychology, 91,* 188–204.

Rehfuss, M. C. (2009). The future career autobiography: A narrative measure of career intervention effectiveness. *The Career Development Quarterly, 58*(1), 82–90.

Rehfuss, M., & Di Fabio, A. (2012). Validating the future career autobiography as a measure of narrative change. *Journal of Career Assessment, 20,* 452–462.

Savickas, M. L. (1995). Current theoretical issues in vocational psychology: Convergence, divergence, and schism. In W. B. Walsh & S. H. Osipow (Eds.), *Handbook of vocational psychology* (2nd ed., pp. 1–34). Hillsdale, NJ: Lawrence Erlbaum Associates.

Savickas, M. L. (1997). Career adaptability: An integrative construct for life-span, life-space theory. *The Career Development Quarterly, 45,* 247–259.

Savickas, M. L. (2001). Toward a comprehensive theory of career development: Disposition, concerns and narratives. In F. T. L. Leong & A. Barak (Eds.), *Contemporary models in vocational psychology: A volume in honor of Samuel H. Osipow* (pp. 295–320). Mahwah, NJ: Lawrence Erlbaum.

Savickas, M. L. (2005). The theory and practice of career construction. In S. D. Brown & R. W. Lent (Eds.), *Career development and counseling: Putting theory and research to work* (pp. 42–70). Hoboken, NJ: Wiley.

Savickas, M. L. (2007). Prologue reshaping the story of career counseling. In K. Maree (Ed.), *Shaping the story. A guide to facilitating narrative counseling* (pp. 1–3). Pretoria, South Africa: Van Schaik Publishers.

Savickas, M. L. (2013). *Life designing in 21st century*. Closing Conference at the IAEVG International Conference, Montpellier, France.

Savickas, M. L. (2015). *Life-design counseling manual*. Rootstown, OH: Author.

Savickas, M. L. (Ed.). (2011). *Career counseling*. Washington, DC: American Psychological Association.

Savickas, M. L., & Porfeli, E. J. (2012). Career adapt-abilities scale: Construction, reliability, and measurement equivalence across 13 countries. *Journal of Vocational Behavior, 80,* 661–673.

Savickas, M. L., Nota, L., Rossier, J., Dauwalder, J. P., Duarte, M. E., Guichard, J., … & Van Vianen, A. E. (2009). Life designing: A paradigm for career construction in the 21st century. *Journal of vocational behavior*, *75*(3), 239–250.

Severy, L. E. (2002). What's the story? Postmodern career counseling in student affairs. *Journal of College Student Development, 43*(1), 84–92.

World Medical Association [WMA]. (2013). *WMA Declaration of Helsinki – Ethical Principles for Medical Research Involving Human Subjects*. Available at: www.wma.net/en/30publications/10policies/b3/.

Chapter 9
Life Design Counseling Intervention: Two Case Studies on Italian Workers Using Career Construction Interview and LAQuA and CCIO as Qualitative Evaluation Tools

Letizia Palazzeschi, Allison Creed, Alessio Gori and Annamaria Di Fabio

Abstract This chapter describes two cases studies. The first case study regards a young male physiotherapist, graduated in France, who decided to move to Italy some months after graduation to find a job in his field of specialization. He was uncertain about his future career, and he did not know the best choice for him. He participated in a life design counseling intervention at the University of Florence where he was required to complete the Life Adaptability Qualitative Assessment (LAQuA) before and after the life design counseling intervention. The second case study is relative to a personnel director of a large company in the center of Italy who participated in a narrative career counseling intervention and filled two new qualitative instruments before and after the intervention: the Life Adaptability Qualitative Assessment (LAQuA) and the Career Counseling Innovative Outcomes (CCIO). The results are discussed for the two studies, underlining the importance of using life design counseling intervention in helping people to understand themselves more deeply, identify their actual objectives, and the necessary steps in order to develop their career and life paths.

L. Palazzeschi · A. Gori · A. Di Fabio (✉)
Department of Education and Psychology (Psychology Section),
University of Florence, Florence, Italy
e-mail: adifabio@psico.unifi.it

A. Creed
School of Linguistics, Adult, and Specialist Education,
University of Southern Queensland, Toowoomba, Australia

© Springer Nature Switzerland AG 2018
A. Di Fabio and J.-L. Bernaud (eds.), *Narrative Interventions in Post-modern Guidance and Career Counseling*, https://doi.org/10.1007/978-3-319-98300-4_9

9.1 Introduction

In the twenty-first century, there is an increasing need to design and implement new approaches in the field of guidance and career counseling (Savickas, 2011) to enable people to timely and adequately respond to the demands of the postmodern society. In a scenario characterized by globalization, requirement of digital skills, constant changes, and reorganizations, people need to develop their knowledge and skills to deal successfully with continuing challenges (Guichard, 2013; Savickas, 2011). New theoretical models and modalities of intervention are required to encourage clients to examine possible career and life paths (Blustein, 2006, 2011; Cochran, 1997; Brott, 2004; McMahon & Watson, 2010, 2011; Oyserman, Bybee, & Terry, 2006; Severy, 2002). The fundamental shift from career development to career management (Savickas, 2013) to life management (Guichard, 2013) in the postmodern era focuses on the responsibility of individuals, and no longer of organizations (Duffy et al., 2012; Duffy, Torrey, Bott, Allan, & Schlosser, 2013; Duarte, 2004), to explore possible selves and external opportunities in order to understand different professional and personal trajectories. These skills help people to navigate potentially unpredictable and chaotic pathways (Savickas, 2011), identifying their actual objectives and the strategies to reach them. The importance of awareness of choice and particularly in knowing how to build our professional and personal life represents fundamental skills in this current uncertain era (Savickas, 2011).

In addition, researchers and practitioners are called to go beyond the positivist approach in guidance and career counseling, related to personality traits and sequential stages of development, and to embrace a hermeneutic approach related to the involvement of individuals in a process of establishing goals and subsequent actions (Blustein, 2006, 2011; Savickas, 2011; Valach & Young, 2004).

Fundamental theoretical frameworks for research and intervention are the Career Construction Theory (Savickas, 2001, 2005), the Self-Construction Theory (Guichard, 2004, 2005, 2008), and the recent evolution in Life Construction Theory (Guichard, 2013). The specificity between these theories can be indicated by two paradigmatic questions. For the Career Construction Theory, the questions are: "What is the meaning of my professional career in my life?" and "How can I use the work role to manifest and advance my life story?" This theory highlights modalities by which the individuals construct their life through career, seeking to unify the present and to construct the future through a reorganization of the past (Guichard, 2013; Savickas, 2013). The Self-Constructing Theory is instead oriented to a wider reference question: "What should give meaning to my life?" This theory does not focus on career construction—its scope is more general. People construct their life "seeking to unify the present through the development of future possibilities" (Guichard, 2013; Savickas, 2013).

Counselors are thereby called to help people give meaning to their professional and personal life through the construction of their own self as a story (Savickas, 2005, 2011). Counselors help clients construct, deconstruct, co-construct, and reconstruct their own stories, as clients are stimulated to reinterpret memories, to analyze present experiences, and to identify future aspirations. Clients' narratives allow them to discover life themes that can bring cohesion and give direction to their lives (Savickas, 2011). Stories become a "biographical" bridge allowing people to unify their plural identities (Guichard, 2013) and facilitate contact with internal and external complexity to positively face frequent transitions (Savickas, 2011). It is increasingly important to consider the connection between work and the other aspects of life (Guichard, 2004, 2009; Guichard & Di Fabio, 2015) as the postmodern era is characterized by a de-regulation of the paths and a proliferation of the directions (Guichard, Bangali, Cohen Scali, Pouyaud, Robinet, 2016; Guichard & Di Fabio, 2015; Savickas, 2013).

The passage from the concept of career project to life project is emblematic of the features of the current society (Di Fabio, 2014a). In terms of the narrative perspective of the twenty-first century (Busacca & Rehfuss, 2016), career counseling consists in a process that helps clients to construct their career and life through narration; stories are guide to give meaning to their experiences, understand them, and choose how to proceed (Savickas, 2011). Narratives allow identity construction, shaping individuals' stories (Maree, 2007; Savickas, 2011), identifying and connecting life themes to construct life portraits (Maree, 2013; Savickas, 2011) through their complex contexts and environments (Savickas, 2001, 2005, 2011, 2015). Life design counseling interventions for the twenty-first century can enable clients to recognize a system of meanings (Di Fabio & Blustein, 2016) according to which they reflect on their experiences, and more in general on the nature of their life, its value and purposes (Bernaud, 2013; Bernaud, Lhotellier, Sovet, Arnoux-Nicolas, & Pelayo, 2016). The identification of life meaning is important as it can give order and consistency (Reker, 2000), coherence, direction, significance, and belonging on one's own way (Di Fabio & Maree, 2016; Schnell, Höge, & Pollet, 2013), and it is associated with the sustainability of the project (Di Fabio, 2017). Life design counselors enable clients to write and rewrite their stories, modifying them according to the perceived changes of their needs, interests, and experiences (Savickas, 2011) in order to build a successful life (Savickas, 2004, 2011, 2015).

According to this background, the Career Adaptability construct is essential. It regards the ability of individuals to anticipate transitions and their future in a changing society (Savickas, 2011). The Career Adaptability construct has four core dimensions: Concern, Control, Curiosity, and Confidence (Savickas, 2001; Savickas & Porfeli, 2012).

1. Concern: this dimension regards the way in which people are oriented toward their own future. It also refers to the planning and the presence of a certain level of optimism regarding the future.
2. Control: this dimension regards the level to which people take the responsibility for and feel capable of constructing of their own careers, that is, the ability to make decisions about themselves autonomously.

3. Curiosity: this dimension regards the ability to analyze many working opportunities present in the belonging context relative to one's own aptitudes and interests. This dimension allows individuals to enter the working environment as it permits an adequate in-depth exploration of both their own aptitudes and their possible connection with the possibilities present in the labor market.
4. Confidence: this dimension regards the trust in the self, relating to the ability of pursuing one's own aspirations and professional objectives even in the face of obstacles and barriers that could be encountered in a career.

Within the current narrative perspective in career counseling (Hartung, 2010, 2012, 2013; Maree, 2007; Rehfuss, 2009; Savickas, 1995, 1997, 2001, 2005, 2011), it is highlighted the importance of new instruments to evaluate the effectiveness of life design counseling interventions (Di Fabio, 2012; Di Fabio & Maree, 2013; Rehfuss, 2009; Rehfuss & Di Fabio, 2012). Due to the limitation of traditional quantitative instruments in evaluating change in self-narratives in career counseling for the twenty-first century, it seems crucial to develop and implement innovative instruments (Blustein, Kenna, Murphy, Devoy, & DeWine, 2005; Rehfuss, 2009; Rehfuss & Di Fabio, 2012). Qualitative evaluation of the effectiveness of life design counseling interventions is strongly endorsed as such interventions are basically narrative interventions (Di Fabio, 2015).

The present chapter discusses two case studies.

9.2 First Case Study

9.2.1 Aim of the Case Study

The first case study is relative to a young male physiotherapist who, at the time of the study, had just moved from Paris to Florence in order to begin a career in his field of specialization. He was confused about the kind of professional he wanted to become and the city where he wished to live and work. He participated in a life design counseling intervention and filled a recent innovative qualitative instrument before and after the intervention.

The case study described the usefulness of a life design counseling intervention in helping the research participant to understand himself more deeply through identifying his actual objectives and the necessary steps to develop his career and life paths.

This case study was guided by the following research questions.

- How the life design counseling intervention was applied to the case of a young man graduated in physical therapy in France who moved to Italy to begin a career in his field of specialization?
- How did the life design counseling help the participant to increase the awareness of himself, to identify clearly his real objectives and the next steps, to develop his career and life paths?

9.3 Materials and Methods

9.3.1 Participant and Context

The male participant in this study, Simone (a pseudonym), was a young male physiotherapist, graduated in France, who decided to move from Paris to Italy some months after graduation to find a job in his field of specialization. He was uncertain about his future career, and he did not know how to make the best choice for himself. He chose to attend a postgraduate course at the University of Florence mainly to develop his communication and coaching skills in order to establish better relationships with his clients. During this course, he participated voluntarily in a life design counseling intervention at the University of Florence to better understand himself, his real purposes, and his resources in order to accurately design his career project. He needed help to resolve some issues such as those concerning the possible city to live and work and possible type of professional to become.

9.3.2 Qualitative Instruments

9.3.2.1 Life Adaptability Qualitative Assessment (LAQuA)

The Life Adaptability Qualitative Assessment (LAQuA, Di Fabio, 2015) is a new qualitative instrument developed to qualitatively evaluate the effectiveness of life design counseling interventions. Specifically, this instrument allows the assessment of adaptability, evaluating change or lack of change in individuals' life narratives before and after the intervention. The LAQuA comprises 12 written questions, and each dimension (Concern, Control, Curiosity, and Confidence) of the Career Adapt-Abilities Inventory—International Version 2.0 (Savickas & Porfeli, 2012)—has three questions. The LAQuA's 12 written questions are given in the following:

Concern: (1a) What does it mean to you to be oriented toward your future? (1b) Do you think you are oriented toward your future? (1c) Why?
Control: (2a) What does it mean to you to take responsibility for your future? (2b) Do you think you do take responsibility for your future? (2c) Why?
Curiosity: (3a) What does it mean to you to be curious about your own future? (3b) Do you think you are curious about your future? (3c) Why?
Confidence: (4a) What does it mean to you to have confidence in your own ability to build your future? (4b) Do you think you have confidence in your ability to build your future? (4c) Why?

In this study, the LAQuA compared the narratives produced by the individuals as answers to 12 questions before and after the intervention. The comparison and analysis of the narratives were realized using 24 qualitative indicators relating to each of the four dimensions of Career Adaptability (Concern, Control, Curiosity, and Confidence):

Anticipating, Predicting, Equipping, Involved, Strategic, and Aware (of choices and transitions to be made) for the Concern dimension of Career Adaptability.

Positive attitude, Autonomous, Conscientious, Assertive, Responsible, and Honest for the Control dimension of Career Adaptability.

Investigative, Developing, Inquisitive, Recognizing/Discovering, Inquiring, and Searching for the Curiosity dimension of Career Adaptability.

Productive, Mindful, Innovative, Capable, Resilient, and Able to work out answers for the Confidence dimension of Career Adaptability.

These qualitative indicators are organized in the LAQuA Coding System into five qualitative analysis change categories. The LAQuA Coding System allows the following five levels of reflexivity change or no change related to the four dimensions of Career Adaptability (Concern, Control, Curiosity, and Confidence).

5. Increased reflexivity: it has two different forms (Type I and Type II). Type I: in narratives produced post-intervention, there is/are an identical descriptor/s present in narratives produced pre-intervention but with more in-depth reflexivity. Type II: in narratives produced pre-intervention, there is a lack of descriptors whereas in narratives produced post-intervention a descriptor appears. So, it emerges an increase in reflexivity in the same descriptor/s (Type I) or an increase in reflexivity with the manifestation of a descriptor/s (Type II).
6. Revised reflexivity: in narratives produced post-intervention, there is a loss of the previous descriptor/s present in narratives produced pre-intervention and the manifestation of new different descriptor/s. So, there is a new concentration on a different facet/s of the specific Career Adaptability dimension.
7. Open reflexivity: in narratives produced post-intervention, there is/are the same identical descriptor/s present in narratives produced pre-intervention and with the same level of reflexivity, but new descriptor/s also emerges/e in addition. So, the previous focus is preserved, and there is also new awareness of a different facet/s of the specific Career Adaptability dimension.
8. Enhanced reflexivity: in narratives produced post-intervention, there is/are identical descriptor/s present in narratives produced pre-intervention but with more in-depth reflexivity, and a new descriptor/s also appears in addition. So, we have an expansion in the complexity regarding the dimension because we have both a depth increase in reflexivity in the same descriptor/s and also a diversification of a different facet/s of the specific Career Adaptability dimension.
9. No change: it has two different forms (Type I and Type II). Type I: in the narratives produced post-intervention, there is/are the same identical descriptor/s present as in the narratives produced pre-intervention and with the same level of reflexivity regarding the descriptor/s. Type II: in the narratives produced pre-intervention, there is a lack of a descriptor/s, and in the narratives produced post-intervention, there is still a lack of descriptors regarding the specific Career Adaptability dimension.

Thus, the LAQuA is an innovative instrument that allows the detection of change comparing narratives pre- and post-intervention in relation to the four Career Adaptability dimensions (Concern, Control, Curiosity, and Confidence).

9.3.3 *Procedure*

The LAQuA was administered before and after a life design counseling intervention (Savickas, 2010, 2011) by a psychologist trained in the administration of this qualitative instrument. Three independent, trained expert reviewers (raters) compared the participant's initial and final answers to the written questions of the LAQuA. An interrater reliability analysis using the Kappa statistic was realized to identify the level of consistency among the raters.

The study was carried out observing the requirements of privacy and informed consent in Italian law (Law Decree DL-196/2003) and the ethical standards for research of the Declaration of Helsinki revised in Fortaleza (World Medical Association [WMA], 2013), followed and approved by the Department of Education and Psychology of the University of Florence (Italy).

Simone took part in a life design counseling intervention that used the framework of the *Career Construction Interview* (Savickas, 2010, 2011), divided into four 1-day session (eight hours a day) in a group context using the modality of the power of the audience (Di Fabio & Maree, 2012). The aim of the life design counseling intervention is to facilitate the participant exploration of his professional and life paths.

9.3.4 *Criteria for Quality Assurance*

The following quality assurance criteria were applied to ensure the trustworthiness of the research findings with regard to methods of data gathering and data analysis: credibility, confirmability, transferability, and dependability (Maree, 2012). Credibility of the data refers to the significance and credibility of the results for participants and readers (Maree, 2012) and was established in the current study through review and verification of the data by external researchers. Confirmability refers to the objectivity and accuracy of the data and procedures, with results being derived from the participants and the research conditions rather than from the opinions and biases of the researcher (Maree, 2012). Confirmability was assessed by external researchers who judged whether the methods and procedures of this study were sufficiently clear and detailed to permit verification. Transferability refers to the extent to which the findings can be generalized to other contexts (Maree, 2012). In the present study, transferability was determined through a thorough and accurate description of the participant's situation and context and the research methods. This detailed information permits other researchers to evaluate the applicability of the findings to other clients and contexts. Dependability refers to the stability, consistency, and degree of control in the research process and methods (Maree, 2012). Dependability was assessed in this study by the examination of the participant's narratives by three independent expert raters.

9.4 Results

In this paragraph, the participant's answers to the written questions of the LAQuA are reported as well as the results of the analysis achieved through the LAQuA qualitative indicators and the different degrees of reflexivity (Increased Reflexivity, Revised Reflexivity, Open Reflexivity, Enhanced Reflexivity, and No Change).

The participant's answer to the first LAQuA question before the life design counseling intervention was: "*To me, to be oriented toward my future means to realize my actions with a general idea of my future, a long-term macro-objective. To me it is important to understand what I want to do in my future because my current choices can influence it*" (qualitative descriptor: Predicting); and after the life design counseling intervention, it was: "*To me, to be oriented toward my future means to understand the current actions, paying attention to the impacts they will have in the future. I think that anchoring to the present is important to build an overview of my future. I decided to move from Paris to Florence because I want to begin to work as a physiotherapist for an important sport organization and/or have a private practice*" (identical qualitative descriptor but more in-depth reflexivity: Predicting. (Increased reflexivity: in the narratives produced after the life design counseling intervention, there were identical descriptors, but they were presented with more in-depth reflexivity.)

The participant's answer to the second LAQuA question before the life design counseling intervention was: "*To me, to take responsibility for my future means knowing that I'm responsible for my actions and that these actions will shape my future*" (qualitative descriptor: Conscientious); after the life design counseling intervention, it was: "*To me, to take responsibility for my future means that I have the responsibility of my actions to shape my future*" (identical qualitative descriptor: Conscientious); "*The person who is responsible for my future is me. I think and act on the basis of my purposes. Achieving successes or failures depend on me*" (new, different qualitative descriptor: Responsible) (Open reflexivity (O): in the narratives produced after the life design counseling intervention, there is an identical descriptor/s—with the same level of reflexivity in presenting the descriptor—plus a new, different descriptor/s.)

The participant's answer to the third LAQuA question before the life design counseling intervention was: "*To me, to be curious about my future means attempting to do different experiences and observing different contexts and ways to do things*" (qualitative descriptor: Recognizing/Developing); after the life design counseling intervention, it was: "*To me, to be curious about my future means asking to myself the right questions about what I really want to do, how to do it, what I'll do to get it and where I will live and work*" (new, different qualitative descriptor: Inquiring). (Revised reflexivity (R): in the narratives produced after the life design counseling intervention, the previous descriptor/s has disappeared, and a new, different descriptor/s has appeared.)

The participant's answer to the fourth LAQuA question before the life design counseling intervention was: "*To me, to have confidence in my own abilities to build my future means understand that I have to work hard to improve my competences to realize my project. Anyway I really don't' know if it is better to create a career in Florence or to move to another city, maybe outside Italy, in order to identify possibilities to become physiotherapist for VIP person in the sport world*" (qualitative descriptor: Capable); after the life design counseling intervention, it was: "*To me, to have confidence in my own abilities to build my future means to work hard to develop my competences for my future*" (identical qualitative descriptor but more in-depth reflexivity: Capable); "*It is important for me to do a balance between positive and critical personal aspects: I can solve my problems counting on my strengths and ameliorate my limitations. It is important for me to make various experiences as physiotherapist in Florence, in my own private practice as an independent consultant. Providing my services for high-level sport organizations, such as in the motoring field, could be useful to improve my knowledge and skills. In particular I understood that I want to live and work in Florence, traveling sometimes abroad to take care of athletes*" (new, different qualitative descriptor: Able to work out answers. (Enhanced reflexivity (E): in the narratives produced after the life design counseling intervention, there is an identical descriptor/s but presented with more in-depth reflexivity plus a new, different descriptor/s.)

9.5 Discussions

This case study showed the value of a life design counseling intervention (Savickas, 2010, 2011) in helping a client to better understand himself, identify his actual objectives and the necessary steps to achieve them, in order to develop his career and life paths. Adequate narrative interventions can thereby address needs of clients who seem at risk of making choices incongruent with their actual values, interests, meanings, and aspirations (Di Fabio & Bernaud, 2014; Di Fabio & Maree, 2013). Timely life design interventions can be very useful as professional support for vulnerable people (Di Fabio & Palazzeschi, 2016), especially young, who are taking responsibility of both their career and life (Guichard, 2009; Savickas, 2011). Life design counseling intervention (Savickas, 2010) is specially aimed at helping people to successfully face continuous transitions and complex situations during the writing of the next chapters of their life in order to achieve positive and satisfying outcomes (Savickas, 2011).

The findings of this case study can be verified through the analysis of the narratives before and after the life design counseling intervention (Savickas, 2010,

2011) detected with the LAQuA (Di Fabio, 2015). The analysis of the answers to the LAQuA questions indicated changes in the participant's reflexivity referring to adaptability before and after the life design counseling intervention. The level of reflexivity in the four dimensions of adaptability (Concern, Control, Confidence, and Curiosity) appeared to have increased. In relation to Concern, the participant underlined the importance of clarifying his objectives and trying to realize them, connecting the present with the future. In relation to Control, the participant highlighted the importance of taking responsibility for shaping his future in order to achieve successes. In relation to Curiosity, the participant realized the importance of asking himself the right questions to envision meaningful work path. In relation to Confidence, the participant understood the importance of the awareness of his resources, counting on them to achieve his objectives.

9.6 Second Case Study

9.6.1 Aim of the Case Study

The present chapter discusses the case of Marta (a pseudonym), a personnel director of a large company in the center of Italy, who participated in a narrative career counseling intervention because she wanted to understand how to develop her career and life paths. This case study was guided by the following research questions.

- How the narrative career counseling intervention was applied to the case of a personnel director of a big company in the center of Italy?
- How did the narrative career counseling intervention help the participant to increase the awareness of herself, to identify clearly her objectives and the next steps, to develop his career and life paths?

Marta was specializing in foreign languages, and she requested to participate in the narrative career counseling intervention because she wanted to improve some personal strengths and to understand her professional and life paths. Marta is 42 years old and comes from a small town in the center of Italy, where her family still lives. She has been living in a medium-sized city in central Italy where her company is located.

9.7 Materials and Methods

For the qualitative evaluation of the effectiveness of intervention, two qualitative instruments have been used: the *Life Adaptability Qualitative Assessment* (Di Fabio, 2015) and the *Career Counseling Innovative Outcomes* (CCIO, Di Fabio, 2016).

Life Adaptability Qualitative Assessment (LAQuA)
The *LAQuA* (2016) is a qualitative instrument developed for the evaluation of the effectiveness of life design counseling interventions. It was described in details above in the chapter for the first case study.

Career Counseling Innovative Outcomes (CCIO)
The CCIO (Di Fabio, 2016) evaluates the outcomes of life design counseling interventions. This measure was conceptualized from the Innovative Moments Coding System (IMCS) used in psychotherapy (Gonçalves, Ribeiro, Mendes, Matos, & Santos, 2011) and was conceptualized to be applied to life design counseling (Cardoso, Silva, Gonçalves, & Duarte, 2014). Whereas the IMCS (Cardoso et al., 2014; Gonçalves et al., 2011) is used to monitor the process of change during psychotherapeutic intervention, the CCIO is instead a measure developed to elicit and analyze specific narratives produced before and after life design counseling.

The CCIO comprises seven questions developed on the basis of the narrative paradigm (Savickas, 2011. These questions provide access to the client's narrative expression at two points in time and allow comparison of how the client organizes these narrations before and after the narrative intervention. The intervention itself seeks to recognize dissonances in clients' occupational plots and reunite them with the main theme of their life stories. The life design intervention involves gaining equilibrium between occupational plot and career theme through a new equilibrium balanced on narrative truth, which opens new pathways that previously were neither perceived nor possible. The new equilibrium enables clients to carry forward their life project more consciously and with more intentionality in shaping the next scenario. The seven CCIO questions are located within the narrative paradigm (Savickas, 2011). They comply with the principle of the emergence of narratives through stimuli and thereby begin the search to understand one's own life. Each question enables the emergence of a specific narrative anchored to specific facets of the narrative paradigm (Savickas, 2011). Accordingly, the CCIO contains seven questions, each modeled after a specific CCI question.

Question 1: In which ways can this intervention be (was this intervention) useful to you? This question is anchored in the first question of the CCI because it aims to reveal the client's presenting problem and basis for requesting the intervention. It also reveals what the client expects to get from the intervention. The first question elicits the client's discourse on the initial situation and the complicating action that leads to the entanglement, or the beginning of the conflict that is the basis of the narrative tension. It provides access to the client's representation of the adversities prompting the client to seek the intervention, resulting from the tension they generated.

Question 2: What are your main useful resources? This question elicits a narrative about how clients represent the personal and contextual strengths that enable their success in navigating the difficult passage of life being faced and about the resources that clients perceive can advance their identities and help them write a new chapter in their life story (Savickas, 2011). The question brings out the client's discourse on the resources perceived to venture toward a transforming action of change in the initial situation and resolution of the narrative tension.

Question 3: What are the main obstacles you encounter? This question elicits the client's narrative about his or her perceptions of the obstacles to be overcome for his or her success in navigating the difficult passage of life being faced. The question evokes a narrative about the obstacles that hinder the client's identity development (Savickas, 2011).

Question 4: Who do you think can be useful to you? This question is oriented toward bringing out the client's narrative about his or her perception in specific reference to the people who can provide support to deal with the transition.

Question 5: What do you think can be useful to you? This question is oriented toward bringing out the client's narrative about his or her perception in specific reference to the means that can be useful in dealing with the transition.

Question 6: What are the main challenges you face? This question is oriented toward evoking the client's narratives about the challenges he or she perceives before the intervention. The main challenges are related to the principle that offers the client the capacity to develop new strategies for life planning, learning, and personal growth. These challenges provide the inspiration to help the client become who he or she wants to become and to write a new chapter in his or her life story (Savickas, 2011). In contrast to Question 3, which is centered on obstacles with a negative connotation, Question 6 focuses on challenges with a positive connotation. If obstacles are problematic matters, on the contrary, challenges are framed as opportunities.

Question 7: What are the main objectives you are hoping to achieve? This question is oriented toward bringing out narratives about future goals, from where the individual is now to where the individual wants to end up. The narrative elicited allows the counselor access to how the client perceived these goals before the intervention. Clients need goals to become something more than they are now; therefore, it is a question that refers to the character arc, as growth in the transformation of needs into goals. This question generates information from the client about what is important to write the next chapter of his or her life story. The narrative data gleaned from this question reveal what the client thinks he or she needs to become who he or she wants to become. Question 7 is focused on explaining something that is also linked with what already emerged through Question 1 through a specific narrative. Question 7 brings out the client's discourse on the object of perceived value, from which the client feels disjointed, and where he or she wants to direct his or her energy to resolve the narrative tension.

The narratives elicited by these seven questions are coded using a system of five categories inspired by Gonçalves et al. (2011). Action refers to actions or particular behaviors related to solving problems; Reflection is composed of two different types (Type 1 Reflection refers to getting away from the problem[s], and Type II Reflection is focused on change); Protest is divided into two different types (Type 1

Protest is a critical analysis of the problems, and Type II Protest is related to the development of a new perspective on the problems); Reconceptualization implies a metacognitive narrative of the process; and Performing Change implies access to different scopes and project for the individual. Gonçalves et al. (2011) apply the coding categories to the verbal responses a client makes during the counseling process. In the present application, the five categories to assess the outcomes of counseling have been used not to monitor the process of change during the career counseling intervention but to evaluate the outcomes of the narrative career counseling intervention by comparing the narratives of the participants before and after the intervention.

9.7.1 Procedure and Data Analysis

The LAQuA and the CCIO were administered before and after the narrative career counseling intervention by a psychologist trained in the administration of qualitative instruments.

Regarding the LAQuA, the narratives produced by Marta as answers to 12 questions before and after the intervention have been compared by three independently trained experts in career counseling. The comparison and analysis of the narratives were done using qualitative indicators relating to each of the four dimensions of Career Adaptability (Concern, Control, Curiosity, and Confidence), organized in the LAQuA Coding System permits the detection of change for each dimension of Career Adaptability at different levels of reflexivity (Increased Reflexivity, Revised Reflexivity, Open Reflexivity, Enhanced Reflexivity, and No Change).

With regard to the CCIO, Marta's initial and subsequent responses to the seven narrative written questions were paired for narrative comparison by three independently trained experts in career counseling. Five steps were carried out in the process of coding innovative moments: (a) training of the raters; (b) consensual definition of the problems by the three raters; (c) identification of innovative moments, defining their onset and offset; (d) categorization of previously identified innovative moments in terms of type; and (e) categorization of previously identified innovative moments in terms of emergence (Gonçalves et al., 2011). An interrater reliability analysis using the Kappa statistic was performed to determine consistency among the raters for both the LAQuA and the CCIO.

The study was carried out observing the requirements of privacy and informed consent in Italian law (Law Decree DL-196/2003) and the ethical standards for research of the Declaration of Helsinki revised in Fortaleza (World Medical Association [WMA], 2013).

Marta took part in a narrative career counseling intervention that used the framework of the *Career Construction Interview* (Savickas, 2010, 2011), divided into four 1-day sessions (eight hours a day) in a group context using the modality of the power of the audience (Di Fabio & Maree, 2012). The aim of the narrative career counseling intervention is to increase self-awareness and the awareness of one's own interests, professional values, aspirations, life themes, to construct autonomously one's own career and life projects (Di Fabio, Maree, & Kenny, in press).

9.7.2 *Criteria for Quality Assurance*

As for the first case study, the following quality assurance criteria were applied in order to fundamentally guarantee the trustworthiness of the research outcomes using different modalities for the data collection and analysis: credibility, confirmability, transferability, and dependability in the data collection and analysis process (Maree, 2012).

9.8 Results

The participant's responses to the written questions of the LAQuA and the CCIO before and after the narrative career counseling intervention are presented in this paragraph.

9.8.1 *LAQuA Results*

Below, the participant's answers to the four core questions of the LAQuA are reported as well as the results of the analysis realized through the LAQuA qualitative indicators and the different levels of reflexivity (Increased Reflexivity, Revised Reflexivity, Open Reflexivity, Enhanced Reflexivity, and No Change).

The participant's response to the first LAQuA set of questions before the narrative career counseling intervention was: "*To me, to be oriented toward my future means to reflect carefully on my current choices because they could influence my future*" (qualitative descriptor: Predicting); and after the narrative career counseling intervention, it was: "*To me, to be oriented toward my future means to acquire now a greater self-awareness particularly about my career because to construct my working future it is important to take today some important decisions. If I wait too much, it may be too late*" (identical qualitative descriptor but more in-depth reflexivity: Predicting); (Open reflexivity (O): in the narratives produced after the narrative career counseling intervention, there were identical descriptors, and with the same level of reflexivity, but a new descriptor appeared in addition.)

The participant's response to the second LAQuA set of questions before the narrative career counseling intervention was: "*To take responsibility for my future means to be actor/constructor of my future*" (qualitative descriptor: Responsible); after the narrative career counseling intervention, it was: "*To take responsibility for my future means to be actor and maker of my future. I can only count on myself if I really want to change something in my work and in my life*" (identical qualitative descriptor but more in-depth reflexivity: Responsible) *and "To take responsibility for my future means also to think of being able to completely take responsibility for my actions*" (new, different qualitative descriptor: *Conscientious).* (Enhanced reflexivity (E): in the narratives produced after the narrative career counseling intervention, there is an identical descriptor/s but presented with more in-depth reflexivity plus a new, different descriptor/s).

The participant's responses to the third LAQuA set of questions before the narrative career counseling intervention was: "*To me, to be curious about my future means learning and doing new things*" (qualitative descriptor: Developing); after the narrative career counseling intervention, it was: "*To be curious about my future means looking for opportunities for learning and doing new things because I have the necessity to grown in my work*" (identical qualitative descriptor but more in-depth reflexivity: Developing) "*because I was always curious about the different opportunities that are offered to me*" (new, different qualitative descriptor: Searching); (Enhanced reflexivity (E): in the narratives produced after the narrative career counseling intervention, there is an identical descriptor/s but presented with more in-depth reflexivity plus a new, different descriptor/s.)

The participant's response to the fourth LAQuA set of questions before the narrative career counseling intervention was: "*To me, to have confidence in my own abilities means believing that have abilities to face with the challenges and the obstacles I can encounter in the future*" (qualitative descriptor: Resilient); after the narrative career counseling intervention, it was: "*To me, to have confidence in my own abilities means believing that working hard I can realize my projects*" (new, different qualitative descriptors: Capable). (Revised reflexivity (R): in the narratives produced after the life construction intervention, the previous descriptor/s has disappeared, and a new, different descriptor/s has appeared; besides, the confidence in the ability has decreased, but the awareness has increased.)

9.8.2 CCIO Results

Below are shown the participant's responses to the seven questions of the CCIO before and after the narrative career counseling intervention as well as the results of the analysis in terms of the five categories (Action, Reflection, Protest, Reconceptualization, and Performing Change) of the CCIO Coding System (Di Fabio, 2016).

Marta's response to the first CCIO question (*How this intervention can be useful for you*?) before the narrative career counseling intervention was: "*This intervention can be useful for me to understand how to build my future career path in a stimulating way*"; after the narrative career counseling intervention, it was: "*This intervention was useful to me to stimulate my reflexivity and to push me to act in order to satisfy my self-realization needs"* (Reflection Type II).

The participant's response to the second CCIO question before the narrative career counseling intervention was: "*I think that my main resource that can help me is curiosity*"; after the narrative career counseling intervention, it was: "*Actually, I think that my main resources that can help me are: creativity; determination; persistence. These resources can help me to introduce innovations in my organization, introducing new practices in human resources management*" (Reflection Type II).

The participant's response to the third CCIO question before the narrative career counseling intervention was: "*My principal obstacles are: living in a small city with little possibilities to succeed in career and only a few interesting entrepreneurial realities*"; after the narrative career counseling intervention, it was: "*If before the intervention I thought that my principal obstacle was living in a small city with little possibilities for my career, now I understand that in reality the obstacles are mainly in myself and not in the context. In fact, my principal obstacles are: poor projectuality; poor capacity to transform a crisis in opportunities*" (Reconceptualisation). "*I'm tired of me to say from others what is best for me. I want to find a solution to my problems and working to improve my situation to be more satisfied*" (Protest Type II).

The participant's response to the fourth CCIO question before the narrative career counseling intervention was: "*I think it could be useful to me a career counseling professional*"; after the narrative career counseling intervention, it was: "*If before the intervention I thought that a professional could be useful to me to give me advice on my future, now I think that also confronting with my family and/or my partner could help me*" (Reconceptualization IM).

The participant's response to the fifth CCIO question before the narrative career counseling was: "*I think that it can be really useful to me new stimuli and more money*"; after the narrative career counseling intervention, it was: "*I think that it can be really useful to me best personal accomplishments and personal satisfaction, continuing to work in her organizations but introducing innovation in resource management*" (Performing Change IM).

The participant's response to the sixth CCIO question before the narrative career counseling intervention was: "*The main challenge that I feel I'm facing at the moment is to understand how to change my career*"; after the narrative career counseling intervention, it was: "*The main challenge that I feel I'm facing at the moment is to be more active/proactive to reach my personal goals and change my career. I'm attending a post graduated course and I would like to find other specialized courses to update my competences in human resources management and to apply them in my organization because only in this way I could be realized*" (Action IM).

The participant's response to the seventh CCIO question before the narrative career counseling intervention was: "*The main objective that I hope is to obtain a more autonomous work, into an organization less structured. I would like to learn new things*"; after the narrative career counseling intervention, it was: "*The main objective that I hope is to improve my competence in human resources management and also my relational competence to change my work context*" (Action IM).

9.9 Discussion

This case study showed the effectiveness of a narrative career counseling intervention using a preventive approach (Di Fabio & Kenny, 2015, 2016; Di Fabio & Palazzeschi, 2016; Di Fabio & Saklofske, 2014a, b; Di Fabio et al., 2016; Kenny & Hage, 2009; Hage et al., 2007) toward people with unsatisfied jobs. Helping people that experience dissatisfaction with their work means promoting positive career outcomes and decency in their lives (Di Fabio & Blustein, 2016). Narrative career counseling is an intervention developed to help people cope with transitions and design new chapters in their lives (Savickas, 2011). In this case study, the evolution of the participant could be seen through the analysis of the narratives before and after the narrative career counseling intervention by the means of the LAQuA (Di Fabio, 2015) and the CCIO (Di Fabio, 2016).

The analysis of the responses to the LAQuA questions showed changes in the participant's reflexivity regarding adaptability before and after the narrative career counseling intervention. The level of reflexivity in the four dimensions of adaptability (Concern, Control, Confidence, and Curiosity) seemed to be increased. In relation to Concern, the participant highlighted the recognition that current choices can influence her future. In relation to Control, the participant underscored the significance of taking responsibility for her actions regarding the future and the importance of counting on herself to realize her aims. In relation to Curiosity, the participant realized the importance of looking for opportunities for learning and growing and being curious about new opportunities. In relation to Confidence, the participant showed trust in herself and in her capacity to overcome obstacles.

The analysis of the five categories of the CCIO (Action, Reflection, Protest, Reconceptualization, and Performing Change) showed changes in the participant's narratives before and after the narrative career counseling intervention. These results can be considered in terms of Action, as the participant would like to update her competences to introduce innovative practices in human resource management in her organization. The results indicated changes in terms of Reflection, referring to the importance to *stimulate her reflexivity and to push her to act in order to satisfy her self-realization needs*. Moreover, the results of the analysis of the narratives described a change in terms of Protest. She wants to autonomously find a solution to her problems and work to improve her situation to be more satisfied. The results of the analysis of the narratives also showed a Reconceptualization regarding the transition between two positions (past before the narrative career counseling intervention and present after the narrative career counseling intervention) (Di Fabio, 2016; Gonçalves et al., 2011). The participant moved from an initial position where she believed that her principal obstacle was *living in a small city with little possibilities for her career to a new position where she understood that the real obstacle is her poor projectuality and not the context.* Finally, the results of the analysis of the narratives indicated Performing Change since the participant recognized new aims in obtaining personal accomplishments and personal satisfaction, continuing to work in her organizations but introducing innovation in resource management.

9.10 Conclusion

The results of the analysis in the two case studies of the narratives before and after the life design counseling intervention revealed changes in the narratives of the participants. They indicate, on the one side, that this type of practice allowed the increase of self-awareness, helping to define personal and professional path more clearly; and on the other side, that the LAQuA and the CCIO are powerful innovative qualitative instruments that can be used for the detection of the effectiveness of recent narrative interventions (Di Fabio, 2015, 2016).

A limit of both the case studies is related to the potential subjective interpretation of the scholar, although the trustworthiness and credibility of the study were ensured. It is important to confirm the results of the studies through a follow-up assessment 6–12 months after the life design counseling intervention. Further studies could be carried out to confirm the effectiveness of the life design counseling intervention.

Despite the aforementioned limitations, the two case studies denote the importance of realizing career counseling interventions for helping clients to respond appropriately to the demands of the postmodern society and qualitative instruments to analyze the effectiveness of this kind of interventions (Di Fabio, 2015; Di Fabio & Blustein, 2016; Duffy et al., 2017; Duffy, Blustein, Diemer, & Autin, 2016). In this way, individuals are considered as a totality with their uniqueness, authenticness, and purposefulness (Di Fabio, 2017). Life design counseling interventions can thereby help people to become aware of their resources and strengths to identify meaningful goals in line with their deep authentic values and interests (Allan, Duffy, & Douglass, 2015; Di Fabio, 2014b, 2015; Di Fabio & Kenny, 2015, 2016; Di Fabio, Palazzeschi, & Bucci, 2017; Douglass, Duffy, & Autin, 2016; Maree & Di Fabio, 2015). Life design counselors can enable clients to develop their adaptability to the current ever-changing context and to enhance reflexivity, promoting also the sustainability of their project (Di Fabio, 2017) and the construction of decent work and decent lives (Blustein, Kenny, Di Fabio, & Guichard, in press).

References

Allan, B. A., Duffy, R. D., & Douglass, R. (2015). Meaning in life and work: A developmental perspective. The Journal of Positive Psychology, 10(4), 323-331.

Bernaud, J.-L. (2013). Career counseling and life meaning: A new perspective life designing for research and applications. In A. Di Fabio & K. Maree (Eds.), *Psychology of career counseling: New challenges for a new era*. New-York: Nova Science Publishers.

Bernaud, J.-L., Lhotellier, L., Sovet, L., Arnoux-Nicolas, C., & Pelayo, F. (2016). *Psicologia dell'accompagnamento. Il senso della vita e del lavoro nell'orientamento professionale* [*Psychologie de l'accompagnement. Concepts et outils pour développer le sens de la vie et du travail*]. (Italian version edited by A. Di Fabio). Trento: Erickson.

Blustein, D. L. (2006). *The psychology of working: A new perspective for career development, counseling and public policy*. NY: Routledge.

Blustein, D. L. (2011). A relational theory of working. *Journal of Vocational Behavior, 79,* 1–17.

Blustein, D. L., Kenna, A. C., Murphy, K. A., DeVoy, J. E., & DeWine, D. B. (2005). Qualitative research in career development: Exploring the center and margins of discourse about careers and working. *Journal of Career Assessment, 13,* 351–370.

Blustein, D. L., Kenny, M. E., Di Fabio, A., & Guichard, J. (in press). Expanding the impact of the psychology of working: Engaging psychology in the struggle for decent work and human rights. *Journal of Career Assessment*. https://doi.org/10.1177/1069072718774002.

Brott, P. E. (2004). Constructivist assessment in career counseling. *Journal of Career Development, 30*(3), 189–200.

Busacca, L., & Rehfuss, M. (Eds.). (2016). *Postmodern career counseling: A handbook of culture, contexts, and cases*. Alexandria: American Counseling Association.

Cardoso, P., Silva, J. R., Gonçalves, M. M., & Duarte, M. E. (2014). Innovative moments and change in career construction counseling. *Journal of Vocational Behavior, 84,* 11–20.

Cochran, L. (1997). *Career counseling: A narrative approach*. London: Sage publications.

Di Fabio, A. (2012, July). *Narratability and career construction: Empirical evidence of intervention effectiveness*. State-of-the-Science Lecture, International Congress of Psychology (ICP), Cape Town, South Africa.

Di Fabio, A. (2014a). Career counseling and positive psychology in the 21st century: New constructs and measures for evaluating the effectiveness of intervention. *Journal of Counsellogy, 1,* 193–213.

Di Fabio, A. (2014b). Intrapreneurial self-capital: A new construct for the 21st century. *Journal of Employment Counseling, 51,* 98–111.

Di Fabio, A. (2015). Life adaptability qualitative assessment (LAQuA): A narrative instrument for evaluating counseling intervention effectiveness. In J. G. Maree & A. Di Fabio (Eds.), *Exploring new horizons in career counselling: Turning challenges into opportunities* (pp. 43–62). Rotterdam, The Netherlands: Sense Publishers.

Di Fabio, A. (2016). Life design and career counseling innovative outcomes (CCIO): A case study. *The Career Development Quarterly, 64,* 35–48.

Di Fabio, A. (2017). The psychology of sustainability and sustainable development for well-being in organizations. In G. Arcangeli, G. Giorgi, N. Mucci, J.-L. Bernaud, & A. Di Fabio (Eds.), Emerging and re-emerging organizational features, work transitions and occupational risk factors: The good, the bad, the right. An interdisciplinary perspective. Research Topic in *Frontiers in Psychology. Organizational Psychology*, *8*, 1534. https://doi: 10.3389/fpsyg.2017.01534.

Di Fabio, A., & Bernaud, J.-L. (Eds.). (2014). *The construction of the identity in 21st century: A Festschrift for Jean Guichard*. New York: Nova Science Publishers.

Di Fabio, A., & Blustein, D. L. (Eds). (2016). *From meaning of working to meaningful lives: The challenges of expanding decent work*. Lausanne: Frontiers Media. https://doi.org/10.3389/978-2-88919-970-9.

Di Fabio, A., & Kenny, M. E. (2015). The contributions of emotional intelligence and social support for adaptive career progress among Italian youth. *Journal of Career Development, 42,* 48–49.

Di Fabio, A., & Kenny, M. E. (2016). From decent work to decent lives: Positive Self and Relational Management (PS&RM) in the twenty-first century. *Frontiers in Psychology, 7,* 361. https://doi.org/10.3389/fpsyg.2016.00361.

Di Fabio, A., & Maree, J. G. (2012). Group-based life design counseling in an Italian context. *Journal of Vocational Behavior, 80,* 100–107.

Di Fabio, A., & Maree, J. G. (Eds.). (2013). *Psychology of career counseling: New challenges for a new era. Festschrift in honour of Prof. Mark Savickas*. New York, NY: Nova Science.

Di Fabio, A., & Maree, J. G. (2016). A psychological perspective on the future of work: promoting sustainable projects and meaning-making through grounded reflexivity. *Counseling. Giornale Italiano di Ricerca e Applicazioni, 9,* 14605.

Di Fabio, A. & Palazzeschi, L. (2016). Marginalization and precariat: The challenge of intensifying life construction intervention. In A. Di Fabio & D. L. Blustein (Eds.), "From meaning of working to meaningful lives: The challenges of expanding decent work". Research topic in *Frontiers in Psychology. Section Organizational Psychology*, *7*, 444. https://doi:10.3389/fpsyg.2016.00444.

Di Fabio, A., Palazzeschi, L., & Bucci, O. (2017). In an unpredictable and changing environment: Intrapreneurial self-capital as a key resource for life satisfaction and flourishing. In G. Arcangeli, G. Giorgi, N. Mucci, J.-L. Bernaud, & A. Di Fabio (Eds.), Emerging and re-emerging organizational features, work transitions and occupational risk factors: The good, the bad, the right. An interdisciplinary perspective. Research Topic in *Frontiers in Psychology. Organizational Psychology*, *8*, 1819. https://doi:10.3389/fpsyg.2017.01819.

Di Fabio, A., & Saklofske, D. H. (2014a). Comparing ability and self-report trait emotional intelligence, fluid intelligence, and personality traits in career decision. *Personality and Individual Differences, 64*, 174–178.

Di Fabio, A., & Saklofske, D. H. (2014b). Promoting individual resources: The challenge of trait emotional intelligence. *Personality and Individual Differences, 65*, 19–23.

Di Fabio, A., Giannini, M., Loscalzo, Y., Palazzeschi, L., Bucci, O., Guazzini, A., & Gori, A. (2016). The challenge of fostering healthy organizations: An empirical study on the role of workplace relational civility in acceptance of change, and well-being. In G. Giorgi, M. Shoss, & A. Di Fabio (Eds.), From organizational welfare to business success: Higher performance in healthy organizational environments. Research Topic in *Frontiers in Psychology. Organizational Psychology*, *7*, 1748. doi: https://doi.org/10.3389/fpsyg.2016.01748

Douglass, R. P., Duffy, R. D., & Autin, K. L. (2016). Living a calling, nationality, and life satisfaction: A moderated, multiple mediator model. *Journal of Career Assessment, 24*(2), 253–269.

Duarte, M. E. (2004). O indivíduo e a organização: Perspectivas de desenvolvimento. [The individual and the organization: Perspectives of development]. *Psychologica (Extra-Série)*, 549–557.

Duffy, R. D., Allan, B. A., England, J. W., Blustein, D. L., Autin, K. L., Douglass, R. P. … Santos, E. J. (2017). The development and initial validation of the Decent Work Scale. *Journal of counseling psychology*, *64*(2), 206.

Duffy, R. D., Blustein, D. L., Diemer, M. A., & Autin, K. L. (2016). The psychology of working theory. *Journal of Counseling Psychology, 63*(2), 127–148.

Duffy, R. D., Foley, P. F., Raque-Bodgan, T. L., Reid-Marks, L., Dik, B. J., Castano, M. C., et al. (2012). Counseling psychologists who view their careers as a calling: A qualitative study. *Journal of Career Assessment, 20*(3), 293–308.

Duffy, R. D., Torrey, C. L., Bott, E. M., Allan, B. A., & Schlosser, L. Z. (2013). Time management, passion, and collaboration: A qualitative study of highly research productive counseling psychologists. *The Counseling Psychologist, 41*(6), 881–917.

Gonçalves, M. M., Ribeiro, A. P., Mendes, I., Matos, M., & Santos, A. (2011). Tracking novelties in psychotherapy process research: The innovative moments coding system. *Psychoteraphy Research, 21,* 497–509.

Guichard, J. (2004). Se faire soi. *L'Orientation Scolaire et Professionnelle, 33,* 499–534.

Guichard, J. (2005). Life-long self-construction. *International Journal for Educational and Vocational Guidance, 5,* 111–124.

Guichard, J. (2008). Proposition d'un schéma d'entretien constructiviste de conseil en orientation pour des adolescents ou de jeunes adultes. *L'Orientation Scolaire et Professionnelle, 37,* 413–440.

Guichard, J. (2009). Self-constructing. *Journal of Vocational Behavior, 75,* 251–258.

Guichard, J. (2013, September). *Which paradigm for career and life designing interventions contributing to the development of a fairer world during the 21st century*. Lecture presented at the IAEVG International Conference, Montpellier, France.

Guichard, J., Bangali, M., Cohen Scali, V., Pouyaud, J., & Robinet, M. L. (2016). *Concevoir et orienter sa vie: Les dialogues de conseil en life design*. Paris: Editions Qui plus est.

Guichard, J., & Di Fabio, A. (2015, June). *How can career and life designing interventions contribute to a fair and sustainable development and to the implementation of decent work over the world?* Invited Keynote at the UNESCO Chair on Lifelong Guidance and Counseling International Conference "How can career and life designing interventions contribute to a fair and sustainable development and to the implementation of decent work over the world?" Florence 2015, University of Florence (Italy) and University of Wroclaw (Poland), Florence, Italy, 4–6 June 2015.

Hage, S. M., Romano, J. L., Conyne, R. K., Kenny, M., Matthews, C., Schwartz, J. P., & Waldo, M. (2007). Best practice guidelines on prevention practice, research, training, and social advocacy for psychologists. *The Counseling Psychologist, 35*, 493–566.

Hartung, P. J. (2010). Practice and research in career counseling and development-2009. *Career Development Quarterly, 59,* 98–142.

Hartung, P. J. (2012). Career development in global context: History, status, and prospects. In M. Watson & M. McMahon (Eds.), *Career development: Global issues and challenges* (pp. 11–26). Hauppauge, NY: Nova Science.

Hartung, P. J. (2013). Career as story: Making the narrative turn. In W. B. Walsh, M. L. Savickas, & P. J. Hartung (Eds.), *Handbook of vocational psychology* (4th ed., pp. 33–52). New York, NY: Routledge.

Kenny, M. E., & Hage, S. M. (2009). The next frontier: Prevention as an instrument of social justice. *The Journal of Primary Prevention, 30*, 1–10.

Maree, J. G. (Ed.). (2007). *Shaping the story: A guide to facilitating narrative career counseling*. Pretoria: Van Schaik.

Maree, J. G. (2012). A (guided) meta-reflection theory of career counselling: A case study. *South African Journal of Higher Education, 26*(4), 661–669.

Maree, J. G. (2013). *Counselling for career construction: Connecting life themes to construct life portraits. Turning pain into hope*. Rotterdam, The Netherlands: Sense.

Maree, J. G., & Di Fabio, A. (Eds.). (2015). *Exploring new horizons in career counselling: Turning challenges into opportunities*. Rotterdam, The Netherlands: Sense Publishers.

McMahon, M., & Watson, M. (2010). Story telling: Moving from thin stories to thick and rich stories. In K. Maree (Ed.), *Career counselling: Methods that work* (pp. 53–63). Cape Town, South Africa: Yuta.

McMahon, M., & Watson, M. (2011). Career counselling: What's the story? In M. McMahon & M. Watson (Eds.), *Career counselling and constructivism: Elaboration of constructs* (pp. 13–24). New York: Nova Science.

Oyserman, D., Bybee, D., & Terry, K. (2006). Possible selves and academic outcomes: How and when possible selves impel action. *Journal of Personality and Social Psychology, 91,* 188–204.

Rehfuss, M. C. (2009). The future career autobiography: A narrative measure of career intervention effectiveness. *The Career Development Quarterly, 58*(1), 82–90.

Rehfuss, M., & Di Fabio, A. (2012). Validating the future career autobiography as a measure of narrative change. *Journal of Career Assessment, 20,* 452–462.

Reker, G. T. (2000). Theoretical perspectives, dimensions and measurement of existential meaning. In G. T. Reker & K. Chamberlain (Eds.), *Exploring existential meaning: Optimising human development across the life span* (pp. 39–55). Thousand Oaks, CA: Sage.

Savickas, M. (2004). Vocational psychology. In C. Spielberger (Ed.), Encyclopedia of Applied Psychology (pp. 655-667). Amsterdam: Elsevier.

Savickas, M. L. (1995). Current theoretical issues in vocational psychology: Convergence, divergence, and schism. In W. B. Walsh & S. H. Osipow (Eds.), *Handbook of vocational psychology* (2nd ed., pp. 1–34). Hillsdale, NJ: Lawrence Erlbaum Associates.

Savickas, M. L. (1997). Career adaptability: An integrative construct for life-span, life-space theory. *The Career Development Quarterly, 45,* 247–259.
Savickas, M. L. (2001). Toward a comprehensive theory of career development: Disposition, concerns and narratives. In F. T. L. Leong & A. Barak (Eds.), *Contemporary models in vocational psychology: A volume in honor of Samuel H. Osipow*. Mahwah, NJ: Lawrence Erlbaum.
Savickas, M. L. (2005). The theory and practice of career construction. In S. D. Brown & R. W. Lent (Eds.), *Career development and counseling: Putting theory and research to work* (pp. 42–70). Hoboken, NJ: Wiley.
Savickas, M. L. (2010, July). *Life designing: Framework and introduction*. Paper presented at the 27th International Congress of Applied Psychology, Melbourne, Australia.
Savickas, M. L. (Ed.). (2011). *Career counseling*. Washington, DC: American Psychological Association.
Savickas, M. L. (2013). *Life designing in 21st century*. Closing Conference at the IAEVG International Conference, Montpellier, France.
Savickas, M. L. (2015). *Life-design counseling manual*. Rootstown, OH: Author.
Savickas, M. L., & Porfeli, E. J. (2012). Career adapt-abilities scale: Construction, reliability, and measurement equivalence across 13 countries. *Journal of Vocational Behavior, 80,* 661–673.
Severy, L. E. (2002). What's the story? Postmodern career counseling in student affairs. *Journal of College Student Development, 43*(1), 84–92.
Schnell, T., Höge, T., & Pollet, E. (2013). Predicting meaning in work: Theory, data, implications. *The Journal of Positive Psychology, 8*(6), 543–554.
Valach, L., & Young, R. A. (2004). Some cornerstones in the development of a contextual action theory of career and counseling. *International Journal of Educational and Vocational Guidance, 4,* 61–81.
World Medical Association [WMA]. (2013). *WMA declaration of Helsinki—Ethical Principles for medical research involving human subjects*. Available at: http://www.wma.net/en/30publications/10policies/b3/.

Chapter 10
Life Meaning Intervention: A Case Study on an Italian Worker Using LAQuA and CCIO as Qualitative Evaluation Instruments

Annamaria Di Fabio and Maureen E. Kenny

Abstract This chapter presents the case study of an operator of an employment office in Tuscany who participated in a life meaning intervention and completed two new qualitative instruments, the Life Adaptability Qualitative Assessment (LAQuA) and the Career Counseling Innovative Outcomes (CCIO), before and after the intervention. The intervention posed questions and reflection about the sources of meaning in her personal life and work to assist her in identifying the principal and meaningful pathways for her future. The evaluation of the life meaning intervention using the LAQuA and CCIO is discussed in this chapter. The findings highlight the effectiveness of the life meaning intervention in helping the employee to increase her self-awareness in terms of her deeply held values and life meaning.

10.1 Introduction

The identification and enhancement of personal strengths is increasingly important for maintaining well-being amidst the high levels of instability and uncertainty that characterize work in the twenty-first century (Di Fabio, 2014a; Di Fabio & Kenny, 2015, 2016; Di Fabio, Kenny, & Claudius, 2016; Douglass, Duffy, & Autin, 2016; Hage et al., 2007; Kenny & Hage, 2009). The rapid spread of technology and accelerated pace of life (Rosa, 2015) require people to do many things quickly in order to maintain their position in society (Di Fabio, 2017a). In this context, finding a stable career while balancing personal and professional life and sustaining meaning in life and work are significant challenges (Di Fabio & Maree, 2016). While change is a source of stress, it can also be an opportunity to learn and

A. Di Fabio (✉)
Department of Education and Psychology (Psychology Section),
University of Florence, Florence, Italy
e-mail: adifabio@psico.unifi.it

M. E. Kenny
Lynch School of Education, Boston College, Chestnut Hill, MA, USA

© Springer Nature Switzerland AG 2018
A. Di Fabio and J.-L. Bernaud (eds.), *Narrative Interventions in Post-modern Guidance and Career Counseling*, https://doi.org/10.1007/978-3-319-98300-4_10

develop new personal knowledge and skills in order to respond in a timely and adequate manner to the demands of the current context (Di Fabio & Gori, 2016b).

As work is a source of identity (Blustein, 2006), it is important that people develop resources to deal successfully with threats to the self presented by the complexities of postmodern society (Di Fabio, 2014c; Di Fabio, Palazzeschi, & Bucci, 2017; Di Fabio et al., 2016; Maree & Di Fabio, 2015). Psychological resources, such as adaptability (Savickas, 2001, 2005) and reflexivity (Di Fabio, 2014b; Di Fabio & Maree, 2016; Di Fabio, Maree, & Kenny, 2018; Guichard, 2004, 2005; Maree, 2012, 2013), for example, can help people to better "read" different situations and contexts, thereby uncovering meanings and themes useful in constructing future pathways (Di Fabio & Maree, 2016).

Given the growing challenges in obtaining decent and satisfying personal and work lives (Blustein, Kenny, Di Fabio, Guichard, in press; Di Fabio & Blustein, 2016; Duffy et al., 2017; Duffy, Blustein, Diemer, & Autin, 2016), understanding how people define meaning in their life and work activities amidst work uncertainty and scarcity is a concern of growing scholarly importance (Di Fabio & Blustein, 2016). Scholars need to explore how people find meaning in their lives so that professionals can provide more effective support to individuals as they strive to construct meaning in their lives (Di Fabio & Blustein, 2016). As such, scholarship and practice in career counseling are shifting from the paradigm of motivation to the paradigm of meaning (Di Fabio & Blustein, 2016; Di Fabio & Maree, 2016).

The concepts of life and work meaning are increasingly crucial (Allan, Duffy, & Douglass, 2015; Bernaud, Lhotellier, Sovet, Arnoux-Nicolas, & Pelayo, 2016; Di Fabio & Blustein, 2016; Savickas, 2011, 2015) and relevant to the design of dialogue interventions, such as the one used in this case study, to assist clients in discovering meaning in their lives and work (Guichard, Bangali, Cohen Scali, Pouyaud, Robinet, 2016; Guichard & Di Fabio, 2015). Life meaning represents a vital dimension of the human condition, related to the individual's reflection on the nature of his/her life and the source of goals and values (Frankl, 1963). Life meaning is also understood as the pursuit of valuable and satisfying objectives, which bring order and consistency to one's life (Reker, 2000). Bernaud et al. (2016) consider meaning as a product of existential reflection and a process involving complex analysis, of the past, present, and future to delineate a valuable future direction for one's own life. Work meaning also seems to have a subjective dimension that is context-dependent (Rosso, Dekas, & Wrzesniewski, 2010). Life meaning encompasses coherence, direction, significance, and belonging (Di Fabio & Maree, 2016a, b; Schnell, Höge, & Pollet, 2013) and fosters sustainability of personal and professional projects in the context of challenge (Di Fabio, 2017b). Within a positive psychology approach to career and life management, the sustainability of personal and professional life projects is anchored to meaningful construction, defined by coherence, direction, significance, and belonging (Di Fabio, 2017b; Schnell et al., 2013).

In dialogue intervention for the twenty-first century, which follows the narrative perspective, clients are seen as responsible for their lives, both personal and professional (Guichard, 2013), and are guided in constructing the self through story (Savickas, 2011). Contemporary narrative intervention focuses the client on making meaning of their life stories (Di Fabio & Blustein, 2016), with the career counselor assisting the client in the discovery of personal and professional meaning through the identification of themes in the narrative (Guichard, 2013; Savickas et al., 2009). This process allows clients to develop consistency, significance, and direction in their personal and professional lives as they cope with ongoing change and transitions (Di Fabio, 2017b; Savickas, 2011, 2015). The application of the narrative perspective in dialogue intervention for the twenty-first century (Guichard, 2013) calls for the use of qualitative assessment instruments to assess the type of change the client is experiencing and to verify the effectiveness of these interventions (Blustein, Kenna, Murphy, Devoy, & DeWine, 2005; Busacca & Rehfuss, 2016; Di Fabio, 2014, 2016; Di Fabio & Maree, 2016; Duffy et al., 2012; Duffy, Torrey, Bott, Allan, & Schlosser, 2013; Rehfuss, 2009; Rehfuss & Di Fabio, 2012).

This article discusses the case study of a female guidance counselor of an employment office who participated in a life meaning intervention. This woman was dealing with the reorganization of the public employment center where she worked (considered as a critical life situation) in an Italian city in Tuscany. This article discusses the effectiveness of the life meaning intervention evaluated through innovative qualitative assessment instruments (LAQuA and CCIO).

10.2 Aim of the Case Study

The case study describes the application of a life meaning intervention (Bernaud et al., 2016) as a means to increase self-awareness and a means of assisting the client in clarifying her next life and career steps as aligned with her authentic values.

The following two research questions guided the case study.

- How was the life meaning intervention applied in the case of a woman dealing with the reorganization of the public employment office where she worked in a city in the Italian region of Tuscany?
- How did the life meaning intervention help the participant to increase her self-awareness with regard to her authentic values and sources of life meaning and to clearly identify her next life and career steps in line with those values and meaning during the reorganization of her employment office?

10.3 Materials and Methods

10.3.1 Participant and Context

The participant in the study, Francesca (a pseudonym), was a 37-year-old woman who completed an undergraduate degree in psychology and worked in an employment center in Florence. The employment office in Italy, at the time of the research, was dealing with reorganization. Francesca understood the importance of maintaining her employability and sought a postgraduate course, enabling her to update and increase her communication and relational knowledge and skills. She also wanted to enhance her personal strengths and deeply explore her professional and personal life paths.

10.3.2 Qualitative Instruments

10.3.2.1 Life Adaptability Qualitative Assessment (LAQuA)

The LAQuA (Di Fabio, 2015) is a new qualitative instrument developed to evaluate the effectiveness of dialogue interventions. This instrument assesses adaptability, evaluating change or lack of change in the individuals' life narratives before and after the intervention. The LAQuA includes 12 written questions, with three questions addressing each dimension (Concern, Control, Curiosity, and Confidence) of the Career Adapt-Abilities Inventory—International Version 2.0 (Savickas & Porfeli, 2012). The LAQuA 12 questions are:

Concern: (1a) What does it mean to you to be oriented toward your future? (1b) Do you think you are oriented toward your future? (1c) Why?
Control: (2a) What does it mean to you to take responsibility for your future? (2b) Do you think you do take responsibility for your future? (2c) Why?
Curiosity: (3a) What does it mean to you to be curious about your own future? (3b) Do you think you are curious about your future? (3c) Why?
Confidence: (4a) What does it mean to you to have confidence in your own ability to build your future? (4b) Do you think you have confidence in your ability to build your future? (4c) Why?

The answers to these 12 questions are compared before and after the intervention with respect to 24 qualitative indicators specified by the LAQuA coding system for each of the four dimensions of the Career Adapt-Abilities Inventory—International Version 2.0 (Savickas & Porfeli, 2012). The LAQuA coding system (Di Fabio, 2015) assesses change or lack of change for each dimension of adaptability in relation to varied levels of reflexivity (Increased Reflexivity, Revised Reflexivity, Open Reflexivity, Enhanced Reflexivity, and No Change.)

10.3.3 Career Counseling Innovative Outcomes (CCIO)

The CCIO (Di Fabio, 2016) is a new qualitative instrument designed to evaluate the outcomes and effectiveness of dialogue interventions. The CCIO was developed based on the innovative moments coding system applied in psychotherapy

(Gonçalves, Ribeiro, Mendes, Matos, & Santos, 2011) and in career construction counseling (Cardoso, Silva, Gonçalves, & Duarte, 2014). While the innovative moments coding system assesses the process of change during psychotherapeutic intervention (Gonçalves et al., 2011) and career construction counseling (Cardoso et al., 2014), the CCIO is designed specifically to examine narratives before and after life interventions. The CCIO comprises seven questions aligned within the narrative paradigm (Savickas, 2011), which the participant is asked to answer before and after the intervention: (1) In which ways can this intervention be/was this intervention useful to you? (2) What are your most useful resources? (3) What are the main obstacles you encounter? (4) Who do you think can be useful to you? (5) What do you think can be useful to you? (6) What are the main challenges you face? (7) What are the main objectives you are hoping to achieve? The narratives elicited by these seven questions are coded using the five categories of the CCIO coding system: Action, Reflection (Type I and Type II), Protest (Type I and Type II), Reconceptualization, and Performing Change (See Kenny & Di Fabio, this volume, for description of these codes).

10.3.4 Procedure

The LAQuA and the CCIO were administered before and after the life meaning intervention by a psychologist trained in the administration of these two qualitative instruments.

Three independent, trained expert reviewers (raters) compared the participant's initial and subsequent responses to the written questions of these two narrative tools. An interrater reliability analysis using the Kappa statistic was carried out to establish the level of consistency among the raters.

The study adhered to the requirements of privacy and informed consent in Italian law (Law Decree DL-196/2003) and the ethical standards for research of the Declaration of Helsinki revised in Fortaleza (World Medical Association [WMA], 2013), followed and approved by the Department of Education and Psychology of the University of Florence (Italy).

Francesca participated in a life meaning intervention (Bernaud et al., 2016), characterized by three 1-day group sessions (eight hours a session) using the modality of the power of an audience (Di Fabio & Maree, 2012). The participants, seated in a circle, interacted with the psychologist one at a time, as individual clients discussed their life meaning intervention responses. In this way, the group members were participants in an individual intervention session, while also reflecting deeply on the stimuli aroused by the intervention across group members. Life meaning interventions seek to facilitate participants' reflections about the meaning of their personal and professional lives to promote new awareness of themselves on which to build their lives.

10.3.5 Criteria for Quality Assurance

Four quality assurance criteria were applied to assess the trustworthiness of the study outcomes: credibility, confirmability, transferability, and dependability across different modalities of data collection and analysis (Maree, 2012). Credibility of the data with regard to the significance and credibility of the results (Maree, 2012) was assessed through review of the data by independent researchers. Confirmability with regard to the objectivity of the data and the absence of research errors (Maree, 2012, p. 142) was also assessed by independent external researchers who evaluated the verifiability and replicability of the research methods and procedures. The transferability or generalizability of the results to other contexts (Maree, 2012) was achieved in the current study by providing sufficient detail concerning the research methods and the participant's condition and context so that other researchers can determine their applicability to other contexts. Dependability with regard to the stability over time and level of internal control and consistency of the research process (Maree, 2012) was assessed through the independent rating of the participant's narratives by three expert researchers.

10.4 Results

The participant's responses to the written questions of the LAQuA and the CCIO before and after the life meaning intervention are reported below, along with analysis of the LAQuA qualitative indicators and levels of reflexivity (Increased Reflexivity, Revised Reflexivity, Open Reflexivity, Enhanced Reflexivity, and No Change.)

The participant's answer to the first LAQuA question before the life meaning intervention was: "*To me, to be oriented toward my future means to think a lot now about my work choices because they will have consequences for my future*" (qualitative descriptor: Predicting); and after the life meaning intervention, it was: "*To me, to be oriented toward my future means thinking very well about my choices relative to work in this period because they shape my future* (identical descriptor: Predicting) *and beginning to plan the steps for achieving my goals*" (new different qualitative descriptor: Strategic). (Open reflexivity (O): in the narratives produced after the life meaning intervention, there is an identical descriptor/s—with the same level of reflexivity in presenting the descriptor—plus a new, different descriptor/s.)

The participant's answer to the second LAQuA question before the life meaning intervention was: "*To me, to take responsibility for my future means being committed to the maximum to improve my life counting on myself*" (qualitative descriptor: Responsible); after the life meaning intervention, it was: "*To me, to take responsibility for my future means following my authentic aims to realize what has real meaning for me*" (new, different qualitative descriptor: Honest). (Revised reflexivity (R): in the narratives produced after the life meaning intervention, the previous descriptor/s has disappeared, and a new, different descriptor/s has appeared.)

The participant's answer to the third LAQuA question before the life meaning intervention was: "*To me, to be curious about my future means imagining various alternatives although I tend to routine*" (qualitative descriptor: Recognizing/Discovering); after the life meaning intervention, it was: "*To me, to be curious about my future means envisaging the new working situation after the reorganization and trying to identify different way to do things in my work, making new hypotheses to develop my career*" (identical qualitative descriptor but more in-depth reflexivity: Recognizing/Discovering). (Increased reflexivity: in the narratives produced after the life meaning intervention, there were identical descriptors, but they were presented with more in-depth reflexivity.)

The participant's answer to the fourth LAQuA question before the life meaning intervention was: "*To me, to have confidence in my own abilities to build my future means believing I am able to obtain good results thanks to my abilities*" (qualitative descriptor: Capable); after the life meaning intervention, it was: "*To have confidence in my own abilities means thinking I can obtain good results thanks to my abilities according to my most profound values and meaning*" (identical qualitative descriptor but more in-depth reflexivity: Capable); "*I have confidence in my abilities because I'm not discouraged in the face of a failure so much as to give up taking the path I desired and that permits to me to feel fully realized according to my life meaning*" (new, different qualitative descriptor: Resilient). (Enhanced reflexivity (E): in the narratives produced after the life meaning intervention, there is an identical descriptor/s but presented with more in-depth reflexivity plus a new, different descriptor/s.)

Below the participant's responses to the seven questions of the CCIO before and after the life meaning intervention are presented along with the results of the analysis based on the five CCIO coding system categories (Action, Reflection, Protest, Reconceptualization, and Performing Change) (Di Fabio, 2016).

The participant's answer to the first CCIO question before the life meaning intervention was: "*I hope this intervention will give me solutions in order to make a choice regarding my work. I mean that I have graduated in psychology and have since worked for ten years in a public employment office that is currently facing a political and economic crisis. Maybe I need to develop new skills and update my knowledge in order to change organizations or become a freelance consultant in guidance psychology. I really don't know what I would like to do*"; after the life meaning intervention, it was: "*This intervention was useful to me because I understood that I need not only to acquire new knowledge and skills but also to increase awareness of myself, to discover my actual values and to reach my values and my meaning in life*" (Reflection Type II IM). "*If before the intervention I thought that I would like to change my work, after I realized that I want to continue to work for the public employment office because I think that my work through career guidance interviews can help people in searching for new career opportunities in public service*" (Reconceptualization IM).

The participant's answer to the second CCIO question prior to the life meaning intervention was: "*I think that my useful resources are the motivation to learn new things, listening skills, putting myself to the test; maybe I will change my work and become a freelance consultant*"; after the life meaning intervention, it was: "*When I began the intervention I thought that I hadn't enough knowledge and skills to start a new job for another organization or as a freelance consultant. Now I reviewed my main aim and I understand that I want to continue to work for the public employment office and I also understand that my principal useful resource is my motivation in helping others to construct their career paths*" (Reflection Type II IM). "*Furthermore, I can continue to increase my competencies to support people who are searching for new opportunities in their careers and lives, continuing to take specialized courses to keep me updated*" (Action IM).

The participant's answer to the third CCIO question before the life meaning intervention was: "*My principle obstacle is the perception of a lack of time to study to increase my knowledge and skills and to offer a new perspective in another organization or as a consultant*"; after the life meaning intervention, it was: "*After the intervention I understood that I have to listen to myself more accurately to become aware of my authentic desires. My principal obstacle is that I have always been too influenced by what my colleagues said about the reorganization, but now it is the time to decide on my own*" (Protest Type I IM). "*Now I really understand that I want to continue to do my work because I feel life meaning when I help others to construct their lives and careers. The principal obstacle could be the uncertainty caused by this reorganization, but now I know what I really want and I don't intend to give up because life satisfaction is fundamental for me*" (Protest Type II IM).

The participant's answer to the fourth CCIO question before the life meaning intervention was: "*I believe that my colleagues are useful in helping me to bear the critical situation of the office. They can also help me understand what I really want to do in my life: I don't know if I would like to continue my current job or if it is time to search for a position in another organization or to become an independent consultant*"; after the life meaning intervention, it was: "*If before the intervention I thought that only my colleagues could help me reflect regarding my work, now I know that good relationships not only with my colleagues but above all with my family, are important in advising me on my future and in supporting me in discovering what I think is the best choice for me*" (Reconceptualization IM). "*In particular, my family was useful because they supported me and helped me to realize that in my future I would prefer to work as a guidance psychologist in a public employment center rather than in a private organization or as an independent consultant. In my life, I would to make a contribution to society by helping people to find their authentic aims and life meaning*" (Performing Change IM).

The participant's answer to the fifth CCIO question before the life meaning intervention was: "*I believe that the practice, gaining further experiences in guidance psychology, could be useful for me, to deeply analyse if I want to change my career life*"; after the life meaning intervention, it was: "*After the intervention I understand that acquiring updated skills in guidance and career counseling could be useful for me, not to change my career, but to improve my competencies and to use them adaptively to face the challenges of this period of reorganization*" (Reflection Type II IM). "*I would like to continue to find new specialized courses and new opportunities of training to improve my knowledge and competencies*" (Action IM).

The participant's answer to the sixth CCIO question before the life meaning intervention was: "*The main challenge for me regards the management of family and work duties. I think that the current critical phase of my work must not affect relationships and activities with my family*"; after the life meaning intervention, it was: "*Now I think that the main challenge is to improve my work strengths in terms of the accuracy and professionalism of the daily activities in which I am engaged*" (Reconceptualization IM). "*In this way I can continue with my current job but be more careful and productive. I can realize my objective to help other people to construct their career and life and thus I could be fully satisfied. So both my clients and my family could have advantages*" (Performing change IM).

The participant's answer to the seventh CCIO question before the life meaning intervention was: "*My principal objectives refer to the accomplishment of courses that I have to attend in line with the indication of my supervisor and my colleagues. I feel confused about the possibility of continuing my current work for the public employment center and committing to complete each task*"; after the life meaning intervention, it was: "*My main objectives now regards the fact that I want to finish the courses that I choose in line with what I understand is important for me to learn and not the courses that my supervisor has forced me to follow.*" (Protest Type II IM). "*To me, it is very important to change and make less mistakes in administrative procedures because they are an important part of my job for the clients who need my help to see new work possibilities*" (Reflection Type II IM). "*I recognize that my main objective in my life is to continue to help people seeking new work opportunities in a public employment center as a guidance psychologist*" (Reflection Type II IM).

10.5 Discussion

This case study shows the value of life meaning intervention following a positive prevention perspective (Di Fabio, 2014a; Di Fabio & Kenny, 2015, 2016; Di Fabio et al., 2016; Hage et al., 2007; Kenny & Hage, 2009) for workers dealing with critical situations in their workplace. Timely interventions administered to vulnerable workers offer professional support for the construction of their careers and lives that will offer fulfillment and meaning (Guichard, 2009; Kenny, Blustein, & Meerkins, 2018; Savickas, 2011). Life meaning interventions (Bernaud et al., 2016) can help workers to discover the real meaning of their life, allowing them to build an authentic framework for their career and life paths (Di Fabio & Blustein, 2016; Di Fabio, 2017a, 2017b; Di Fabio & Maree, 2016). Life meaning counseling (Bernaud et al., 2016) is aimed at helping people to successfully face transitions and critical situations to achieve positive career outcomes and be able to write the next chapters of their professional and personal lives according to important sources of meaning.

In this case study, the narratives obtained from the participant can be evaluated through their analysis before and after the life meaning intervention (Bernaud et al., 2016) elicited and coded through the LAQuA (Di Fabio, 2015) and the CCIO (Di Fabio, 2016).

The analysis of the responses to the LAQuA questions showed changes in the participant's reflexivity regarding adaptability before and after the life meaning intervention. The assessed level of reflexivity across the four dimensions of adaptability (Concern, Control, Confidence, and Curiosity) increased. In relation to Concern, the participant highlighted the importance of identifying new objectives and trying to pursue them. In relation to Control, the participant underscored the significance of independently shaping her future, putting all of her effort to achieve success. In relation to Curiosity, the participant realized the importance of envisioning new situations, making new work hypotheses in order to obtain a more stable job in the future. In relation to Confidence, the participant showed trust in herself, being able to use different strategies for satisfying her objectives notwithstanding difficulties.

The analysis using the five categories of the CCIO (Action, Reflection, Protest, Reconceptualization, and Performing Change) showed changes in the participant's narratives before and after the life meaning intervention. These results can be considered in terms of Action as the participant would like to improve her skills to continue to do well her job in the public employment office. The results indicated also changes in Reflection referring to the importance for the participant to continue with her current job so that she can follow her authentic values in helping people to find new career perspectives. She understood that further experiences in guidance psychology and the improvement of administrative procedures can help to build her skills and to enhance her professional identity. Moreover, the results of the analysis of the narratives described a change in term of Protest. She was realizing her authentic aims without being influenced by the opinions of her colleagues or her supervisor. Before the life meaning intervention, the participant in the case study was confused about what she really wanted to do in her life. In response to the current crisis of the public employment office in which she worked, she thought it might be the right time to start a new job for another organization or to become an independent consultant as guidance psychology. After the life meaning intervention, she stated that in line with her authentic self and life meaning, she intended to continue her current work in the public employment center. The analysis of the narratives also showed Reconceptualization regarding the transition between her past and present perspectives (past before the life meaning intervention and present after the life meaning intervention) (Di Fabio, 2016; Gonçalves et al., 2011). The participant, after engaging in deep reflection about the authentic meaning of her work and life, moved from a confused condition in which she didn't know what she had to do, toward a condition in which she was more aware of what she understands as her career mission, namely helping people to identify new work opportunities. She recognized that this mission could affect her personal and professional identity and her future choices. She also knew that now she was able to construct her career and life path according to her explicit mission, being able also to balance the work and family domains of her life. Finally, analysis of the narratives revealed development in Performing Change as the participant clarified her life and career project as a result of the change process (Di Fabio, 2016; Gonçalves et al., 2011). In particular, she understood that remaining in the current public employment office had positive benefits with regard to choosing training courses that could refine and update her skills, knowledge, and competencies and use this expertise to help people to find work alternatives.

10.6 Conclusion

Overall, the analysis of the narratives before and after the life meaning intervention revealed changes in the narratives of the participant, indicating that the intervention increased her awareness of her true values and life meaning and helped her to identify clear next steps for her career and life in line with her authentic self. The explicit intention of the participant to remain in her current employment center could be considered in terms of her authentic self (Di Fabio, 2014d) and purposeful identitarian awareness (Di Fabio, 2014d), or capacity to maintain a sense of coherence and to unify, based on a sense of meaning, authenticity, and autonomous self-direction, the plural identities that emerged in an unstable situation. The case study also underscored how through life meaning intervention (Bernaud et al., 2016), a critical job situation can be turned in a positive situation with the support of resources including relationships with colleagues, support of family, and the opportunity to attend training courses that offer new knowledge and updating of current skills. This new knowledge could be applied in her current position to construct a more desirable life and career (Di Fabio, 2017a; Guichard, 2009).

Although the results of this case study highlighted changes in the narratives produced by the participant before and after the life meaning intervention, the effectiveness of the intervention needs to be confirmed by further evaluation. The trustworthiness and credibility of the study were ensured, but a limitation could be the subjective interpretation of the scholar and client. A follow-up assessment 6–12 months after the life meaning intervention would be valuable to confirm the findings of the study. It would be important to verify, for example, that the participant chose to continue in her current position and has experienced enhanced life meaning, fulfillment, and life–work balance in this pathway.

Notwithstanding the above limitations, the study reveals the importance of life meaning intervention (Di Fabio & Blustein, 2016) in a positive preventive perspective (Di Fabio, 2014a; Di Fabio & Kenny, 2015, 2016; Di Fabio et al., 2016; Hage et al., 2007; Kenny & Hage, 2009) for helping workers in complex workplace situations to construct meaningful life and career paths (Di Fabio, 2017a; Guichard, 2009). Life meaning intervention (Bernaud, 2013; Bernaud et al., 2016) could be offered to all workers in complex situations and to workers that are dealing with career dilemmas. Timely interventions can reduce risks and increase protective factors, including self-awareness and support from others, to help workers make adaptive decisions and self-realization (Blustein, 2006, 2011) in line with their real self and their authentic values (Di Fabio, 2014d) for their self-realization. Workers could be empowered to build frameworks rich with meaning (Bernaud et al., 2016) for writing the next self-attuned chapters of their lives (Di Fabio, 2014d; Savickas, 2011).

References

Allan, B. A., Duffy, R. D., & Douglass, R. (2015). Meaning in life and work: A developmental perspective. *The Journal of Positive Psychology, 10*(4), 323–331.

Bernaud, J.-L. (2013). Career counseling and life meaning: A new perspective life designing for research and applications. In A. Di Fabio & K. Maree (Eds.), *Psychology of Career Counseling: New challenges for a new era*. New-York: Nova Science Publishers.

Bernaud, J.-L., Lhotellier, L., Sovet, L., Arnoux-Nicolas, C., & Pelayo, F. (2016). *Psicologia dell'accompagnamento. Il senso della vita e del lavoro nell'orientamento professionale* [*Psychologie de l'accompagnement. Concepts et outils pour développer le sens de la vie et du travail*]. (Italian version edited by A. Di Fabio). Trento: Erickson.

Blustein, D. L. (2006). *The psychology of working: A new perspective for career development, counseling and public policy*. NY: Routledge.

Blustein, D. L. (2011). A relational theory of working. *Journal of Vocational Behavior, 79*(1), 1–17.

Blustein, D. L., Kenna, A. C., Murphy, K. A., DeVoy, J. E., & DeWine, D. B. (2005). Qualitative research in career development: Exploring the center and margins of discourse about careers and working. *Journal of Career Assessment, 13*(4), 351–370.

Blustein, D. L., Kenny, M. E., Di Fabio, A., & Guichard, J. (in press). Expanding the impact of the psychology of working: Engaging psychology in the struggle for decent work and human rights. *Journal of Career Assessment.* https://doi.org/10.1177/1069072718774002.

Busacca, L. A., & Rehfuss, M. C. (Eds.). (2016). *Postmodern career counseling: A handbook of culture, context, and cases*. John Wiley & Sons.

Cardoso, P., Silva, J. R., Gonçalves, M. M., & Duarte, M. E. (2014). Innovative moments and change in career construction counseling. *Journal of Vocational Behavior, 84,* 11–20.

Di Fabio, A. (2014a). Career counseling and positive psychology in the 21st century: New constructs and measures for evaluating the effectiveness of intervention. *Journal of Counsellogy, 1,* 193–213.

Di Fabio, A. (2014b). "Constructing my future purposeful life": A new life construction intervention. In A. Di Fabio & J.-L. Bernaud (Eds.), *The construction of the identity in 21st century: A Festschrift for Jean Guichard* (pp. 219–239). New York: Nova Science Publishers.

Di Fabio, A. (2014c). Intrapreneurial self-capital: A new construct for the 21st century. *Journal of Employment Counseling, 51,* 98–111.

Di Fabio, A. (2014d). The new purposeful identitarian awareness for the twenty-first century: Valorize themselves in the life construction from youth to adulthood and late adulthood. In A. Di Fabio & J.-L. Bernaud (Eds.), *The construction of the identity in 21st century: A Festschrift for Jean Guichard* (pp. 157–168). New York: Nova Science Publishers.

Di Fabio, A. (2015). Life adaptability qualitative assessment (LAQuA): A narrative instrument for evaluating counseling intervention effectiveness. In J. G. Maree & A. Di Fabio, A. (Eds.), *Exploring new horizons in career counselling: Turning challenges into opportunities* (pp. 43–62). Rotterdam, The Netherlands: Sense Publishers.

Di Fabio, A. (2016). Life design and career counseling innovative outcomes (CCIO): A case study. *The Career Development Quarterly, 64,* 35–48.

Di Fabio, A. (2017a). Positive healthy organizations: Promoting well-being, meaningfulness, and sustainability in organizations. In G. Arcangeli, G. Giorgi, N. Mucci, J.-L. Bernaud, & A. Di Fabio (Eds.), Emerging and re-emerging organizational features, work transitions and occupational risk factors: The good, the bad, the right. An interdisciplinary perspective. Research Topic in *Frontiers in Psychology. Organizational Psychology*, *8,* 1938. https://doi:10.3389/fpsyg.2017.01938.

Di Fabio, A. (2017b). The psychology of sustainability and sustainable development for well-being in organizations. In G. Arcangeli, G. Giorgi, N. Mucci, J.-L. Bernaud, & A. Di Fabio (Eds.), Emerging and re-emerging organizational features, work transitions and occupational risk factors: The good, the bad, the right. An interdisciplinary perspective. Research Topic in *Frontiers in Psychology. Organizational Psychology*, *8*, 1534. https://doi:10.3389/fpsyg.2017.01534

Di Fabio, A., & Blustein, D. L. (Eds). (2016). *From meaning of working to meaningful lives: The challenges of expanding decent work*. Lausanne: Frontiers Media. https://doi.org/10.3389/978-2-88919-970-9.

Di Fabio, A., & Gori, A. (2016a). Assessing workplace relational civility (WRC) with a new multidimensional "mirror" measure. In A. Di Fabio & D. L. Blustein (Eds.), From meaning of working to meaningful lives: The challenges of expanding decent work. Research Topic in *Frontiers in Psychology. Section Organizational Psychology*, *7*, 890. https://doi:10.3389/fpsyg.2016.00890.

Di Fabio, A., & Gori, A. (2016b). Developing a new instrument for assessing Acceptance of Change. *Frontiers in Psychology. Section Organizational Psychology, 7,* 802. https://doi:10.3389/fpsyg.2016.00802.

Di Fabio, A., & Kenny, M. E. (2015). The contributions of emotional intelligence and social support for adaptive career progress among Italian youth. *Journal of Career Development, 42,* 48–49.

Di Fabio, A., & Kenny, M. E. (2016). From decent work to decent lives: Positive self and relational management (PS&RM) in the twenty-first century. *Frontiers in Psychology, 7,* 361. https://doi.org/10.3389/fpsyg.2016.00361.

Di Fabio, A., Kenny, M. E., & Claudius, M. (2016). Preventing distress and promoting psychological well-being in uncertain times through career management intervention. In M. Israelashvili & J. L. Romano (Eds.), *Cambridge handbook of international prevention science*. Cambridge: Cambridge University Press.

Di Fabio, A., & Maree, J. G. (2012). Group-based Life Design Counseling in an Italian context. *Journal of Vocational Behavior, 80,* 100–107.

Di Fabio, A., & Maree, J. G. (2016). A psychological perspective on the future of work: Promoting sustainable projects and meaning-making through grounded reflexivity. *Counseling. Giornale Italiano di Ricerca e Applicazioni, 9*(3).

Di Fabio, A., Maree, J. G., & Kenny, M. E. (2018). Development of the life project reflexivity scale: A new career intervention inventory. *Journal of Career Assessment*, 1–13. https://doi.org/10.1177/1069072718758065.

Di Fabio, A., Palazzeschi, L., & Bucci, O. (2017). In an unpredictable and changing environment: Intrapreneurial self-capital as a key resource for life satisfaction and flourishing. In G. Arcangeli, G. Giorgi, N. Mucci, J.-L. Bernaud, & A. Di Fabio (Eds.), Emerging and re-emerging organizational features, work transitions and occupational risk factors: The good, the bad, the right. An interdisciplinary perspective. Research Topic in *Frontiers in Psychology. Organizational Psychology*, *8*, 1819. https://doi:10.3389/fpsyg.2017.01819.

Douglass, R. P., Duffy, R. D., & Autin, K. L. (2016). Living a calling, nationality, and life satisfaction: A moderated, multiple mediator model. *Journal of Career Assessment, 24*(2), 253–269.

Duffy, R. D., Allan, B. A., England, J. W., Blustein, D. L., Autin, K. L., Douglass, R. P., …, & Santos, E. J. (2017). The development and initial validation of the decent work scale. *Journal of Counseling Psychology, 64*(2), 206.
Duffy, R. D., Blustein, D. L., Diemer, M. A., & Autin, K. L. (2016). The psychology of working theory. *Journal of Counseling Psychology, 63*(2), 127–148.
Duffy, R. D., Foley, P. F., Raque-Bodgan, T. L., Reid-Marks, L., Dik, B. J., Castano, M. C., et al. (2012). Counseling psychologists who view their careers as a calling: A qualitative study. *Journal of Career Assessment, 20*(3), 293–308.
Duffy, R. D., Torrey, C. L., Bott, E. M., Allan, B. A., & Schlosser, L. Z. (2013). Time management, passion, and collaboration: A qualitative study of highly research productive counseling psychologists. *The Counseling Psychologist, 41*(6), 881–917.
Frankl, V. (1963). *Man's search for meaning* (Rev ed.). London, UK: Hodder & Stoughton.
Gonçalves, M. M., Ribeiro, A. P., Mendes, I., Matos, M., & Santos, A. (2011). Tracking novelties in psychotherapy process research: The innovative moments coding system. *Psychoteraphy Research, 21,* 497–509.
Guichard, J. (2004). Se faire soi. *L'Orientation Scolaire et Professionnelle, 33,* 499–534.
Guichard, J. (2005). Life-long self-construction. *International Journal for Educational and Vocational Guidance, 5,* 111–124.
Guichard, J. (2009). Self-constructing. *Journal of Vocational Behavior, 75*(3), 251–258.
Guichard, J. (2013, September). *Which paradigm for career and life designing interventions contributing to the development of a fairer world during the 21st century*. Lecture presented at the IAEVG international conference, Montpellier, France.
Guichard, J., Bangali, M., Cohen Scali, V., Pouyaud, J., & Robinet, M. L. (2016). *Concevoir et orienter sa vie: Les dialogues de conseil en life design*. Paris: Editions Qui plus est.
Guichard, J., & Di Fabio, A. (2015, June). *How can career and life designing interventions contribute to a fair and sustainable development and to the implementation of decent work over the world?* Invited keynote at the UNESCO Chair on lifelong guidance and counseling international conference "How can career and life designing interventions contribute to a fair and sustainable development and to the implementation of decent work over the world?" Florence 2015, University of Florence (Italy) and University of Wroclaw (Poland), Florence, Italy, 4–6 June 2015.
Hage, S. M., Romano, J. L., Conyne, R. K., Kenny, M., Matthews, C., Schwartz, J. P., et al. (2007). Best practice guidelines on prevention practice, research, training, and social advocacy for psychologists. *The Counseling Psychologist, 35,* 493–566.
Kenny, M. E., Blustein, D. L., & Meerkins, T. M. (2018). Integrating relational perspectives in career counseling practice. *The Career Development Quarterly, 66*(2), 135–148.
Kenny, M. E., & Hage, S. M. (2009). The next frontier: Prevention as an instrument of social justice. *The Journal of Primary Prevention, 30,* 1–10.
Maree, J. G. (2012). A (guided) meta-reflection theory of career counselling: A case study. *South African Journal of Higher Education, 26*(4), 661–669.
Maree, J. G. (2013). *Counselling for career construction: Connecting life themes to construct life portraits. Turning pain into hope*. Rotterdam, The Netherlands: Sense Publishers.
Maree, J. G., & Di Fabio, A. (Eds.). (2015). *Exploring new horizons in career counselling: Turning challenges into opportunities*. Rotterdam, The Netherlands: Sense Publishers.
Rehfuss, M. C. (2009). The Future Career Autobiography: A narrative measure of career intervention effectiveness. *The Career Development Quarterly, 58*(1), 82–90.
Rehfuss, M. C., & Di Fabio, A. (2012). Validating the future career autobiography as a measure of narrative change. *Journal of Career Assessment, 20*(4), 452–462.
Reker, G. T. (2000). Theoretical perspectives, dimensions and measurement of existential meaning. In G. T. Reker & K. Chamberlain (Eds.), *Exploring existential meaning: Optimising human development across the life span* (pp. 39–55). Thousand Oaks, CA: Sage.
Rosa, H. (2015). *Accelerazione e alienazione. Per una teoria critica del tempo nella tarda* modernità (Trad. it. E. Leonzio). Torino: Einaudi.

Rosso, B. D., Dekas, K. H., & Wrzesniewski, A. (2010). On the meaning of work: A theoretical integration and review. *Research in Organizational Behavior, 30,* 91–127.
Savickas, M. L. (2001). Toward a comprehensive theory of career development: Disposition, concerns and narratives. In F. T. L. Leong & A. Barak (Eds.), *Contemporary models in vocational psychology: A volume in honor of Samuel H. Osipow* (pp. 295–320). Mahwah, NJ: Lawrence Erlbaum.
Savickas, M. L. (2005). The theory and practice of career construction. In S. D. Brown & R. W. Lent (Eds.), *Career development and counseling: Putting theory and research to work* (pp. 42–70). Hoboken, NJ: Wiley.
Savickas, M. L. (Ed.). (2011). *Career counseling*. Washington, DC: American Psychological Association.
Savickas, M. L. (2015). *Life-design counseling manual*. Rootstown, OH: Author.
Savickas, M. L., Nota, L., Rossier, J., Dauwalder, J. P., Duarte, M. E., Guichard, J., …, & Van Vianen, A. E. (2009). Life designing: A paradigm for career construction in the 21st century. *Journal of Vocational Behavior, 75*(3), 239–250.
Savickas, M. L., & Porfeli, E. J. (2012). Career adapt-abilities scale: Construction, reliability, and measurement equivalence across 13 countries. *Journal of Vocational Behavior, 80,* 661–673.
Schnell, T., Höge, T., & Pollet, E. (2013). Predicting meaning in work: Theory, data, implications. *The Journal of Positive Psychology, 8*(6), 543–554.
World Medical Association [WMA]. (2013). *WMA Declaration of Helsinki—Ethical principles for medical research involving human subjects*. Available at: http: www.wma.net/en/30publications/10policies/b3/.

Chapter 11
Intrapreneurial Self-Capital Training: A Case Study of an Italian University Student

Peter McIlveen and Annamaria Di Fabio

Abstract This chapter presents a case study which describes the application of the Intrapreneurial Self-Capital Training with a final-year postgraduate female biology student, Erica. The chapter presents an overview of the theory that is relevant to the world of work and the conceptual dimensions of Intrapreneurial Self-Capital (ISC). Training for ISC aims to assist young people to identify their personal strengths in terms of intrapreneurship and career adaptability. A qualitative instrument, the Life Adaptability Qualitative Assessment (LAQuA), was administered before and after the training to detect meaningful changes in the participant's narratives about career adaptability and enhanced reflexivity. The LAQuA coding system revealed enhancements to the participant's awareness about her personal intrapreneurial resources and career adaptability. The relevance of ISC to employability and career services in education contexts is discussed along with recommendations for research into ISC training.

Keywords Intrapreneurship · Intrapreneurial Self-Capital · Life Adaptability Qualitative Assessment, LAQuA · Career adaptability

11.1 Introduction

The twenty-first century is characterized by instability and unpredictability in the world of work. The pace of change (Rosa, 2015) requires people to respond more effectively and efficiently to societal demands (Guichard, Bangali, Cohen Scali, Pouyaud, Robinet, 2016), all the while adapting to change as an opportunity to

---

P. McIlveen
School of Linguistics, Adult, & Specialist Education,
University of Southern Queensland, Toowoomba, Australia

A. Di Fabio (✉)
Department of Education and Psychology (Psychology Section),
University of Florence, Florence, Italy
e-mail: adifabio@psico.unifi.it

© Springer Nature Switzerland AG 2018

A. Di Fabio and J.-L. Bernaud (eds.), *Narrative Interventions in Post-modern Guidance and Career Counseling*, https://doi.org/10.1007/978-3-319-98300-4_11

grow and to learn knowledge and skills to deal with inherent challenges in contemporary society (Di Fabio, 2014a, 2014b). People are required to use flexibility, creativity, innovation, to express their talents, and potentiality to reach a satisfying and productive life (Blustein, 2006, 2011; Guichard, 2013; Savickas, 2011, 2015). Yet, young people feel often uncertain about the myriad paths they could follow to a positive future for themselves and to contribute fruitfully to society (Di Fabio, Kenny, & Claudius, 2016). They are unsure, for example, about their university degree qualifications providing for career opportunities after graduation (Peiró, Sora, & Caballer, 2012). In this paper, we argue that it is important to assist young people to manage increasingly numerous challenges in transitions in the world of work. It seems important, therefore, that scholars, particularly in the psychological fields, develop new constructs, measures, and interventions to enhance the capacity of people to adapt to the contemporary world of work (Blustein, Kenna, Murphy, DeVoy, & DeWine, 2005; Duffy et al., 2012, 2017; Duffy, Torrey, Bott, Allan, & Schlosser, 2013) and construct decent work and decent lives (Blustein, Kenny, Di Fabio, Guichard, in press). To that end, we articulate the construct Intrapreneurial Self-Capital (ISC, Di Fabio, 2014c) as a tool for scholars and practitioners to address the complex world of work.

11.2 Conceptual Foundations of Intrapreneurial Self-Capital

ISC represents a *core* of individual intrapreneurial attributes that allow people to deal with career and life construction changes through the creation of innovative solutions to critical situations, and to turn constraints into resources (Di Fabio, 2014c, p. 100). ISC is based on the notion *intrapreneur*—those individuals who develop and make efforts to implement innovative ideas within the organization in which they work, knowing both its limitation and possibilities (Honig, 2001). In summary, ISC can be described as self-perceptions with regard to: a positive self-evaluation; commitment, control, and challenge in one's own life; abilities to creatively solve problems; abilities to cope with adversity in an adaptive way; a pursuit to develop one's skills; ability to use decision-making skills in every context and to make decisions accurately and adaptively (Di Fabio, 2014c). Thus, ISC refers to individuals as *intrapreneurs* of their lives. This perspective is conceptually useful with respect to their creating new chapters of their life stories that are meaningful for confronting perceived discrepancies in their life amidst their contextual constraints (Di Fabio & Van Esbroeck, 2016).

ISC is a higher-order construct composed of seven constructs: core self-evaluation, hardiness, creative self-efficacy, resilience, goal mastery, decisiveness, and vigilance (Di Fabio, 2014c). Core self-evaluation (Judge, Erez, Bono, & Thorensen, 2003) represents a positive self-concept in terms of self-esteem, self-efficacy, the locus of control, and the absence of pessimism. Hardiness denotes an individual combination of beliefs about the self and the world and how to interact with this world; it includes three dimensions: commitment, control, and challenge (Maddi, 1990). Creative self-efficacy refers to an individual's perception of the ability to deal with and creatively solve problems. It involves the perception to have problem-solving skills and to be able to produce new ideas (Tierney & Farmer, 2002). Resilience regards the perceived ability to cope adaptively with difficulties and to apply adaptive strategies to face discomfort and troubles (Tugade & Fredrickson, 2004). Goal mastery is related to constantly evolving skills and achieving the best level of performance in activities that are conducive to this result (Midgley et al., 2000). Decisiveness denotes the perceived ability to timely make decisions in any life environment. Vigilance can be considered as an adaptive decision-making style described as an accurate and adaptive search for significant information and the careful examination of each option before making a choice (Mann, Burnett, Radford, & Ford, 1997). The Intrapreneurial Self-Capital Scale (ISCS, Di Fabio, 2014c) was developed to measure ISC.

These constructs selected to reflect ISC are associated with career outcomes, such as performance, employability, career decision-making self-efficacy, and the lack of career decision-making difficulties (Di Fabio, 2014c). Thus, ISC is a key protective factor important for reducing risks of career and self-decision-making troubles, distress, and failures, rather than focusing on explicit problems (Di Fabio, 2014c). ISC can promote adaptations particularly for exploring future challenges and changing schemas toward more flexibility (Di Fabio & Van Esbroeck, 2016) in order to achieve successful results, meaningful objectives (Di Fabio, 2014c), and well-being (Di Fabio, Palazzeschi, & Bucci, 2017). ISC is conceptually situated in a preventive perspective (Hage et al., 2007; Kenny & Di Fabio, 2009; Kenny & Hage, 2009; Kenny, Horne, Orpinas, & Reese, 2009) and a lifelong development perspective (Allan, Duffy, & Douglass, 2015; Di Fabio & Kenny, 2016). Having summarized the conceptual foundations of ISC and its potential utility for career self-management, we now turn to the challenge of enhancing individuals' ISC by a specific training regime.

11.3 Training for ISC

According to a positive preventive perspective (Di Fabio & Kenny, 2015; Di Fabio et al., 2016; Hage et al., 2007; Kenny & Hage, 2009), it is important to emphasize and enhance personal strengths (Di Fabio, 2014c, 2015a; Di Fabio & Blustein, 2016; Di Fabio & Kenny, 2012a, 2012b, 2016; Di Fabio & Palazzeschi, 2016; Di Fabio & Saklofske, 2014a, 2014b). Therefore, ISC training should be administered early and before transitions, especially to young people in uncertain conditions, such as students who are dealing with an important transition from the university to the world of work (Di Fabio, 2014c).

ISC training involves individuals reflecting on their career and life (Di Fabio & Van Esbroeck, 2016). ISC training begins with a first session focused on the exercise "The Book of My Life Story" to encourage reflection on one's whole life.

This exercise also comprises reflection on "The Future Chapter of My Life Story." The next three sessions regard the elements of ISC. The second session addresses positive self-concept and hardiness, the third session is about creative self-efficacy and resilience, and the fourth session is related to goal mastery, decisiveness, and vigilance. The exercises within each session are prepared in three levels: a first level to inspire reflection for the self-evaluation of each ISC element, a second level to encourage the detection of specific positive aspects in relation to each ISC element, and a third level to recognize aspects within past, present, and future chapter/s in the individual's life story, in order to positively explicit the elements of ISC. The chapter/s has/have to be graphically highlighted and subsequently used to deeply analyze motivations and dimensions that can be exploited to define accurately ISC elements. Furthermore, specific exercises to enhance each particular element are administered to the participants. The fifth session addresses thought validation to reach new authorship in constructing the next chapter in individual's life story. Attention is paid to personal strategies to reach clear expression and enhancement of intrapreneurial resources. At one level, the process of ISC training (e.g., reflective story) resembles other narrative career counseling approaches focused on the creation of new perspectives and stories that foster career adaptations in response to conflicts and challenges (e.g., My Career Chapter; McIlveen, 2015, 2017). The feature that distinguishes ISC training from these other approaches is its focus on enhancing qualities of intrapreneurship.

In this chapter, we describe the case study of a female student, Erica, who was concerned about her job placement and work possibilities. The case study describes how Intrapreneurial Self-Capital Training was applied and how it helped the participant to increase her awareness of personal intrapreneurial resources.

11.4 The Case of Erica

Erica (a pseudonym) was 24 years old and is close to master's degree in biology at the University of Florence in Italy. Erica was very worried about her job placement and unsure about her career resources, so she attended the career service of the School of Psychology at the University of Florence. Erica felt unsure about how to leverage the knowledge and skills acquired during her university education. Erica participated in Intrapreneurial Self-Capital (ISC) Training to resolve her concerns and confusion, discover her personal intrapreneurial attributes and resources, and facilitate self-awareness (Di Fabio, 2014c; Di Fabio & Van Esbroeck, 2016).

11.5 Evaluation Instrument

Life Adaptability Qualitative Assessment (LAQuA). The LAQuA (Di Fabio, 2015b) is a new qualitative instrument that can be used to evaluate the effectiveness of career counseling and education interventions. LAQuA qualitatively assesses career adaptability by using 12 written questions about *Concern*, *Control*, *Curiosity*, *Confidence*, which are the dimensions of the Career Adapt-Abilities Inventory-International Version (CAAS, Savickas & Porfeli, 2012). There are three questions for each career adaptability dimension. The 12 written questions of the LAQuA are the following.

- Concern: (1a) What does it mean to you to be oriented toward your future? 1b) Do you think you are oriented toward your future? (1c) Why?
- Control: (2a) What does it mean to you to take responsibility for your future? (2b) Do you think you do take responsibility for your future? (2c) Why?
- Curiosity: (3a) What does it mean to you to be curious about your own future? (3b) Do you think you are curious about your future? (3c) Why?
- Confidence: (4a) What does it mean to you to have confidence in your own ability to build your future? (4b) Do you think you have confidence in your ability to build your future? (4c) Why?

Responses to the LAQuA questions given before and after training are compared. The method of comparison for evaluation uses 24 qualitative indicators related to each of the four dimensions of career adaptability. These indicators reflect the 24 items of the CAAS.

- Concern: Anticipating, Predicting, Equipping, Involved, Strategic, Aware (of choices and transitions to be made).
- Control: Positive Attitude, Autonomous, Conscientious, Assertive, Responsible, and Honest.
- Curiosity: Investigative, Developing, Inquisitive, Recognizing/Discovering, Inquiring, and Searching.
- Confidence: Productive, Mindful, Innovative, Capable, Resilient, Able to Work Out Answers.

These 24 qualitative descriptors are used for the LAQuA coding system, organized in five qualitative analysis change categories that allow detection of any changes or lack of change for each dimension of career adaptability at different levels of reflexivity (Increased Reflexivity, Revised Reflexivity, Open Reflexivity, Enhanced Reflexivity, and No Change.)

1. Increased Reflexivity: It appears in two different forms (Type I and Type II). Type I: Within the narratives produced post-intervention, there are the identical descriptor/s present within the narratives produced pre-intervention but with more in-depth reflexivity. Type II: Within the narratives produced pre-intervention, there is a lack of descriptors, whereas a descriptor of reflexivity appears within narratives produced post-intervention. Thus, there is a depth increase in reflexivity in the same descriptor/s (Type I) or an increase in reflexivity with the appearance of a descriptor/s (Type II).
2. Revised Reflexivity: Descriptor/s present in narratives produced pre-intervention are no longer present at post-intervention; however, there are

new or different descriptor/s. Thus, now there is a new focus on different facets of career adaptability.

3. Open Reflexivity: In narratives produced post-intervention, there is identical descriptor/s present in narratives produced pre-intervention and with the same level of reflexivity, but there is/are new descriptor/s in addition. Thus, the previous focus is preserved and a new awareness of a different facet/s of the specific career adaptability dimension rises.
4. Enhanced Reflexivity: In narratives produced post-intervention, there is the identical descriptor/s present in narratives produced pre-intervention but with more in-depth reflexivity, and there is/are a new descriptor/s in addition. Thus, there is an expansion in the complexity regarding the dimension because there are both a depth increase in reflexivity in the same descriptor/s and also a diversification of a different facet/s of the specific career adaptability dimension.
5. No Change: There are two forms of No Change (Type I and Type II). Type I: Within the narratives produced post-intervention, there is the same identical descriptor/s present as in the narratives produced pre-intervention and with the same level of reflexivity related to the descriptor/s. Type II: Within the narratives produced pre-intervention, there is a lack of a descriptor/s, and in the narratives produced post-intervention there is still a lack of descriptors relating to the specific career adaptability dimension.

The LAQuA is, therefore, an instrument that may detect change (or lack of change) within narratives pre- and post-interventions specifically for the four career adaptability dimensions (Concern, Control, Curiosity, and Confidence). Moreover, change is indicated by levels of reflexivity.

11.6 Procedure

The aim of the ISC training is to facilitate the reflection of individual for self-evaluation in relation to each component of the intervention; to encourage the recognition of positive personal aspects regarding each dimension of the intervention; and to sustain the analysis of the past through the present toward the future for identifying in individual life story the chapter/s in which the components of the ISC are expressed in a favorable manner.

Erica participated in the ISC training (Di Fabio, 2014c; Di Fabio & Van Esbroeck, 2016) which was delivered as five sessions, of 8 hours per session, over a period of 5 weeks. Training occurred in a group setting (Di Fabio, 2013) using the methology of the power of the audience (Di Fabio & Maree, 2012). The members were arranged in a circle, communicated in turn with the psychologist facilitator one at a time, deepening the individual's training outcomes. Thus, the group participants were treated as individuals in a one-to-one intervention session, but, at the same time, they could reflect on themselves and the stimuli from observing other participants in the intervention.

The LAQuA was administered before and after the ISC training by a psychologist trained in the administration of this assessment tool. Three independent, trained expert reviewers (raters) compared the participant's responses to the 12 written questions of the LAQuA produced by the client before and after the intervention. An interrater reliability analysis using the Kappa statistic was carried out to establish the level of consistency among the raters.

The study adhered to the requirements of privacy and informed consent in Italian law (Law Decree DL-196/2003) and the ethical standards for research of the Declaration of Helsinki revised in Fortaleza (World Medical Association [WMA], 2013), followed and approved by the Department of Education and Psychology of the University of Florence (Italy).

11.7 Results

The analysis of the narratives produced by Erica before and after the ISC training was carried out by examining the LAQuA 24 qualitative indicators corresponding to Concern, Control, Curiosity, and Confidence. The change or lack of change in the narratives before and after the intervention relying on the identified qualitative descriptors was examined using the levels of reflexivity (Increased Reflexivity, Revised Reflexivity, Open Reflexivity, Enhanced Reflexivity, and No Change).

Erica's response to the first LAQuA question before the ISC training was: "*To me, to be oriented toward my future means being aware of what I want to do in my life, both personal and professional, and by aware of the personal and professional choices I have to made*" (qualitative descriptor: Involved); and after the ISC training, it was: "*To me be oriented toward my future means to having shaped a precise project both personal and professional. After the intervention, I'm more looking positively to the future, I think to have useful tools and resources to construct my life and career project according to my values and ideals. I think that I could use my skills to search for different job opportunities and, also for a specialized internship in Italy or outside Italy. I understand that I want to improve my knowledge and competences in biology*" (identical qualitative descriptor but more in-depth reflexivity: Involved; Increased Reflexivity: in the narratives produced after the ISC training, there were identical descriptors, but they were described with more in-depth reflexivity).

Erica's response to the second LAQuA question before the ISC training was: "*To me, to take responsibility for my future means being ready to perform autonomously the tasks and the duties that I will encounter during my path*" (qualitative descriptor: Responsible); and after the ISC training, it was: "*To me, to take responsibility for my future now means counting on myself to fulfil the activities in which I'm involved that I consider as challenge for my growth*" (identical qualitative descriptor but more in-depth reflexivity: Responsible). "*It is important for me to do different tasks and activities to test myself and to make decisions autonomously without accepting passively the advices by others*" (a new, different qualitative descriptor: Autonomous). "*For me it is important to make choices carefully, being aware of the consequences for me and others*" [a new, different qualitative descriptor: Conscientious; Enhanced Reflexivity (E): in the narratives produced after the ISC training, there is an identical descriptor/s but described with more in-depth reflexivity plus a new, different descriptor/s].

Erica's response to the third LAQuA question before the ISC training was: "*To me, to be curious about my future means 'leaving open the door' to many different career possibilities and gathering many information about post-graduate courses or internships*" (qualitative descriptor: Searching); and after the ISC training, it was: "*Now I think to be very curious about my future, and I want to know more in-depth post-graduate courses or internships for opening career opportunities*" (identical qualitative descriptor: Searching); "*I would like to examine different career fields where I could express my talents, for example doing internships in specific organization to observe the context and the ways in which people do their work*" [a new, different qualitative descriptor: Recognizing/Discovering; Open Reflexivity (O): in the narratives produced after the ISC training, there is an identical descriptor/s—with the same level of reflexivity in presenting the descriptor—plus a new, different descriptor/s].

Erica's response to the fourth LAQuA question before the ISC training was: "*To me, to have confidence in my own abilities to build my future means to be aware of my skills and the ways in which they can be used to construct my life*" (qualitative descriptor: Capable); and after the ISC training, it was: "*I think that to have confidence in my own abilities to build my future means to deal successfully with the daily activities and to accept the challenges in my personal and professional life. I think that learning new skills and updating my knowledge is important to identify more career opportunities*" [a new, different qualitative descriptor: Productive; Revised Reflexivity R: in the narratives produced after the ISC training, the previous descriptor/s has disappeared, and a new, different descriptor/s has appeared].

11.8 Discussion

The value of this case study regards the importance of enhancing personal resources of young people who deal with uncertain and unsecure context within a positive preventive perspective (Di Fabio & Kenny, 2015; Di Fabio et al., 2017; Hage et al., 2007; Kenny & Hage, 2009). Students who are close to graduation have to overcome a relevant transition from the university to the world of work. They need thereby to become more aware of their personal strengths and the possibility to improve them (Di Fabio & Kenny, 2016; Di Fabio et al., 2016). The ISC training is an intervention to help young people to enhance their individual resources in order to timely answer to the demands of the twenty-first century (Di Fabio, 2014c; Di Fabio & Van Esbroeck, 2016).

In this case study, the analysis of the narratives produced by Erica before and after the intervention, through the LAQuA coding system (Di Fabio, 2015b), denoted the evolution of her beliefs about herself and her career. The increase in the level of reflexivity is evident in all the four dimensions of adaptability (Concern, Control, Curiosity, and Confidence). With respect to Concern, Erica understood that she is engaged in identifying and realizing her personal and professional project. As for Control, for Erica is important to being able to accomplish her tasks and activities, to make decision independently and to take the responsibility for the possible consequences. In her Curiosity, Erica stressed the importance of open different career opportunities, collecting much information on postgraduate courses and internships in order to learn new knowledge and skills through particular training and direct experiences in specialized organizations. As for her Confidence, Erica understood that she could use her knowledge and skills to deal successfully with her tasks and to accept changes and challenges; she realized also that she could improve her competences after her master's graduations through different ways. After the training, Erica's narratives of awareness and the potential of her intrapreneurial resources are useful for a successful career and life management. Overall, the changes in the narratives before and after the ISC training indicated the effectiveness of the intervention for Erica.

11.9 Limitations

This case study revealed changes in the narratives produced by the participant after her ISC training. An $N = 1$ case study is informative with respect to the intervention's effects for the participant's self-perceptions reflective of career adaptability; however, the generalizable effectiveness of the intervention for others needs to be confirmed by research with larger samples. Furthermore, future research should implement both qualitative and quantitative indicators of change so as to explore the evolution of narrative content (Busacca & Rehfuss, 2016) and reflexivity (Di Fabio, Maree, & Kenny, 2018), changes in scores for common measures of career constructs (e.g., career adaptability, self-efficacy), and, apposite to ISC, the Intrapreneurial Self-Capital Scale (ISCS, Di Fabio, 2014c). In the case of Erica, it may be informative to conduct a follow-up LAQuA evaluation 12 months after the ISC training to ascertain further evolution in her narratives.

11.10 Implications for Practice

Erica's engagement with and personal benefits from ISC suggest that being near to graduation does not limit the personal effectiveness of the program. Nonetheless, in an ideal situation, ISC should be completed in the early years of a student's studies so as to provide them more opportunities to explore and test their narratives in an educational context that is focused on their career. Career counseling interventions effectively assist clients to identify and develop their talents by enhancing key career self-management factors such as self-awareness and self-efficacy (Whiston, Li, Goodrich Mitts, & Wright, 2017). Higher education scholars argue that enhanced self-awareness about human capital (Clarke, 2017), a sense of career ownership, and good career advice may have positive effects for students' perceptions of employability (Clarke, 2017; Donald, Baruch, & Ashleigh, 2017). Thus, career counseling practitioners working in educational settings may deliver ISC as a career education program, either independent of curricula or integrated within curricula. Case studies, such as the present one, can be useful training resources for practitioners wish to learn about ISC and its training.

11.11 Conclusion

The world of work demands higher-order cognitive and behavioral competencies, particularly in knowledge-intensive industries and organizations in which intrapreneurship is valued. Employers, universities and colleges, trainers, and educators are interested in novel perspectives and tools to meet those demands. Training for these higher-order competencies may enhance a person's employability and career sustainability. In this regard, ISC is a useful construct for conceptualizing, designing, and delivering career counseling and education that aims to develop intrapreneurship within students and workers.

References

Allan, B. A., Duffy, R. D., & Douglass, R. (2015). Meaning in life and work: A developmental perspective. *The Journal of Positive Psychology, 10*(4), 323–331.

Blustein, D. L. (2006). *The psychology of working: A new perspective for career development, counseling and public policy*. NY: Routledge.

Blustein, D. L. (2011). A relational theory of working. *Journal of Vocational Behavior, 79,* 1–17.

Blustein, D. L., Kenna, A. C., Murphy, K. A., DeVoy, J. E., & DeWine, D. B. (2005). Qualitative research in career development: Exploring the center and margins of discourse about careers and working. *Journal of Career Assessment, 13*(4), 351–370.

Blustein, D. L., Kenny, M. E., Di Fabio, A., & Guichard, J. (in press). Expanding the impact of the psychology of working: Engaging psychology in the struggle for decent work and human rights. *Journal of Career Assessment.* https://doi.org/10.1177/1069072718774002.

Busacca, L., & Rehfuss, M. (Eds.). (2016). *Postmodern career counseling: A handbook of culture, contexts, and cases*. American Counseling Association.

Clarke, M. (2017). Rethinking graduate employability: The role of capital, individual attributes and context. *Studies in Higher Education*, 1–15. https://doi.org/10.1080/03075079.2017.1294152.

Di Fabio, A. (2013). Applying career construction in group-based contexts with adults. In A. Di Fabio & J. G. Maree (Eds.), *Psychology of career counseling: New challenges for a new era. Festschrift in honour of Prof. Mark Savickas* (pp. 83–99). New York: Nova Science Publishers.

Di Fabio, A. (2014a). Career counseling and positive psychology in the 21st century: New constructs and measures for evaluating the effectiveness of intervention. *Journal of Counsellogy, 1,* 193–213.
Di Fabio, A. (2014b). "Constructing my future purposeful life": A new life construction intervention. In A. Di Fabio & J.-L. Bernaud (Eds.), *The construction of the identity in 21st century: A Festschrift for Jean Guichard* (pp. 219–239). New York: Nova Science Publishers.
Di Fabio, A. (2014c). Intrapreneurial self-capital: A new construct for the 21st century. *Journal of Employment Counseling, 51,* 98–111.
Di Fabio, A. (2015a). Beyond fluid intelligence and personality traits in social support: The role of ability based emotional intelligence. *Frontiers in Psychology, 6*, 395. https://doi.org/10.3389/fpsyg.2015.00395.
Di Fabio, A. (2015b). Life adaptability qualitative assessment (LAQuA): A narrative instrument for evaluating counseling intervention effectiveness. In J. G. Maree & A. Di Fabio, A. (Eds.), *Exploring new horizons in career counselling: Turning challenges into opportunities* (pp. 43–62). Rotterdam, The Netherlands: Sense Publishers.
Di Fabio, A., & Blustein, D. L. (Eds). (2016). *From meaning of working to meaningful lives: The challenges of expanding decent work.* Lausanne: Frontiers Media. https://doi.org/10.3389/978-2-88919-970-9.
Di Fabio, A., & Kenny, M. E. (2012a). The contribution of emotional intelligence to decisional styles among Italian high school students. *Journal of Career Assessment, 20,* 404–414.
Di Fabio, A., & Kenny, M. E. (2012b). Emotional intelligence and perceived social support among Italian high school students. *Journal of Career Development, 39,* 461–475.
Di Fabio, A., & Kenny, M. E. (2015). The contributions of emotional intelligence and social support for adaptive career progress among Italian youth. *Journal of Career Development, 42,* 48–49.
Di Fabio, A., & Kenny, M. E. (2016). From decent work to decent lives: Positive self and relational management (PS&RM) in the twenty-first century. *Frontiers in Psychology*, *7*(361). https://doi.org/10.3389/fpsyg.2016.00361.
Di Fabio, A., Kenny, M. E., & Claudius, M. (2016). Preventing distress and promoting psychological well-being in uncertain times through career management intervention. In M. Israelashvili & J. L. Romano (Eds.), *Cambridge handbook of international prevention science*. Cambridge: Cambridge University Press.
Di Fabio, A., & Maree, J. G. (2012). Group-based life design counseling in an Italian context. *Journal of Vocational Behavior, 80,* 100–107.
Di Fabio, A., Maree, J. G., & Kenny, M. E. (2018). Development of the Life project reflexivity scale: A new reflexivity inventory. *Journal of Career Assessment*.
Di Fabio, A., & Palazzeschi, L. (2016). Marginalization and precariat: The challenge of intensifying life construction intervention. In A. Di Fabio & D. L. Blustein (Eds.), From meaning of working to meaningful lives: The challenges of expanding decent work. Research topic in *Frontiers in Psychology. Section Organizational Psychology*. https://doi.org/10.3389/fpsyg.2016.00444.
Di Fabio, A., Palazzeschi, L., & Bucci, O. (2017). In an unpredictable and changing environment: Intrapreneurial self-capital as a key resource for life satisfaction and flourishing. In G. Arcangeli, G. Giorgi, N. Mucci, J.-L. Bernaud, & A. Di Fabio (Eds.), Emerging and re-emerging organizational features, work transitions and occupational risk factors: The good, the bad, the right. An interdisciplinary perspective. Research Topic in *Frontiers in Psychology. Organizational Psychology*, *8*, 1819. https://doi.org/10.3389/fpsyg.2017.01819.
Di Fabio, A., & Saklofske, D. H. (2014a). Comparing ability and self-report trait emotional intelligence, fluid intelligence, and personality traits in career decision. *Personality and Individual Differences, 64,* 174–178.
Di Fabio, A., & Saklofske, D. H. (2014b). Promoting individual resources: The challenge of trait emotional intelligence. *Personality and Individual Differences, 65,* 19–23.
Di Fabio, A., & Van Esbroeck, R. (2016). Intrapreneurial self-capital: A concept fitting a life-designing intervention. *Counseling. Giornale Italiano di Ricerca e Applicazioni, 9*(2).

Donald, W. E., Baruch, Y., & Ashleigh, M. (2017). The undergraduate self-perception of employability: Human capital, careers advice, and career ownership. *Studies in Higher Education*, 1–16. https://doi.org/10.1080/03075079.2017.1387107.

Duffy, R. D., Allan, B. A., England, J. W., Blustein, D. L., Autin, K. L., Douglass, R. P., …, & Santos, E. J. (2017). The development and initial validation of the decent work scale. *Journal of Counseling Psychology*, *64*(2), 206.

Duffy, R. D., Foley, P. F., Raque-Bodgan, T. L., Reid-Marks, L., Dik, B. J., Castano, M. C., et al. (2012). Counseling psychologists who view their careers as a calling: A qualitative study. *Journal of Career Assessment, 20*(3), 293–308.

Duffy, R. D., Torrey, C. L., Bott, E. M., Allan, B. A., & Schlosser, L. Z. (2013). Time management, passion, and collaboration: A qualitative study of highly research productive counseling psychologists. *The Counseling Psychologist, 41*(6), 881–917.

Guichard, J. (2013, September). *Which paradigm for career and life designing interventions contributing to the development of a fairer world during the 21st century*. Lecture presented at the IAEVG international conference, Montpellier, France.

Guichard, J., Bangali, M., Cohen Scali, V., Pouyaud, J., & Robinet, M. L. (2016). *Concevoir et orienter sa vie: Les dialogues de conseil en life design*. Paris: Editions Qui plus est.

Hage, S. M., Romano, J. L., Conyne, R. K., Kenny, M., Matthews, C., Schwartz, J. P., et al. (2007). Best practice guidelines on prevention practice, research, training, and social advocacy for psychologists. *The Counseling Psychologist, 35,* 493–566.

Honig, B. (2001). Learning strategies and resources for entrepreneurs and intrapreneurs. *Entrepreneurship Theory and Practice, 26,* 21–35.

Judge, T. A., Erez, A., Bono, J. E., & Thoresen, C. J. (2003). The core self-evaluations scale: Development of a measure. *Personnel Psychology, 56,* 303–331.

Kenny, M., & Di Fabio, A. (2009). Prevention and career development. *Risorsa Uomo Rivista di Psicologia del Lavoro e dell'Organizzazione, 15,* 361–374.

Kenny, M. E., & Hage, S. M. (2009). The next frontier: Prevention as an instrument of social justice. *The Journal of Primary Prevention, 30,* 1–10.

Kenny, M. E., Horne, A. M., Orpinas, P., & Reese, L. E. (2009). Social justice and the challenge of preventive interventions: An introduction. In M. E. Kenny, A. M. Horne, P. Orpinas, & L. E. Reese (Eds.), *Realizing social justice: The challenge of preventive interventions* (pp. 3–14). Washington, DC: American Psychological Association.

Maddi, S. R. (1990). Issues and interventions in stress mastery. In H. S. Friedman (Ed.), *Personality and disease* (pp. 121–154). New York: Wiley.

Mann, L., Burnett, P., Radford, M., & Ford, S. (1997). The Melbourne decision making questionnaire: An instrument for measuring patterns for coping with decisional conflict. *Journal of Behavioral Decision Making, 10,* 1–19.

McIlveen, P. (2015). My career chapter and the career systems interview. In M. McMahon & M. Watson (Eds.), *Career assessment: Qualitative approaches* (pp. 123–128). Rotterdam, The Netherlands: Sense Publishers.

McIlveen, P. (2017). Using my career chapter with a Malaysian engineer to write and tell a career story. In L. A. Busacca & M. C. Rehfuss (Eds.), *Postmodern career counseling. A Handbook of culture, context, and cases* (pp. 105–117). Alexandria, VA: American Counseling Association.

Midgley, C., Maehr, M. L., Hruda, L. Z., Anderman, E., Anderman, L., Freeman, K. E., …, Urdan, T. (2000). *Manual for the patterns of adaptive learning scales*. Retrieved from University of Michigan website: http://www.umich.edu/~pals/PALS%202000_V13Word97.pdf.

Peiró, J. M., Sora, B., & Caballer, A. (2012). Job insecurity in the younger Spanish workforce: Causes and consequences. *Journal of Vocational Behavior, 80,* 444–453.

Rosa, H. (2015). *Accelerazione e alienazione. Per una teoria critica del tempo nella tarda* modernità (Trad. it. E. Leonzio). Torino: Einaudi.

Savickas, M. L. (Ed.). (2011). *Career counseling*. Washington, DC: American Psychological Association.

Savickas, M. L. (2015). *Life-design counseling manual*. Rootstown, OH: Author.

Savickas, M. L., & Porfeli, E. J. (2012). Career adapt-abilities scale: Construction, reliability, and measurement equivalence across 13 countries. *Journal of Vocational Behavior, 80,* 661–673.

Tierney, P., & Farmer, S. M. (2002). Creative self-efficacy: Its potential antecedents and relationship to creative performance. *Academy of Management Journal, 45,* 1137–1148.

Tugade, M. M., & Fredrickson, B. L. (2004). Resilient individuals use positive emotions to bounce back from negative emotional experiences. *Journal of Personality and Social Psychology, 86,* 320–333.

Whiston, S. C., Li, Y., Goodrich Mitts, N., & Wright, L. (2017). Effectiveness of career choice interventions: A meta-analytic replication and extension. *Journal of Vocational Behavior, 100,* 175–184. https://doi.org/10.1016/j.jvb.2017.03.010.

World Medical Association [WMA]. (2013). *WMA declaration of Helsinki—Ethical principles for medical research involving human subjects.* Available at: http: //www.wma.net/en/30publications/10policies/b3/.

Chapter 12
Constructing My Future Purposeful Life as a New Life Construction Dialogue Intervention: A Case Study on an Italian Worker Using Comparatively FCA, LAQuA, and CCIO as Qualitative Evaluation Instruments

Violetta Drabik-Podgórna, Marek Podgórny and Annamaria Di Fabio

Abstract This chapter presents the case study of an employee of the didactic and guidance office of a public graduate school and research institute in Italy who participated in a new life construction dialogue intervention entitled "Constructing My Future Purposeful Life" and filled qualitative instruments for verifying the effectiveness of this intervention: the Future Career Autobiography (FCA), the Life Adaptability Qualitative Assessment (LAQuA), and the Career Counseling Innovative Outcomes (CCIO). The qualitative instruments were administered before and after the life construction dialogue intervention. The results of the case study underscored the effectiveness of the Constructing My Future Purposeful Life intervention evaluated through different qualitative instruments and highlighted the value of enhancing new dialogue interventions to strengthen client's reflexivity and increase purposeful identitarian awareness.

12.1 Introduction

In the postmodern era, the concept of "career" as a predictable evolution of steps in a stable organization (Super, 1957, 1980) or a sequence of vocational activities in the life span of an individual (Osipow, 2012) is no longer applicable because the world of work is unstable and flexible, and organizations are fluid (Hartung, 2012; Savickas, 2011). In a liquid society (Bauman, 2000; Guichard & Di Fabio, 2015),

A. Di Fabio (✉)
Department of Education and Psychology (Psychology Section),
University of Florence, Florence, Italy
e-mail: adifabio@psico.unifi.it

V. Drabik-Podgórna · M. Podgórny
Institute of Pedagogy, University of Wrocław, Wrocław, Poland

© Springer Nature Switzerland AG 2018

A. Di Fabio and J.-L. Bernaud (eds.), *Narrative Interventions in Post-modern Guidance and Career Counseling*, https://doi.org/10.1007/978-3-319-98300-4_12

career no longer belongs to the organization but to the person (Duffy et al., 2012; Duffy, Torrey, Bott, Allan, & Schlosser, 2013; Duarte, 2004). Accordingly, career management can be conceptualized as how "people go about constructing their lives through work, always bearing in mind … that the career of an individual is a faithful record of his/her life" (Duarte, 2009, p. 264). This perspective refers to the process by which individuals are encouraged to develop, implement, and monitor their objectives and strategies for their career (Greenhaus, Callanan, & Goodshalk, 2010; Savickas, 2011). Paradoxically, a lack of clearly defined trajectories multiplies the possible occupations and identities (Guichard, 2013; Savickas, 2013). In this complex scenario (Blustein, 2006), there are a few points of reference for self-orientations (Guichard, 2007, 2009a) because people have to deal with the narrow interconnection between work and other personal activities (Guichard, 2004, 2005, 2008, 2009b). Thus, the concept "life management" is thus introduced as fundamental for people to develop skills and strategies in order to achieve their life objectives (Guichard, 2004, 2005). Together, career and life management represent crucial challenges in the postmodern era regarding self-realization both in personal and in professional dimensions (Busacca & Rehfuss, 2016; Di Fabio, 2014b, d, e; Guichard, Bangali, Cohen Scali, Pouyaud, & Robinet, 2016). Individuals have to balance the different aspects of their life through adaptability, intentionality, lifelong learning, autobiographical reasoning and meaning (Savickas, 2011, 2013). They are entirely responsible for shaping their life as accountable for their biographical decisions (Savickas, 2011, 2013).

In career and life management, relationships acquire a key value according to the relational theory of working (Blustein, 2011). Work is an inherently relational act as each decision, experience, and interaction in a work context are understood, influenced, and shaped by relationships. A perspective of intervention responsive to changes and transitions of the postmodern society underscores the importance of helping people, especially to construct their lives through work and relationships considered as main contexts (Duffy et al., 2017; Duffy, Blustein, Diemer, & Autin, 2016; Maree & Di Fabio, 2015; Richardson, 2012). The principle shift can be outlined from career project to life project that is an inherently relational act (Di Fabio, 2014c). Knowing how to choose and, above all, knowing how to construct can be considered as important skills in the Career Construction Theory (Savickas, 2005). The concept of self as a project in a relational form is essential, as self-construction is considered as not an individual process but a social construction —as a co-construction through the collaboration with the close social group and the larger community (Savickas, 2011). In the Self-Construction Theory (Guichard, 2004, 2005), people are seen as plural entities and the individual identity is associated with a dynamic system of subjective identity forms. People interact in different contexts and have various experiences, developing plural self-images, assuming many roles and implementing diverse selves (Guichard, 2004, 2005). They can reach a more unified self by integrating their experiences and shaping fundamental future expectations. In the recent evolution of the Self-Construction Theory (Guichard, 2004, 2005), the Life Construction Theory (Guichard, 2013), it is underlined that individuals are able to unify themselves by linking their different life experiences through the narration of future events, thus favoring the attribution of sense and meaning to their lives.

Moreover, as the postmodern era is characterized by a deregulation of life paths and an increase in the opportunities and directions (Guichard, 2013; Savickas, 2013), it important to stress the importance of the connection among various life dimensions. The relational theory of working (Blustein, 2011) authorizes another movement from career and life management (Guichard, 2013; Savickas, 2013) toward career and life management through self and relational management (Di Fabio, 2014e; Di Fabio & Kenny, 2016). The career and life management process are influenced by the relationships and the contexts where individuals are involved; accordingly, these processes may be enhanced by preventive interventions (Di Fabio, 2014a; Di Fabio & Kenny, 2016; Kenny & Hage, 2009) that aim at constructing personal strengths for adapting to changes in professional and personal life (Di Fabio, Kenny, & Minor, 2014). Individuals are required to improve their psychological resources (Di Fabio, 2014d) to maintain their personal and social well-being through economic, structural, and social changes (Di Fabio & Kenny, 2016; Di Fabio, Palazzeschi, & Bucci, 2017; Douglass, Duffy, & Autin, 2016). This new vision places the interventions in a new and early preventive perspective (Blustein, 2006, 2011; Kenny & Hage, 2009) and underlines the value of effective career and life construction interventions for individuals responsible for their life (Guichard & Di Fabio, 2015).

New postmodern interventions are necessary to timely and effectively answer to the demands of the twenty-first century. They can be developed within the recent taxonomy of Guichard (2013): information, guidance, and dialogue. Information interventions aim at increasing the skills of individuals to search for relevant and reliable information in relation to the world of work. Guidance intervention aims at developing client employability promoting the construction of an adaptable and vocational self-concept. Dialogue interventions aim at helping clients identify a personal life meaning, encouraging them in the construction of their lives within an unstable context.

An innovative dialogue intervention, "Constructing My Future Purposeful Life" (Di Fabio, 2014b), was developed with the aim of enhancing two key meta-competencies: *adaptability* (Savickas, 2001), as the ability to anticipate the future in a constant changing environment (Savickas, 2001), and *identity* (Guichard, 2004, 2010) related to the concept of the self as a story representing inner bearings to face multiple transitions that can be enhanced by narratability, biographicity, and reflexivity. The new intervention aims also to strengthen a purposeful *identitarian awareness* (Di Fabio, 2014e) toward an increased authentic intentionality (Di Fabio, 2014d). The main goal of the intervention is to facilitate recognition of life and career meaning (Di Fabio, 2014d, f) so as to manage the experiential challenges to become and not only to decide. This involves enabling individuals to write a successful new chapter of their life in the new postmodern reality (Guichard & Di Fabio, 2015; Savickas, 2013, 2015) in relation to the complexity of working (Blustein, 2006, 2011).

The new dialogue intervention "Constructing My Future Purposeful Life" is articulated in three modules (Di Fabio, 2014b) that aim to achieve specific level of reflexion. The fundamental concept stages of this intervention are rooted in the principal career theories of the twenty-first century (Guichard & Di Fabio, 2010). The first module is established principally in the Career Construction Theory (Savickas, 2001, 2005, 2011) and on the Life Construction Theory as well (Guichard, 2013). The second module is concentrated on self-reflection, self-advising (Guichard, 2013), guided meta-reflection (Maree, 2013), and reflexivity (Di Fabio & Maree, 2013; Guichard, 2009b; Maree, 2013). The third module aims "To make oneself self" (Guichard, 2004), as well as to continue and enhance reflexivity processes.

The first module consists of two activities. The first activity, the "Life Design Genogram," comprises two genograms: the Career Construction Genogram related to the Career Construction Theory (Savickas, 2005, 2011) and the Life Construction Genogram related to the Life Construction Theory (Guichard, 2013). Clients are required to reflect on the career motto and life motto of the father's line and the mother's line to produce "My career motto" and "My life motto." The second activity of the first module, "Me and the Future," refers to a reflection on the adaptability dimensions that strengthen this meta-competence in relation to the personal mottos produced in the previous part (Savickas, 2001; Savickas & Porfeli, 2012). For each of the four dimensions of adaptability, the following questions are asked: "How much interest do I have for myself in the future? Why?" (Concern); "How much do I feel in control of my future? Why?" (Control); "How much curiosity do I have to build my future? Why?" (Curiosity), and "How much confidence do I have to build my future? Why?" (Confidence). For each of the four dimensions of adaptability, the client is also required to indicate the personal characteristics that describe him or her by concluding the following sentence from a given list: "With respect to the future I am…" These characteristics are drawn from the 24 items of the Career Adaptability Scale (Savickas & Porfeli, 2012).

The second module of the intervention, "Self-advising the Future Self," enhances reflection on life roles. Through self-advising, the individual is stimulated to explicate the authentic self (Di Fabio, 2014e) by increased reflectivity on the past to unify the present through the development of future prospects and a future self. This process is rooted on the Self-Construction Theory (Guichard, 2005, 2010, 2013) to achieve a full meaningfulness (Di Fabio, 2014b, c). The individual is required to indicate future personal life roles in order of importance (the first order). Afterward, the process of self-advising begins: The individual is first asked to read and comprehend those roles and then to propose important advice to himself or herself. Then, the person is required to change the order of the roles (the second order) if they have changed. If the order did not change, the person is required to explain the reasons why. At the same time, if the order changed, the person is required to explain why it changed. The individual is also required to detect the roles perceived as less authentic for him or her in the first order; in the second order, the individual is also required to detect the roles considered the most authentic. The individual then is asked to answer the following questions: "Which meaningful changes do I want to make in how to act my roles?" and "Why?"; finally, the individual is required to recognize the most authentic elements of his or her future self.

The third module, "Constructing the Purposeful Self," is related to the process called "To make oneself self" (Guichard, 2004). Clients, through narration, unify themselves by connecting their different life experiences, and then they can extend this reflection to their future projects promoting authentic intentionality. This module is in part drawn from a theoretical view on the personal success formula of Savickas (2011), which highlights the importance of finding individuals' values and goals in constructing their professional and life system that is actual satisfying and meaningful. Moreover, this module is related to the importance of early reflection and identity awareness connected with individuals' aspired SIF and to the secondary SIF as core elements within individuals' SSIF (Guichard, 2010). This third module actualized the practical passage from helping people develop a career to helping people construct lives (Richardson, 2012), facilitating the construction of a career project and a life project. The third module regards a guided meta-reflection of a high aspiration, of a minimal aspiration, and of designing individuals' reality in relation to both career and life. Particularly, the narrative attempts to facilitate the reflexivity of clients in both career and life through the following questions: "What I would like if I could? And why?" (the ideal plan); "[What is] the minimum objective without which I would strongly unsatisfied? ("minimum satisfaction for me" and "why," indicating the minimum aspiration level), and "[What are the] possible/probable concrete results?" and "why?" (the real plan). Afterward, individuals design the first concrete project for their purposeful self and the A and B life-vest projects for sustaining this purposeful self. Then, clients engage in the first level of meta-guided reflection on the purposeful self and its actual strengths. Clients are at the same time encouraged to think about their relational networks and the contexts where they live and work, being involved in positive self and relational management (PS&RM) (Di Fabio & Kenny, 2016).

Finally, the second level of meta-reflection elicits life meaningfulness through an ongoing verification of the core of the individual. At the end of this level, clients are required to answer the following question "What [can] I take away for me [that] is particularly helpful for me to remember?" The resulting finding encourages the individual to construct a purposeful perspective on career, self, and life meaningfulness.

The effectiveness of "Constructing My Future Purposeful Life" was evaluated (Di Fabio, 2014b) with a combined quali+quanti approach (Di Fabio, 2013; Di Fabio & Maree, 2012, 2013; Maree, 2012, 2013). The study showed qualitative changes in themes relative to life and career, detected through the Future Career Autobiography (FCA, Rehfuss, 2009; Rehfuss & Di Fabio, 2012) and the Career Counseling Innovative Outcomes (CCIO, Di Fabio, 2016). The study also presented a quantitative increase in positive self-concept in terms of self-esteem, self-efficacy, locus of control, and the absence of pessimism, as detected through the Italian version (Di Fabio & Busoni, 2009) of the Core Self-Evaluation Scale (Judge, Erez, Bono, & Thorensen, 2003). In addition, there was enhanced self-awareness about projects more congruent with the self, as detected through the Italian version (Di Fabio, 2014f) of the Authenticity Scale (Wood, Maltby, Baliousis, Linley, & Joseph, 2008).

12.2 Case Study: Sara

This case study examined the process and usefulness of the "Constructing My Future Purposeful Life" intervention in involving the research participant (client) to deeply understand her problems, to overcome the difficulties, and to better design the next chapters of her life. The case study also described the narrative changes related to the intervention. The participant in the study was Sara (a pseudonym), a 49-years-old employee of the didactic and guidance office of a public graduate school and research institute in Italy. She was graduated in information science, and at the time of the research, she was looking for a postgraduate course with the aim of implementing her guidance and communication knowledge and skills. She felt unsure about her career future as she was facing a dilemma in terms of change type of work or change role in the current organization. She was very confused about the next step, and she thought that the updating through a postgraduate course could be useful to accomplish her daily work activities and to clarify her objectives. Sara participated in the "Constructing My Future Purposeful Life" intervention, characterized by three 1-day sessions (8 hours a session) in a group modality using the methodology of the power of an audience (Di Fabio & Maree, 2012). The intervention aims to strengthen participants reflexivity (Di Fabio, Maree, & Kenny, 2018), improving their ability to elaborate through narratives their personal and professional problems, to identify real meanings, and to design more effective projects in different contexts.

12.3 Qualitative Instruments

12.3.1 Future Career Autobiography (FCA)

The *Future Career Autobiography* (FCA, Rehfuss, 2009; Rehfuss & Di Fabio, 2012) is a narrative instrument developed to qualitatively assess the effectiveness of narrative career interventions. The FCA narratively detects an individual's motivations, values, and future direction. The FCA consists of a sheet of paper at the beginning of which clients can write their name and read specific instructions: "Please use this page to write a brief paragraph about where you hope to be in life and what you hope to be doing occupationally five years from now" (Rehfuss, 2009). Moreover, clients are orally instructed to complete the form in 10 minutes. The duration of FCA administration is intentionally limited as the desired outcome is a focused and brief narrative (Rehfuss, 2009). A concise narrative helps the practitioner to understand the clients' life and occupational themes and goals, and then facilitates comparison between the narratives produced before and after the intervention in order to recognize change or lack of change (Rehfuss, 2009). The analysis of FCA can be done by concentrating on the following Eight Degrees of Change identified by Rehfuss (2009).

1. General Fields and Desires to Specification and Exploration, which describe a shift from general fields and desires to specific themes;
2. General Interests to More Specification, in which clients begin with multiple general interests, but over time refine their FCAs;
3. Non-description to Specification, where clients' initial FCAs start with general themes and then concentrate on personal and professional themes;
4. Disregard to Direction, where clients ignore the life and career parts of their initial FCAs and are apparently unable to finish the task. In their subsequent FCAs, nonetheless, they tackle the same task with specificity and direction;
5. Vagueness to Focus, in which the clients' FCAs moved from an initial perception of insecurity about their personal and professional life to a narrative more detailed and focused;
6. Hindered to Hopeful, where an initial perception of worry or indifference toward work is substituted with specificity;
7. Fixation to Openness, where clients have hastily ignored a personal situation or an occupation and are surprised by the incongruence between their life/career goals and their skills. In subsequent FCAs, they attempt to overcome this dilemma;
8. Stagnation, when there are no changes from initial to subsequent FCAs.

12.3.2 Life Adaptability Qualitative Assessment (LAQuA)

The *Life Adaptability Qualitative Assessment* (LAQuA, Di Fabio, 2015) is a narrative instrument developed to qualitatively evaluate the effectiveness of career and life construction interventions. This instrument permits to evaluate adaptability, assessing change or lack of change in individuals' narratives before and after the intervention. The LAQuA consists of 12 written questions with three questions for each dimension (i.e., Concern, Control, Curiosity, Confidence) of the Career Adapt-Abilities Inventory-International Version 2.0 (Savickas & Porfeli, 2012). The LAQuA 12 written questions (Di Fabio, 2015) are:

Concern: (1a) What does it mean to you to be oriented toward your future? (1b) Do you think you are oriented toward your future? (1c) Why?

Control: (2a) What does it mean to you to take responsibility for your future? (2b) Do you think you do take responsibility for your future? (2c) Why?

Curiosity: (3a) What does it mean to you to be curious about your own future? (3b) Do you think you are curious about your future? (3c) Why?

Confidence: (4a) What does it mean to you to have confidence in your own ability to build your future? (4b) Do you think you have confidence in your ability to build your future? (4c) Why?

The answers to the 12 questions are compared before and after the intervention with respect to 24 indicators for Concern, Control, Curiosity, and Confidence. The comparison and analysis of the narratives were carried out through these qualitative indicators organized into in the LAQuA coding system (Di Fabio, 2015), structured into five qualitative analysis change categories. The LAQuA coding system addresses change or lack of change for each dimension of adaptability regarding different levels of reflexivity (Increased Reflexivity, Revised Reflexivity, Open Reflexivity, Enhanced Reflexivity, and No Change).

12.3.3 Career Counseling Innovative Outcomes (CCIO)

The *Career Counseling Innovative Outcomes* (CCIO, Di Fabio, 2016) is a narrative instrument, developed for qualitatively assessing career and life construction intervention outcomes and evaluating the effectiveness of the intervention. The CCIO was informed by the psychotherapeutic Innovative Moment Coding System (IMCS, Gonçalves, Ribeiro, Mendes, Matos, & Santos, 2011) and its application in career construction counseling (Cardoso, Silva, Gonçalves, & Duarte, 2014). The IMCS is used to observe the process of change during psychotherapeutic intervention (Gonçalves et al., 2011) and during career construction counseling intervention (Cardoso et al., 2014) through an examination of transcripts, audio recordings, or video recordings to detect narrative changes after each session. Instead, the CCIO aims at eliciting, exploring, and comparing specific narratives produced before and after the intervention. The CCIO comprises the following seven questions, developed on the basis of the narrative paradigm (Savickas, 2011) that are administered both before and after the intervention.

1. In which ways can/was this intervention (be) useful to you?
2. What are your main useful resources?
3. What are the main obstacles you encounter?
4. Who do you think can be useful to you?
5. What do you think can be useful to you?
6. What are the main challenges you face?
7. What are the main objectives you are hoping to achieve?

The narratives elicited by these seven questions are coded using the same five—category system proposed by Gonçalves et al. (2011) in their psychotherapeutic research model. These five categories are: Action, Reflection (type I and type II), Protest (type I and type II), Reconceptualization, and Performing Change.

12.3.4 Procedure

The FCA, LAQuA, and CCIO were administered before and after the intervention by a psychologist specialized in the administration of these qualitative instruments. Three trained expert reviewers (raters) independently compared the participant's initial and subsequent responses to the written questions of the three qualitative tools. An interrater reliability analysis using the Kappa statistic was used to calculate the level of consistency among the raters. The research was realized adhering to the requirements of privacy and informed consent in Italian law (Law Decree DL-196/2003) and the ethical standards for research of the Declaration of Helsinki revised in Fortaleza (World Medical Association [WMA], 2013), followed and approved by the Department of Education and Psychology of the University of Florence (Italy).

12.3.5 Criteria for Quality Assurance

It is important to apply the following quality assurance criteria in order to guarantee the trustworthiness of the research results using different modalities for gathering and analyzing the data: credibility, confirmability, transferability, and dependability (Maree, 2012). Credibility of data is related to "factors such as the significance of results and their credibility for participants and readers" (Maree, 2012, p. 141). Credibility in the present study was assured by verification of the outcomes by external researchers. Confirmability regards "the objectivity of the data and the absence of research errors. Results can be regarded as confirmable when they are derived from the participants and the research conditions rather than from the (subjective) opinion of the researcher" (Maree, 2012, p. 142). Confirmability was guaranteed by external researchers who evaluated whether the methods and procedures of the study had been explained clearly enough to allow verification. Transferability refers to "the extent to which the results can be 'exported' and generalised to other contexts" (Maree, 2012, p. 142). Transferability in this study was achieved through the detailed presentation of the participant's situation and the methodologies used to elicit the narratives. Detailed information was involved also in the context of the study allowing external researchers to assess the applicability of the results to other contexts. Dependability pertains "the stability and consistency of the research process and methods over time and influences the degree of control in a study" (Maree, 2012, p. 141). Dependability was based on the independent evaluation of the participant's narratives by three expert raters.

12.4 Results

Below, the life and occupational themes of the narratives produced by Sara through the FCA administered before and after the intervention are presented.

Regarding life themes, the participant's answer before the intervention was: "*I hope to continue to stay in the city where I live now,*" and after the intervention, it was: "*I hope to continue to live in the same city where I live now because I stay very well and I have all my relatives and my friends with me. Even if I will decide the change my work, I would like to continue to live in my city*" (Non-description to Specification: the initial client's FCA begins with general themes, and in the narrative produced after the intervention, client focuses on personal theme).

With regard to occupational themes, the participant's answer before the intervention was: "*I hope that I will be doing the same job or another job five years from now, in this city or in another city, that gratifies me from the point of view of lifelong learning. I need cultural stimuli also in my job,*" and after the intervention, it was: "*I hope that I will be doing a different job five years from now, in the same city, that gratifies me and permit me to be fully satisfied*" (General Interests to More Specification: the initial client's FCA starts with a variety of general occupational interests, and in the narrative produced after the intervention, client refines them).

Below, the participant's answers to the four questions of the LAQuA are provided as well as the results of the analysis obtained through the LAQuA qualitative indicators and the different levels of reflexivity (Increased Reflexivity, Revised Reflexivity, Open Reflexivity, Enhanced Reflexivity, and No Change).

The participant's answer to the first LAQuA question before the intervention was: "*To me, to be oriented toward my future means to be able to deal successfully with the different events in my life*" (qualitative descriptor: Equipping); after the intervention, it was: "*To me, to be oriented toward my future means to plan how to achieve my goals using my resources and strengths*" (a new, different qualitative descriptor: Strategic) (Revised Reflexivity R: in the narratives produced after the intervention, the previous descriptor/s has disappeared, and a new, different descriptor/s has appeared).

The participant's answer to the second LAQuA question before the intervention was: "*To me, to take responsibility for my future means not being overwhelmed by events that I encounter in my life*" (qualitative descriptor: Positive Attitude); after the intervention, it was: "*To me, to take responsibility for my future means not being overcome by the different situations and happenings in my life*" (identical qualitative descriptor: Positive Attitude). "*For me it is important to can count on myself using my self-awareness in relation to my skills and knowledge to face adaptively my future*" (a new, different qualitative descriptor: Responsible) (Open Reflexivity (O): in the narratives produced after the intervention, there is an identical descriptor/s—with the same level of reflexivity in presenting the descriptor—plus a new, different descriptor/s).

The participant's answer to the third LAQuA question before the intervention was: "*To me, to be curious about my future means to be able to catch opportunities for increasing my reflexion and growing*" (qualitative descriptor: Developing); after the intervention, it was: "*To me, to be curious about my future means to be able to reflect and grown learning from each experience. It means to take advantage of every opportunity to learn and continue to build a professionalism attending many training courses*" (identical qualitative descriptor but more in-depth reflexivity:

Developing) (Increased Reflexivity: in the narratives produced after the intervention, there were identical descriptors, but they were presented with more in-depth reflexivity).

The participant's answer to the fourth LAQuA question before the intervention was: "*To me, to have confidence in my own abilities to build my future means to be able to learn new skills useful for my work*" (qualitative descriptor: Innovative); after the intervention, it was: "*I think that it is important for me to be able to learn new skills and exploit them in my work. These new skills can permit me to find new ways for achieving my work objectives*" (identical qualitative descriptor but more in-depth reflexivity: Innovative); "*I feel unblock, I think to have made a break through the impasse in which I could not make decisions about my life. Now I'm thinking about how use my resources and strengths in the best way possible to act in order to enter new organization and renew my work life*" (a new, different qualitative descriptor: Capable. Enhanced Reflexivity (E): in the narratives produced after the intervention, there is an identical descriptor/s but presented with more in-depth reflexivity plus a new, different descriptor/s).

The participant's answers to the seven questions of the CCIO before and after the intervention are described below, as well as the results of the analysis based on the five categories (Action, Reflection, Protest, Reconceptualization, and Performing Change) of the CCIO coding system (Di Fabio, 2016).

The participant's answer to the first CCIO question before the intervention was: "*I hope that this intervention will help me to better understand what I really want to do in this period of my life. I have a graduation in information science and I work for didactic and guidance office of a public graduate school and research institute in Tuscany since many years. Now I don't know whether I should continue this job, require another role in the same organization or change job*"; after the intervention, it was: "*This intervention was useful to me because finally I understood that I desire to change work entering a new organization*" (Reflection Type II IM). "*If before the intervention I was very confuse about what I would like to do professionally, now I feel that I began a reflexion process about my strengths and weaknesses and about how to use my resources to find new work objectives. I think that I've started a change process, characterized by small steps in order to find a new, satisfying and meaningful job*" (Reconceptualization IM).

The participant's answer to the second CCIO question before the intervention was: "*I think that I could have the resources of resilience, curiosity, lateral thinking and the support from my parents and my husband*"; after the intervention, it was: "*At the beginning of this intervention I though to not have the necessary knowledge and skills to renew my work life. Furthermore I was confused about the possibility that my current position would give me satisfactory results. Now I am more confident in myself: on a one side to accomplish my daily tasks that I feel to be more fatiguing and on another side to identify more clearly my future work objectives, and to be able to search for a new job examining different options*" (Reconceptualization IM). "*The intervention help me also to understand that I have many resources, such as resilience, skills of analysis and synthesis, curiosity about the general culture, autonomy. I have to exploit them in order to change my working life finding real meanings*" (Reflection Type II IM). "*Now I have the new aim of examining the work possibilities in the city where I currently live in line with my graduation in information science and my experience as guidance operator*" (Performing Change IM). "*Furthermore now I think that attending a postgraduate course is crucial to update my knowledge and skills and to learn something new to realize this my new project*" (Action IM).

The participant's answer to the third CCIO question before the intervention was: "*My principal obstacles are the tendency to avoid the problems, the introversion. I don't know if it is better for me to continue working for my current organization, ask my supervisor to change my role in the same organization, or to change work life*"; after the intervention, it was: "*I realized that now it's time to turn my excessive rationalization, introversion, and lack of intrapreneurship in resources to use for building my life in line with my authentic self*" (Protest Type I IM). "*I finally understood that it is important to find new work starting from my strengths and improving my weaknesses to renew my life giving it a deep real meaning. I don't intend to give up because my work satisfaction is crucial for me*" (Protest Type II IM). "*After attending a useful postgraduate course at the University of Florence, I begin to collect information about work opportunities in my city and also other training courses in order to make the best choice for me and to maintaining my employability*" (Action IM).

The participant's answer to the fourth CCIO question before the intervention was: "*I think that advise from the other individuals especially my family are important for helping me to better understand what I really want to do in my future*"; after the intervention, it was: "*If at the beginning of the intervention I thought that others and particularly my family are important for helping me to better understand myself, now I think that the only person that can really help me was I. The lifelong learning is fundamental in order to update my knowledge and skills maintain my employability. Also my relationships with others are important not only to exchange opinions and reflect on the situations but also to have direct experiences from which I can learn something useful for my life*" (Reconceptualization IM). "*I have the new objective to find a new job, in line with my education and my work expertise and that stimulate me to grow further*" (Performing Change IM).

The participant's answer to the fifth CCIO question before the intervention was: "*I think that the most important thing now is to understand how to continue my career. I need some new stimuli in order to cope with the problems*"; after the intervention, it was: "*I think that it can be really useful to me to search carefully for information about work possibilities in my city, to do multiple job interviews, to speak with professionals working in my field to clearly recognize my purposes and then to make the appropriate choice*" (Action IM). "*Now my aim is find a new job and so it is important to start from micro-situations allowing me to better understand both which new job is interesting for me an in line with my values and which training courses could be important for my wealth of resources and strengths*" (Performing Change IM).

The participant's answer to the sixth CCIO question before the intervention was: "*The main challenge that I feel I'm dealing with at the moment is to become sure about my future working life. I'm really confused about what kind of choice will be actual satisfying for me*"; after the intervention, it was: "*If at the beginning of intervention I was unsure about my future working life, now I feel more determined about the next career choice. After the intervention I realize the best micro-steps I need to do in order to actualize my project*" (Reconceptualization IM). "*I think to be in the right path to overcome my limitations, to turn them into resources and to reflect more deeply to my real choice*" (Reflection Type II IM).

The participant's answer to the seventh CCIO question before the intervention was: "*My main objective is to clarify what is the best choice for me in this moment of my life, to improve my decisional skills and to be more strong in making decision*"; after the intervention, it was: "*Now my main objective is to finish the post-graduate course at the University of Florence, to accomplish my tasks in the office where I currently work until the end of the academic year. In the meantime I've just begin to collect some information about opportunities in the world of work that characterizes my city; I'll speak with professionals in the same field of mine or in close fields and I continue to search for training courses to maintain my employability*" (Action IM). "*My main issue is to find a new job entering a different organization in the city where I currently live to express my wealth of skills and to achieve meaningful goals in line with my authentic perspective*" (Reflection Type II IM).

12.5 Discussion

The case study presented in this chapter showed the value of "Constructing My Future Purposeful Life" (Di Fabio, 2014b) for increasing the key meta-competencies adaptability (Savickas, 2001) and identity (Guichard, 2004, 2010). Helping people to clarify their objectives, to discover authenticity and meanings in their life by using innovative effective postmodern interventions, could be useful for promoting the construction of desirable lives and careers (Allan, Duffy, & Douglass, 2015; Di Fabio & Blustein, 2016; Di Fabio & Palazzeschi, 2016; Guichard, 2009b). Dialogue interventions (Guichard, 2013) are specific interventions to help people deal with difficulties and write the next chapters of their life with more intentionality (Di Fabio, 2014d), through the increase of their purposeful identitarian awareness (Di Fabio, 2014e).

In this case study, the movement of the participant could be discovered through the analysis of the narratives before and after the intervention by means of the FCA (Rehfuss, 2009), the LAQuA (Di Fabio, 2015), and the CCIO (Di Fabio, 2016).

The FCA analysis narratively detected Sara's personal and career motivations, values, and future direction, in particular her life and occupational themes. The results reflect the development of herself and her life and career objectives. This movement in themes applied to some relevant Degrees of Change (Rehfuss, 2009):

Non-description to Specification and General Interests to More Specification. Regarding Non-description to Specification, the initial client's FCA started with general themes and then client focused on personal theme, identifying the importance to continue living in the city where there are her relatives and her friends. These relationships and the familiarity of the city seem to give stability to her life. Regarding General Interests to More Specification, the initial client's FCA started with a variety of general occupational interests and then client was able to refine them, recognizing the desire to change her job instead of continuing the current job that could really gratify her.

The LAQuA analysis allowed the detection through narrative of Sara's adaptability in terms of her ability to anticipate challenges and her future (Savickas, 2001) and envision the necessary steps to obtain her objectives through the difficulties of the 543 ever-changing world of work. The level of reflexivity in all the four dimensions of adaptability (Concern, Control, Confidence, and Curiosity) was observed. In relation to Concern, the participant underlined the importance of planning how to achieve her goals and identifying her resources and strengths to shape her future. In relation to Control, the participant highlighted the significance of relying on herself and on her resources, knowing to adaptively use her knowledge and skills to achieve positive results in her life. In relation to Curiosity, the participant realized the importance of learning something from each situation, especially from work experiences and training courses, and applying her knowledge to shape her future on the basis of a positive vision of herself. In relation to Confidence, the participant felt more confident in her knowledge and skills, being able to use them for satisfying her objectives and obtaining the best work position for her, overcoming the obstacles.

The CCIO analysis permitted to narratively detect Sara's novelties that emerged in contrast to her problematic self-narratives (Di Fabio, 2016). The results indicated a new way of understanding her life pattern, unifying herself in the construction of her future. Client is enabled to try to realize her life project more consciously and with more intentionality in shaping her next steps. These results emerged in terms of Action as the participant actively started to explore solutions (Di Fabio, 2016; Gonçalves et al., 2011) gathering information on new training courses for further improving her knowledge and skills, on work opportunities in the city where she has always lived, and to speak with other professionals in the same or close fields of her, to be able to make the right choice for her life and maintain her employability. The results also showed changes in terms of Reflection related to the choice of continuing to work for the current organization or asking to have a new role in the same organization or change job and organization in order to come to terms with her new emerging identities (Gonçalves et al., 2011). The participant could rely on new adaptive self-instructions on the basis of her greater self-awareness about her resources and strengths that she will exploit in her new future job as a guidance worker. The analysis of the narratives also presented Protest aspects (Di Fabio, 2016; Gonçalves et al., 2011): The first type was related to the issue of being aware of her weaknesses and turning them into resources; the second type regards client's stated intention to find a new job as guidance operator in line with her most authentic inner aspects. There were also changes in Sara's narratives in terms of

Reconceptualization regarding the movement from a past position to a present position (Di Fabio, 2016; Gonçalves et al., 2011). The participant moved from a confused condition, not knowing about continued work for the current organization, toward a position of greater awareness in relation to the importance of finding a new, satisfying, and meaningful job to construct her career path (Di Fabio, 2016; Gonçalves et al., 2011). Finally, the analysis of the narratives showed Performing Change referring to the participant's endeavors as a result of the change process (Di Fabio, 2016; Gonçalves et al., 2011). Particularly, she started to exam in the work opportunities in the city where she resided, particularly those opportunities aligned to her graduation in information science, her expertise as guidance operator, and mostly with her values and authentic self. She also realized the importance of attending other training to constantly update her knowledge and skills and to maintain her employability.

12.6 Conclusion

This case study highlights that through the "Constructing My Future Purposeful Life" intervention (Di Fabio, 2014b) the self-awareness of the participant was increased, helping her to transform her limitations into resources and to use her enhanced strengths to clarify her objectives, values, personal and professional themes to design the useful actions to renew her life. In this way, she can ask herself fundamental questions regarding the problems she faces in order to make authentic choices to obtain desirable career and life outcomes. The ability to design a new purposeful self (Di Fabio, 2014e) permitted her to build a bridge from the past to the present, all the while anticipating the future in the complex scenario of working (Blustein, 2006, 2011; Kenny, Blustein, & Meerkins, 2018). Thanks to her increased reflexivity, now she is able to unify herself by connecting her multiple experiences through the narration of future events, thus favoring the attribution of sense and meaning to her lives (Guichard, 2013).

Despite these results showing changes in the narratives produced by the participant before and after the intervention, the effectiveness of the intervention needs confirmation by further studies. The trustworthiness and credibility of the study were assured, but a limitation could be the subjective interpretation of the author. A follow-up session out of 6 weeks after the intervention showed that Sara began to implement her new intentions to find a new job, by gathering information, speaking with other professionals, and, at the same time, finding new training courses. She spoke also with her family who supported her. Nonetheless, a follow-up assessment of 6–12 months after the intervention would be useful to confirm the results achieved in this study.

Despite the above limitations, the study indicated the value of enhancing life construction dialogue intervention, particularly for worker but also for young people who deal with key choices and transitions, helping them construct positive life and career and identities. The new dialogue intervention, "Constructing My

Future Purposeful Life" by Di Fabio (2014b), strengthens the two key meta-competencies for the twenty-first century (Guichard, 2013; Savickas, 2013): adaptability and identity. These are fundamental for enhancing purposeful identitarian awareness (Di Fabio, 2014b, e). The intervention also encourages the possibility of reaching greater personal congruence by designing one's own life through the purposeful self by planning more coherently and authentically, and by establishing attuned goals. In conclusion, the aim of this intervention is to enable individuals to design and redesign their plural identities and pathways for an authentic, effective, and decent construction (Blustein, Kenny, Di Fabio, & Guichard, in press; Guichard & Di Fabio, 2015).

References

Allan, B. A., Duffy, R. D., & Douglass, R. (2015). Meaning in life and work: A developmental perspective. *The Journal of Positive Psychology, 10*(4), 323–331.

Bauman, Z. (2000). *Liquid modernity*. Cambridge, UK: Polity Press.

Blustein, D. L. (2006). *The psychology of working: A new perspective for career development, counseling and public policy*. NY: Routledge.

Blustein, D. L. (2011). A relational theory of working. *Journal of Vocational Behavior, 79*(1), 1–17.

Blustein, D. L., Kenny, M. E., Di Fabio, A., & Guichard, J. (in press). Expanding the impact of the psychology of working: Engaging psychology in the struggle for decent work and human rights. *Journal of Career Assessment*. https://doi.org/10.1177/1069072718774002.

Busacca, L., & Rehfuss, M. (Eds.) (2016). *Postmodern career counseling: A handbook of culture, contexts, and cases*. American Counseling Association.

Cardoso, P., Silva, J. R., Gonçalves, M. M., & Duarte, M. E. (2014). Innovative moments and change in career construction counseling. *Journal of Vocational Behavior, 84*, 11–20.

Di Fabio, A. (2013). Applying career construction in group-based contexts with adults. In A. Dsi Fabio & J. G. Maree (Eds.), *Psychology of career counseling: New challenges for a new era. Festschrift in honour of Prof. Mark Savickas* (pp. 83–99). New York: Nova Science Publishers.

Di Fabio, A. (2014a). Career counseling and positive psychology in the 21st century: New constructs and measures for evaluating the effectiveness of intervention. *Journal of Counsellogy, 1*, 193–213.

Di Fabio, A. (2014b). "Constructing my future purposeful life": A new life construction intervention. In A. Di Fabio & J.-L. Bernaud (Eds.), *The Construction of the Identity in 21st Century: A Festschrift for Jean Guichard* (pp. 219–239). New York: Nova Science Publishers.

Di Fabio, A. (2014c). Due meta-competenze chiave narrative per la nuova consapevolezza identitaria purposeful nel XXI secolo. *Counseling. Giornale Italiano di Ricerca e Applicazioni, 7*, 133–141.

Di Fabio, A. (2014d). Intrapreneurial self-capital: A new construct for the 21st century. *Journal of Employment Counseling, 51*, 98–111.

Di Fabio, A. (2014e). The new purposeful identitarian awareness for the twenty-first century: Valorize themselves in the life construction from youth to adulthood and late adulthood. In A. Di Fabio & J.-L. Bernaud (Eds.), *The Construction of the identity in 21st century: A Festschrift for Jean Guichard* (pp. 157–168). New York: Nova Science Publishers.

Di Fabio, A. (2014f). Authenticity Scale: Un primo contributo alla validazione della versione italiana. *Counseling Giornale Italiano di Ricerca e Applicazioni, 7*, 231–238.

Di Fabio, A. (2015). Life adaptability qualitative assessment (LAQuA): A narrative instrument for evaluating counseling intervention effectiveness. In J. G. Maree & A. Di Fabio, A. (Eds.),

Exploring new horizons in career counselling: Turning challenges into opportunities (pp. 43–62). Rotterdam, The Netherlands: Sense Publishers.

Di Fabio, A. (2016). Life design and career counseling innovative outcomes (CCIO): A case study. *The Career Development Quarterly, 64,* 35–48.

Di Fabio, A., & Blustein, D. L. (Eds). (2016). *From meaning of working to meaningful lives: The challenges of expanding decent work.* Lausanne: Frontiers Media. https://doi.org/10.3389/978-2-88919-970-9.

Di Fabio, A., & Busoni, L. (2009). Proprietà psicometriche della versione italiana della Core Self-Evaluation Scale (CSES) con studenti di scuola secondaria. *Counseling. Giornale Italiano di Ricerca e Applicazioni, 2,* 73–83.

Di Fabio, A., & Kenny, M. E. (2016). From decent work to decent lives: Positive self and relational management (PS&RM) in the twenty-first century. *Frontiers in Psychology, 7,* 361. https://doi.org/10.3389/fpsyg.2016.00361.

Di Fabio, A., Kenny, M. E., & Minor, K. (2014). Emotional intelligence: School-based research and practice in Italy. In M. J. Furlong, R. Gilman, & E. S. Huebner (Eds.), *Handbook of positive psychology in the schools* (2nd ed., pp. 450–464). New York: Routledge, Taylor and Francis.

Di Fabio, A., & Maree, J. G. (2012). Group-based life design counseling in an Italian context. *Journal of Vocational Behavior, 80,* 100–107.

Di Fabio, A., & Maree, J. G. (Eds.). (2013). *Psychology of career counseling: New challenges for a new era. Festschrift in honour of Prof. Mark Savickas.* New York: Nova Science Publishers.

Di Fabio, A., Maree, J. G., & Kenny, M. E. (2018). Development of the Life Project Reflexivity Scale: A new career intervention inventory. *Journal of Career Assessment,* 1–13. https://doi.org/10.1177/1069072718758065.

Di Fabio, A. & Palazzeschi, L. (2016). Marginalization and precariat: The challenge of intensifying life construction intervention. In A. Di Fabio & D. L. Blustein (Eds.), *From meaning of working to meaningful lives: The challenges of expanding decent work. Research topic in Frontiers in Psychology. Section Organizational Psychology.* https://doi.org/10.3389/fpsyg.2016.00444.

Di Fabio, A., Palazzeschi, L., & Bucci, O. (2017). In an unpredictable and changing environment: Intrapreneurial self-capital as a key resource for life satisfaction and flourishing. In G. Arcangeli, G. Giorgi, N. Mucci, J.-L. Bernaud, & A. Di Fabio (Eds.), *Emerging and re-emerging organizational features, work transitions and occupational risk factors: The good, the bad, the right. An interdisciplinary perspective.* Research Topic in *Frontiers in Psychology. Organizational Psychology, 8,* 1819. https://doi:10.3389/fpsyg.2017.01819.

Douglass, R. P., Duffy, R. D., & Autin, K. L. (2016). Living a calling, nationality, and life satisfaction: A moderated, multiple mediator model. *Journal of Career Assessment, 24*(2), 253–269.

Duarte, M. E. (2004). O indivíduo e a organização: Perspectivas de desenvolvimento. [The individual and the organization: Perspectives of development]. *Psychologica (Extra-Série),* 549–557.

Duarte, M. E. (2009). The psychology of life construction. *Journal of Vocational Behavior, 75,* 259–266.

Duffy, R. D., Diemer, M. A., Perry, J. C., Laurenzi, C., & Torrey, C. L. (2012). The construction and initial validation of the Work Volition Scale. *Journal of Vocational Behavior, 80,* 400–411.

Duffy, R. D., Torrey, C. L., Bott, E. M., Allan, B. A., & Schlosser, L. Z. (2013). Time management, passion, and collaboration: A qualitative study of highly research productive counseling psychologists. *The Counseling Psychologist, 41*(6), 881–917.

Duffy, R. D., Blustein, D. L., Diemer, M. A., & Autin, K. L. (2016). The Psychology of Working Theory. *Journal of Counseling Psychology, 63,* 127–148.

Duffy, R. D., Allan, B. A., England, J. W., Blustein, D. L., Autin, K. L., Douglass, R. P., ... & Santos, E. J. (2017). The development and initial validation of the Decent Work Scale. *Journal of Counseling Psychology, 64*(2), 206–221.

Gonçalves, M. M., Ribeiro, A. P., Mendes, I., Matos, M., & Santos, A. (2011). Tracking novelties in psychotherapy process research: The innovative moments coding system. *Psychoteraphy Research, 21,* 497–509.
Greenhaus, J. H., Callanan, G. A., & Godshalk, V. M. (2010). *Career management* (4th ed.). Thousand Oaks: SAGE Publications Inc.
Guichard, J. (2004). Se faire soi. *L'Orientation Scolaire et Professionnelle, 33,* 499–534.
Guichard, J. (2005). Life-long self-construction. *International Journal for Educational and Vocational Guidance, 5,* 111–124.
Guichard, J. (2007). L'impact de la mondialisation sur le conseil en orientation des adultes. *Risorsa Uomo, 13*(3), 423–442.
Guichard, J. (2008). Proposition d'un schéma d'entretien constructiviste de conseil en orientation pour des adolescents ou de jeunes adultes. *L'Orientation Scolaire et Professionnelle, 37,* 413–440.
Guichard, J. (2009a). Problematiche e sfide dell'orientamento nelle società industriali globalizzate all'inizio del XXI secolo. In A. Di Fabio (Ed.), *Career counseling e bilancio di competenze: Prospettive internazionali* (pp. 11–28). Firenze: Giunti O.S. Organizzazioni Speciali.
Guichard, J. (2009b). Self-constructing. *Journal of Vocational Behavior, 75,* 251–258.
Guichard, J. (2010, March). *Les théories de la construction des parcours professionnels et de la construction de soi: Deux approches de la construction de la vie individuelle*. Paper presented at Colloque International INETOP, Paris, France.
Guichard, J. (2013, September). *Which paradigm for career and life designing interventions contributing to the development of a fairer world during the 21st century*. Lecture presented at the IAEVG International Conference, Montpellier, France.
Guichard, J., Bangali, M., Cohen Scali, V., Pouyaud, J., & Robinet, M. L. (2016). *Concevoir et orienter sa vie: Les dialogues de conseil en life design*. Paris: Editions Qui plus est.
Guichard, J., & Di Fabio, A. (2010). Life-designing counseling: Specificità e integrazioni della teoria della costruzione di carriera e della teoria della costruzione di sé. *Counseling. Giornale Italiano di Ricerca e Applicazioni, 3,* 277–289.
Guichard, J., & Di Fabio, A. (2015, June). *How can career and life designing interventions contribute to a fair and sustainable development and to the implementation of decent work over the world?* Invited Keynote at the UNESCO Chair on Lifelong Guidance and Counseling International Conference "How can career and life designing interventions contribute to a fair and sustainable development and to the implementation of decent work over the world?" Florence 2015, University of Florence (Italy) and University of Wroclaw (Poland), Florence, Italy, 4–6 June 2015.
Hartung, P. J. (2012). Career development in global context: History, status, and prospects. In M. Watson & M. McMahon (Eds.), *Career development: Global issues and challenges* (pp. 11–26). Hauppauge, NY: Nova Science.
Judge, T. A., Erez, A., Bono, J. E., & Thoresen, C. J. (2003). The core self-evaluations scale: Development of a measure. *Personnel Psychology, 56,* 303–331.
Kenny, M. E., Blustein, D. L., & Meerkins, T. M. (2018). Integrating relational perspectives in career counseling practice. *The Career Development Quarterly, 66*(2), 135–148.
Kenny, M. E., & Hage, S. M. (2009). The next frontier: Prevention as an instrument of social justice. *The Journal of Primary Prevention, 30,* 1–10.
Maree, J. G. (2012). A (guided) meta-reflection theory of career counselling: A case study. *South African Journal of Higher Education, 26*(4), 661–669.
Maree, J. G. (2013). *Counselling for career construction: Connecting life themes to construct life portraits. Turning pain into hope*. Rotterdam, The Netherlands: Sense.
Maree, J. G., & Di Fabio, A. (Eds.). (2015). *Exploring new horizons in career counselling: Turning challenges into opportunities*. Rotterdam, The Netherlands: Sense Publishers.
Osipow, S. H. (2012). Career Development. *Enciclopedia human behaviour*, 430–433.
Rehfuss, M. C. (2009). The *future career autobiography*: A narrative measure of career intervention effectiveness. *The Career Development Quarterly, 58*(1), 82–90.

Rehfuss, M., & Di Fabio, A. (2012). Validating the future career autobiography as a measure of narrative change. *Journal of Career Assessment, 20,* 452–462.
Richardson, M. S. (2012). Counseling for work and relationship. *The Counseling Psychologist, 40* (2), 190–242.
Savickas, M. L. (2001). Toward a comprehensive theory of career development: Disposition, concerns and narratives. In F. T. L. Leong & A. Barak (Eds.), *Contemporary models in vocational psychology: A volume in honor of Samuel H. Osipow* (pp. 295–320). Mahwah: NJ: Lawrence Erlbaum.
Savickas, M. L. (2005). The theory and practice of career construction. In S. D. Brown & R. W. Lent (Eds.), *Career development and counseling: Putting theory and research to work* (pp. 42–70). Hoboken, NJ: Wiley.
Savickas, M. L. (2009). Career studies as self-making and life designing. *Career Research & Development, 24,* 15–17.
Savickas, M. L. (Ed.). (2011). *Career counseling*. Washington, DC: American Psychological Association.
Savickas, M. L. (2013). *Life designing in 21st century*. Closing Conference at the IAEVG International Conference, Montpellier, France.
Savickas, M. L. (2015). *Life-design counseling manual*. Rootstown, OH: Author.
Savickas, M. L., & Porfeli, E. J. (2012). Career adapt-abilities scale: Construction, reliability, and measurement equivalence across 13 countries. *Journal of Vocational Behavior, 80,* 661–673.
Super, D. E. (1957). *The psychology of career*. New York: Harper.
Super, D. (1980). A life-span, life-space approach to career development. *Journal of Vocational Behavior, 16,* 282–298.
Wood, A. M., Linley, P. A., Maltby, J., Baliousis, M., & Joseph, S. (2008). The authentic personality: A theoretical and empirical conceptualization and the development of the authenticity scale. *Journal of Counseling Psychology, 55*(3), 385–399.
World Medical Association [WMA] (2013). *WMA declaration of Helsinki—Ethical principles for medical research involving human subjects*. Available at: http://www.wma.net/en/30publications/10policies/b3/.

Chapter 13
Qualitative SIFS Evaluation for Future (QSEF) Coding System

Annamaria Di Fabio and Peter McIlveen

Abstract This chapter presents a new qualitative tool for evaluating the effectiveness of dialogue-based interventions: the Qualitative SIFS Evaluation for Future (QSEF). This tool is developed on the basis of the Self-Construction Theory (Guichard in L'Orientation Scolaire et Professionnelle, 33, 499–534, 2004; in International Journal of Education and Vocational Guidance, 5, 111–124, 2005) and the Life Construction Theory (Guichard in Lecture presented at the IAEVG International Conference, Montpellier, France, 2013). The chapter also presents a case study that describes the application of the QSEF to evaluate the effectiveness of a dialogue intervention with a worker in a public organization. The QSEF was administered before and after the intervention to appraise the client's changes. The results of the analysis using the QSEF indicate that the dialogue intervention allowed the participant to have a greater awareness of herself in terms of Subjective Identity Forms System (SIFS), core Subjective Identity Form, and aspired Subjective Identity Form to autonomously develop her own career and life path.

Keywords Self-construction · Life construction · Dialogue intervention effectiveness · Qualitative SIFS evaluation for future (QSEF)

13.1 Introduction

Research into the effectiveness of career counseling interventions builds the evidence base for its efficient and effective utilization (Di Fabio, Bernaud, & Kenny, 2013). Conventionally, quantitative methods are used to verify the effectiveness of

A. Di Fabio (✉)
Department of Education and Psychology (Psychology Section),
University of Florence, Florence, Italy
e-mail: adifabio@psico.unifi.it

P. McIlveen
School of Linguistics, Adult and Specialist Education,
University of Southern Queensland, Queensland, Australia

© Springer Nature Switzerland AG 2018
A. Di Fabio and J.-L. Bernaud (eds.), *Narrative Interventions in Post-modern Guidance and Career Counseling*, https://doi.org/10.1007/978-3-319-98300-4_13

career counseling interventions and, to that end, successive meta-analytic studies attest to the positive effects of career counseling (Whiston, Goodrich Mitts, & Wright, 2017). Scholars have increasingly called for evaluation methodologies that utilize qualitative approaches (Blustein, Kenna, Murphy, DeVoy, & DeWine, 2005), particularly those methods appropriate to evaluate narrative career counseling (Busacca & Rehfuss, 2016; Brott, 2004; Cochran, 1997; Di Fabio & Maree, 2013; Rehfuss, 2009; Rehfuss & Di Fabio, 2012; McMahon & Watson, 2010, 2011; Severy, 2002). For this reason, specific qualitative tools to identify changes after career counseling interventions have developed, for example, the *Future Career Autobiography* (FCA; Rehfuss, 2009; Rehfuss & Di Fabio, 2012), the *Life Adaptability Quality Assessment* (LAQuA; Di Fabio, 2015), and the *Career Counseling Innovative Outcomes coding system* (CCIO; Di Fabio, 2016). Amidst the emergent panoply of qualitative career counseling methods, there is a relative lack of specially constructed qualitative evaluations tools. Thus, in this chapter, we present a new qualitative evaluation framework with specific theoretical foundations, the framework of Self-Construction Theory (Guichard, 2004, 2005), and Life Construction Theory (Guichard, 2013).

The Self-Construction Theory (Guichard, 2004, 2005) considers the life construction of an individual in different contexts and the processes that organize these contexts. In the Self-Construction Theory, people are considered as plural beings and individual identity is seen as a dynamic *Subjective Identity Forms Systems* (SIFSs). Individuals unify themselves, construct expectations about their future, and draw meaning from their own personal experiences. The theory posits individuals a multiplex entity imbued with different facets:

- Individuals interact in different *contexts*,
- have different experiences,
- through which they may develop different self-images,
- acting different roles,
- that vary in different environments.

The construct SIF represents each self that an individual develops in a specific context. An SIF corresponds to a specific social role. An SIF includes the way in which individuals perceived themselves in a specific role and in a specific context. Some SIFs regard contexts where the individuals interact in a specific period of their lives; other SIFs are relative to ways in which individuals imagine themselves in the future or are relative to past experiences. The SIFS of an individual is dynamic, and some SIFs are more relevant than others. The fundamental SIFs generally produce Aspired SIFs. These stimulate individuals to imagine their own future, giving priority to those perspectives that give consistency to all the SIFs of a person.

The Self-Construction Theory responds to the following fundamental question that Guichard (2010) identified: “What could be meaningful to my life?” From this question comes the Life Construction Theory (Guichard, 2013) that emphasizes self-management to build a life full of meaning for the individual. In this framework, the concept of *Core SIF* was introduced. A Core SIF wants to satisfy a need for self-actualization. It corresponds to a life domain in which the person wants to attain a certain state of excellence as it gives his/her life meaning. The Core SIF is linked to an expectation of reaching an objective that has value for the person (Guichard, 2013), an objective full of meaning, and in the process of life construction, it constructs the meaningfulness of life. In Life Construction Theory, dialogue counseling (Guichard, 2008, 2009; Collin & Guichard, 2011) is centered on forms of reflexivity to raise awareness of one's own SIFS to make individuals able to design and re-design themselves (Guichard, 2013). Guichard (2004, 2005) individuates two different forms of reflexivity: dual and ternary. The process of dual reflexivity refers to the processes of identification that regards the construction of the individual as images of the other in the attempt to become as this model (or not to become like this model in terms of specific counter-model). The process of ternary reflexivity regards the dialogue with the self in which individual occupies three possible positions: the "I" assumes a certain position, the "you" who responds, and the "he/she" as a third person's point of view. Individuals have the possibility to elaborate alternative interpretations of their experiences, taking away from them and their immediate meaning in defining future goals and building their own self in this way (Di Fabio, Maree, & Kenny, 2018).

Dialogue counseling works on SIFs and SIFS. In this theoretical framework, the transition from career project to life project underlines the Subjective Identity Forms System in relation to the roles individuals attributed to themselves. This happens not only in a professional context but in all contexts of life, thus defining a wider project that considers individuals in their complexity and plurality. The evolution of Self-Construction Theory and Life Construction Theory indicates that in postmodern societies, individuals unify themselves by connecting their different life experiences with the narratives of future events, thus contributing to the meaning of their lives.

13.2 Purpose of the Study

The Qualitative SIFS Evaluation for Future (QSEF) is based on the Self-Construction Theory and the Life Construction Theory. QSEF was developed as a new narrative qualitative tool for verifying the effectiveness of dialogue in career counseling. The QSEF is intended to respond to the current need for qualitative tools to determine the effectiveness of the dialogue career counseling interventions for the twenty-first century. A case study was presented to demonstrate the QSEF and its coding system as a method for assessing client change after a dialogue intervention "Constructing my Future Purposeful Life" (Di Fabio, 2014a). Two questions guided the case study: (a) Can the QSEF be used to assess for client change after a dialogue intervention? and (b) Can the QSEF be used to describe the sort of changes that may be facilitated by a dialogue intervention?

13.3 Method

13.3.1 Participant and Context

The participant in this study, Monica (a pseudonym), was a 47-year-old worker in a public organization that offers guidance intervention and training. Her work regards in particular the design of guidance and training interventions, but also in some cases the provision of services to users. She decided to participate in a "Constructing Future Purposeful Life" intervention because she felt the necessity to reflect on her professional and personal life and to find the energy and motivation to continue to work in a working reality that imposes many constraints.

13.4 Qualitative SIFS Evaluation for Future (QSEF)

The QSEF comprises six questions administered before and after the dialogue career counseling intervention, providing access to the client's narrative expression at two points in time and allow comparison of how the client organizes these narrations before and after the narrative intervention. There are four primary questions and two additional control questions administered before and after the intervention:

1. What are your main goals for the future?
2. What are your main doubts for the future?
3. What are the main obstacles?
4. What is your dream?
5. How do you imagine the future in the short-, medium-, long-terms?
6. What are your key resources to use?

The narratives elicited by these six questions are coded according to nine categories:

1. From "Decisional disinterest" to "Decisional involvement in examining own SIFS to design own life";
2. From "Unawareness" to "Identification" (System of Subjective Identity Forms —SSIF, Aspired SIF, Core SIF);
3. From "Identification" to "Specification" (SSIF, Aspired SIF, Core SIF);
4. From "Rigidity" to "Openness about how to realize himself/herself";
5. From "Simple vision" to "Expert vision (Openness to complexity)" in constructing the new chapter of own life in terms of diverse paths, objectives, possibilities;
6. From "Openness to complexity" to "Acceptance of change";
7. From "Acceptance of change" to think about "Challenges as opportunities";

8. From "Opportunities in challenges" to "Hardiness/Resilience/Think out of the box" about himself/herself for the new chapter of own life;
9. "Rumination or absence of change in reading into himself/herself and the situation."

13.4.1 Procedure

The QSEF was administered before and after the dialogue career counseling intervention by a psychologist trained in the administration of qualitative instruments. Monica's initial and subsequent responses to the six narrative written questions were also paired for narrative comparison by three independently trained experts in career counseling.

Monica participated in a "Constructing my Future Purposeful Life Intervention" (Di Fabio, 2014a). The intervention aims to strengthen participants' reflexivity, improve their ability to elaborate through narratives their personal and professional problems, identify real meanings, and design projects in different contexts more effectively. The intervention is articulated in three modules.

The first module of intervention is composed of two exercises. The first, the "Life Design Genogram" consists of two genograms: the Career Construction Genogram based on the Career Construction Theory (Savickas, 2005, 2011) and the Life Construction Genogram based on the Life Construction Theory (Guichard, 2013). The second exercise "Me and the future" seeks to improve the meta-competence of adaptability in relation to these personal mottos. The second module is called "Self-advising the Future Self"; this enhances reflection on life roles. The third module is called "Constructing the Purposeful Self" and refers to the process "To make oneself self" (Guichard, 2004).

13.4.2 Ethics

Steps were taken to ensure Monica's well-being throughout the study. She was given feedback by the career counselor during the dialogue career counseling session. The intervention was conducted in accordance with Italian Privacy Law, and the anonymity was guaranteed.

13.5 Criteria for Quality Assurance

In relation to qualitative assurance, it is fundamental to guarantee the trustworthiness of the results using various strategies during the data collection and analysis: credibility, confirmability, transferability, and dependability (Maree, 2012).

Credibility of data refers to "factors such as the significance of results and their credibility for participants and readers" (Maree, 2012, p. 141). The credibility was ensured by external verification of the results, which enables the researcher to assess the credibility of the results. This was achieved by submitting the documentation to researchers who did not participate in the research and asking them to assess the way in which the conceptual analysis was carried out. Confirmability refers to "the objectivity of the data and the absence of research errors. Results can be regarded as confirmable when they are derived from the participants and the research conditions rather than from the (subjective) opinion of the researcher" (Maree, 2012, p. 142). Confirmability was achieved from external researchers in guidance and career counseling, who did not participate in the study and who assessed whether the methods and general procedures of the study were described clearly and in sufficient detail to allow for data verification. Furthermore, the data obtained, the methods used, and the decisions made during the intervention were fully documented. Transferability refers to "the extent to which the results can be 'ex-ported' and generalised to other contexts" (Maree, 2012, p. 142). Transferability was ensured by providing an accurate description of Monica's personal situation and the techniques used to elicit data. Also, information was provided in the context of the case to enable readers to judge the applicability of the findings to other settings. It is important to underline that the research was based on comprehensive descriptions of the case study without any attempts at generalization. Dependability refers to "the stability and consistency of the research process and methods over time and influences the degree of control in a study" (Maree, 2012, p. 141). Dependability was ensured through the independent analysis of Monica's QSEF by three experts to enhance the accuracy of the deductive process and to ensure that the identified themes accurately represented the data.

13.6 Results

What follows is a summary of Monica's responses to the six questions of the QSEF before and after the "Constructing my Future Purposeful Life" intervention and the results of the analysis through the QSEF coding system based on the QSEF nine categories. The verbatim responses of the participant have been lightly edited to preserve their authenticity.

Monica's initial answer to the first QSEF question "What are your main goals for the future?" was: "My main goal for the future is improve my professional situation but I don't know how can I do"; after the intervention, she stated: "My main goal for the future is to offer to clients services and interventions really useful for them. I think that I understand that my work is fundamental for my self-realization but only if I'm able to do something that is really useful for others" (Category 2: From "Unawareness" to "identification").

Monica's answer to the second QSEF question, "What are your main doubts for the future?" was: "My principal doubts for the future are relative to the situation of changes and instability that characterizes my organizations in this moment but it is the reality and I have to consider it in developing my future project." Her subsequent answer to the second QSEF question was as follows: "The intervention permitted me to reflect about my role and about I would like to construct my future. I think that in this moment I concentrate especially on my professional life and on this situation of change in my organization. I perceive this situation as an opportunity because my organization is giving me some responsibilities in the reorganization of services for clients. So I have the opportunity to introduce new services more anchored to recent scientific theories in my field. Therefore I think that this can be really useful to help clients" (Category 7: From "Acceptance of change" to think about "Challenges as opportunities").

Monica's initial answer to the third QSEF question "What are the main obstacles?" was: "I think that my principal obstacles both personal and professional are relative to my self-esteem and my professional self-efficacy, and there is no possibility to improve these aspects." Her subsequent answer to the third QSEF question after the intervention was as follows: "After the intervention I understand that I have much more resources that I could image. Sometimes I get discouraged because I have low self-esteem and self-efficacy and this may be an obstacle. However, I have had many successes in my personal and professional life and I can count on relationships with my family and colleagues. In this moment of my life in which I am realized in all my familiar roles, I feel that I can fully invest in my work. I would like to actively participate in the reorganization of the guidance and training service and have a management role. I think that to fully realize myself it is important to make sure that my work will be really useful for others. I realize myself if I'm able to help others" (Category 4: From "Rigidity" to "Openness about how to realize himself/herself").

Monica responded to the fourth QSEF question "What is your dream?" prior to the intervention by stating the following: "Sincerely, I don't have a professional or personal dream." Her subsequent answer to the fourth QSEF question was as follows: "The intervention permitted me to reflect on my different roles and perhaps to think about my dream. On personal point of view I would like to maintain all my roles as life partner, daughter, friends. I'm fully satisfied of my personal life. My dream is thus to improve my professional life perhaps having a leadership and management role and to do something concrete to be useful for other and helping them" (Category 1: From "Decisional disinterest" to "Decisional involvement in examining own SIFS to design own life").

Monica's initial answer to the fifth QSEF question "How do you imagine the future in the short-, medium-, long-terms?" was as follows: "I'm this moment there are so many changes in my organization and I have to understand how to cope with this challenge and complexity." Her subsequent answer to the fifth QSEF question was as follows: "From a professional point of view I think that in the short-term I have to face with the change in my organization and restructuring my daily work according to the new bureaucratic norms. For example I have to rethink the structure of the guidance and training intervention on the based of the new bureaucratic and economic constraints. So I have the same role but in a new framework. In a medium-term I would like to improve my competences perhaps also my managerial competences because I would like in a long-term assume a management role in my organization in order to be able to decide and act politically for realizing services really useful to others. Regarding my personal life I would like that always remain in this way also in the future" (Category 6: From "Openness to complexity" to "Acceptance of change").

Monica's initial answer to the sixth QSEF question "What are your key resources to use?" consisted of the following: "My key resource used to face this challenging period is my professional experience, matured in many year of work in my organization." Her subsequent answer to the sixth QSEF question was as follows: "I realized that I have many resources not only my professional experience. They are my desire to acquire even more competences, my curiosity for the future, and also the good relationships with my colleagues. I can use all these resources to face the complex situation of change that regards my organizations and the changes in bureaucratic rules. I recognize this complexity as a challenge for my professional growth and to try to be useful to improve the quality of the offered service and be really useful for client. I would be have a role in the reorganization of services and interventions for clients provided by my organization to offer a concrete contribution to society" (Category 5: From "Simple vision" to "Expert vision (Openness to complexity) in constructing the new chapter of own life").

13.7 Discussion

The results of this case study indicate that the QSEF and its coding system provide a promising tool for assessing growth in the dialogue career counseling. In this case, the client showed an evolution across a number of important dimensions in particular of her work life, as reflected in a comparison of the narrative before and after the "Constructing my Future Purposeful Life" intervention.

From the analysis, it emerged that Monica presented changes in narratives in terms of different categories of the QSEF coding system. She showed a change from "Decisional disinterest" to "Decisional involvement in examining own SSIF to design own life" (Category 1). It is possible to recognize a decisional disinterest in the fact that before intervention, Monica stated that she had no dream. Instead after the intervention that permits a reflection on her different life and work roles, she has the possibility to reflect on her Subjective Identity Forms System (SIFS) and to understand that in this moment of her life her role as worker has a central position in her system. Monica showed a change from "Unawareness" to "Identification" (Category 2). In fact before the intervention, she did not know how to improve her professional situation and she had thus no clear self-awareness. After the intervention, she identified the central role of work in her life and she realized that her work is fundamental for her realization only if permitting to obtain something that it is really useful for others. Monica presented also a change from "Rigidity" to "Openness about how to realize himself/herself" (Category 4). At the beginning of the intervention, she saw only internal obstacles. After the intervention, Monica realized that she has internal resources to realize her identified Aspired SIF relative to have a management role in her organization to do something really useful for other people. Furthermore, Monica showed a change from "Simple vision" to "Expert vision (Openness to complexity) in constructing new chapter of own life" (Category 5). Before the intervention, she recognized only her professional experience as a resource to face this challenging period of her working life. After the intervention, she recognized that she has many resources such as her professional competences, her curiosity for the future, her good relationships with her colleagues. Above all, she started from the analysis of the complexity of her current work situation to understand the importance for her to have a role in the reorganization of services and interventions for clients to offer a concrete contribution to help them and the society as a whole. Monica showed also a change from "Openness to complexity" to "Acceptance of change" (Category 6). At the beginning of intervention, she recognized and she is stimulating by the complexity of her current working situation, and after the intervention, she was able to project her future in short-, medium-, and long-terms, projecting different Aspired SIFs in the future. Finally, Monica presented a change from "Acceptance of change" to think about "Challenges as opportunities" (Category 7). Before the intervention, she considered her working role only in relation to the issue of change in her organization, and after the intervention, she was able to identify the current changing situation as an opportunity for the development of her professional self (Di Fabio, 2014b; Di Fabio, Palazzeschi, & Bucci, 2017).

The "Constructing my Future Purposeful Life" intervention (Di Fabio, 2014a) appears to be a useful intervention modality. A follow-up session carried out 6 weeks after the end of intervention revealed that there was some implementation of the new intentions. Monica was a member of the team that had the task to reorganize all the guidance and training services offered by her organization. She started a course to better understand the new bureaucratic norms and to acquire management competences in public organizations. It would be important to conduct a follow-up assessment 6–12 months after the intervention to confirm the stability of the results obtained.

At the end of the "Constructing my Future Purposeful Life" intervention, Monica was more aware of her SSIF that includes also different SIFs relative to personal aspects (e.g., life partner, daughter, friends) but, above all, her Core SIF is relative to her work role. The Core SIF is in fact a SIF within which the person wants to achieve a need for self-actualization. It corresponds to a life domain in which the person wants to realize his/her life meaning. The Core SIF is linked to an expectation of reaching an objective that has value and is full of meaning for the person and permits to realize his/her life meaningfulness (Guichard & Di Fabio, 2015; Guichard, Bangali, Cohen Scali, Pouyaud, & Robinet, 2016). The Core SIF constitutes the basis and generates Aspired SIF, the projection into the future of meaningful roles for the individual. In this regard, Monica expressed her Aspired SIF relative to the desire to assume a management role in her organization in order to be able to decide and act politically for realizing services really useful to others. Overall, the analysis that compared Monica's pre- and post-dialogue career counseling intervention narratives showed the presence of narrative change using the QSEF coding system, thus also underlining the effectiveness of the "Constructing my Future Purposeful Life" intervention (Di Fabio, 2014a).

The case study has some limitations. Although steps were taken to enhance the trustworthiness and credibility of the study, future research should not only test the "Constructing my Future Purposeful Life" intervention with a multitude of other clients but also use the QSEF coding system to evaluate its utility. This single case may have benefits with respect to practitioners using the case to reflect on their own practices and generate new perspectives; however, quantitative studies involving pre- and post-test measures would provide a more convincing test of its effectiveness. Although the QSEF coding system is bespoke to Guichard's theory, it may be evaluated by using it with other narrative approaches to career counseling.

Analysis of this case study revealed client change after a dialogue career counseling through the use of the QSEF coding system. This case study presents a new qualitative tool that has the potential to provide important information for counselors seeking to assess the outcomes of dialogue career counseling. This new tool is specially constructed upon the framework of Self-Construction Theory (Guichard, 2004, 2005) and Life Construction Theory (Guichard, 2013). This dialogue intervention allows individuals to reflect on their SSIF, Core SIF, and Aspired SIF (Guichard, 2004, 2005, 2013) to construct life and work project where people fully achieve their self-realization and reach objectives that are worthy and full of meaning for them (Allan, Duffy, & Douglass, 2015; Blustein, 2006, 2011; Blustein, Kenny, Di Fabio, & Guichard, in press; Duffy, Blustein, Diemer, & Autin, 2016; Maree & Di Fabio, 2015; Savickas, 2015), permitting them to realize a whole life meaningfulness (Di Fabio & Blustein, 2016; Guichard, 2013).

References

Allan, B. A., Duffy, R. D., & Douglass, R. (2015). Meaning in life and work: A developmental perspective. *The Journal of Positive Psychology, 10*(4), 323–331.

Blustein, D. L. (2006). *The psychology of working: A new perspective for career development, counseling and public policy.* NY: Routledge.

Blustein, D. L. (2011). A relational theory of working. *Journal of Vocational Behavior, 79,* 1–17.

Blustein, D. L., Kenna, A. C., Murphy, K. A., DeVoy, J. E., & DeWine, D. B. (2005). Qualitative research in career development: Exploring the center and margins of discourse about careers and working. *Journal of Career Assessment, 13,* 351–370.

Blustein, D. L., Kenny, M. E., Di Fabio, A., & Guichard, J. (in press). Expanding the impact of the psychology of working: Engaging psychology in the struggle for decent work and human rights. *Journal of Career Assessment.* https://doi.org/10.1177/1069072718774002.

Brott, P. E. (2004). Constructivist assessment in career counseling. *Journal of Career Development, 30*(3), 189–200.

Busacca, L., & Rehfuss, M. (Eds.) (2016). *Postmodern Career Counseling: A Handbook of Culture, Contexts, and Cases.* American Counseling Association.

Cochran, L. (1997). *Career counseling: A narrative approach.* London: Sage Publications.

Collin, A., & Guichard, J. (2011). Constructing self in career theory and counseling interventions. In P. J. Hartung & L. M. Subich (Eds.), *Constructing self in work and career. Concepts, cases and contexts* (pp. 89–106). Washington, DC: American Psychological Association.

Di Fabio, A. (2014a). "Constructing my future purposeful life": A new life construction intervention. In A. Di Fabio & J.-L. Bernaud (Eds.), *The construction of the identity in 21st century: A festschrift for Jean Guichard* (pp. 219–239). New York: Nova Science Publishers.

Di Fabio, A. (2014b). Intrapreneurial self-capital: A new construct for the 21st century. *Journal of Employment Counseling, 51,* 98–111.

Di Fabio, A. (2015). Life Adaptability Qualitative Assessment (LAQuA): A narrative instrument for evaluating counseling intervention effectiveness. In J. G. Maree & A. Di Fabio, A. (Eds.), *Exploring new horizons in career counselling: Turning challenges into opportunities* (pp. 43–62). Rotterdam, The Netherlands: Sense Publishers.

Di Fabio, A. (2016). Life design and career counseling innovative outcomes (CCIO): A case study. *The Career Development Quarterly, 64,* 35–48.

Di Fabio, A., Bernaud, J.-L., & Kenny, M. E. (2013). Perceived career counselor relational and technical behaviors and outcomes among Italian university students. *Journal of Career Assessment, 21,* 190–199. https://doi.org/10.1177/1069072712466721.

Di Fabio, A., & Blustein, D. L. (Eds). (2016). *From meaning of working to meaningful lives: The challenges of expanding decent work.* Lausanne: Frontiers Media. https://doi.org/10.3389/978-2-88919-970-9.

Di Fabio, A., & Maree, J. G. (Eds.). (2013). *Psychology of career counseling: New challenges for a new era. Festschrift in honour of Prof. Mark Savickas.* New York: Nova Science Publishers.

Di Fabio, A., Maree, J. G., & Kenny, M. E. (2018). Development of the life project reflexivity scale: A new career intervention inventory. *Journal of Career Assessment*, 1–13. https://doi.org/10.1177/1069072718758065.

Di Fabio, A., Palazzeschi, L., & Bucci, O. (2017). In an unpredictable and changing environment: Intrapreneurial Self-Capital as a key resource for life satisfaction and flourishing. In G. Arcangeli, G. Giorgi, N. Mucci, J.-L. Bernaud, & A. Di Fabio (Eds.), *Emerging and re-emerging organizational features, work transitions and occupational risk factors: The good, the bad, the right. An interdisciplinary perspective. Research Topic in Frontiers in Psychology. Organizational Psychology*, *8*, 1819. https://doi:10.3389/fpsyg.2017.01819

Duffy, R. D., Blustein, D. L., Diemer, M. A., & Autin, K. L. (2016). The psychology of working theory. *Journal of Counseling Psychology, 63*(2), 127–148.

Guichard, J. (2004). Se faire soi. *L'Orientation Scolaire et Professionnelle, 33,* 499–534.

Guichard, J. (2005). Life-long self-construction. *International Journal of Education and Vocational Guidance, 5,* 111–124.

Guichard, J. (2008). Proposition d'un schéma d'entretien constructiviste de conseil en orientation pour des adolescents ou de jeunes adultes. *L'Orientation Scolaire et Professionnelle, 37,* 413–440.

Guichard, J. (2009). Self-constructing. *Journal of Vocational Behavior, 75,* 251–258.

Guichard, J. (2010, March). *Les théories de la construction des parcours professionnels et de la construction de soi: Deux approches de la construction de la vie individuelle*. Paper presented at Colloque International INETOP, Paris, France.

Guichard, J. (2013, September). *Which paradigm for career and life designing interventions contributing to the development of a fairer world during the 21st century.* Lecture presented at the IAEVG International Conference, Montpellier, France.

Guichard, J., Bangali, M., Cohen Scali, V., Pouyaud, J., & Robinet, M. L. (2016). *Concevoir et orienter sa vie: Les dialogues de conseil en life design.* Paris: Editions Qui plus est.

Guichard, J., & Di Fabio, A. (2015, June). *How can career and life designing interventions contribute to a fair and sustainable development and to the implementation of decent work over the world?* Invited Keynote at the UNESCO Chair on Lifelong Guidance and Counseling International Conference "How can career and life designing interventions contribute to a fair and sustainable development and to the implementation of decent work over the world?"

Florence 2015, University of Florence (Italy) and University of Wroclaw (Poland), Florence, Italy, 4–6 June 2015.
Maree, J. G. (2012). A (guided) meta-reflection theory of career counselling: A case study. *South African Journal of Higher Education, 26*(4), 661–669.
Maree, J. G., & Di Fabio, A. (Eds.). (2015). *Exploring new horizons in career counselling: Turning challenges into opportunities*. Rotterdam, The Netherlands: Sense Publishers.
McMahon, M., & Watson, M. (2010). Story telling: Moving from thin stories to thick and rich stories. In K. Maree (Ed.), *Career counselling: Methods that work* (pp. 53–63). Cape Town, South Africa: Yuta.
McMahon, M., & Watson, M. (2011). Career counselling: What's the story? In M. McMahon & M. Watson (Eds.), *Career counselling and constructivism: Elaboration of constructs* (pp. 13–24). New York: Nova Science.
Rehfuss, M. C. (2009). The future career autobiography: A narrative measure of career intervention effectiveness. *The Career Development Quarterly, 58*(1), 82–90.
Rehfuss, M., & Di Fabio, A. (2012). Validating the future career autobiography as a measure of narrative change. *Journal of Career Assessment, 20,* 452–462.
Savickas, M. L. (2005). The theory and practice of career construction. In S. D. Brown & R. W. Lent (Eds.), *Career development and counseling: Putting theory and research to work* (pp. 42–70). Hoboken, NJ: Wiley.
Savickas, M. L. (Ed.). (2011). *Career counseling*. Washington, DC: American Psychological Association.
Savickas, M. L. (2015). *Life-design counseling manual*. Rootstown, OH: Author.
Severy, L. E. (2002). What's the story? Postmodern career counseling in student affairs. *Journal of College Student Development, 43*(1), 84–92.
Whiston, S. C., Li, Y., Goodrich Mitts, N., & Wright, L. (2017). Effectiveness of career choice interventions: A meta-analytic replication and extension. *Journal of Vocational Behavior, 100,* 175–184. https://doi.org/10.1016/j.jvb.2017.03.010.

Conclusions

The chapters in this book contribute to progress toward a system of evaluation for postmodern guidance and career counseling narrative interventions for the twenty-first century characterized by a dialogical perspective. The volume was developed under the UNESCO UNITWIN Network Life Designing Interventions (counseling, guidance, education) for decent work and sustainable development. The book demonstrates the value of a new qualitative approach with specific innovative qualitative tools to evaluate interventions' effectiveness. Thus, the book enables reflection on accountability and evidence-based practice.

The economic crisis in the twenty-first century has indeed highlighted the need to follow principles of accountability in terms of attention to service costs, the effectiveness of interventions, and best practices supported by research (Whiston, 2001). According to these principles, it appears essential to offer effective guidance and career counseling interventions without dispersing the available limited economic resources (Whiston, 1996, 2001). Currently, postmodern guidance and career counseling interventions are based on psychological approaches to narrative (Savickas, 2005, 2011, 2015) expressed in narrative counseling (Savickas, 2005, 2011) and also in dialogue interaction (Guichard, 2005, 2013). Traditionally, quantitative tools were employed to evaluate the effectiveness of guidance and career counseling interventions. However, the current postmodern interventions have been inherently narrative and qualitative (Busacca & Rehfuss, 2016; Di Fabio, 2015, 2016; Rehfuss, 2009; Rehfuss & Di Fabio, 2012). For this reason, it has been necessary to develop new qualitative tools specifically realized to identify changes in clients' narratives after guidance and career counseling narrative interventions (Blustein, Kenny, Murphy, Devoy, & DeWine, 2005; Di Fabio, 2015, 2016).

The present volume focused on accountability in postmodern guidance and career counseling narrative interventions, offering a review of case studies and innovative qualitative approaches. The first part of this book presented new perspectives, a new intervention, and new approaches in a different context with a strongly international focus. The introductory chapter by Di Fabio and Bernaud described the framework of reference of accountability principles and the issue of the evaluation of effectiveness

© Springer Nature Switzerland AG 2018

A. Di Fabio and J.-L. Bernaud (eds.), *Narrative Interventions in Post-modern Guidance and Career Counseling*, https://doi.org/10.1007/978-3-319-98300-4

of postmodern guidance and career counseling narrative interventions in the twenty-first century, and some contributions regarding case studies and qualitative approaches in different international contexts were presented. The case study proposed by Kobus Maree showed the value of career construction counseling for a South African postgraduate student in psychology who experienced career indecision, and demonstrated how this intervention can help clients to face with decisional challenges. Jean-Luc Bernaud and Dominique Guédon presented a case study whose results stressed in particular a quali+quanti approach to the evaluation of psychosocial risks, and showed the value of a counseling method to evaluate resources. Also in the French context, Lin Lhotellier, Caroline Arnoux-Nicolas, and Laurent Sovet presented a case study about a Life Meaning Intervention to underline both the qualitative and quantitative effects of this kind of intervention. Peter McIlveen and Allison Creed introduced a new approach to counseling case formulation as metaphor with a specific focus on this professional practice as a highly specialized aesthetic of counseling practice. The case study prepared by Afonso Ribeiro, Guilherme de Oliveira Silva Fonçatti, and Maria da Conceição Coropos Uvaldo revealed the impact of a group-based career counseling model for unskilled adults in crisis in the Brazilian context showed through a qualitative non-structured method an increased reflexivity and a clear process of narrative changes during the counseling.

All the chapters of the first part of the present volume contributed to broadening the perspective of postmodern guidance and career counseling narrative interventions (Blustein, 2006, 2011; Blustein & Di Fabio, 2016; Blustein, Kenny, Di Fabio, & Guichard, in press; Duffy, Blustein, Diemer, & Autin, 2016; Kenny, Blustein, & Meerkins, 2018) and their effectiveness evaluated through qualitative approaches. The chapters offered precious points of view to continue and improve the research on these issues in the perspective of dialogic interventions.

After the introductory chapter of the section by Maureen E. Kenny and Annamaria Di Fabio, the second part of the book offered to readers a wide range of case studies regarding different narrative career interventions for the twenty-first century and different innovative qualitative tools to evaluate the effectiveness of such interventions, including: Career Interest Profile (CIP) as a Life Design Counseling Intervention evaluated using both FCA and LAQuA as qualitative evaluation tools in the case study by Ornella Bucci, Allison Creed, and Annamaria Di Fabio; narrative career counseling intervention based on Career Construction Interview evaluated using LAQUA and CCIO in the two case studies by Letizia Palazzeschi, Allison Creed, Alessio Gori, and Annamaria Di Fabio; Life Meaning Intervention evaluated using LAQuA and CCIO in the case study by Annamaria Di Fabio and Maureen E. Kenny; Intrapreneurial Self-Capital Training evaluated using LAQuA in the case study by Peter McIlveen and Annamaria Di Fabio; Constructing My Future Purposeful Life evaluated using comparatively FCA, LAQuA, and CCIO in the case study by Violetta Drabik-Podgórna, Marek Podgórny, and Annamaria Di Fabio; and Constructing My Future Purposeful Life evaluated using a new qualitative tool (QSEF) in the case study by Annamaria Di Fabio and Peter McIlveen.

The contributions of the present volume thus offered a range of stimuli to reflect on the issue of the evaluation of the effectiveness of interventions in an accountability framework. The aim of the present book was to propose new perspectives regarding this issue by showing case studies and innovative qualitative approaches and tools. Although there is still much to be done to answer the call for accountability in postmodern guidance and career counseling narrative interventions, we hope that this volume provides renewed impetus toward accountability.

Annamaria Di Fabio and Jean-Luc Bernaud

References

Blustein, D. L. (2006). *The psychology of working: A new perspective for career development, counseling and public policy*. NY: Routledge.

Blustein, D. L. (2011). A relational theory of working. *Journal of Vocational Behavior, 79,* 1–17.

Blustein, D. L., Kenny, M. E., Di Fabio, A., & Guichard, J. (in press). Expanding the impact of the psychology of working: Engaging psychology in the struggle for decent work and human rights. *Journal of Career Assessment.* https://doi.org/10.1177/1069072718774002.

Blustein, D. L., Kenna, A. C., Murphy, K. A., DeVoy, J. E., & DeWine, D. B. (2005). Qualitative research in career development: Exploring the center and margins of discourse about careers and working. *Journal of Career Assessment*, *13*(4), 351–370.

Busacca, L., & Rehfuss, M. (Eds.) (2016). *Postmodern Career Counseling: A Handbook of Culture, Contexts, and Cases*. American Counseling Association.

Di Fabio, A. (2015). Life Adaptability Qualitative Assessment (LAQuA): A narrative instrument for evaluating counseling intervention effectiveness. In J. G. Maree & A. Di Fabio, A. (Eds.), *Exploring new horizons in career counselling: Turning challenges into opportunities* (pp. 43–62). Rotterdam, The Netherlands: Sense Publishers.

Di Fabio, A. (2016). Life design and career counseling innovative outcomes (CCIO). *The Career Development Quarterly*, *64*, 35–48.

Di Fabio, A., & Blustein, D. L. (Eds). (2016). *From meaning of working to meaningful lives: The challenges of expanding decent work*. Lausanne: Frontiers Media. https://doi.org/10.3389/978-2-88919-970-9.

Duffy, R. D., Blustein, D. L., Diemer, M. A., & Autin, K. L. (2016). The Psychology of Working Theory. *Journal of Counseling Psychology*, *63*(2), 127–148.

Guichard, J. (2005). Life-long self-construction. *International Journal for Educational and Vocational Guidance, 5,* 111–124.

Guichard, J. (2009). Self constructing. *Journal of Vocational Behavior*, *75*, 251–258.

Guichard, J. (2013, November). *Career guidance, education, and dialogues for a fair and sustainable human development*. Inaugural conference of the UNESCO chair of Lifelong guidance and counseling, University of Wroclaw, Poland.

Kenny, M. E., Blustein, D. L., & Meerkins, T. M. (2018). Integrating relational perspectives in career counseling practice. *The Career Development Quarterly*, *66*(2), 135–148.

Rehfuss, M., & Di Fabio, A. (2012). Validating the Future Career Autobiography as a measure of narrative change. *Journal of Career Assessment, 20,* 452–462.

Savickas, M. L. (2005). The theory and practice of career construction. In S. D. Brown & R. W. Lent (Eds.), *Career development and counseling: Putting theory and research to work* (pp. 42–70). Hoboken, NJ: Wiley.

Savickas, M. L. (Ed.). (2011). *Career counseling*. Washington, DC: American Psychological Association.

Savickas, M. L. (2015). Life-design counseling manual. *Rootstown, OH: Author*.
Whiston, S. C. (1996). Accountability through action research: Research methods for practitioners. *Journal of Counseling & Development*, *74*, 616-623.
Whiston, S. C. (2001). Selecting career outcome assessments: An organizational scheme. *Journal of Career Assessment*, *9*(3), 215–228.

MIX
Papier aus verantwortungsvollen Quellen
Paper from responsible sources
FSC® C105338

If you have any concerns about our products,
you can contact us on
ProductSafety@springernature.com

In case Publisher is established outside the EU,
the EU authorized representative is:
Springer Nature Customer Service Center GmbH
Europaplatz 3, 69115 Heidelberg, Germany

Printed by Libri Plureos GmbH
in Hamburg, Germany